PCWEEK

Microsoft Windows NT Security

System Administrator's Guide

PCWEEK

Microsoft Windows NT Security

System Administrator's Guide

Nevin Lambert and Manish Patel

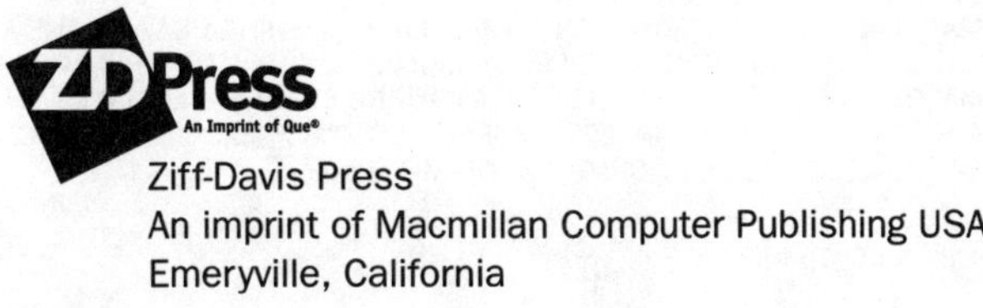

Ziff-Davis Press
An imprint of Macmillan Computer Publishing USA
Emeryville, California

Publisher	Stacy Hiquet
Associate Publisher	Steven Sayre
Acquisitions Editor	Brett Bartow
Author Assistant	Dawn Lambert
Development Editor	Paula Hardin
Copy Editor	Carol Henry
Production Editor	Edith Rex
Proofreader	Jeff Barash
Cover Illustration and Design	Megan Gandt
Book Design	Paper Crane Graphics, Berkeley
Page Layout	Janet Piercy
Indexer	Valerie Robbins

Ziff-Davis Press imprint books are produced on a Macintosh computer system with the following applications: FrameMaker®, Microsoft® Word, QuarkXPress®, Adobe Illustrator®, Adobe Photoshop®, Adobe Streamline™, MacLink® *Plus*, Aldus® FreeHand™, Collage Plus™.

Ziff-Davis Press, an imprint of
Macmillan Computer Publishing USA
5903 Christie Avenue
Emeryville, CA 94608
510-601-2000

ISBN 1-56276-457-8

Manufactured in the United States of America
10 9 8 7 6 5 4 3 2 1

Contents at a Glance

Table of Contents

■ Acknowledgments

This book has been long in the making and has undergone many mishaps. The fact that it has been published is a tribute to the Ziff-Davis Press staff and our desire to get them out of our hair ☺. Officially, we would like to thank the Ziff-Davis Press staff for their diligence and hard work, and the opportunity to work with them.

We would like to thank Microsoft Corporation for creating the diverse and successful operating system, Windows NT, and all the BackOffice products.

Further, we would like to thank our loved ones—Diane, Kyle, Marcela, and Anita—for their patience, support, and understanding.

We thank our business partner Lisa Parker for understanding our lack of attention to her work.

Dawn Lambert deserves more than a passing acknowledgment for her efforts on this book. Dawn was instrumental in the early development work, all writing and editing phases, and in moral support for the authors. Her work on this book cannot be understated.

And of course to Brett, who never once criticized us.

Introduction

First we would like to thank *you* for purchasing our book. We expect this book to become a valuable guide for your understanding and implementation of Windows NT security.

We realize that not every book will cover every topic that every reader wants, and we have done our best to provide the proper focus for administrators of NT security. We are interested in your feedback, so, please feel free to e-mail us or send mail to the following addresses:

NevinL@pacts.com
ManishP@pacts.com
PACTS, 5515 N. 7th St., Ste. 5-441, Phoenix, AZ 85014

Although NT has been out for several years now, there has not yet been a real guide to security specifically for NT administrators. We have watched as NT matured and gained huge market share, and in fact helped spur that market on. We have seen Windows NT Workstation become a viable desktop operating system, and NT begin to really give UNIX flavors a run for their money. Now in Version 4.0, NT is finding much acceptance and use.

The nice thing about version 4.0 of NT is its ease of use. Although there is much to security, you do not have to grasp much to start creating your security environment. You can learn as you build. (But do not learn slowly or you'll learn the hard way.)

Intended Audience

Who should read this book?

- New network administrators of any size network
- New NT Administrators (If you are new to NT, this is a must-read!)
- Experienced network administrators of other operating systems
- Experienced NT administrators who have not yet implemented security or need better understanding of how security works
- Administrators who have implemented security but have not utilized auditing
- Everyone who wants to learn more about auditing
- Those who have a basic administrator knowledge of Windows NT 4.0, and, of course, a desire for learning NT security aspects and implementation

You will find the pertinent information you need to get going fast as you delve into this book.

Our Coverage of Security

First we'll define *security*. How about that deep peaceful feeling you get when things are just as they should be, or the alarm that screeches when anyone gets to close to your car? Or maybe you have a large person who goes everywhere you go? No? Well, security is certainly subjective.

With regard to computer security, some would say that every administrative action and capability affects some aspect of security, but it is more than that to us.

Our idea of security is protection against threats. Security protects against the actions of invaders—either through direct online activities or by programs that create malicious attacks.

What about honest mistakes, or just old bumbling mistakes? Security also offers protection from legitimate users who accidentally or on purpose attempt to exceed the limits placed on their actions. The protections we suggest will be effective against those kinds of individuals (just don't make them administrators).

Since this is not a "learn-all-know-all" NT operating system book, we do not concern ourselves with certain aspects of NT. We don't cover protection against hardware failure in any detail, such as disk striping, mirroring, or many other robust NT features. Such components are valuable but do not fall into our definition of security in this book.

We will not judge or compare NT against other systems. When we reference another system, it is more for descriptive purposes.

So *security* just might become that deep peaceful feeling—that is, after you have a thorough understanding of the security features, how to use them, and implement them.

Overview of Major NT Security Concepts

The following is an overview of concepts that permeate NT and are used throughout this book.

Authentication

Since we believe that computers are here to serve us, and that *we* are actually the source of moving and creating information, we need to secure *ourselves*. Well, sort of.

The very first rule of computer security is to identify whom is being served by the system. This is what we call authentication and validation. Authentication and validation is usually seen as the request for a username and password before you can use the system, (called logging on). The security controls are based on the assumption that you should be the only one who knows your password, so if you present the proper password for your name, the computer assumes you are who you say you are and validates you. After logon, security systems should, and NT does, associate and control all your actions on the system using your authenticated logon name or account. When you finish work on a computer you log off so no other user can use the computer with your account.

Your account is defined on the system by information about you, including the name by which the system knows you and your password. This security account also holds any special capabilities you may be granted on the system.

Malicious Software and Viruses

Viruses. Don't panic, but be careful. Just because your users might be trusted doesn't mean the people who wrote the programs you use can. Many virus attacks are seemingly innocent applications in disguise (A screen saver that looks cool but really penetrates your system and corrupts data). You will learn about and use access control to help avoid and limit the damage that such programs can do.

The Trusted/Secure Path

One of the particularly nasty things a malicious program, sometimes referred to as a Trojan horse, can do is pretend to be a legitimate program so as to "trick" you into entering some sensitive information like your password. The Trusted Path is a traditional method to protect you from such situations.

I like to think of the trusted path as "the secure path" because the Trusted Path is a special window, entitled Windows NT Security, that you call up with a reserved key-combination: the Ctrl, Alt, and Delete keys pressed simultaneously. When you press this key-combination, NT guarantees that the window that appears is legitimate and a safe entry point for information. Therefore, the changing of information (entering passwords) are secure transactions. This is why I call it a secure path. You must use the secure path for certain security-critical operations, such as logging on, unlocking your workstation after you lock it, and changing your password.

The Windows NT Security window (secure path) will never appear unless you enter the Ctrl+Alt+Del key-combination. Thus, it is your job to ensure that all users know *never* to interact with what looks like a secure path window, without first entering the key sequence. You should not perform a secure path function, such as changing your password, by any other means.

The Network Environment and the Internet

There are two aspects of "network security." The first is simply that security enforcement by individual computers must be coordinated in today's highly inter-connected computer environments. Important objectives of this are that critical security information is centralized and that user identity controls user actions on all machines across the network. The cornerstone for coordination in Windows NT is called the *domain*.

The second aspect of network security is protecting data in transit between computer systems and securely identifying remote communicants. The only practical way to do this is through various encryption techniques, which are ways of secretly encoding data so networking eavesdroppers can't see or tamper with it. The current interest in the Internet brings these technologies to the foreground, and no system is leading the way more than Windows NT with its strong, secure base on which such network security can be constructed.

It is time for you to begin your journey into the realm of secure computing. Enjoy!

- *Controls for Access, Actions, and Auditing*
- *Security Levels*
- *The C2 Evaluation Process*

CHAPTER

1

Network Security and Windows NT

TODAY, COMPUTER NETWORKS ARE INDISPENSABLE TO MOST businesses. Networked computer systems are used to share and access key information and resources among millions of users throughout all types and sizes of organizations. Frequently, the information stored on these systems is confidential and/or intended for use only by specific authorized individuals. The ability of the network system to prevent unauthorized access and control authorized access to such information is critical to both the security and competitiveness of an organization.

Network security comprises all aspects of protection for all components of a computer network system (hardware, software, and stored data). This includes protection from damage, theft, and unauthorized access. A system policy that is well designed, precisely implemented, and carefully audited makes authorized access of system resources simple, and unauthorized access nearly impossible.

Protecting confidential, sensitive data from being lost or exposed is a top priority for any organization. Whether it's a large corporation, a SOHO (small office/home office), a bank, or the government of a country, those in charge want to be assured that critical data is protected from malicious tampering, unauthorized access, and user errors. With the use of Windows NT Workstation and Windows NT Server, such assurance is real.

Windows NT provides a full range of security options. The security implementation is easy for both administrators and end-users: A simple password-based logon procedure gives users access to authorized resources. Users do not see the internal complexities of system-level encryption; they just log on.

This chapter discusses some of the components of NT security. It describes three security categories—low, medium, and high—and provides some background into U.S. government security ratings.

Controls for Access, Actions, and Auditing

Microsoft included security as part of the initial design specifications for Windows NT, and it is prevalent throughout the operating system. Windows NT is loaded with features and tools that make it easy to customize security for your needs. The security model includes components to

- Govern access to objects (such as files and printers)
- Control actions an individual user can take on objects (such as Read or Write access)
- Specify which events are audited

Access to objects is the key objective of the Windows NT security model. The security model maintains security information for all user and group accounts as well as all objects. Access is controlled by the assignment of permissions. Owners or other authorized users may, at their discretion, change permissions and the use of user accounts. You can create an almost unlimited number of accounts or groups of accounts. You can permit or restrict an account's access to any computer resource. An administrator assigns permissions to users and groups to grant or deny access to particular objects.

For every account, a range of security attributes can be set on a per-file or per-directory basis. These attributes can be on a per-user or per-group basis. In addition to controlling access, these mechanisms allow you to identify access attempts that are made directly by a user, or indirectly by a program or another process that is running.

In support of all this control over the actions of a large number of users, it's important to maintain consistent, reliable desktop environments that provide the flexibility for network users to accomplish their daily tasks via a friendly interface. Policies and profiles are used for this in the NT Security subsystem.

You can define security policies that apply to the domain as a whole. The *Trust Relationships policy* defines relationships with other domains. The *User Rights policy* controls access rights given to groups and user accounts. The *Account policy* controls how user accounts use passwords. The *Audit policy* controls the types of events recorded in the security log.

Auditing is built into Windows NT. This allows you to track which user account was used to attempt a particular kind of access to files or other objects. Auditing also can be used to track logon attempts, system shutdowns and restarts, and similar events. These features support the monitoring of events related to system security, helping you identify any security breaches and determine the extent and location of any damage. The level of audited events is customizable to your needs. The security log in the Event Viewer can list audited events by category and by event ID.

Security Levels

Windows NT provides a full range of security options, from no security at all to the C2 level of security required by many U.S. government agencies. This section describes three security categories—low (or none), medium, and maximum—and the security measures used to obtain each level. These categories are arbitrary, and you will probably combine characteristics of these categories in creating your own security policy.

How Much Security Does Your Network Need?

There is much hullabaloo in the computer industry about security and levels of security. Why not just set maximum security at all times? Setting various limits on access to computer resources complicates users' work with those resources. It is also extra work for security administrators to set up and maintain the various levels.

Here's what can happen: Suppose only members of the Accounts Payable user group are allowed to access AP records. A new person is hired into that group. For starters, someone needs to create an account for the new user and add that account to the Accounts Payable group account. If the new account gets created but not added to Accounts Payable group, the new user cannot access the AP records and will be prevented from contributing any meaningful work. Or, if the account is created and made a member of the Accounts Payable group, you'll need to consider what other access privileges are thereby granted to this new person.

Another possible problem may occur when the security is too tight: Users will try to "beat the system" in order to get work done. Take passwords, for instance. You might decide to make them long and require that they be changed often. Users may find it hard to remember their password and will write it down to avoid forgetting it and being locked out of the network. Another dangerous password workaround is a very common occurrence in corporate environments: Users who are denied access from files they truly need to use are "loaned" other employees' accounts and passwords so that work can get done.

Now let's take a look at what's involved in achieving the three levels of security.

Low Security

Security may not be of much concern to you or your organization when the computer is not used to store or access sensitive data, or if the machine is in a very secure location. For example, if a computer is in the SOHO of a sole-proprietor business, or if it is used as a testing machine within a locked lab, then security precautions might be unnecessary. Windows NT allows you to fully access the system with no security protection at all, if you so desire.

Physical Considerations for Low-Level Security

For the simplest level of security, take the same precautions you would with any piece of valuable equipment to protect against casual theft. This can include locking the room when no one is using the computer, or using a locked cable to attach the unit to a wall. You might also want to establish procedures for moving or repairing the computer so that the hardware cannot be stolen or altered under false pretenses.

Use a surge protector or power conditioner to protect the computer and all peripherals from power spikes. Also, perform regular disk scans and defragmentation. Always maintain backups of important data.

Configuration for Low-Level Security

For low security, none of the Windows NT security features are used. You might even allow automatic logon to the Administrator account (or any other user account). This allows anyone with physical access to the computer to turn it on and immediately have full access to its resources.

Caution

Even if you choose low-level security, don't let a bug get you! Take adequate precautions against viruses—they can damage your data and prevent programs from operating. And that virus may spread from your low-security computer to a more secure machine.

Bear in mind that low security is not the norm. Most computers are used to store sensitive and/or valuable data. This could be financial data, personnel files, confidential correspondence…just about anything. In addition, most computers need to be protected against configuration changes, whether accidental or deliberate.

Finally, if you do choose low security, keep in mind that the computer's users need to be able to do their work, with minimal barriers to the resources they need.

Medium Security

Most environments require more than low security. Although every implementation of security will be different, we have outlined a broad spectrum of security requirements that we call medium security. For most implementations of security, however, you will want to ensure you include all of the following guidelines and suggestions.

Warning Banners

To protect against intrusion is, of course, the goal of all security systems; unfortunately, however, simply making the system secure may not be enough. You may also decide you need to post warnings that it is against company policy or even against the law to intrude upon your system. In recent court cases, the argument has been put forth that a logon screen "invites" you to log on, and therefore a clever hacker is "justified" in working hard to accomplish what you invited.

Before a user logs on to the system, Windows NT can display a message box with the caption and text of your choice. This mechanism is often used to issue a warning message that users will be held legally liable if they attempt to use the computer without authorization. We consider such a warning necessary for both medium- and high-security implementations.

Physical Considerations for Medium Security

As with low-level security, the medium-security computer should be physically secured and protected like any other valuable equipment. Keep the computer in a locked environment—particularly if it is a server. A building that is locked to unauthorized users, as most homes and offices are, is generally acceptable.

If you use a physical lock (a cable from the computer to a wall for instance), keep the key in a safe place for additional security. Remember, if the key is lost or unavailable, authorized users might be unable to work.

Configuration for Medium-Level Security

First, security system administrators must set up appropriate account policies. Users must form good logon habits, such as logging off at the end of each day and memorizing (rather than writing down) their passwords.

In the NT Security system, a series of specific steps are taken to set up and ensure medium-level security. Following are brief descriptions of these concepts, with the technical and implementation components left to later chapters.

Set Up User Accounts and Groups In the medium-security environment, a user account and password are required to use a computer. Windows NT provides a GUI tool, the User Manager, for creating, deleting, and disabling user accounts. User Manager also allows you to set password policies and other security system policies, and to organize user accounts into Groups.

Maintain Separate Administrative and User Accounts The *least-privilege use* axiom is used at the medium-security level. This axiom advocates that, to avoid accidental changes to secured resources, the account with the least privilege that can accomplish the task should be used. You use separate accounts for administrative activity and user activity. All administrators should have two user accounts: one for administrative tasks and one for general activity. For example, viruses can do much more damage if activated from an account with Administrator privileges.

The built-in Administrator account must be renamed to something else. This account is the only one that can never be locked out and is thus attractive to hackers. By renaming the account, you force hackers to guess the account name as well as the password.

The Guest Account In medium security, it is not necessarily required that the Guest account be disabled. However, the Guest account should be prohibited from writing or deleting any files, directories, or Registry keys. If the computer is for public use, the Guest account can be used for public logons.

Precautions for Logging On and Logging Off Under medium security, *all* users should *always* press Ctrl+Alt+Del before logging on. "Trojan horse" programs are designed to collect account passwords while appearing as a logon screen. Pressing Ctrl+Alt+Del foils such programs and provides a secure logon screen. Users should also either log off or lock the workstation if they will be away from the computer for any length of time.

Passwords In medium security, protected usernames and passwords are your greatest ally. Anyone who knows a username and the correct password can log on. Here are a few tips for using passwords:

- Change passwords frequently, and don't reuse passwords.
- Avoid passwords that are easily guessed or common words that appear in the dictionary. A phrase or a combination of letters and numbers works well.
- Don't write a password down; choose one that is easy to remember.

Protect Files and Directories The NTFS file system provides more security features than the FAT system and should be used whenever security is a concern.

Backups for Medium-Level Security

Regular backups are a must to protect your data from hardware failures, accidents, viruses, and other malicious tampering. Since files must be read to be backed up, and they must be written to be restored, backup rights should be limited to administrators and backup operators. Also, you'll want to assign accountability for the proper operation of the backup and restore procedures.

Protecting the Registry

All the initialization and configuration information used by Windows NT is stored in the Registry. Under medium security, you'll need to ensure that the Registry Editor will be used only by individuals who thoroughly understand the tool, the Registry itself, and the effects of changes to various keys in the Registry. Mistakes made in the Registry Editor can render part or all of the system unusable.

Auditing for Medium Security

When you establish an audit policy, you'll need to consider the overhead in disk space and CPU usage of the auditing options against the advantages of these options. For medium security, you'll want to at least audit failed logon attempts, attempts to access sensitive data, and changes to security settings.

Maximum Security

Although medium security is sufficient for most installations, additional security precautions are required for computers that contain highly sensitive data, or that are at high risk for theft or malice.

Physical Considerations for High-Level Security

In addition to the physical security considerations for low- and medium-security configurations, the requirements for high-level security include examining your physical network links, where the lines come into your office or building. You may also want to control who has physical access to the computer.

As soon as you put a computer on the network, you add a funnel or route to your system. This access port must be secured. Maintenance of user account validation and object permissions is sufficient for medium-level security, but for maximum security you'll need to make sure the network itself is secure.

The two risks to network connections are unauthorized network users and unauthorized network taps. By containing the network entirely within a secure building, you prevent or at least minimize the chance of unauthorized taps. If the cabling must pass through unsecured areas, use optical fiber links rather than twisted pair, to foil attempts to tap the wire and collect transmitted data. Use data encryption techniques on all transmissions outside your site.

Controlling Access to the Computer No computer will ever be completely secure if people other than authorized users can physically access it. For maximum security on a computer that is not physically secure (locked safely away), consider the following security measures:

- Disable or remove the floppy disk drive.
- The CPU should have a case that cannot be opened without a key. Store the key in a safe location away from the computer.
- The entire hard disk should be NTFS.

Controlling Access to the Power Switch Users without shutdown rights should be barred from the computer's power or reset switches. The most secure computers (other than those in locked and guarded rooms) expose only the computer's keyboard, monitor, mouse, and (when appropriate) printer to users. The CPU and removable media drives can be locked away where only authorized personnel can access them.

On many of today's new machines, the system can be protected using a *power-on password*. This prevents unauthorized users from starting an operating system other than Windows NT. Power-on passwords are a function of the computer hardware, not the operating system, so check with your hardware venders for choices.

Other Maximum Security Options

Some maximum-security options can be implemented only by using the Registry Editor. The following list of topics also need to be addressed for maximum security. Bear them in mind as you read this book.

- Assigning user rights
- Protecting files and directories
- Protecting the Registry
- Using the Schedule Service (AT Command)
- Hiding the last username
- Restricting the boot process
- Allowing only logged-on users to shut down the computer
- Controlling access to removable media

The C2 Evaluation Process

The most recognized (at least, in the U.S.) baseline measurement for a secure operating system is the U.S. Department of Defense (DOD) criteria for a C2-level secure system. C2 security is a requirement for many U.S. government installations, and its standards are of immense value to all organizations concerned about the security of business-sensitive data.

Orange Book Standards

The requirements for a C2 secure system are defined by the U.S. DOD's National Computer Security Center (NCSC), a division of the National Security Agency (NSA). These requirements are published in the *Trusted Computer System Evaluation Criteria*, also known as the "Orange Book." All systems desiring certification for C2 security, whether network operating systems or stand-alone operating systems, are evaluated under the criteria set forth in the Orange Book. Windows NT Server was designed from the ground up to comply with the C2 requirements.

Let's take a look at some of the most important requirements of C2-level security.

- **Discretionary Access Control.** The owner of a resource such as a file must be able to control access to the resource.
- **Object Reuse.** The operating system must protect data stored in memory for one process so that other processes do not improperly use it. For example, Windows NT Server protects memory so that its contents cannot be read after a process frees it. In addition, when a file is deleted, users must not be able to access the file's data even when the disk space used by that file is allocated for use by another file. This protection must also extend to the disk, monitor, keyboard, mouse, and any other devices.

- **Identification and Authentication.** Users must uniquely identify themselves. With Windows NT Server, this is achieved by each user's typing a unique logon name and password before being allowed access to the system. The system must be able to use this unique identification to track the activities of the user.
- **Auditing.** System administrators must be able to audit security-related events and the actions of individual users. Access to this audit data must be limited to authorized administrators.

Is the Windows NT C2 Secure?

The NCSC has determined that Windows NT Workstation and Windows NT Server version 3.5, combined with Service Pack 3 for Windows NT 3.5, satisfy all of the specified requirements of the criteria as class C2. This applies to both stand-alone machines and networked installations. According to Microsoft, there have been no changes in Windows NT 4.0 that should change the status of its C2 rating. This rating process is very lengthy and complex, and it is expected that NT 4.0 will be explicitly certified.

As of January 31, 1997, NT has also received an FC2/E3 security rating, the European equivalent of C2 security. This evaluation means that Windows NT Server is the first and only PC-based server operating system to have a fully networked C2 or FC2 security evaluation from either ITSEC or the NSA. In our opinion, Windows NT is the most secure PC-based server operating system available.

Windows NT Server C2 Implementation

The Windows NT Server C2 implementation is entirely software based. This means users will not have to install additional hardware on either their servers or clients to meet C2 security requirements.

Some other vendors of network technology, most notably Novell, include a hardware component that provides some of the C2 security characteristics. In fact, our research shows that NetWare has not completed an evaluation from any internationally recognized security council. Windows NT (both the server and the workstation), by comparison, was designed from the beginning to be C2-secure. Every process and feature was designed with C2 security in mind. In fact, Windows NT Server is so secure that certain processes (identification and authentication, and the ability to separate users from their functions) meet B2 security requirements, a level of security that is even more exacting than C2.

Designing an operating system this way—as opposed to adding components on top of an already complete operating system—provides benefits such as cost efficiency, reliability, and robustness. As the NCSC says in the

Final Evaluation Report of the Windows NT operating system, "...[W]hen security is not an absolute requirement of the initial design, it is virtually impossible through later add-ons to provide the kind of uniform treatment to diverse system resources that Windows NT provides." Windows NT Server is fundamentally secure.

Caution

> *No operating system can provide* physical *security for your computers. External media drives (floppy disk, CD-ROM, and so on) provide the physical means for anyone to bypass Windows NT and gain access to your files.*

Summary

A security policy is required for all system administrators—whether your objective is to create the Fort Knox of networking or simply to protect your own private SOHO. We now know that many components work together to make up the big picture of security in Windows NT. Let's move on to finding out how this whole thing works.

- *Pre-NT History*
- *The Beginnings of Windows NT*
- *Windows NT and the Concept of Objects*
- *The Windows NT Architecture*
- *Workgroups and Domains*
- *The Windows NT Domain Model*
- *Domains and Security*

CHAPTER

2

Operating Systems and NT

MICROSOFT HAS FOR YEARS WORKED AT CREATING AN OPERATING system that is resilient, efficient, and easy for the user to understand and operate. It began with MS-DOS and has culminated with Windows NT 4.0.

Pre-NT History

MS-DOS made its debut in 1981 when IBM introduced the IBM PC. The original operating system was intended for simplistic platforms, such as the IBM XT (8088). However, the operating system failed to take advantage of the more advanced AT model computers (80286 and 80386).

DOS supports a single user running a single process; it does that in real mode, using only 640K of memory, regardless of how much the machine has. There is no multitasking, no swapping, no protection, and no virtual memory (these terms are discussed later in the chapter). There is no network support and no security. Yet, due to its simplicity, MS-DOS became a very popular application development platform. The PC became an enormous commercial success, and hence MS-DOS came to be very well established.

Windows 3.*x* was Microsoft's breakthrough environment. It sported a Graphical User Interface(GUI) that was much friendlier to use than MS-DOS. It also allowed users to run multiple processes simultaneously in separate "windows." The graphical environment was also easier to use for development. Windows-based applications flourished, and Windows took off as a choice operating environment.

One of the drawbacks to Windows was its continuing reliance on MS-DOS. Windows was initially conceived as a desktop environment, and Microsoft did not include any built-in networking support early on. Eventually, Microsoft added peer-to-peer networking and released Windows for Workgroups 3.11. The Windows product was never intended to function as a network client; therefore, Microsoft decided to create a new 32-bit desktop client that was meant for networking.

Windows 95 succeeded MS-DOS, Windows 3.1, and Windows for Workgroups 3.11 as a standard desktop client. The goals of this new OS were simple:

- To be easy to use
- To be faster and more powerful
- To provide robust network connectivity
- To be compatible with existing applications

Microsoft met these goals by providing a 32-bit, multitasking, multithreaded operating system that presents an intuitive interface. At the same time, it supports full backward compatibility with legacy hardware and software. Microsoft also included support for multiple network redirectors, thus allowing greater connectivity in heterogeneous environments.

OS/2 LAN Manager was a joint project by Microsoft and IBM. LanMan was the predecessor to Windows NT (you could even call it NT's father). Microsoft's first network operating system, LanMan was designed primarily for a small LAN rather than large enterprise networks—as evidenced by its reliance on NetBEUI- or NetBIOS-based protocols. Many of Windows NT's networking concepts stem from OS/2 LanMan.

The Beginnings of Windows NT

Windows NT is the flagship of Microsoft's network operating systems. The company had several goals in mind when they set out to create this OS. They wanted reliability, stability, good performance, and top-notch security. In Windows NT they have all of that and more.

Most Microsoft applications, including Word, Excel, and Windows 95, are designed solely for the single workstation. They work fine across a network but were not designed with that primarily in mind. The Windows 3.1 and 95 versions were fundamentally designed as graphical interfaces between the user and the OS. With Windows NT, however, a whole new approach to a Microsoft operating system took shape.

The original mission of Windows NT was born back in 1988, when Microsoft wanted to design a new operating system from the ground up. Not satisfied with MS-DOS or OS/2, the company looked to a totally new system to take PCs into the 1990s. The primary goals of this New Technology operating system are outlined below.

Distributed Computing	NT has enhanced networking capabilities built in, including management of hardware resources such as disk space and processing power.
Government-Certifiable Security	NT is built with the Class C2 level of computer security, the NCSC standard for government security compliance.
Multiprocessing and Scalability	NT can run the same application on single and multiprocessor computers.
Portability	NT was designed in a language that allows it to be easily ported to different architectures—for example, from CISC processors to RISC-based systems.
POSIX Compliance	NT meets the U.S. government procurement standard of POSIX (Portable Operating System Interface)[1] so that it is flexible across many platforms and application environments.

1. POSIX began as an effort by the IEEE community to promote the portability of applications across UNIX environments. Today it is not limited to the UNIX environment; it can be implemented on non-UNIX operating systems, as was done with the IEEE Std. 1003.1-1990 (POSIX.1) implementation on the VMS, MPE, and CTOS operating systems. POSIX actually consists of a set of standards that range from POSIX.1 to POSIX.12.

Windows NT and the Concept of Objects

Although the NT design goals shape the product and help us understand NT's use and capabilities, understanding how it is constructed—its architecture—is key to understanding the security system. NT's architecture model is based on the concept of objects.

Software *objects* are a combination of computer instructions and data that models the behavior of things. Objects are run-time instances of a particular *object type* that can be manipulated by an operating system process. The object type includes

- A system-defined data type
- A list of operations that can be performed upon the object (such as Wait, Create, or Cancel)
- A set of object attributes

Objects themselves are composed of

- Attributes, which define the object's state
- Behavior, which modifies the attributes
- An identity, which distinguishes one object from all others

Objects interact by passing messages back and forth. The sending object is known as the *client,* and the receiving object is known as the *server*. The client requests, and the server responds. In the course of conversation, the client and server roles often alternate between objects.

Windows NT is not an object-oriented system in the strictest sense, but it does use objects to represent internal system resources. NT uses an *object metaphor* that is prevalent throughout the architecture of the system. When viewed using Windows NT, all of the following appear as ordinary objects:

- Printers
- Keyboard
- Mouse
- Tape devices
- Storage devices
- Folders and directories
- Processes and threads
- Shared memory segments
- Access rights

As you can see from this list, virtually all things in Windows NT are considered objects and can be manipulated as such. Throughout this book, consider this list when we refer to objects.

The Windows NT Architecture

A working knowledge of the functionality of Windows NT security begins with an understanding of the system architecture. In a multitasking, multithreaded operating system such as Windows NT, applications share a variety of system resources, including the computer's memory, I/O devices, files, and system processors.

Windows NT's set of security components ensures that applications cannot access these resources without authorization—also a C2 requirement. Windows NT uses two modes of operation for these security components—User mode and Kernel mode—to maintain operating efficiency and integrity. Figure 2.1 displays Windows NT 4.0's architecture.

Figure 2.1

Windows NT 4.0's architecture

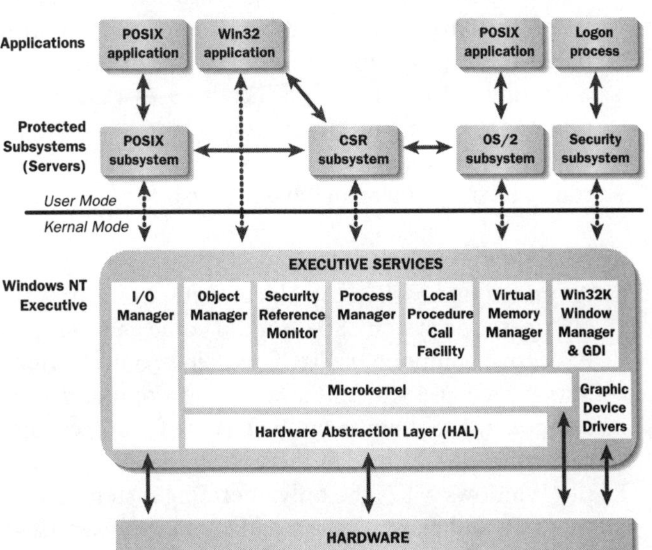

NOTE. *One of the changes to Windows NT 4.0's internal architecture is the relocation of the Graphical Device Interface (GDI) and user interface from the Win32 subsystem in User mode to the Windows NT Executive Services in Kernel mode. (NT Executive will be defined later in this chapter.) This change provides increased performance to multimedia applications and other graphically intensive programs. These changes have no effect on NT's security or reliability.*

User Mode

Applications and the subsystems that support them run in User mode. User mode processes are limited by the following:

- No direct access to hardware.
- Assigned address space is limited.
- Hard disk space may have to be used as virtual RAM.
- Kernel mode components have a higher priority.

User Mode processes cannot directly access resources. The Kernel mode component must grant resource access requests, which provide protection against unauthorized users and malfunctioning applications. User mode processes are typically lower in priority than Kernel mode processes. Therefore, Kernel mode processes have more access to CPU cycles than User mode processes.

Kernel Mode

The Windows NT Executive Services are central to all major operating system functions. Because of this, it is important to protect them from User mode applications and subsystems. The Executive Services are protected by operating in Kernel mode, which isolates a memory area securely from all other applications yet provides access to all of the memory on the computer. Only Kernel mode components can access resources directly. Processes that run at Kernel mode can have higher priority and thus can be faster.

NT Executive

As mentioned earlier, the object metaphor is prevalent within the Windows NT operating system. So it should come as no surprise that the Kernel and Executive components are based on an object-oriented model. This model allows for a consistent and uniform view of security, right down to the essential components that make up the basics of the operating system. This is a significant concept. Because of this tight integration of operating system and security, Windows NT is the only operating system that has practical commercial uses (file and print services, and application services) and also provides a security model that is truly inherent in every operation performed.

Windows NT uses the same routines for both access validation and audit checks of all protected objects. That is, whether someone is trying to access a file/folder (object) on the disk or a process (object) in memory, there is one component in the system that is required to perform access checks, regardless of the object type.

The Executive, except for a user interface, is a complete operating system unto itself; it is never modified or recompiled by the system Administrator. The Executive is actually a group of objects sometimes called *managers.* Each manager object is a software component that provides basic operating-system services to the protected subsystems and to other managers. The Executive object managers are as follows:

- I/O Manager
- Object Manager
- Security Reference Monitor
- Process Manager
- Local Procedure Call Facility (LPC)
- Virtual Memory Manager
- Window Manager
- Graphics Device Interface (GDI)
- Graphics Device Drivers (GDD)

The Executive components and services communicate through controlled interfaces and are completely independent of one another. This object model allows existing Executive objects and managers to be replaced with ones that implement new features or technologies. As long as the integrity of the existing interface is maintained, the operating system integrity remains secure.

The Executive services that deal primarily with security and security related issues are the Object Manager, the Process Manager, the Virtual Memory Manager, and the Security Reference Monitor.

Object Manager

Objects are run-time instances of a specific object type that can be manipulated by an operating system process. As explained earlier, the object type includes a system-defined data type, a list of operations that can be performed upon it (such as Wait, Create, or Cancel), and a set of object attributes.

Before a process can manipulate a Windows NT object, the process must first acquire a *handle* to the object. An *object handle* includes access control information and a pointer to the object itself. All object handles are created through the Object Manager.

In addition to creating handles, the Object Manager manages the global *namespace* for Windows NT and tracks the creation and use of objects by any process. This namespace facilitates access to all named objects that are contained in the local computer environment. Some of the objects that can have names include the following:

- Directory objects
- Symbolic link objects
- Semaphore and event objects
- Process and thread objects
- Section and segment objects
- Port objects
- File/folder objects

The object name space is modeled after a hierarchical file system, in which directory names in a path are separated by a backslash (\).

Process Manager

The *Process Manager* is the component that tracks two types of objects: process objects and thread objects.

- A *process object* is defined as an address space, a set of objects (resources) visible to the process, and a set of threads that run in the context of the process.
- A *thread* is the most basic entity that can be scheduled in the system.

The Process Manager provides a standard set of services for creating, deleting, and using threads and processes in the context of a particular subsystem environment.

The Windows NT process model works in conjunction with the security model and the Virtual Memory Manager (defined just below) to provide interprocess protection. Each process is assigned a *security access token*. When a thread within a process references a protected object, the Windows NT access-validation routines use the object's access tokens to determine rights of execution and handling. (For more information about how Windows NT uses access tokens, see Chapters 5 and 6.)

The Virtual Memory Manager

The *Virtual Memory Manager* (VMM) maps virtual addresses in the process's address space to physical pages in the computer's memory. In doing so, it hides the physical organization of memory from the process's threads. This ensures that the thread can access its process's memory as needed, but not the memory of other processes. (For further information on VMM, see the Windows NT Resource Kit.)

The Security Reference Monitor

The Windows NT security model discussed in Chapter 5 consists of the Security Reference Monitor component plus two user mode services: the protected subsystems called Logon Process and Security.

The Security Reference Monitor (SRM) is responsible for enforcing the access-validation and audit-generation policy defined by the local Security subsystem. SRM provides services to both Kernel and User modes for validating access to objects, checking user privileges, and generating audit messages.

The User mode's protected subsystems, Logon Process and Security, are the other two components of the Windows NT security model and are discussed further in Chapter 5.

Changes to Protected Subsystems in Windows NT 4.0

The protected subsystems are User mode services that are started when Windows NT is started. There are two types of protected subsystems: integral and environment. An *integral subsystem* is a service that performs an important operating system function, such as security. An *environment subsystem* is a service that provides support to applications written for operating system environments, such as OS/2.

Windows NT 3.5*x* differs slightly from NT 4.0 in that it has three environment subsystems: the Win32® subsystem, the POSIX subsystem, and the OS/2 subsystem. The Win32 (or 32-bit Windows) subsystem is the native subsystem of Windows NT 3.5*x*. It provides the most capabilities and efficiencies to its applications. The POSIX and OS/2 subsystems provide compatibility environments for their respective applications and have fewer features than the Win32 subsystem.

Windows NT 4.0 has two environment subsystems and the CSR (Client Server) subsystem. Components of the Win32 subsystem have been moved down into the kernel. These changes are transparent to applications and users, but result in a variety of improvements to graphics performance and memory requirements. They also simplify the design of the Windows NT Win32 subsystem.

Changes to the code that operates in the *Kernel* or *privileged* mode of any operating system can be of concern to the continued stability of the product and to application designers and system architects. Because such changes potentially affect the operating system's compatibility with existing applications, as well as its portability and reliability, such changes should be explained and justified. Microsoft has done so in a white paper called "Kernel-mode User and GDI," which is included on both the NT 4.0 Server and NT 4.0 Workstation CDs.

In essence, the changes in the Kernel, GDI, and Win32 subsystems have had no effect on the security of NT. Furthermore, since security is in no way dependent on those changed components, the workings of the security model are identical to the NT 3.5*x* system.

Workgroups and Domains

Windows NT-based computers operate in either a domain or a workgroup. The difference, as you will see in later chapters, is where security validation occurs. In this section we will define workgroup and domains, describe the four domain models, and discuss the pros and cons of workgroup and domain models.

Workgroups (Independent Management)

A workgroup is a collection of computers and users arranged primarily for sharing resources such as files/folders and printers. As part of a workgroup, a Windows NT-based computer has its own security accounts database (Microsoft now calls this the *directory database*). Resources and accounts are managed at each computer in the workgroup.

Workgroups function well for small numbers of computers that share resources with users on other computers. A workgroup does not offer any advantages for security. Its basic role is to provide a logical grouping of computers for browsing purposes. This model is ideal for three to five computers on a local area network (LAN).

A workgroup can contain Windows NT Workstations and Windows NT Member Servers. The workgroup model is a networking arrangement in which there is no centralized management of resources, administration, and security. Since every computer has its own accounts, administration, and security policies, each Windows NT machine in the workgroup requires an individual to maintain its own security policies and User accounts.

Administration of other machines in the workgroup (including computers running MS-DOS, Windows for Workgroups (WFW), or Windows 95) is separate, different, and possibly nonexistent.

Domains (Centralized Management)

A domain is a logical grouping of computers and users that all share a central or common database; the database stores security and User account information for the domain. As a member of a domain, a Windows NT-based computer can share resources, but the domain provides a centralized approach to administration, security, and account maintenance. The centralized management and common database are handled by one or more Windows NT Server domain controllers and are titled the Windows NT Directory Services.

Windows NT Directory Services

Windows NT Directory Services (NTDS) manage a secure, distributed directory database and provide services for both end-users and network administrators. For users, NTDS supports authentication services that allow users to log on from any desktop on the network with a single Logon ID and password.

The same ID/password are used for access to services, applications, and resources located anywhere else on the network. For administrators, NTDS provides graphical management tools, auditing, and security services that simplify the creation and maintenance of user identities and rights, and resource access protection.

Trusts

Trusts are a mechanism in Windows NT that allow domains to access the resources of other domains. Trusts allow administrators to easily extend a Windows NT model to reflect the structure of the organization. Once trust relationships are established, they are used to validate users between domains and assign permissions to Users and groups.

By default, no administrative control is passed when a trust is established. Furthermore, no user or group is automatically granted access into the other domain. This has to be given by an Administrator.

Trusts enable Windows NT Directory Services to keep a centralized management of accounts even when there are multiple domains. Users can log on from any machine in the network, as long as their account is defined in the correct domain.

There are two type of domains in a trust relationship: trusted and trusting.

- The *trusted domain*, also called the *accounts domain,* contains the User accounts. The trusted domain may physically consist of just a single machine, but it may have 40,000 users defined in it.
- The *trusting domain* contains the resources the users are accessing. Trusting domains usually represent the logical or functional structure of your organization (the Sales and Accounting divisions, for instance) or possibly regional areas (Phoenix, Chicago).

When designers create multiple trusts, various models are created. In the next section, we provide an overview the four domain models but do not attempt to explore the complex world of multidomain networking. These subjects are covered in depth in many NT books, including Microsoft's Resource Kits and System Administrator Guides.

The Windows NT Domain Model

The administrative unit of the Windows NT Directory Services is a domain. In a domain, workstations and servers perform secure logon validation via NTDS. They also provide resource access to Users in the common directory database. In addition, they function as part of the centrally administered group of computers.

In a domain, Window NT Server machines work either as domain controllers (Primary or Backup) or as stand-alone servers. Each domain maintains its own directory database and has one and only one Primary Domain Controller (PDC). An Administrator needs to create a User account only once in the directory database, and the PDC will synchronize the directory database with all Backup Domain Controllers (BDCs). When users log on to a domain, a domain controller validates the logon. The domain controller checks the directory database for the username, password, and logon restrictions.

When a resource is shared on a Window NT-based computer, permissions can be assigned to the User accounts that exist in the domain's User account database. Since this database is centralized, all the administration operations are centralized.

The Four Domain Models

All domain installations stem from four basic domain models: Single Domain, Master Domain, Multiple Master Domain, and Complete Trust. The model chosen depends on the type of administration your company needs (centralized or decentralized). The other major criterion is the organization of the network's resources (dispersed or centralized). Table 2.1 presents guidelines for choosing a model.

Table 2.1

Domain Models

NETWORK CHARACTERISTICS:	SINGLE DOMAIN	MASTER DOMAIN	MULTIPLE MASTER	COMPLETE TRUST
Centralized administration	x	x	x	
Decentralized administration				x
Centralized resources	x			
Dispersed resources		x	x	x
More than 15,000 accounts			x	

Single Domain Model

A single domain model is used when your company requires centralized account/security administration and centralized resource management. This model suits small, single-site environments.

Compared with the other three domain models, the setup of a single domain model is quite simple. No trust relationships are necessary. The disadvantage of this model is its lack of scalability. If the number of accounts grows considerably in this environment, network may become difficult to manage. This model offers no way of logically dividing up down departments and allowing them to manage their own resources. The domain Administrators control everything in this model. If you have a centralized MIS department that is in control of everything, this model is optimal.

Master Domain Model

A master domain model is used when your company requires centralized accounts/security administration and decentralized resource management. This model is used when each department in your organization wants to manage its own resources, but an MIS department manages all the users.

Each user is defined in the master domain. Resources such as database applications, e-mail servers, and printers are placed in resource domains based on which department the resource belongs to. One-way trusts are established between the resource domains and the master domain. This gives all accounts that only exist in the master domain access to resources in the entire enterprise.

Multiple Master Domain Model

A multiple master domain model is used when your organization requires centralized accounts/security administration and decentralized resource management, but the number of users exceeds 15,000. This model offers the greatest flexibility and scalability. Each user will be defined on one of the master domains and will be able to access any of the resource domains.

Complete Trust Model

A complete trust model offers no centralized administration and decentralized resource management. In this model, the staff of every department will maintain the User accounts as well as the resources. There generally is no central group of Administrators or MIS department that will manage the users. This model works best in organizations that demand departmental independence.

The disadvantage of the complete trust model is the lack of centralized administration. This model demands cooperation between the various Administrators. The other major disadvantage is that a great number of trust relationships must be established and maintained.

Domains and Security

When choosing among the various domain models, here are a few things to keep in mind as you develop your environment:

- When a trust is developed between two domains, no administrative consent is exchanged. Administrators from both sides must grant the other set of administrative rights to manage the trusting domain.
- When trusts are established, Windows NT requires several levels of security, including a password that both sides must enter. Windows NT also establishes a password that it will check to verify that the original trust has not been compromised.
- When providing access to your domain for groups from other domains, you are directly relying on the Administrators of the trusted domain to make sure the correct users are in the proper groups.
- The trusted domain Administrators are also relying on the trusting Administrators to correctly use the groups and give them access to the resources they were intended to access.
- Always draw your domain model using some sort of flowcharting program. This will give you an idea of what your environment looks like at all times. Remember to also list all groups and the resources to which they are to be granted access.

Summary

This chapter has given you the background you need to understand the Windows NT structure and its architecture. This client/server, modularized architecture gives Windows NT its flexibility and its stability. You've also learned about trusts and their role in the Windows NT environment. Trusts are a basic tool that allows two domains to share resources. By combining multiple trusts together, we end up with one of four domain models.

Every Windows NT domain implementation takes the form of one of these domain models, or often a blend of models. The model you choose will greatly influence your security policy. It is necessary to understand these fundamental concepts if you are going to be able to implement security in Widows NT.

The next chapter takes you through the first step in dealing with users and groups.

- *User Manager for Domains*
- *Users and User Accounts*
- *Groups and Group Accounts*
- *User Account Properties*
- *Creating Users and Groups*
- *Developing a Group Strategy*
- *Summary*

CHAPTER

3

User and Group Administration

ONE OF THE FUNDAMENTAL RESPONSIBILITIES OF SYSTEM administrators is tracking who is on the network and what they are doing. Windows NT 4.0 requires every individual who needs access to resources to properly identify themselves before they are granted any rights or permissions on the system. The management of these individuals is a challenge. Thus it is critical for system administrators to have a complete understanding of user accounts and groups, in order to accomplish a high-level security model in Windows NT. Creating a secured environment in which these individuals can access and store resources is an equal challenge.

In this chapter we will examine how the Windows NT tool, User Manager for Domains, helps you to create user accounts and group accounts, to meet both these challenges efficiently. And we've also coined our own special acronym for its unwieldy name—in this chapter, UM4D will mean User Manager for Domains.

User Manager for Domains

User Manager for Domains (see Figure 3.1) is a GUI-based administrative utility tool for managing user and group accounts. The tool is also used to develop security policies and manage trust relationships in the Windows NT environment. Any user may launch UM4D, but to effectively use it you must be a member of either the Administrators or Account Operators group. Individual users may also use the tool to create local groups.

Figure 3.1

User Manager for Domains

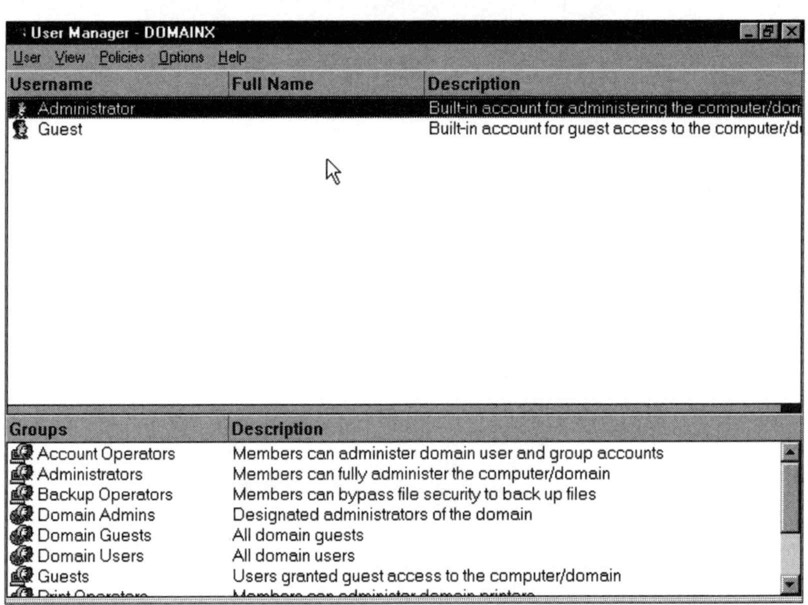

Windows NT installs UM4D only on domain controllers. However, the tool may be loaded on any NT Workstation or NT Server. This is done by adding the Server Tools from the \Support\Srvtools directory on the NT Server 4.0 CD.

Users and User Accounts

A *user* is anyone who accesses the Windows NT machine, either interactively from the console or across the network. Users may include administrators, common users—even Windows NT itself may be a user at times.

Each user who needs access to the network should have a user account that identifies the individual as a unique person to Windows NT. Each user account has all the pertinent information Windows NT will need to grant the user access to the system and its resources. The individual will need a username and password for validation by the system. User accounts are then used by administrators to control what each unique person may do on the network or local computer.

There are three types of users in Windows NT, as described in Table 3.1.

Table 3.1

Types of NT Users

USER ACCOUNT	DESCRIPTION
Administrator	This account has complete control of the entire domain. The account comes built in to Windows NT. It cannot be deleted, but it may be copied and renamed. The Administrator account cannot be denied access to Windows NT.
Guest	This account is to give occasional users access to Windows NT. The account is built in to Windows NT. It cannot be deleted, but it may be copied and renamed. The Guest account is disabled, by default, on domain controllers.
User	These accounts are created for each person who wishes to access Windows NT. User accounts have no inherent rights or permissions. They are given access to specific resources or allowed to perform specific tasks. User accounts can be deleted, copied, or renamed.

Access to the Administrator account must be carefully controlled. As mentioned earlier, the two requirements to accessing a computer are a username and password. Since the Administrator account is a Built-In account, it should be renamed and the description should be modified. This prevents unauthorized users from obtaining either of the two keys they need to gain administrative access to the system.

The Guest account, because it can be a potential security risk, is disabled by default on Windows NT Server 4.0. If a user attempts to gain access to Windows NT without a valid username, the system will attempt to grant the user access through the Guest account. If the Guest account is enabled, the user would gain access to the NT system or domain under this account. (A technical description of this process is covered in Chapter 5.) If you choose to enable the Guest account, take care in choosing the access privileges granted.

User accounts are accounts used by individuals and internally by NT, enabling access to system resources. Normal security procedures will require each user to have their own account. This is primarily for auditing purposes and discretionary access control, which may differ from user to user.

Caution

Users or administrators may ask to share the same account to implement a specific task—for example, when several users have the task of backing up the system. You may be asked to consider a special shared user account for backup operations, to be used only when the backup routines are run. However, this and most other similar situations are actually excuses for poor security practices. There is rarely, if ever, a need to share a user account, especially when groups are appropriately set up and there is understanding and use of other back-office products, such as SQL, SMS, and Exchange.

User Rights

User rights authorize users or groups of users to perform certain tasks on each system. User rights are granted from within UM4D, with commands in the Policies menu. These rights must be allocated on each system that a user needs to access. User rights are different from *permissions,* which are applied to a resource.

Rights are generally applied to groups but can be applied to individual users as well. It is better, however, to assign rights to a group rather than to individuals (as explained later in the chapter). Once you have granted a right to a group, all members of the group inherit that right.

Figure 3.2 shows the User Rights Policy dialog. There are two types of user rights: basic and advanced. Basic rights are generally given to users for everyday tasks. Advanced rights are generally given to Windows NT system components, such as services or the kernel; some advanced rights are for programmers, such as the ability to debug programs. To view advanced rights, click on the Show Advanced User Rights check box.

Table 3.2 identifies some of the basic rights and what they allow.

Examples of some uses of basic rights are covered in the "Developing a Group Strategy" section at the end of this chapter.

Now that you have a basic understanding of user accounts, let's jump to the subject of Group accounts. Groups play a large part in user configurations, so we'll study them before we learn how to create accounts.

Figure 3.2

User Rights Policy dialog

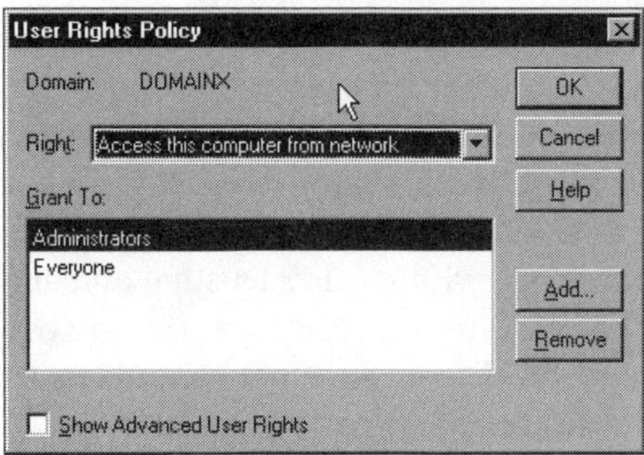

Table 3.2

Summary of Basic User Rights

BASIC RIGHTS	WHAT IS ALLOWED
Access this computer from network	Connect over the network to this computer.
Back up files and directories	Overrides NTFS permissions for backup purposes only.
Change the system time	Set the time for the internal clock of the computer.
Log on locally	Log on to the system from the keyboard interactively.
Manage Auditing and Security Log	View and clear the audit logs through Event Viewer. User may also specify which types of events and resources will be audited. This right does not allow user to enable/ disable systemwide audit policies; that may only be done by an administrator.
Restore files and directories	User can override all NTFS permissions for the purpose of restoration only.
Shut down the system	User can initiate a system shutdown while logged on locally.
Take ownership of files or other objects	Take ownership of any object under NT, regardless of user's actual permissions.

Groups and Group Accounts

A *group* is a collection of users who all need access to similar resources and/or user rights. User groups make it easier to manage domain administration because you can assign permissions to users by group and set system policies based on membership of these groups. Users with the same functional requirements are placed into groups. If some aspect of the group's administrative requirements change, you make the change on one group and thus change permissions for all the users in the group.

User groups are either *local* or *global*. The terms local and global refer not to the type of group membership, but to the extent of the group's availability to be assigned rights. Specifically, a local group may be granted access to resources only within the security context in which it was created. A global group is granted access to resources within the domain in which the group was created and within other trusting domains.

Account Names: Group account names may be up to 20 characters and are not case sensitive. The group names should be as descriptive as possible. Typically these groups are going to be used by various individuals throughout the domain to grant access to resources. Keeping a standard naming convention will prevent confusion and a possible break in security.

The account name may not contain any of the following characters:

```
" / \ ? > < + = * [ ] ; :
```

Local Groups

A local group can contain user accounts or global group accounts from the domain in which the group is located, or from any trusted domain. The chart in Figure 3.3 illustrates the process of determining membership in a local group.

As stated above, local groups operate within the security context in which they were created. What this means is, local groups created on an NT Workstation or an NT Member Server are available only on the computer where they were created.

Domain controllers in the same domain share the Security Accounts database, as referenced in Chapter 2. Therefore, a local group created in the Accounts database is available on all domain controllers.

Predefined Local Groups

Several predefined local groups are created on Windows NT machines during installation. Table 3.3 describes the predefined local groups that are common to NT Workstations, NT Member Servers, and NT Domain Controllers. Table 3.4 lists the predefined groups available on all Windows NT Workstations and Windows NT Member Servers. Table 3.5 details the predefined local groups that are available only on Windows NT domain controllers.

NOTE. *It is important to note the allowed operations for each group on its respective machines. When a user is a member of multiple groups, that user's privileges are cumulative. Consistent group strategy is discussed later in this chapter.*

Figure 3.3

What goes in a local group?

Local Group Membership

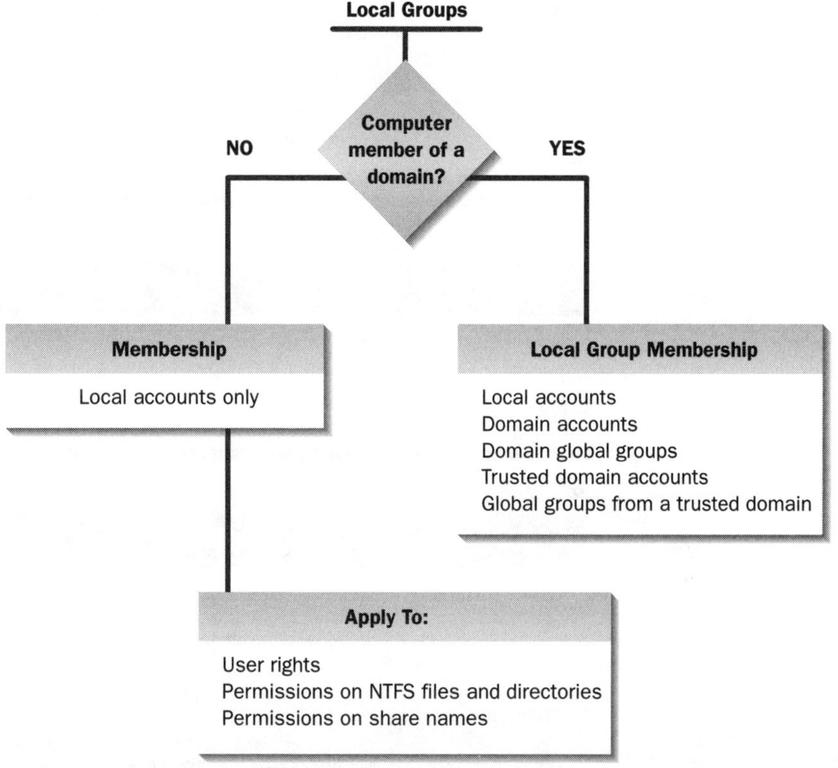

Table 3.3

Common Built-In Local Groups

GROUP	DESCRIPTION
Administrators	Members of this group have complete control over the entire system, including managing users/groups, creating/deleting partitions, managing security policies, backing up/restoring the system, and many more tasks. The Administrators group may not be denied access to the machine. This group contains the global group Domain Admins by default.
Guests	Members of this group are given access to limited resources. By default, the Guest account is disabled on NT domain controllers. This group contains the global group Domain Guests by default.
Users	Members of this group are common users within the domain. This group contains the global group Domain Users by default.

Table 3.3 (Continued)

Common Built-In Local Groups

GROUP	DESCRIPTION
Backup Operators	Members of this group can back up and restore files that they would not normally have access to. For backup purposes only, NT ignores security and allows a member of this group to use a Win32-compliant backup program to back up any file, regardless of NTFS security.
Replicator	Reserved for the Directory Replication service under NT. User accounts should not be placed in this group.

Table 3.4

NT Workstation and NT Member Server Built-In Groups

GROUP	DESCRIPTION
Power Users	Members of this group manage the resources on their local machine only, including network shares, printers, users, system shutdown, and backup/restore of the system.

Table 3.5

Windows NT Domain Controllers Built-In Groups

GROUP	DESCRIPTION
Server Operators	Members have all the rights to manage all the domain controllers, including creating network shares, backing up/restoring files, shutting down servers, and promoting/demoting domain controllers.
Account Operators	Members can manage all the user accounts within the domain's database, but cannot modify any of the administrator or operator accounts.
Print Operators	Members can manage printers on the domain controllers.

Predefined local groups have certain Built-In abilities that cannot be altered. These groups also have predefined User rights that can be changed in UM4D as described previously. Administrators should be cautious when changing these established User rights.

Global Groups

A global group is used to organize domain users into functional administrative units. It contains only individual user accounts (no groups) from the domain in which the global group is created. The chart in Figure 3.4 illustrates the process of determining membership in a global group.

Once created, a global group may be assigned permissions and rights, either in its own domain or in any trusting domain. For example, in a trusting

Figure 3.4

What goes in a global group?

Global Groups Membership

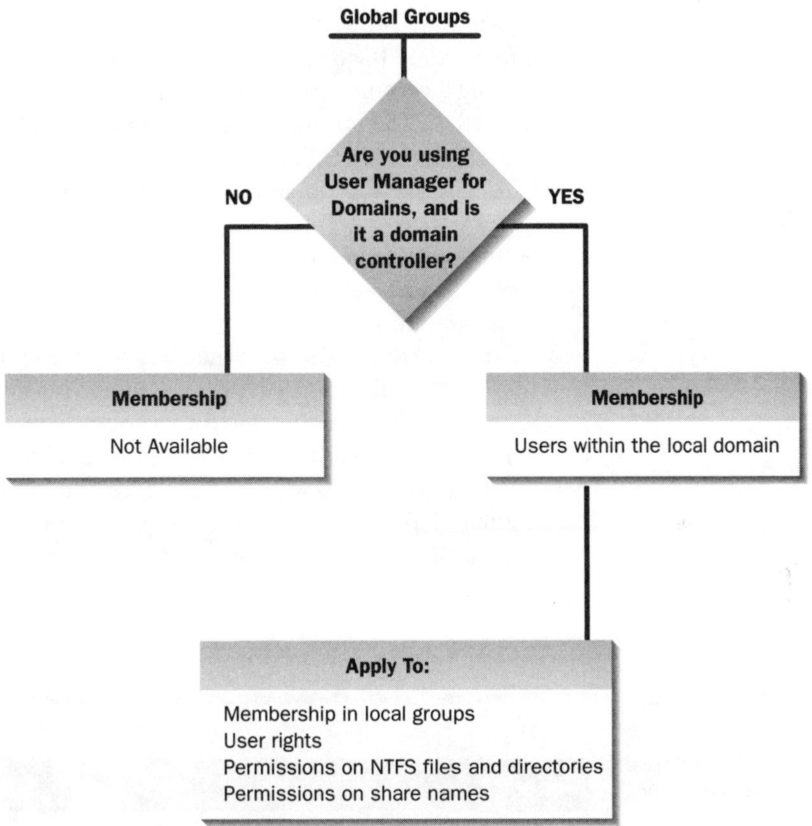

domain you may grant the same permissions for a particular resource to a global group; all members of that group have those permissions.

Global groups are available only on Windows NT domain controllers. Although there are some Built-In global groups, they do not have any inherent rights. By placing user accounts into global groups and global groups inside local groups, the user accounts inherit the rights of the local group.

When Windows NT Server is installed as a domain controller, it has three predefined global groups, as described in Table 3.6.

Each of the predefined groups in Table 3.6 has no inherent rights or Built-In abilities. They simply have a list of users. The users gain rights and privileges through the local group of which the global group is a member.

Security Identifiers (SIDs)

The Windows NT security model assigns every user account a unique number, called the Security Identifier (SID). User SIDs are created by NT using a combination of user information, time, date, and domain information. The following is an example of a SID:

S-1-5-21-126509790-576281716-852295783-500

As you can see, the number is quite complex. These values are used only by Windows NT itself to represent the user throughout the system. The number is analogous to the magnetic encoded strip on the back of your bank card—hard to decipher but full of important, valuable, and confidential information.

Groups have SIDs, too. When a new group is created in UM4D, Windows NT will create a SID. This numerical value will then be used to track the group's membership for various resources.

If a group is ever renamed, the SID remains the same; thus all users in the renamed group will still have access to all resources that the original group had access to. The only way to remove the SID permanently is to delete the group. According to Microsoft, no two SIDS will ever be the same.

Table 3.6

Windows NT Server Built-In Global Groups

GROUP	DESCRIPTION
Domain Administrators	These members need complete control over all machines in the domain. The Administrator account is a default member of this group and cannot be removed from this group. This group is a member of the Local Administrators Group.
Domain Guests	Contains domain users who require limited guest access. The Guest account is a default member of this group. This group is a member of the local Guests group.
Domain Users	Contains all the domain users. Every domain account is initially placed in this group when created. This group is a member of the local Users group.

User Account Properties

To create an effective group strategy for your NT environment, it helps to understand the bigger picture of user properties. Let's examine these properties before we see how to actually create user and group accounts.

User Properties Dialog

User accounts can be assigned properties that provide for various security levels when the user is accessing the domain. Properties are set within UM4D, with the User Properties dialog (see Figure 3.5). This dialog has many optional and some required fields. We'll first discuss the text fields in the top of the dialog, then the check boxes in the middle, and then the large property buttons at the bottom.

Figure 3.5

User Properties dialog

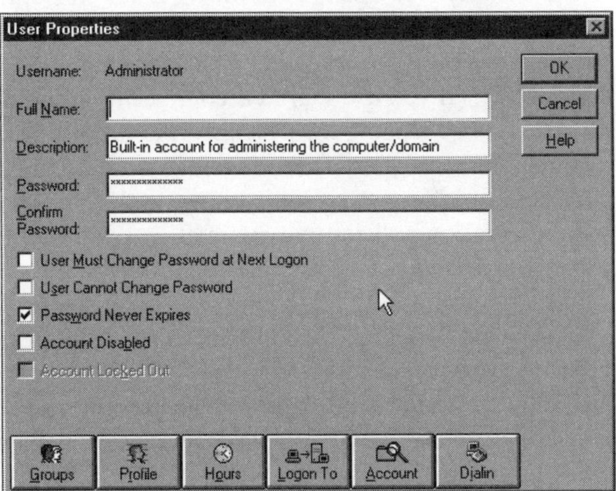

UserName. An entry in the UserName field is required. The UserName must be a unique name within the database, up to 20 characters. It is not case sensitive. The name cannot contain any of the following characters:

< > " / \ [ ] : ; + ? * , =

Full Name. The Full Name file is optional; you can enter the actual name of the user. It is recommended that you use *last name, first name* as the format.

NOTE. *There are only two ways to sort users within User Manager for Domains: by Username and Full Name.*

Description. Another optional field, Description can contain information about the user, such as department, location, or type of work.

Password and Confirm Password. Password is a mandatory field that, if left blank, defaults to null. Here you enter a password of up to 14 characters. The password is case sensitive. When user accounts are viewed in UM4D, the password always appears as 14 asterisks. This masks the actual password to prevent anyone from identifying any characteristics of the user's password. After typing an entry in the Password field, you must reenter it in the Confirm Password box to verify the previous entry.

User Must Change Password at Next Logon. When you check this check box to turn on the User Must Change Password… option, the user is forced to change the password at their next logon. This sustains complete security from the creation of the new account to the initial logon of the user.

How does this work? An administrator, when creating a new account, assigns it a password. The user is informed of the temporary password and, upon initial logon, must create a new unique password known only to that user. This procedure makes unauthorized access difficult.

User May Not Change Password. When this option is turned on, it overrides any account policies and prevents the user from changing the password. The responsibility for changing passwords then becomes a management responsibility. (If you use shared accounts, this is a good way to prevent any single user from changing the password. As stated earlier, however, we caution against the use of shared accounts.)

Password Never Expires. Turning on this option circumvents any password expiration policies that are in effect. You should check this option for all service accounts, and you may want to turn it on for an Administrator account if you want to provide your own back door.

Account Disabled. This option temporarily prevents the account from being accessed and should be turned on whenever the user will be gone for an extended period time. Disabling an account prevents it from being used at all. All the account's rights/permissions are preserved.

Property Buttons

The User Properties dialog contains six button items (see the bottom of Figure 3.5) to help you configure accounts.

Groups Button The Groups button is used to add the user to local and global groups. Strategies for this will be discussed later in this chapter.

Profile Button and Options Several options become available when you click the Profiles button, including Logon Script, Home Directory, and User Profile Path. These options appear in the User Environment Profile dialog.

Logon Script. The Logon Script option allows the administrator to set a customized logon script for the user. The logon script must be run from the machine that validates the user. (For more information on user validation, see Chapter 5.) Windows NT supports MS-DOS batch, Perl 5, and REXX as batch languages for the creation of logon scripts.

Logon scripts run from the following directory:

```
\winnt_root\system32\repl\import\scripts
```

(Note that this is the import\scripts directory, *not* the export\scripts directory.) Windows NT will accept any valid .EXE, .BAT, or .CMD file as a logon script.

Logon scripts are primarily used for standardizing drive mappings and printer connections and for launching system support applications or services. They also provide backward compatibility for MS-DOS, Windows 3.*x*, and LAN Manager users who may not use profiles for setting their network connections (for file access and printing).

NOTE. *This book does not provide in-depth coverage of logon scripts and their distribution. Logon scripts are created once and placed on the PDC in the \winnt_root\system32\repl\export\scripts directory. Then they are replicated to all BDCs and the PDC itself to the winnt_root\system32\repl\import\scripts directory. Thus they are available to all users upon logon. For more information, refer to the System Administrator Guide and NT Resource Kit.*

Home Directory. The Home Directory option allows you to specify a local or network directory as the user's home directory path. If you choose Local Path, you must provide a relative path name such as C:\USERS*username,* where *username* is the user's logon name. If you choose Connect, you can provide a drive letter for the redirection and a UNC (Universal Naming Convention) pathname such as \\\\Server1\Users*username.*

NOTE. *There are many options for deploying home directories for the convenience of end-users, but these options have no real bearing on security. For more information, see the NT 4.0 Resource Kit.*

Hours. You may need to limit the hours of access available to users. The Logon Hours dialog (see Figure 3.6) allows the administrator to set specific times when each authorized user may log on to the network. This can be an effective security tool because it prevents users from accessing data outside their normal working hours.

Logon To Button The Logon To button allows you to specify the computers (by computer name) at which a user may log on. Clicking this button displays a dialog where you can designate up to eight computers that are accessible by the user. If a user then tries to log on from another computer not in the list, the validating computer (PDC or BDC) will deny access. If you do not use this control, a user is allowed to log on from any network computer.

Figure 3.6

Logon Hours dialog

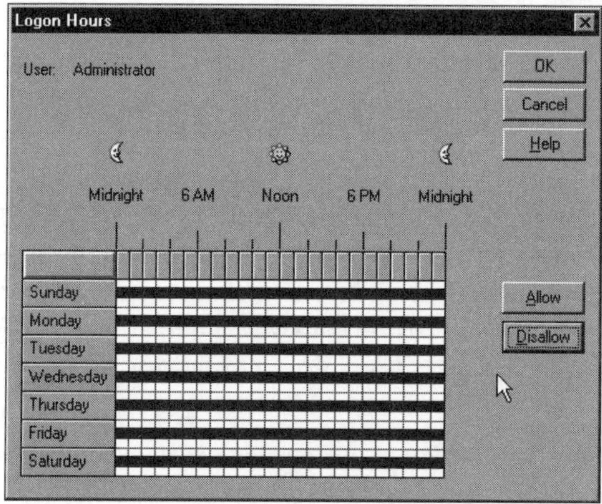

This is an effective security measure. When used appropriately, it can prevent "interoffice hopping," which often leads to a breakdown in security from users' revealing their account names and passwords to others.

Account Button The settings available from the Account button are Account Expires and Account Type.

The Account Expires setting lets the administrator designate a date on which the account will become disabled. At that point, the account's properties can be changed and the expiration date extended. This setting is useful for temporary accounts.

The Account Type setting determines the scope of the account. Global Account is a normal account that can be used to interactively log on to the domain. Local Account is used to provide nondomain accounts (accounts whose domain has no trust relationship access to local resources). A local account can only be used across the network by a nondomain user.

Dialin Button The Dialin button lets you provide remote users with the permissions required to use Windows NT Remote Access Service (RAS, or Dial-Up Networking). The Dialin Information dialog (see Figure 3.7) also lets you place callback security on a per-user basis. A user must meet this criterion before NT will allow remote access.

Copying User Accounts

You can copy any user account to create a new unique account. When you copy a user account, the new account will have only properties that are set within the User Properties dialog (as discussed in the preceding section).

Figure 3.7

The Dialin Information dialog

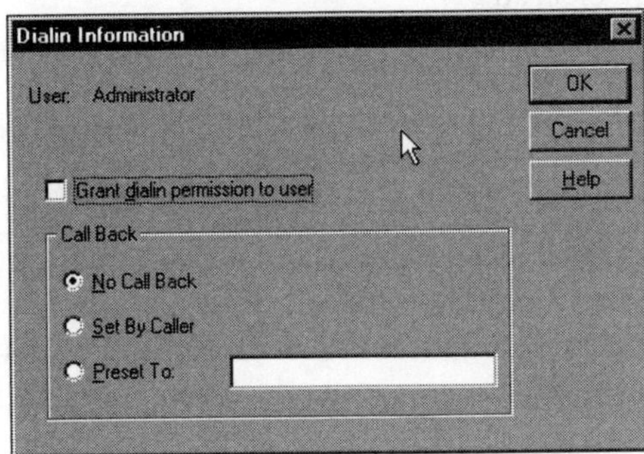

Creating a new user account by copying does *not* copy rights assigned to files, folders or directories, and other objects.

You may want to copy a user account to create multiple user accounts with similar account properties; this is often called a *template*. The administrator can use templates for creating quick and consistent user accounts. This method takes less time and may also reduce errors in assigning proper rights/ permissions to an account.

It is recommended that a template be created for each type of user. For example, you might create a template with all the appropriate options and group memberships established for users in the Engineering department. This template can then be used whenever a new user is added in that department. Just copy the template and modify the new account according to what is appropriate for the new user.

What Gets Copied and What Doesn't

When you copy a user account record to create another user account, not all of the items in the User Properties dialog are copied to the new account.

The following items are copied directly from an existing user account to a new user account:

- Description text.
- Group account memberships.
- Profile button settings, such as Home Directory (good if you use variables). See the Windows NT 4.0 Resource Kits for more information.
- Status of the User Cannot Change Password option.
- Status of the Password Never Expires option.

When you copy an existing user account to create a new user, the following items are cleared:

- Username and Full Name.
- Status of the User Must Change Password at Next Logon option.
- Status of the Account Disabled option.

Bear in mind that any rights and permissions that have been granted to an existing user account do not get copied. User rights are not inherited. Users gain rights by membership to groups. A new user will obtain immediate rights based on the group memberships applied to the user.

Renaming User Accounts

When an account is renamed, all rights and permissions granted to the account are retained. The Security Identifier (SID) never changes; only the user's name changes. (This is like changing your last name when getting married; your Social Security number remains the same.)

The only way to remove a SID is to delete the user account altogether. If you wish to preserve an account's security information when its assigned user changes, simply disable the account when the user leaves the company. You can rename the account with the new user's name when the employee is replaced.

Copying Group Accounts

Here are the rules for copying group accounts:

- You can copy group accounts but you cannot rename them.
- The predefined, Built-In groups described in the section "Group Accounts" can never be deleted.
- Additional group accounts created by administrators can always be deleted. When a group account is deleted, the user accounts that it contains are not deleted. If you wish to remove the user accounts as well, you must manually delete each account.
- Group accounts may not have the same name as any other group account (local or global) or any username on a user account.

What Gets Copied and What Doesn't

When you copy a group account, the Description and the member accounts are copied from the original account. The Group Name is cleared and made available for the new group.

Special/System Groups

There are several special/system groups in Windows NT. Their membership cannot be altered except by internal Windows NT processes. Each special group represents a state the user may be in. For example, a user with a network connection to a server from a workstation is automatically placed in the Network group. A user physically logged on to a server is a member of the Interactive Group. By limiting access to special/system groups, you can provide additional, tighter security measures in a Windows NT environment. Table 3.7 describes the special/system groups.

Table 3.7

Special/System Groups

GROUP	DESCRIPTION
Everyone	Represents all local and network users. Every user with an account on the domain database is a member of the Everyone group; no user may be excluded. If access to a resource is given to this group, all users including the Guest account gain access to the resource. If access to a resource is denied to the group, all users including administrators are denied access.
Interactive Group	Represents all users who are currently logged on physically or interactively on that computer.
Network Group	Represents all users who are accessing the system from the network, through a LAN, WAN, or remote access connection.
Creator/ Owner	Represents the creator or current owner of an object. By default, the original creator of an object is the owner unless ownership is taken by an administrator or other user who has been granted that ability.

Special/system groups are given access to resources just as local groups are given access.

Caution

Be careful when granting access of special/system groups. You may inadvertently grant access to a user who shouldn't have access to a particular resource. By default, the Everyone group is given full control on many resources.

Creating Users and Groups

Users and groups are created, modified, and deleted using UM4D. To create and modify accounts, you will need to be logged on to a domain controller with Administrator or Account Operator permission.

- Any administrator may modify users and groups in the domain.
- A member of the Account Operator group cannot modify or delete the Domain Administrators Global Group, or the Administrators, Account Operators, Backup Operators, Print Operators, or Server Operators local groups, or any global groups belonging to these local groups. Account operators cannot modify the accounts of members of any of these groups and cannot administer Policies.
- Users may create local groups and may only modify the groups they create.

The procedures in this section describe the creation and modification of accounts for the following example users and groups:

- Users named SuSmith, MaPatel, NeLambert, KyTrenton, and JaHunter
- Global groups named HPColorPrinter and Managers
- Local groups named HPColorJet, Production, and Marketing

Now that you have studied the roles and properties of user accounts and group accounts in the NT Security system, this section contains the step-by-step procedures for creating those accounts. We will examine the procedures for creating user accounts and local and global group accounts, copying and renaming user accounts, and copying local and global groups.

Creating User Accounts

In this section we step through the process for creating users.

1. Click the Start menu, point to Programs, point to Administrative Tools, and select UM4D.
2. Select User/New User to open the New User dialog.
3. Based on the definitions and explanations earlier in this chapter, configure the following options for user SuSmith. See the New User dialog in Figure 3.8.

Username:	SuSmith
Full Name:	Smith, Susanne
Description:	Sales Manager
Password:	Just type in the word password, using all lowercase
Confirm Password:	Reenter password

4. Select the appropriate password options. In this case, check the User Must Change Password at Next Logon check box.

Figure 3.8

Configure the new user SuSmith to match this screen.

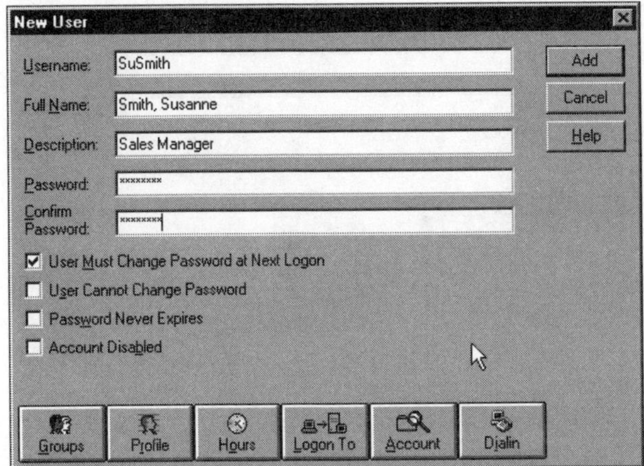

5. Click the Add button to create SuSmith's account. The New User dialog reappears with all fields cleared so that you can add another user.
6. Repeat steps 3 through 5, to create user accounts for the following:

For Username NeLambert:	Lambert, Nevin; Vice President; Password Never Expires
For Username MaPatel:	Patel, Manish; Production Manager; Must Change Password at Logon

7. Close the New User dialog and return to the UM4D main window.

Creating Global Groups

Here are the steps for creating a global group.

1. From UM4D, select User/New Global Group. The New Global Group dialog appears (see Figure 3.9).
2. In the Group Name box, type **HPColorPrinter**.
3. In the Description box, type **Printer.**
4. In the Not Members list on the right, select SuSmith and MaPatel. Click the Add button, and these users will appear as members in the Members list on the left. Click OK when you're done.
5. Repeat steps 2 through 4 to create the Managers group.

When you're done, you'll see the newly created groups in the Groups section of the UM4D window, preceded by globe icons.

Figure 3.9

New Global Group dialog

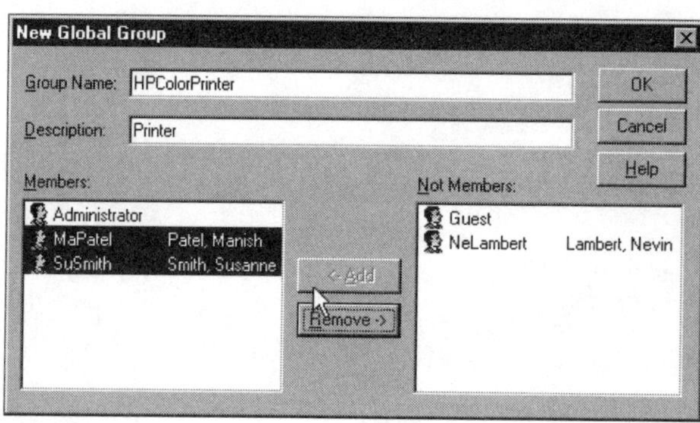

Creating Local Groups

Now here are the steps for creating a local group.

1. In UM4D, select User/New Local Group. The New Local Group dialog appears (see Figure 3.10).

Figure 3.10

Adding the HPColorJet as a new local group

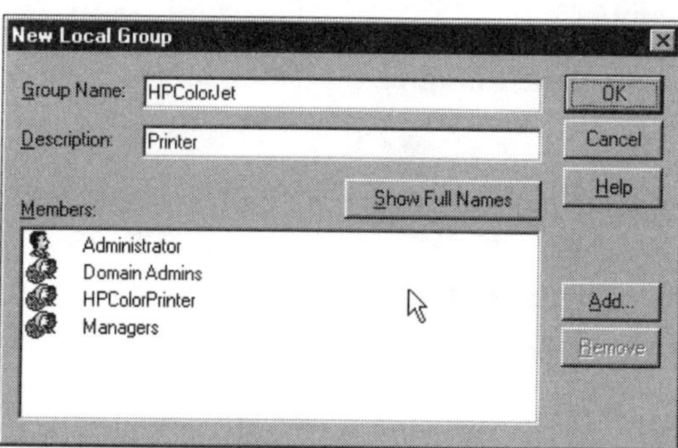

2. In the Group Name box, type HPColorJet.
3. In the Description box, type Printer.
4. Click on the Add button. The Add Users and Groups dialog appears (see Figure 3.11).
5. In the Names list, select the global groups Domain Admins, HPColor-Printer, and Managers. (As usual in Windows applications, you can hold the Ctrl key and click to select multiple users.)
6. Click the Add button, and the names appear in the Add Names box.

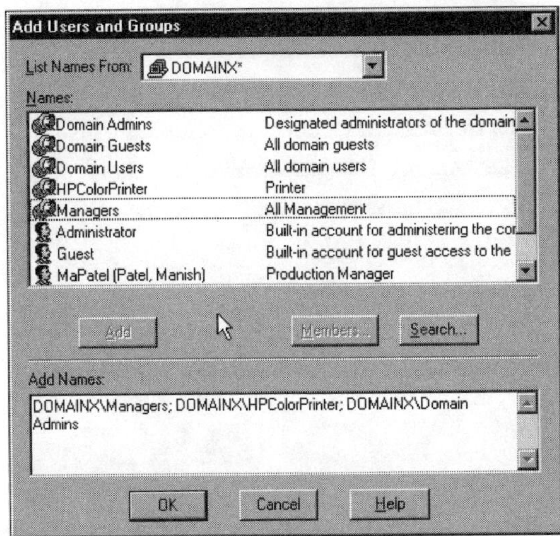

Figure 3.11

Add Users and Groups dialog

7. Click OK. Note that the new group members are now listed in the New Local Group dialog.
8. Repeat steps 2 through 7 to add the Production group.

Copying User Accounts

Currently, you have user accounts for SuSmith, NeLambert, and MaPatel. Now let's use the technique of copying user accounts to create accounts for the other sample users.

1. In UM4D, highlight SuSmith.
2. Select User/Copy. A copy of SuSmith's account appears with most fields cleared, as shown in Figure 3.12.
3. Create a user account for KyTrenton by filling in the account record as follows:

Username:	KyTrenton
Full Name:	Trenton, Kyle
Password:	password

4. Click the Groups button at the bottom of the dialog. In the Group Memberships dialog (see Figure 3.13), notice that KyTrenton has the same group memberships as SuSmith.

Figure 3.12

Copy of SuSmith account, ready to be copied for another user

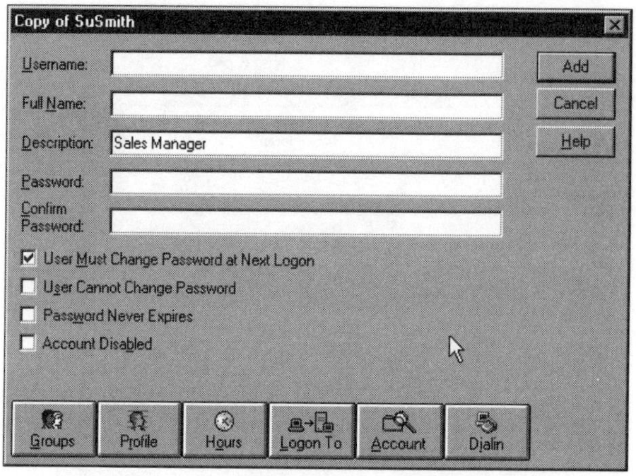

Figure 3.13

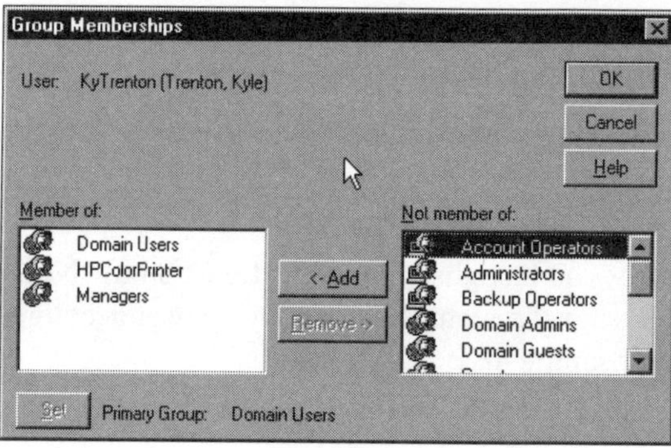

Group Memberships dialog for user KyTrenton

5. Click OK to return to the Copy of SuSmith dialog, and click the Add button to add the KyTrenton account.
6. Click Close.

Renaming a User Account

Follow these steps to rename the SuSmith user account and make it the JaHunter account.

1. In UM4D, highlight SuSmith.
2. Select User/Rename to open the Rename dialog (see Figure 3.14).
3. In the Change To box, type in the new user name JaHunter and click the OK button.

Figure 3.14

Renaming a user account

4. Double-click on JaHunter and change the full name to **Hunter, Jamie.** If you want, change the Description, too.
5. Click on the Groups button, and notice that JaHunter has the same groups that SuSmith had (see Figure 3.15).

Figure 3.15

JaHunter has the same group memberships as SuSmith.

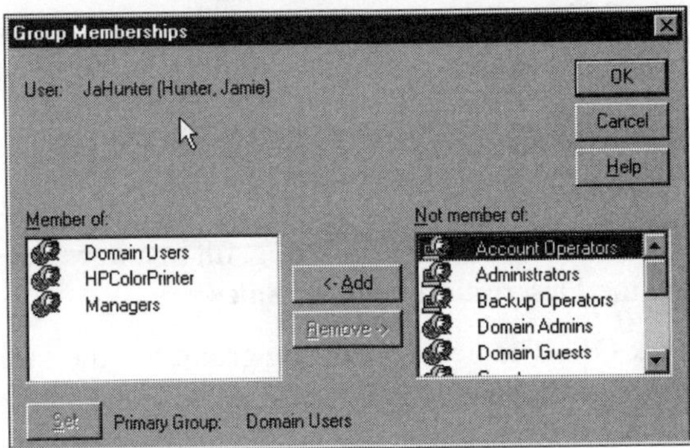

Modifying User Accounts

Let's modify the NeLambert user account to make Lambert a member of the Domain Admins group.

1. In UM4D, double-click on NeLambert.
2. In the User Properties dialog, click the Groups button.
3. In the Group Memberships dialog, select Domain Admins in the Not Member Of list and click the Add button. Domain Admins appears in the Member Of list on the left (see Figure 3.16).
4. Click OK to close the Group Memberships dialog, and then again to close the User Properties dialog.

Figure 3.16

Domain Admins is now in the Member Of list.

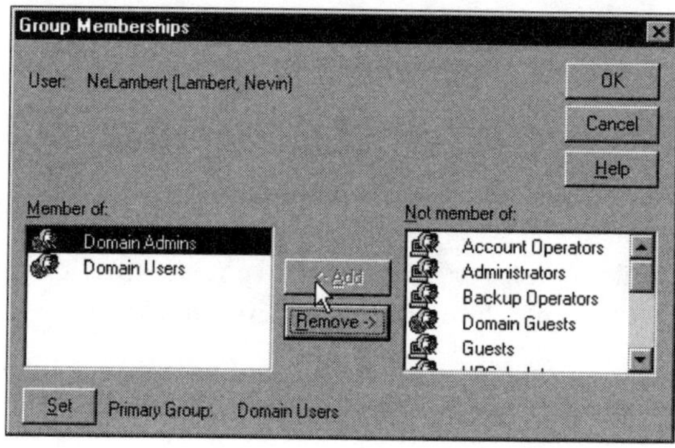

Copying Groups

The process for copying groups is similar to that of copying users.

1. In UM4D, highlight the group Production.
2. Select User/Copy.
3. In the New Local Group dialog, fill in a new Group Name, **Marketing**; and the Description **Product Sales**.
4. Click OK. The new Marketing group has the same membership as the Production group.

■ Developing a Group Strategy

The group strategy we want to use is simple, and can be followed using these steps:

1. Create users in the domain. (SuSmith, MaPatel)
2. Create global groups in the domain, based on similar needs. (HPColor-Printer, Managers)
3. Place the users in the global groups. (SuSmith, MaPatel ‡ HpColor-Printer, Managers)
4. Create a local group at the resource. (HPColorJet, Production)
5. Place the global group in the local group. (HPColorPrinter ‡ HPColorJet)
6. Assign the local groups to the resource. (HPColorJet ‡ Resource)

This may seem like a lot of work, but the steps you followed for creating the user accounts, global accounts, and local accounts in the "Creating Users and Groups" section were set up in this order. Not too much work after all, right? The idea is to develop a consistent group policy and stick to it. The steps outlined in this chapter have been proven effective in both small and enterprise networks. Keeping it consistent allows for tighter security and salability for the future.

Helpful Tip

An easy way to remember the steps of a consistent group strategy is with the acronym UGLY:

- *Users into*
- *Global groups into*
- *Local groups, which are assigned rights*
- *Y? Because that's the way you do it.*

By maintaining user accounts in global groups, you always have one place to go to designate users' access (or denial of access) to certain resources. Local groups are assigned rights to resources. When you need to change the level or type of access to a particular resource, you always change the local group rights.

As an example, suppose we create a new user account JaHunter and assign it to the global group named Managers. The Production local group has full access to the directory Monthly Reports, and Read access to Quarterly Reports. Later we determine that the members of Managers need to have Write access to Quarterly Reports. We also determine that JaHunter requires Print access to the HPColor LaserJet. How do we solve this?

First, on the Quarterly Reports resource, we change the Production local group's Read access to Read/Write access. That gives all Production's members Read/Write access; therefore, the Managers global group, which is member of Production, also gains access to Quarterly Reports. We know where to go to make the change because of UGLY. Quarterly Reports is a resource that requires access privilege changes, and UGLY tells us that rights are granted to local groups.

Second, we add JaHunter to the global group HPColorLaser Users (HPCLU); this gives JaHunter Print access to the printer resource via global group membership in local group HPCLU. We know to do this because UGLY says that users belong in global groups. This is not a resource permission change, so we have to identify a global group that provides such access.

This example using JaHunter and the various groups will bear fruit in later chapters, when we create printers and directories and set the permissions for these resources.

Summary

As you have seen in this chapter, Windows NT maintains strict control in matters of user and group administration. It is important for any administrator who is going to plan and implement a successful security policy to understand how users and groups perform in the Windows NT system.

Naming conventions, user properties, group strategies (remember UGLY), the ability to copy and rename accounts and thereby create templates—all these are components that allow the administrator to maintain an efficient, secure system.

Remember that the users and groups created in the examples of this chapter have been for administrative/organizational purposes. Other than the user NeLambert being assigned to the Domain Admins global group, none of the users have yet gained any rights to resources. In the upcoming chapters, we will continue to construct a secure environment, using the foundation we have built thus far.

- *Microsoft's File Systems*
- *Protection of Data Integrity*
- *Fault Tolerance*
- *Implementing Fault Tolerance*
- *Emergency Boot Disks*

CHAPTER 4

Security for File Systems

UNDERSTANDING MICROSOFT WINDOWS NT SECURITY REQUIRES knowledge of the file systems used on Windows NT-based computers. This chapter does not provide exhaustive coverage of the substantial technical information about the Microsoft FAT and NTFS file systems. Rather, we will concentrate on the security aspects of Windows NT file systems, and identify some important differences between FAT and NTFS.

Microsoft's File Systems

Microsoft first introduced MS-DOS in 1981. It was a new operating system that ran on IBM's first personal computer, containing a 16-bit 8088 processor chip and two drives for low-density floppy disks. The MS-DOS file system, FAT (named for its File Allocation Table), provided more than enough power to format these small disk volumes and to manage hierarchical directory structures and files.

The FAT file system continued to meet the needs of personal computer users as hardware and software power increased year after year. FAT never offered security, however, and continues to struggle even today with file searches and data retrieval that take significantly longer on large hard disks than on the original low-density floppy disks of the early IBM PCs.

In 1990, a high-performance file system (HPFS) was introduced as a part of the OS/2 version 1.*x* operating systems, also designed by Microsoft. This file system was designed specifically for large hard disks on 16-bit processor computers. On the heels of HPFS came HPFS386, announced as part of Microsoft LAN Manager and designed to take advantage of the 32-bit 80386 processor chip. HPFS never met its design goals, and support for HPFS has been dropped from Microsoft Windows NT version 4.0.

Today personal computers include very fast processor chips and can accommodate multiple, huge hard disks. The new Windows NT file system, NTFS, is designed for optimal performance on these computers.

Because of features such as speed and universality, FAT and NTFS file systems currently are both popular and widely used. NTFS offers consistency with FAT file systems, plus advanced functionality needed by corporations interested in greater flexibility and in data security.

Table 4.1 lists the file systems in Windows NT and the operation systems that support them.

Table 4.1

NT File Systems

FILE SYSTEM	SUPPORTING OPERATING SYSTEMS
File Allocation (FAT)	Windows NT, Microsoft Windows 95, Microsoft MS-DOS, and IBM OS/2
Windows NT File System (NTFS)	Windows NT
CD-ROM File System (CDFS)[1]	Windows NT and Windows 95

1. CDFS is used to read from CD-ROM drives. Because CDFS is a read-only, special-purpose file system, it is not described in this book.

Security Needs for Advanced File Systems

Advanced, flexible file systems do not stand alone. The security provided by Windows NT is effective only when the operating system is running. If you dual boot (running another operating system), or if the computer is not absolutely protected from physical access by an unauthorized person, then obviously Windows NT cannot provide protection.

Windows NT does provide protection when it is operating, and when data resides on hard drives formatted with one of NT's file systems.

Partitioning

Before a drive can be formatted, the physical hard disk must be partitioned. Partitioning is the process of dividing a physical drive into one or more logical drives that can be formatted and used independently.

Partitions are created from unused or, as shown in Disk Administrator, *free space.* Free space can be divided into primary and extended partitions.

Primary Partitions

A *primary partition* is a section of disk that can be marked as active and used by the machine to boot the operating system. There is a limit of four primary partitions per disk. A primary partition cannot be further subdivided into smaller logical units.

The advantage of having multiple primary partitions is that they allow separation of different operating systems, such that one machine could boot both NT and UNIX if each OS were loaded on separate primary partitions.

Windows NT system partitions must be primary partitions. The system partition is the partition with NTLDR and the system files required to find the OS files. The partition on which the OS files are located is called the *boot partition;* it can be either primary or extended.

The FAT file system is used on NT primary system partitions for dual-boot purposes (dual-boot meaning the ability to run either NT or Windows 95, for example).

On RISC-based machines such as the DEC ALPHA, the primary partition created by the configuration program (system BIOS) must be a FAT file system of at least 2MB.

Extended Partitions

The *extended partition* is used to avoid the four-partition limit imposed for primary partitions. An extended partition is created from free space, just as a primary partition is. There can be only one extended partition per disk, but the partition can be subdivided into multiple segments. Each segment is seen as a logical drive. This allows more than four drives per disk. The boot partition can be on a logical drive in an extended partition.

Although Windows NT supports many types of partitions—stripe sets and volume sets, primary and extended partitions, and fault-tolerant sets—this chapter discusses only the file systems (FAT and NTFS) and the fault-tolerant sets. The other partitioning schemes provide no fault tolerance or security enhancements.

Supported File Systems in Windows NT

File systems are a critical component to most operations in an OS. Every action from the time the computer boots to the time it is shut down has some relationship to the file system. Since the OS itself is simply files on the hard drive, you need to be able load the file system drivers before you even load the OS.

The FAT file system was developed before the requirements of security, distributed processing, and large file/print service demand reached what they are today. On the other hand, over 55 million machines are still using FAT. Windows NT's answer is to incorporate FAT and a new file system, NTFS. Thus backward compatibility is maintained while accommodating more demanding tasks that require a more robust file system. In the following sections, we'll take a closer look at FAT and NTFS.

The Skinny on the FAT File System

The File Allocation Table (FAT) file system is a modified version of the file system that has been used for years with DOS-based computers. FAT is required for both Windows 95 and MS-DOS. This means the system partition must be formatted with the FAT file system, in order to support the dual boot option on a Windows NT-based computer running the Windows 95 or MS-DOS operating systems. (FAT32, an enhanced version of the FAT file system available on some versions of Windows 95, is not supported under Windows NT.)

FAT does impose restrictions on naming conventions and file partition size. In terms of security, as well, the FAT file system has important limitations. FAT under NT uses a *lazy-write file system.* This means it uses an intelligent cache-management strategy and provides a way to recover data (such as the Chkdsk program) if there is an error when writing to the disk. All data are accessed via the file cache. While the user searches folders or reads files, data to be written to disk accumulates in the file cache. If the same data are modified several times, all those modifications are captured in the file cache. The result is that the file system needs to write to disk only once to update the data.

The danger of this arrangement is that if the system fails, critical files can become corrupt unless there is a transaction logging scheme, which FAT does not have. A FAT partition cannot be protected by the local file or directory security features of Windows NT. FAT is inherently unsecure, and thus Windows 95 and MS-DOS based machines are also unsecure.

Although a file system can greatly influence system security, it is not the only factor. To be secure, a file system must operate under or within the confines of a secure operating system.

NTFS Is Fat Free

NTFS provides a combination of performance, reliability, and compatibility not found in FAT. It is designed to quickly perform standard file operations such as read, write, and search, as well as advanced operations such as file system recovery, on very large drives. NTFS also includes security features required for file servers and high-end personal computers in a corporate environment.

NTFS has a simple yet very powerful design. From the file system perspective, everything on the NTFS volume is a file or part of a file. Every allocated sector on an NTFS volume belongs to some file. Even the file system metadata is part of a file. (Metadata is information that describes the file system itself.)

NTFS views each file (or directory) as a set of file *attributes*. Particulars such as the file's name, its security information, and even its data are all file attributes. Each attribute is identified by an attribute type code and, optionally, an attribute name. As an attribute-based file system, NTFS supports object-oriented applications by treating all files as objects that have user- and system-defined attributes.

NTFS Security

NTFS is the most secure and robust file system for Windows NT. It is a recoverable file system, combining the speed of a lazy-write file system with virtually instant recovery.

NTFS provides security for servers and personal computers. It supports access control and ownership rights important to basic security. Folders shared by a Windows NT-based computer can have assigned permissions (called *share-level permissions*), but NTFS files and folders can have assigned permissions whether or not they are shared. NTFS is the only file system on Windows NT that allows permissions to be assigned to specific files and folders.

Types of Permissions

On NTFS volumes, you can set specific permissions for groups and users. These permissions control access to files and folders, as well as the level of access permitted. NTFS file and folder permissions apply to users accessing the file over the network, as well as to users working at the computer where the file is stored. With NTFS you can also set *share-level permissions*, which operate on shared folders in combination with file and folder permissions.

FAT volumes, too, can have shared folders, although you cannot set any permissions on the individual files and folders. The only security on shared folders under FAT is in the form of share-level permissions that are set on the entire share and only function over the network. Once you share a folder, you can protect it by specifying share-level permissions to apply to all files and subfolders.

Setting share-level permissions is similar to setting file and folder permissions in NTFS. But because share-level permissions apply to all files and folders in the share, these permissions offer less flexibility and no local protection at all, compared to the file and folder permissions used for NTFS volumes. Chapter 7 covers implementation of shares and share-level permissions. NTFS file and directory permissions are covered in Chapter 6.

Share-level permissions apply to both NTFS and FAT volumes. They are enforced by the operating system, not the individual file system.

Protection of Data Integrity

Permission structures are very important to security, but the integrity of the data is crucial as well. File corruption has caused as much damage as viruses and hackers. NT and NTFS offer three built-in, transparent functions that provide for data integrity: transaction logging, sector sparing, and remapping of bad clusters. Although NTFS provides security for files and directories, currently Microsoft does not provide file encryption with NT, leaving that market open to third-party support.

This section presents a technical overview of the data integrity components in the Windows NT file systems.

Transaction Logging

Although it doesn't guarantee the protection of user data, NTFS guarantees the consistency of volumes by using transaction logging and recovery techniques. As mentioned, NTFS includes a lazy-write technique, plus a volume-recovery method, that typically takes only a second or two to ensure the integrity of all NTFS volumes each time the computer is restarted.

Transaction-based recoverability is a recoverable file system that uses transaction logging to log all directory and file updates automatically. This logging information is used to roll forward (commit) or roll back (end) operations that failed due to system failure, power loss, and the like.

Each I/O operation that modifies a file on the NTFS volume is viewed by the file system as a transaction and can be managed as an individual unit processed by the Log File service. This is a function of the I/O Manager. When a user updates a file, the Log File service logs all redo and undo information for the transaction.

- Redo information tells NTFS how to repeat the transaction.
- Undo information tells how to roll back the transaction that was incomplete or had an error.

If a transaction is completed successfully, the file update is committed. If the transaction is incomplete, NTFS ends or rolls back the transaction by following instructions in the undo information. The transaction is also rolled back if NTFS detects an error in the transaction.

If the system crashes, NTFS recovers in three phases: an *analysis phase*, a *redo phase*, and an *undo phase*. During the analysis phase of recovery, NTFS appraises the damage and determines exactly which clusters must now be updated, per the information in the log file. The redo phase performs all transaction steps logged from the last checkpoint. The undo phase backs out any incomplete (uncommitted) transactions.

Every few seconds, NTFS checks the cache to determine the status of the lazy writer and marks the status as a checkpoint in the log. If the system crashes subsequent to that checkpoint, the system knows to back up to that checkpoint for recovery. This method provides for more expedient recovery times by saving on the number of queries required during recovery.

Users do not have to run a disk repair utility on an NTFS partition. Indeed, few (if any) truly worthy repair utilities exist. Older versions of repair utilities for MS-DOS, Windows, and Windows 95 will not function on NTFS volumes. No harm is done to files if you do try to run one of these programs, though you will get an access violation or exception violation error.

The transaction logging done by the NTFS to enable recovery of data protects only NTFS metadata. A power failure can still cause corruption. So can turning off your computer without going through the shutdown process.

NOTE. *This level of recoverability protects metadata. User data can still be corrupted in the case of power and/or system failure.*

Sector Sparing

Sector sparing is a dynamic data-recovery technique that is only available on SCSI disks configured as part of a fault-tolerant volume. Sector sparing works on fault-tolerant volumes because a copy of the data on the erroneous sector can be regenerated. (Fault tolerance is discussed later in this chapter.)

When a disk-read error occurs, Windows NT Server obtains a spare sector from the disk device driver to replace the bad sector. NT Server then recovers the data by recalculating it from a stripe set with parity or by reading the sector from the mirror drive, and writes the data to the new sector.

Cluster Remapping

When Windows NT returns a bad sector error to the NTFS file system, which contains no fault tolerance, the NT fault-tolerant driver dynamically replaces the cluster containing the bad sector and allocates a new cluster for the data. Under Windows NT, a cluster is an allocation unit. Hard drives are usually physically separated into sectors (512 bytes or 1024 bytes). The NTFS partition can contain one sector per cluster. This is the minimum data size that is allocated to each file copied. For example, if a copied file contained 500 bytes, NT would still have to allocate 512 bytes to it, thus wasting 12 bytes. If the file were 900 bytes, then Windows NT would allocate two clusters (1,024 bytes), wasting 124 bytes. A file system such as FAT has to allocate a minimum of 16 sectors per cluster (8,192 bytes).

If the error occurs during a read on a volume that is not fault tolerant, NTFS returns a read error to the calling program and the data are lost. When the error occurs during a write, NTFS writes the data to the new cluster and no data are lost.

NTFS puts the address of the cluster containing the bad sector in its Bad Cluster File so the bad sector will not be reused.

Table 4.2 provides a summary of the events surrounding occurrences of bad sectors. In this table, FtDisk (fault-tolerant disk driver) is the device driver that handles I/O to volume sets, stripe sets, mirror sets, and stripe sets with parity. (FtDisk is explored further later in this chapter.) Volume sets and stripe sets are not fault tolerant, so processing of an error on one of these volumes falls into the non-fault-tolerant volume row.

Fault Tolerance

Windows NT Server 4.0 includes several fault-tolerant capabilities. *Fault tolerance* is the ability to provide real-time data redundancy. The data redundancy will help in case of hardware failures, software corruption, and other unexpected disasters.

Windows NT implements fault tolerance via the FTDISK.SYS (fault tolerant) driver. This software solution provides a highly efficient, cost-effective method of redundancy. There is, however, a slight degradation in system performance because Windows NT must use its own CPU and memory for the fault tolerance operations. In contrast, hardware-based solutions provide their own CPU and memory, and operate independently of the computer system's resources.

There are two forms of fault tolerance available under Windows NT: disk mirroring (RAID 1) and disk striping with parity (RAID 5).

Table 4.2

What Happens When a Sector Goes Bad

VOLUME TYPE	FTDISK+SCSI DISK WITH SPARE SECTORS	FTDISK+NON-SCSI DISK OR DISK WITH NO SPARE SECTORS	NO FTDISK+ANY KIND OF DISK
Fault-tolerant volume (Windows NT Server only)	1. FtDisk recovers data. 2. FtDisk replaces bad sector. 3. File system doesn't know about error.	1. FtDisk recovers data. 2. FtDisk sends data and bad-sector error to file system. 3. NTFS does cluster remapping. 4. FAT doesn't do anything about error.	N/A
Non-fault tolerant-volume	1. FtDisk can't recover data. 2. FtDisk sends bad-sector error to file system. 3. NTFS performs cluster remapping. On a read, data are lost. 4. FAT loses data on both read and write.	1. FtDisk can't recover data. 2. FtDisk sends bad-sector error to file system. 3. NTFS performs cluster remapping. On a read, data are lost. 4. FAT loses data on both read and write.	1. Disk driver returns bad-sector error to file system. 2. NTFS does cluster remapping. On a read, data are lost. 3. FAT loses data on both read and write.

The RAID Solution

RAID stands for Redundant Arrays of Inexpensive Disks. RAID is a disk array in which part of the storage device contains redundant information about data stored on the remainder of the storage device. In Windows NT, this process is implemented through a fault-tolerant driver (FtDisk.SYS). Redundant information allows for the regeneration of data in the event that one of the RAID devices fails. Thus, the RAID solution accommodates two primary concerns in issues of data storage:

- Improving I/O performance
- Improving the reliability of data storage

There are five levels of RAID implementations (RAID 1 to RAID 5). Windows NT implements two of these solutions: RAID 1 and RAID 5. RAID 2, 3, and 4 are evolutionary steps toward RAID 5 and are not implemented under Windows NT. See Table 4.3.

Table 4.3

RAID Levels

LEVEL	FUNCTIONALITY
RAID 1	Disk mirroring
RAID 2	Disk striping with error correction code (ECC)
RAID 3	Disk striping with ECC stored as parity
RAID 4	Disk striping large blocks; parity stored on one drive
RAID 5	Disk striping with parity distributed across multiple drives

Disk Mirroring (RAID 1)

Disk mirroring involves the writing of data simultaneously to two separate physical storage devices. On a read failure of either drive, the fault-tolerant driver reads the data from the other drive in the mirror set. On a write failure of one drive in the mirror set, the fault-tolerant driver uses the remaining drive for all accesses. See Figure 4.1.

Figure 4.1

Disk mirroring (RAID 1)

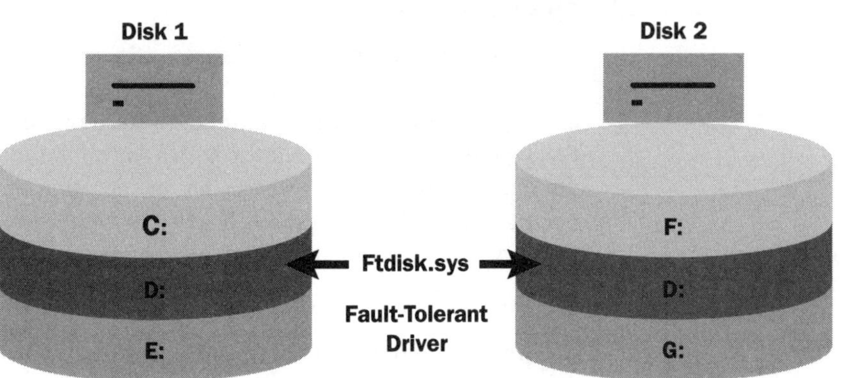

Stripe Set with Parity (RAID 5)

In the RAID level 5, stripe set with parity, data is written evenly in strips over an array of disks, making a *stripe*. Up to 32 disks can participate in one stripe set.

One strip in the stripe set contains parity information. The parity information is used to regenerate the data should one of the disk devices in the stripe set fail.

RAID 5 uses one strip in *each* stripe for parity; thus the equivalent of one disk is used for storing the parity strips. Further, the parity strip is distributed across all the drives in the group. The data and parity information are arranged on the disk array so that parity is evenly distributed across the array.

In Figure 4.2, the first strip on disk 1 is the parity strip for the four data strips in stripe 1. In stripe 2, the parity strip is on disk 2, and so on.

Figure 4.2

RAID 5 and parity stripes

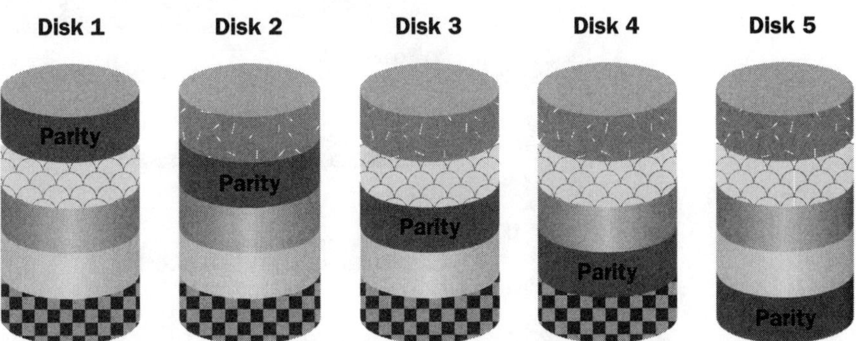

If one of the disk devices in a RAID 5 set fails, no data are lost. When a read operation requires data from the failed disk, the system reads all of the remaining good data strips in the stripe and the parity strip. The fault-tolerant driver users an algorithm that derives the lost data.

Implementing Fault Tolerance

A simple yet effective way to set up fault tolerance on your system is to consider mirroring the system and boot partitions and creating one or more stripe sets with parity for your data and applications. A boot disk is often necessary, and always useful to have when working with NTFS and fault-tolerant drives. The procedure for creating a boot disk is provided at the end of this section.

Procedure for Implementing Disk Mirroring

Disk mirroring is the only fault-tolerance protection you can set on the system and boot partitions.

1. Log on as Administrator or with Administrator Privileges.
2. From the Start menu, select Programs/Administrative Tools/Disk Administrator. You are now in the Disk Administrator dialog (see Figure 4.3).

NOTE. *You may see a message indicating this is the first time you have used this tool and that Disk Administrator wants to write a nondestructive signature to the disk. This is fine for all drives unless you are using a third-party hardware solution that specifies not to use Disk Administrator.*

Figure 4.3

Disk Administrator dialog

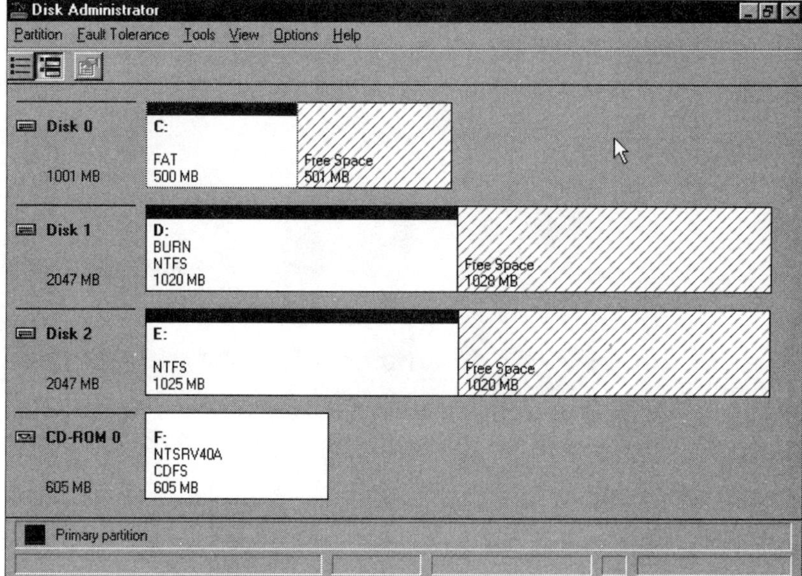

3. In the Disk 0 line, click on partition 1, labeled as drive C.
4. In the Disk 1 line, hold down the Ctrl key and click the area of free space on Disk 1. The Free Space box is now selected. The area must be equal to or greater than the partition selected in step 3.
5. Click in the menu bar to open the Fault Tolerance menu, and select Establish Mirror (the only choice available).

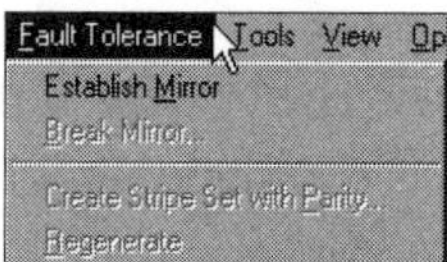

6. You will see the following message screen; click the OK button in this box.

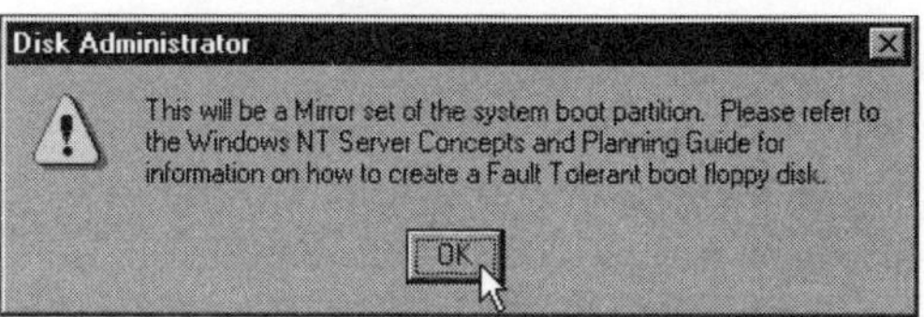

7. Notice that the Disk 0 and Disk 1 partitions now have the same drive letter (C) and are highlighted (see Figure 4.4). This indicates that they are part of a mirrored set.

Figure 4.4

Disk 0 and 1 show a partition C, a mirrored set.

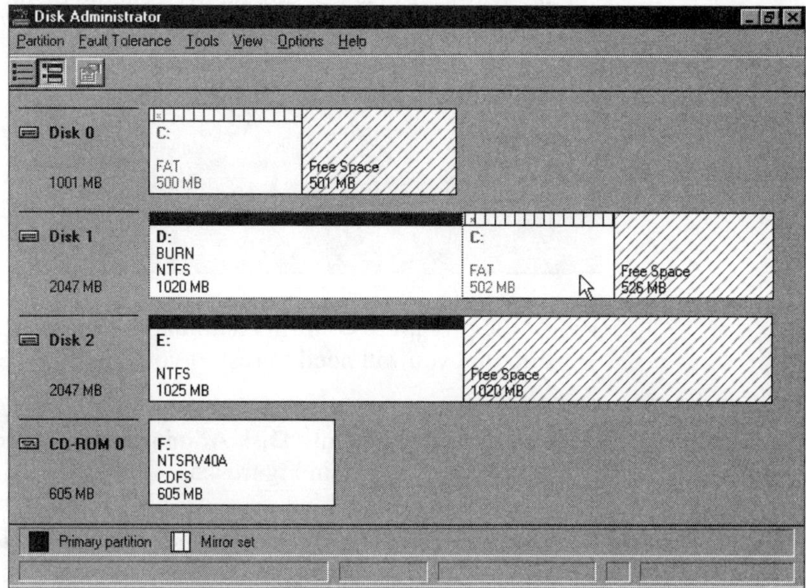

At this point you have only finished the setup to make this mirror. Nothing has been established yet and you can still back out if need be, by exiting Disk Administrator without saving changes. If you're ready, continue with step 7 to finish creating the mirror.

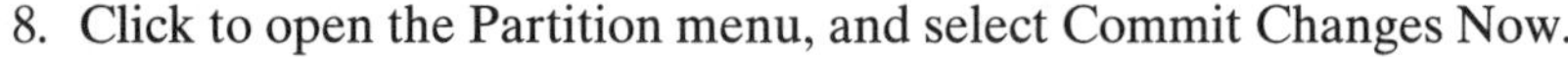

8. Click to open the Partition menu, and select Commit Changes Now.

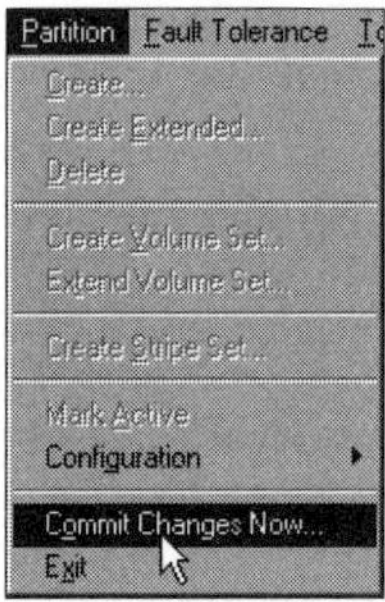

9. When prompted to save your changes, click Yes. You will be notified by the following message box that you should update your Emergency Repair Disk.

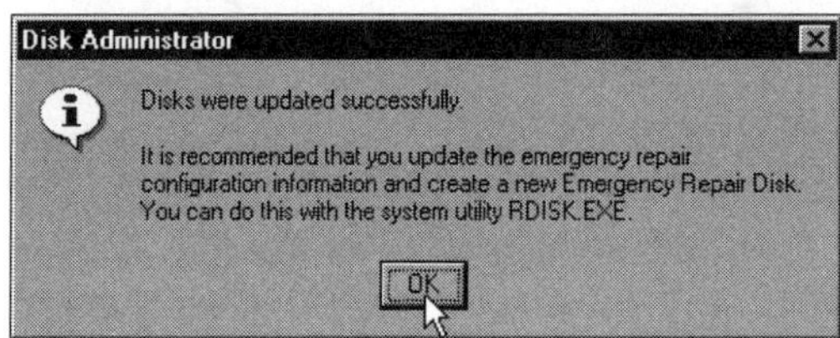

10. At the prompt to confirm continuation, click OK. At the prompt to confirm that you will need to restart your computer, click OK.
11. When the computer comes back up, log on with Administrative Privileges and get back into Disk Administrator. Notice the mirrored set is established, as shown in Figure 4.5.

Procedure for Configuring Disk Striping with Parity (RAID 5)

As stated earlier, disk striping with parity is recommended for use on your data and application drives. Even in low-cost servers, putting in three or more hard drives and striping with parity across them is a thrifty yet efficient way to protect your system for data loss.

1. Log on as Administrator or with Administrator Privileges.
2. From the Start menu, select Programs/Administrative Tools/Disk Administrator to get the Disk Administrator dialog (shown earlier in Figure 4.3).
3. Now you need to select three portions of free disk space to create the RAID 5 set. On Disk 0, click the area of free space.

Figure 4.5

Disk mirror up and running

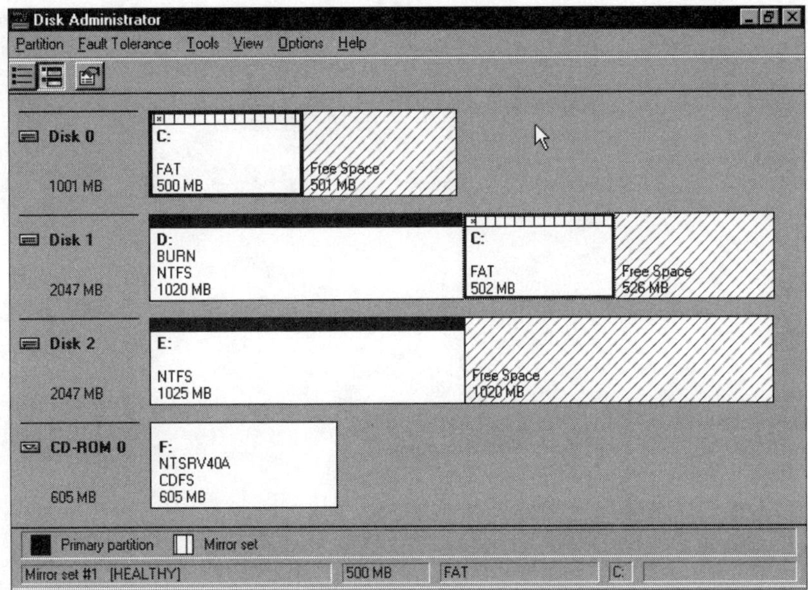

4. While holding the Ctrl key down, click on the area of free space in the lines for Disk 1 and Disk 2. These will be used for the stripe set with parity. As shown in Figure 4.6, all the free space areas are now selected.

5. Click in the menu bar to open the Fault Tolerance menu, and select Create Stripe Set With Parity.

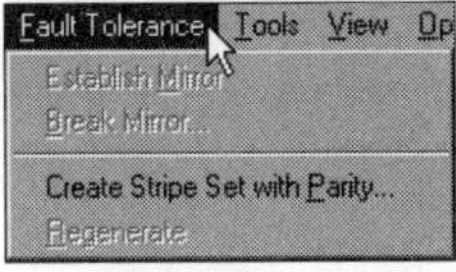

6. The Create Stripe Set With Parity dialog appears (Figure 4.7). The default stripe set size is three times the size of the smallest selected area of free space. We will stick with the default, 1,503MB, so click OK.

7. Notice that the partitions now have the same drive letter (G) and are highlighted with the same pattern. This indicates they are part of a stripe set with parity, as explained in the legend at the bottom of the Disk Administrator (Figure 4.8).

8. Click to open the Partition menu, and select Commit Changes Now.

Figure 4.6

All the drives selected for parity

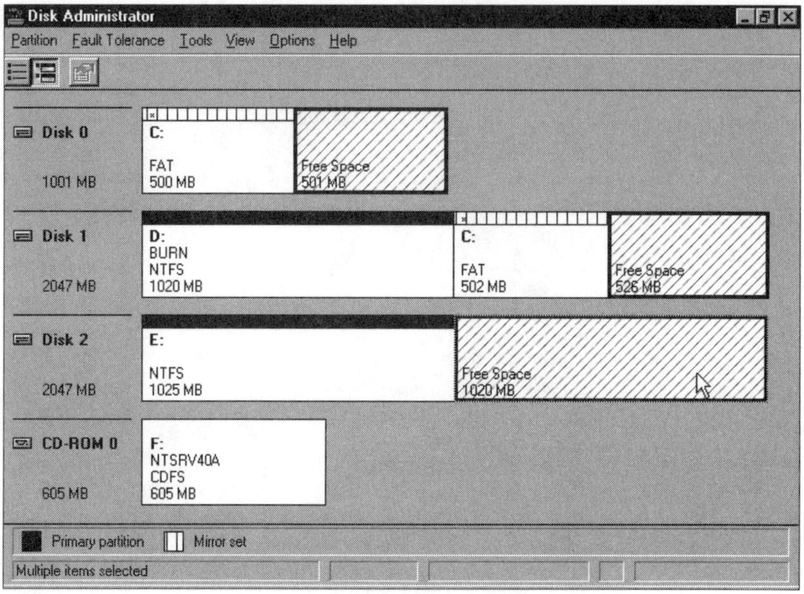

Figure 4.7

The default stripe set size is three times the size of the smallest selected area of free space.

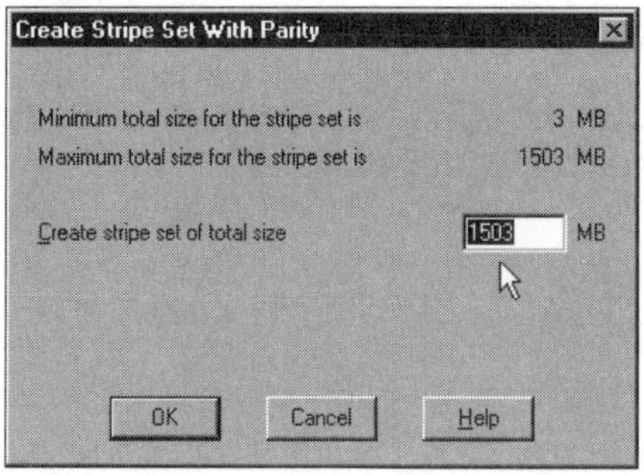

9. Click Yes in the Confirm dialog, and click OK in the Emergency Repair dialog. You are returned to the Disk Administrator; rebooting is not required.
10. Notice that the file system type is Unknown (Figure 4.9). We still have to format this Fault Tolerant Stripe Set. From the Tools menu, choose Format.
11. In the Format dialog (Figure 4.10), choose NTFS in the File System drop-down list and click the Start button.
12. In the Information dialog that appears, click OK.

Figure 4.8

The parity drives; note the legend on the bottom of the screen

Disk Administrator
Partition Fault Tolerance Tools View Options Help
Disk 0
1001 MB
C:
FAT
500 MB
G:
Unformatted
501 MB
Disk 1
2047 MB
D:
BURN
NTFS
1020 MB
C:
FAT
502 MB
G:
Unformatted
502 MB
Free Space
24 MB
Disk 2
2047 MB
E:
NTFS
1025 MB
G:
Unformatted
502 MB
Free Space
518 MB
CD-ROM 0
605 MB
F:
NTSRV40A
CDFS
605 MB
Primary partition
Stripe set with parity
Mirror set

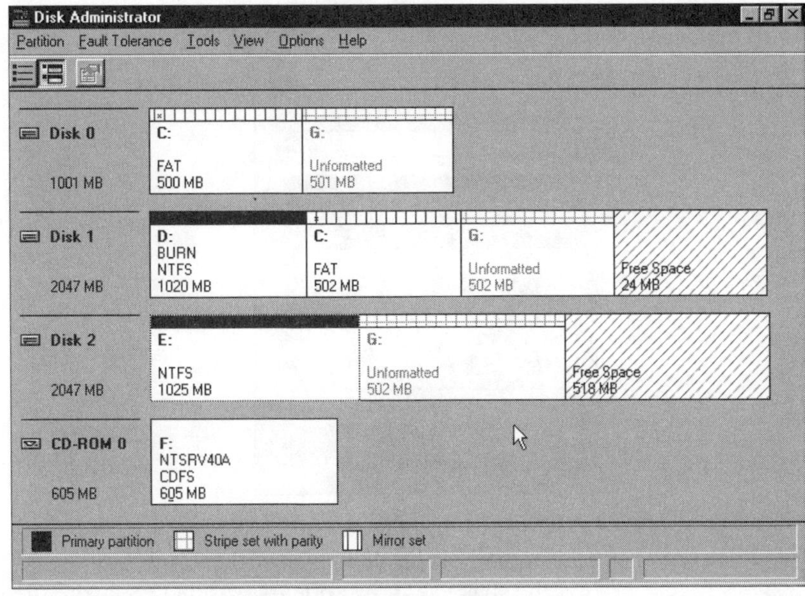

Figure 4.9

The file system type is Unknown on the G drive.

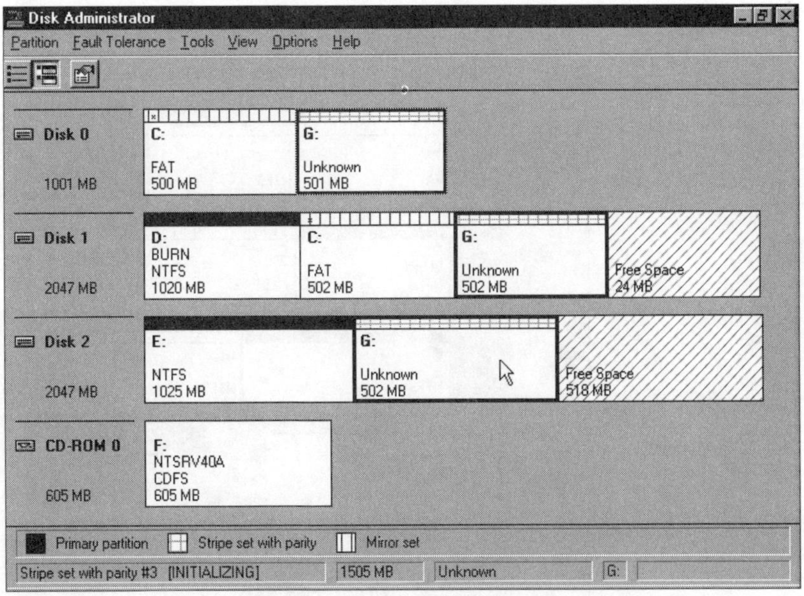

Disk Administrator
Partition Fault Tolerance Tools View Options Help
Disk 0
1001 MB
C:
FAT
500 MB
G:
Unknown
501 MB
Disk 1
2047 MB
D:
BURN
NTFS
1020 MB
C:
FAT
502 MB
G:
Unknown
502 MB
Free Space
24 MB
Disk 2
2047 MB
E:
NTFS
1025 MB
G:
Unknown
502 MB
Free Space
518 MB
CD-ROM 0
605 MB
F:
NTSRV40A
CDFS
605 MB
Primary partition
Stripe set with parity
Mirror set
Stripe set with parity #3 [INITIALIZING]
1505 MB
Unknown
G:

Figure 4.10

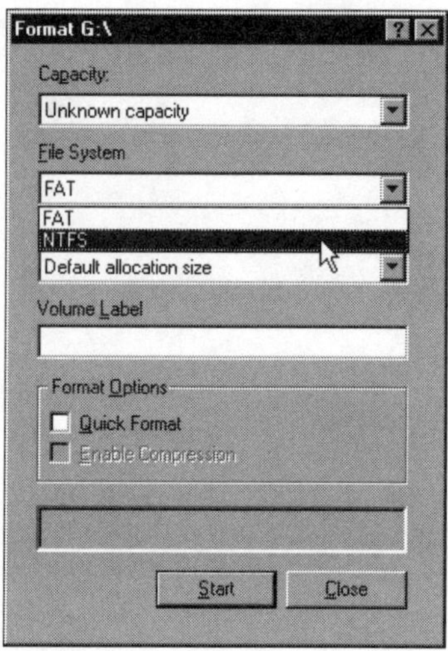

Choose NTFS as the File System for the G drive.

13. In the Format dialog, click the Close button. As shown in Figure 4.11, the stripe set now appears with NTFS as the file system type.

Figure 4.11

The stripe set appears as NTFS file system type.

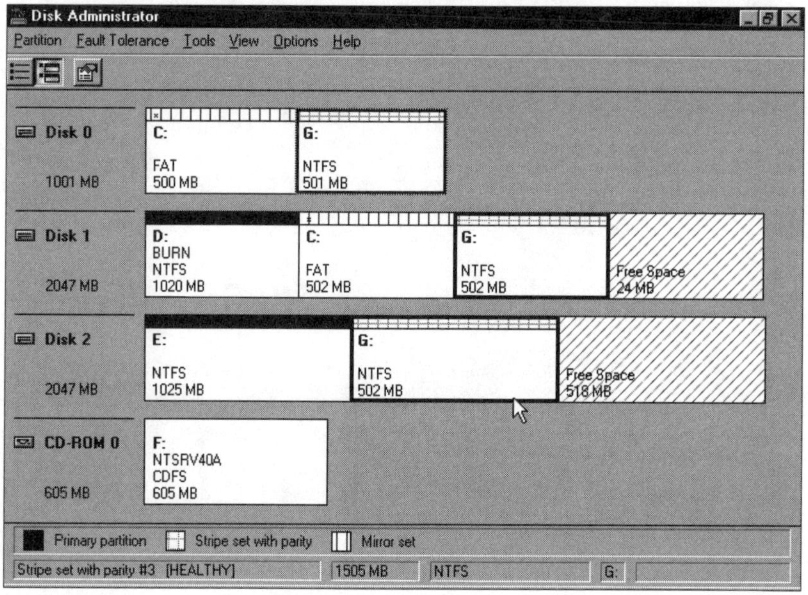

If you now view the system in Explorer, as shown in Figure 4.12, you will notice that there is no indication of the mirror set. Drive G does appear and is approximately 1GB in size.

Figure 4.12

The mirror set does not appear, but the stripe set drive does.

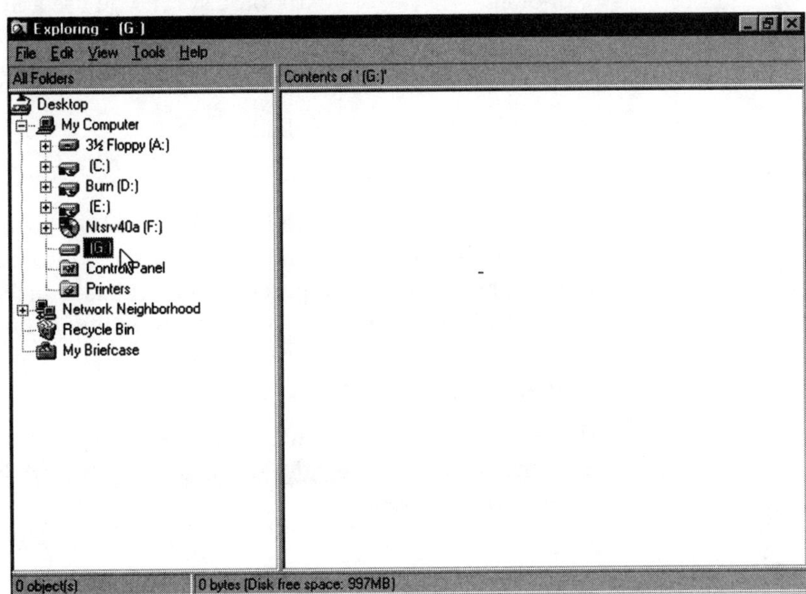

NOTE. *Why is the stripe set only 1GB? When we created the set, we used three chunks of disk space of about 500MB each, thus creating a 1.5GB partition. But because we are using a stripe set with parity, we lose one strip in each stripe and thus one-third of our disk space. If we had eight drives of 500MB each, we would still lose just 500MB, or one-eighth of our storage space.*

Emergency Boot Disks

If NT's boot sector should become corrupted but the OS is undamaged, you can still boot NT if you have a boot disk. To create a boot disk, you need to understand the difference between the system and boot partitions (discussed in the "Partitioning" section earlier in this chapter).

- The system partition contains the system files on an active primary partition that are required to find the OS files.
- The partition where the OS files are located is called the boot partition. The OS files for NT are in the Installation directory.

The system files required for access to the boot drive of NT differ for Intel and RISC architectures. For Intel X86-based machines the following files are required:

Ntldr	Ntdetect.com
Boot.ini	Ntbootdd.sys (if you use a SCSI adapter with the BIOS disabled)

RISC-based computers require the following files:

Osloader.exe	Hal.dll
All *.pal files	

In addition to the above-listed files, the boot disk must be formatted on a Windows NT-based machine. This way, the boot sector appropriately calls and runs Ntldr. If the computer is an Intel-based machine, the ARC (Advanced RISC Computing) path in the Boot.ini file may need to be edited.

Editing the Boot.ini File

The Boot.ini file contains information that Ntldr uses during the boot sequence of NT—specifically, the location of the OS boot files. Here is an example of a Boot.ini file:

```
[boot loader]
timeout=30
default=multi(0)disk(0)rdisk(1)partition(1)\WINNT
[Operating Systems]
multi(0)disk(0)rdisk(1)partition(1)\WINNT="Windows NT Server Version 4.00"
multi(0)disk(0)rdisk(1)partition(1)\WINNT="Windows NT Server Version 4.00 [VGA
mode]" /basevideo /sos
C:\="Microsoft Windows"
```

The fifth line of the preceding Boot.ini file contains an example of an ARC name:

```
multi(0)disk(0)rdisk(1)partition(1)\WINNT="Windows NT Server Version 4.00"
```

Let's examine the contents of this line.

- The first part of the name identifies the drive adapter as either "multi" or SCSI. "Multi" indicates any drive adapter other than a SCSI adapter with BIOS disabled. The (0) is the ordinal number of the hardware adapter.
- The "disk(0)" is the SCSI bus number, or "rdisk(1)" for the ordinal number of the disk (depending on whether the drives are SCSI or IDE).
- The last section, "partition(1)\WINNT," defines the partition number of the drive and the directory location of the OS kernel.

Note that Multi, rdisk, and disk parameters start from 0, and the partition number starts from 1. In other words, the first adapter and first disk would be labeled as 0, and the first partition is labeled as 1.

Consequently, the example ARC name line we are analyzing says that there is an NT installation on the first adapter, second disk, and first partition in directory WINNT.

Procedure for Creating the Book Disk

To create a boot disk, you'll first format a disk under Windows NT. You can do this from Windows Explorer, the command prompt, the Run command, and probably several other ways. Once the disk is formatted, copy the appropriate files for the platform (as described just above) to the disk. These files are located in the root directory of the system partition. Finally, edit the Boot.ini file to reflect the location of your OS files.

For a system that has mirrored system and boot partitions, you should make two boot disks, one for each mirrored partition. Thus if either drive fails, you have a boot disk that will work. On a RISC-based system, you will have to modify the following firmware variables, replacing *x* with the appropriate component number.

OSLOADER	Multi(*x*)disk(*x*)rdisk(*x*)\Osloader.exe
SYSTEMPARTITION	Multi(*x*)disk(*x*)fdisk(*x*)
OSLOADERPARTITION	Path to the secondary mirrored partition
OSLOADFILENAME	Path to the NT root directory

■ Summary

Performance, extensibility, reliability, and security features together make NTFS the preferred file system on Windows NT. Look back at the design goals of NT in Chapter 2, and you will find all of these elements mentioned there as goals and customer requests. Although NTFS is a major component to security on NT, it is nevertheless just another cog in the wheel. For more system security information, you'll want to continue on to Chapter 5, "The NT Security Subsystem (LSA)" and then to Chapter 6, "Local Resource Security."

- *The NT 4.0 Security Model*
- *The Steps of NT Access*
- *Beyond the Steps: Connecting to Network Resources*
- *A Little About Trusts*

CHAPTER

5

The NT Security Subsystem (LSA)

UP TO THIS POINT WE HAVE DISCUSSED NT ARCHITECTURE, domains, users and groups, and file systems. In the next two chapters we will bring them all together to form a detailed description of the NT security model and its systems.

We start this chapter by breaking down the NT security model into components. We will look at the Local Security Authority (LSA) and its significant role in the security system. In addition, we will walk through the NT logon process, which will give us an understanding of tokens—their uses and how NT creates them.

NOTE. *By now you understand that the NT security model has* ***not*** *changed much since NT's inception (version 3.1), so everything you learn in this chapter is applicable in all versions of NT.*

The NT 4.0 Security Model

The NT security model is made up of several components that work together to provide logon and access-control (ACL) security for the Windows NT operating system.

- The *Local Security Authority (LSA)*, which ensures that users have permission to access the system, is the nucleus of the Windows NT security subsystem. It creates access tokens, administers the local security policy, and provides user authentication services. LSA also controls audit policy and logs the audit messages generated by the Security Reference Monitor (SRM) component.
- The *logon process* accepts logon requests from users, including interactive logon and remote logon processes. Windows NT requires each user to provide a unique username and password to log on to a computer. This mandatory logon process cannot be disabled and is the first line of defense against intrusion.
- The NetLogon service is a component of NT that helps carry out the actions of the logon process. The NetLogon service has other responsibilities that will be discussed in this chapter. Perhaps its most vital role, however, is its support of the logon process. Without a properly functioning NetLogon service, the logon process cannot succeed.
- The *Security Account Manager (SAM),* also known as the *directory services database* (discussed in Chapter 2), maintains the user accounts database. This database contains the information for all User and group accounts. The SAM provides user validation services to the LSA component.
- The *Security Reference Monitor (SRM)* checks user permissions for access, and user rights to manipulate objects. It enforces access validation and the audit generation policy defined by the LSA component. SRM also generates audit messages.

The NT security model is what is referred to as the *security subsystem.* It is an integral subsystem, not an environmental subsystem, because it permeates and acts upon the entire Windows NT operating system.

The Steps of NT Access

There are two ways to access an NT server or workstation: by interactive access, and by remote or network access.

Interactive access means a user is physically interacting with the machine running NT, using the keyboard and mouse to access the physical computer and thus the NT operating system installed locally on that machine.

Remote access is the process of connecting to a NT machine from another machine. This could be Local Area Network (LAN) access, Internet access, or even remote dial-up access.

What Happens When You Log On

Before you can interact with a Windows NT system, you must log on to the system. To start a logon process, you are prompted to press Ctrl+Alt+Del. This action spawns the Winlogon process, which has nine steps:

1. The user presses Ctrl+Alt+Del.
2. The user provides a username and a password, and the logon process calls the LSA.
3. The LSA runs the appropriate authentication package.
4. The authentication package checks the domain entry from the Logon dialog to see if the account is local. If it is, the username and password are verified against those held in the local SAM database. If the account is not local, the authentication package requests help from the NetLogon service to retrieve the required information.
5. When the account has been validated, SAM returns the user's security ID and the security IDs of any global groups to which the user belongs.
6. The authentication package creates a logon session and then passes the logon session and the security IDs associated with the user to LSA.
7. If the logon is not rejected, an access token is created containing the user's security ID and the security IDs of Everyone and other groups. This access token is returned to the logon process with a success status. If the logon is rejected, the logon session is deleted, and an error is returned to the logon process.

8. The logon session calls the Client Server subsystem (CSR) to create a process and attach the access token to that process, thus creating a *subject* for the user account. (Subjects are described in the section "Subjects and Impersonation" later in this chapter.)
9. Finally, the logon process spawns a call to the CSR, and the CSR subsystem starts the desktop for the user.

These nine steps are a summary of what is a lengthy technical process. Let's take this big-picture view and break it down step by step. As you read, you may want to refer to this nine-step summary periodically, to reorient yourself to where we are in explaining the process. (We did!)

Step 1: The Function of Ctrl+Alt+Del

The user presses Ctrl+Alt+Del.

As you've learned, NT is *inherently* secure, and this security starts even before user logon. NT tries to prevent all types of improper access and protects its logon process, as well. By requiring a Ctrl+Alt+Del keypress before logon, NT accomplishes several things at once. Within NT, the Ctrl+Alt+Del suspends all interactive operations except those performed by the security subsystem. Thus only the Winlogon process can interact with the user. This setup prevents a Trojan horse attack.

What's a Trojan horse attack? If some clever hacker creates a logon screen that looks like the logon screen you are used to seeing, and you enter your name and password as usual, the hacker's program can capture the name and password and store them locally or remotely for retrieval later. The Trojan horse also passes the name and password through to the real logon screen, thus capturing your name and password without your knowing anything illegal has occurred.

NT prevents this. The suspension of all operations other than Winlogon will lock up any other process; thus the Trojan horse is not only disabled, but it is disabled *before* you ever give it your name and password.

A DOS Trojan horse is prevented in like manner. In that case, Ctrl+Alt+Del reboots a DOS environment; thus the hacker's screen would get rebooted. There are ways to suppress Ctrl+Alt+Del actions in DOS, but all would still lead to the same preventive actions as described for NT's Trojan-horse protection.

NOTE. *You can make several Registry changes to affect the logon screen. This is covered in Chapter 10 on the NT Registry.*

Step 2: Physically Logging On

The user provides a username and a password, and the logon process calls the LSA.

In the Logon Information dialog, a username and a password are required for logging on. Windows NT grants or denies access based upon the information the user provides.

Windows NT uses the username for identification and the password for validation. The logon process requires users to identify themselves to the domain or the computer. The username and password entered in the dialog are checked against either the computer directory database or the domain directory database. The decision on which database to check is based on the information provided in the Domain box of the Logon dialog; or it defaults to the local machine if the computer is not a member of a domain.

The Domain drop-down list contains the options available for the user's selection when logging in. These options may include the name of the local computer (from which the user pressed Ctrl+Alt+Del) as well as any domains to which this computer can log on. The domains listed include the computer's membership domain and any trusted domains of that domain. If the computer is a member of a workgroup and not a domain, the Logon Information dialog does not provide a place for the domain name.

Table 5.1 compares user logon options on a computer running Windows NT in a workgroup, in a domain, and in a domain with a trust relationship. Column 3 describes the unique identifier used by Windows NT after logon, depending on the location of the SAM database that is accessed for the user's logon. Any network connection requests sent elsewhere on the network will include this unique identifier (as described later in this chapter).

When the user logs on, the logon process passes the user credentials entered in the Logon dialog (name, password, and the domain name, if any) to the LSA and asks for an access token in return.

Table 5.1

Logon Authentication

COMPUTER LOCATION	DATABASES THAT CAN BE ACCESSED	UNIQUE IDENTIFIER
Workgroup	Local	Computer name and username
Domain	Local Domain	Computer name and username Domain name and username
Domain with a trust relationship	Local Home domain Trusted domain	Computer name and username Domain name and username Trusted domain name and username
Domain without a trust relationship	Local Untrusted domain	Computer name and username Untrusting domain name and username

Step 3: Authentication Package

The LSA runs the appropriate authentication package.

What actually happens in this step? When the NT access process called the LSA in step 2, it also specified the MSV1_0 authentication package (MSV1_0.DLL) as the authentication package to use. MSV1_0 understands and can process the type of user attributes passed by the logon process.

Windows NT can support other authentication packages, as well, that are implemented as DLLs. Other logon applications might accept attributes in another form, such as data read by a smart card or a retina scan. In that case, the application would need to specify an authentication package other than MSV1_0 that would understand and know how to process the specified attribute type. This flexibility allows third-party software vendors to integrate custom authentication packages with Windows NT.

So in step 3, the LSA forwards the credentials to the MSV1_0 authentication package on the local system, and asks for the user's account security ID (SID) and global SIDs to be returned.

Step 4: Local or Remote Validation

The authentication package checks the domain entry from the Logon dialog to see if the account is local. If it is, the username and password are verified against those held in the local SAM database. If the account is not local, the authentication package requests help from the NetLogon service to retrieve the information it requires.

If the Domain box in the Logon dialog indicates the local user account database (that is, if the user selected the workstation's computer name), MSV1_0 calls the SAM on the local station. From the SAM, the account security identifiers (SIDs) and global group SIDs are retrieved. (SIDs are covered in Chapter 6.)

If the Domain box indicates a remote database (a domain), this tells MSV1_0 that the user account database from which to obtain the account and global group SIDs is not located on the local station. Consequently, MSV1_0 calls (and passes the credentials to) the NetLogon service on the local system.

The NetLogon service considers the domain name and probably already knows the computer name of a domain controller (DC) on the domain. With this computer name, NetLogon uses a Remote Procedure Call (RPC) to forward the credentials to the NetLogon service on a DC.

Should the NetLogon service not know a name for a DC, it has to find one using a process called *discovery*. Once a DC is discovered, it is used for subsequent user-account authentication. (There is an implicit trust between the workstation and DCs in the workstation's own domain.)

NOTE. *The discovery process, although interesting, is not necessarily relevant to this discussion of logon process security. For an in-depth description of the discovery process, please refer to the Windows NT Server 4.0 Resource Kit, Networking Guide, Chapter 2.*

After discovery, the NetLogon services from both computers exchange *challenges* to verify the existence of their valid computer accounts. (These accounts can be viewed in Server Manager.) Once verification is complete, a secure communication session is set up between the computers and used to pass user-identification data.

The NetLogon service maintains security on these communication channels by employing user-level security to create the channel. Three special internal user "trust accounts" are created: workstation, server, and interdomain. *Workstation trust accounts* allow a domain workstation to perform pass-through authentication (described later in this chapter) for a computer running Windows NT in the domain. *Server trust accounts* allow computers running Windows NT Server to get copies of the master-domain database from the DC. *Interdomain trust accounts* allow a computer running Windows NT Server to perform pass-through authentication to another domain. (See "A Little About Trusts" at the end of this chapter.)

On DCs, the NetLogon service, after it is started and discovery is complete, attempts to set up a secure channel. If the channel cannot be established, NetLogon retries every 15 minutes or whenever an action requiring pass-through authentication occurs. To reduce network overhead for trusted domains, the NetLogon service on a DC creates a secure channel only when it is needed.

The first time a user logs on to a domain account from a workstation, a DC downloads validated logon information (from the domain directory database) to the workstation. This information is cached on the workstation. If a DC is not available at the time of subsequent logons, the user can log on to the domain account using the cached logon information.

Computers running Windows NT Workstation and Windows NT Server store the information authenticating the last several users (the default number is ten) who logged on in the local directory database.

Step 5: The Security Account Manager (SAM)

When the account is validated, SAM returns the user's security ID and the security IDs of any global groups to which the user belongs.

Up to this point, the authentication package (MSV1_0) on the computer at which we are logging in has called to the local NetLogon Service requesting the credentials of a user from a domain. Then, in step 3, the two NetLogon Services talk. Now we are working on the DC and attempting to get logon validation. Keep in mind that all of the following occurs on the same machine: the domain controller (DC).

NOTE. *Throughout this chapter we will use the acronym OTDC to represent* ***O****n* ***T****he* ***D****omain* ***C****ontroller.*

The NetLogon service OTDC calls its authentication package (again, this is MSV1_0), passing the credentials (username and password received from the NT requesting workstation) and asking for account and global group SIDs from the DC.

The authentication package OTDC calls and passes the credentials to the SAM locally. The authentication package asks the SAM to use the local (DC) user-accounts database (data contained in a secured Registry key) to do the following:

- Look up the specified user account name and retrieve the associated account SID.
- Compare the specified password with that stored in the database.
- Retrieve the SIDs of all global groups of which this user is a member.

The SAM returns the account SID and global group SIDs to the authentication package OTDC, MSV1_0.

NOTE. *Internally, the MSV1_0 authentication package is split into two halves. The top half executes on the machine where logon (or connecting) is occurring. The bottom half executes on the machine that contains the user account. When both machines are the same machine, the MSV1_0 authentication package's top half simply calls the bottom half without involving the NetLogon service. When the top half recognizes that pass-through authentication is needed (because the domain name received is not its own domain name), MSV1_0 passes the request to the NetLogon service, which routes the request to the NetLogon service on the appropriate machine, which in turn passes the request to the bottom half of the MSV1_0 authentication package on that machine.*

Still OTDC, the authentication package returns the account and global group SIDs to the NetLogon service, which returns these SIDs via RPC to the NetLogon service on the originating system. Now we are finally back on the machine where we physically started our logon process.

At this point, then, the NetLogon service from the DC has passed back to the NetLogon Service on the local workstation the account and group SID information, and NetLogon returns them to the authentication package (MSV1_0) on our local machine.

Although we are about to create an access token, none has yet been created on the domain controller.

Step 6: The Hand-Off

The authentication package creates a logon session and then passes the logon session and the security IDs associated with the user to the LSA.

The LSA on the local workstation uses the local (our system) LSA policy database and data contained in a secured Registry key to retrieve local group SIDs and user rights. The LSA searches the local LSA policy database for all local groups that contain the account SID and/or one or more of the global group SIDs. (These are the account and global group SIDs obtained from the user-account database on the domain controller.)

Now the LSA has collected the account SID, all global group SIDs, and all local group SIDs that apply to the specified username. With all of these SIDs, LSA searches the local LSA policy database for all user rights that have one or more of these SIDs associated. What we have here are the makings of an access token.

NOTE. *When you use User Manager to assign rights to accounts or groups, you first select the user right, and then associate user accounts or groups with this user right; see Chapter 6.*

Step 7: Token Generation

If the logon is not rejected, an access token is created containing the user's security ID and the security IDs of Everyone and other groups. This access token is returned to the logon process with a success status. If the logon is rejected, the logon session is deleted, and an error is returned to the logon process.

The LSA takes all that it has collected thus far and creates the structure called the *access token*. The access token will be attached to all processes spawned by the user in step 8. The LSA returns this token to the logon process, which called the LSA to begin with (see step 2).

We're not finished yet!

Step 8: The Subject

The logon session calls the Client Server Subsystem (CSR) to create a process and attach the access token to that process, thus creating a subject for the user account.

The logon process creates a new process in which the CSR is run (unless another shell has been specified in the Registry). The token is attached to that process. Any process that is created by CSR (that is, any program that the user runs from the desktop) inherits the same token.

Subjects and Impersonation This now brings in the process of *subjects* and *impersonation*. One objective of the Windows NT security model is to ensure that the programs run by a user have no more access to objects than the user does. That is, if a user is granted read-only access to a file, then a program run by that user cannot write to the file. The program, like the user, is granted read-only permission.

A *subject* is the combination of the user's access token and the program that is acting on the user's behalf. Windows NT uses subjects to track and manage permissions for the programs users run. When a program or process runs on the user's behalf, it is said to be running in the *security context* of that user. The security context controls what access the subject has to objects and system services.

There are two classes of subjects within the Windows NT security architecture:

- A *simple subject,* which is a process that was assigned a security context when the corresponding user logged on. It is not acting in the capacity of a protected server, which may have other subjects as clients.
- A *server subject,* which is a process implemented as a protected server (such as the CSR subsystem). A server subject has other subjects as clients. In this role, a server subject typically has the security context of those clients available for use when acting on their behalf.

When a subject calls an object service through a protected subsystem, the subject's token is used within the service to determine who made the call and to decide whether the caller has sufficient access authority to perform the requested action.

Windows NT allows one process to take on the security attributes of another through a technique called *impersonation*. For example, a server process typically impersonates a client process. This is in order to complete a task involving objects to which the server does not normally have access, or—in some client/server applications—to ensure that the user has the rights to carry out the action.

Some organizations want NT to have a different look and feel, other than the default desktop environment established after logon. In these cases the CSR may be run with a custom front-end—for example, a kiosk program or oil refinery processing system. Users should not be forced to navigate Windows NT in order to start the kiosk program. Or the NT machine can be customized for one specific use—that of controlling oil flow through a refinery, perhaps—so the machine would always boot to the refinery process and not to any desktop user interface.

Step 9: The Desktop

Finally, the logon process spawns a call to the CSR, and the CSR subsystem starts the desktop for the user.

Whenever the user opens a resource (such as a folder, an application, or a network resource connection), the file system that manages that resource will be given the token attached to the process that initiated the request to open the resource. A local file system such as NTFS can compare the SIDs in the token to the SIDs in the access control list (ACL) of the specified file to determine whether the user has the right to open the file in the manner indicated—that is, for read privileges or for write privileges or for read/write privileges. (This process is discussed in Chapter 6.)

■ Beyond the Steps: Connecting to Network Resources

You've just finished working your way through the steps that are followed to access Windows NT, including the logon process and generation of an access token. Before we can move on to study the access control list (ACL) and bring the local (NTFS) security into the picture (see Chapter 6), we need to tie up a few loose ends. So put on your TechnoGeek T-shirt, and let's take a look at the networking acceptance of access tokens.

Connecting to a Server

We have logged in, been validated by a domain controller, and have our desktop before us. Now, continuing with the NT access scenario, we need to connect to a server on the network. We can do this by issuing a NET USE command from the command line, or we can work with a GUI tool such as Windows Explorer.

When a NET USE command is executed, or the Network Connection command in Explorer (an open resource connection request), that command travels down the network architecture layers to the network redirector file system. The redirector does not use the token to check ACLs. Rather, the redirector (with help from the security subsystem's SRM, LSA, and other elements) resolves the token back to the user credentials (username, password, domain name) originally passed to the logon process when the local user logged on (that is, when this token was generated).

The token isn't passed back out to other machines or to domain controllers, however. The redirector uses a Server Message Block (SMB) request [Session Setup] to pass the user credentials to the server specified in the NET USE command or Explorer session.

Remote Authentication

Okay, let's say we are trying to connect to a domain controller (DC) on the network, but not the one that just validated us. The DC's Server service receives the incoming call from our redirector, and does just what the logon process did on our machine when we originally logged on: It calls its own

LSA—remember OTDC—and passes the credentials, and then requests a token. But this time we are not logging in; we have been validated already. We just need this server to check our authentication. This time the DC's LSA builds the token as previously described.

Because this server is a DC in the specified domain (our domain, which has validated us), that means the account SID, global group SIDs, local group SIDs, and user rights all come from the local user-account database (OTDC) and the DC's LSA policy database. In this case, the user account and LSA policy databases are the domain user account and LSA policy databases, which are kept up-to-date dynamically via directory synchronization (see Chapter 2) by the NetLogon service. This is controlled by the primary domain controller (PDC) but replicated to all backup domain controllers.

The token has now been created on the domain controller, and the DC's LSA returns the token to the DC's Server service. The Server service saves the token in its internal "user session" list and passes an *index* (or pointer) into that list. This is a user ID or UID in the [SessionSetup] SMB response that goes back to our workstation's redirector.

Our workstation redirector saves the UID in its internal list, with reference to the drive letter (or UNC name) just requested and redirected. When we open a file on the redirected drive, the file system that gets the request is, again, the redirector. The redirector forwards the Open request (through an "Open" SMB request), the drive letter, and the associated UID (or pointer to the index) to the server we are connecting to (the DC).

The DC's Server service uses the Open SMB-indicated UID (index pointer) to find the associated "user session" list entry so that it can retrieve the appropriate token. When the server opens the file locally (OTDC), this token passes to NTFS or other local file system that manages the file being opened. The file system can compare the token SIDs with the SIDs contained in the ACL of the specified file to determine whether the (remote workstation) user has the right to open the file (object). That process is described in Chapter 6.

If we try this process on the DC that validated us or on any other NT machine that participates in the same domain, the above process is repeated. Take note that tokens are not passed. They are created locally (by the LSA and friends) and stored locally, although components may have been retrieved from the network as explained in our original logon process.

What if we wanted to make another connection to the DC to which we connected earlier? We do another NET USE command to another resource on that same DC. When that resource connection request and the token reach the local redirector (on our machine), the redirector notes the secured user session (with a UID) that's already established to the specified server on behalf of the user. This is indicated by its token—that's us. The redirector therefore uses the already obtained UID in subsequent SMBs to create the resource connection and gain access to objects on that (redirected drive) resource. This is why you cannot establish two connections to the same machine under different security contexts. (See Chapter 6.)

Remote User Authentication

With a computer running Windows NT Workstation, or a non-DC computer running Windows NT Server, the NetLogon service is called upon to process logon requests for the local computer and pass them through to a DC.

The NetLogon service authenticates a logon request in three steps:

1. Discovery
2. Secure channel setup
3. Pass-through authentication (where necessary)

We have already discussed the first two actions, in step 4 of the logon process. So let's take a look at the pass-through authentication—it's time to delve back into the depths of NT!

Pass-Through Authentication

Pass-through authentication occurs in the following three scenarios:

1. A user interactively logs on at a Windows NT workstation or server as a member server, and the Domain name in the Logon Information dialog is not the computer name.
2. A user logs on interactively at the domain controller, but the Domain name is not the domain to which the controller belongs.
3. A user already logged on remotely to a domain accesses a computer over the network that is not in the same domain.

In scenario 1, the logon computer sends the logon request to a DC in the domain to which the computer account belongs (keep in mind that a computer account is not a user account). The DC first checks the domain name. If it matches the DC's domain, the controller authenticates the logon credentials and allows access as described previously.

If the domain does not match the DC's domain, the DC determines whether the domain is a trusted domain. If it is, the DC passes the logon request through to a DC in the trusted domain. That DC authenticates the username and password against the domain directory database and passes the account identification back to the initial DC, which sends it back to the logon computer. If the logon credentials supplied match the account identification information, logon succeeds; otherwise, logon fails.

Pass-through authentication in this scenario is much like the pass-through process that takes place between the local workstation and the DC that we discussed earlier. Another hop has simply been added to the process.

In scenario 2, the DC checks the domain name to see if it is a trusted domain. The DC does not check for a computer name, because the DC's directory database contains only domain accounts. If the domain is a trusted domain, the DC passes the logon information to a DC in the trusted domain for authentication. If the trusted domain's DC authenticates the account, the logon information is passed back to the initial DC, and the user is logged on. If the account is not authenticated, the logon fails.

In scenario 3, if the user is logged on to a computer or domain account and then tries to make a network connection to another computer, pass-through authentication proceeds as in interactive logons. The logon credentials used at interactive logon are also used for pass-through authentication.

Exceptions

There are a couple of exceptions to this process, however, if a user overrides the credentials. A special dialog that allows entry of a different username and domain or computer name appears under the following circumstances:

- When the user types an entry in the Connect As field in the Map Network Drive dialog.
- When the user clicks Run in the Start menu, and types the UNC path at the command prompt, using the syntax \\servername\sharename.

For example, let's say MaPatel wants to access a computer in the Phoenix domain. Because the Phoenix domain trusts DomainX, it asks the DomainX to authenticate MaPatel's account information.

Let's examine the logon process for this example. If MaPatel tries to make a network connection to a remote computer in an untrusted domain, the logon proceeds as if MaPatel were connecting to an account on the remote computer. That computer authenticates the logon credentials against its directory database. If the account is not defined in the directory database but the Guest account on the remote computer is enabled, and if the Guest account has no password established, the user will be logged on with guest privileges. If the Guest account is not enabled, the logon fails.

A Little about Trusts

When one domain is permitted to trust another, User Manager for Domains (see Chapters 2 and 3) creates an interdomain trust account in the directory database (SAM) of the trusted domain. A trusted-domain object is created in the LSA of the trusting domain, and a secret object is created in the LSA of the trusting domain. This account is like any other global user account, except that the USER_INTERDOMAIN_TRUST_ACCOUNT bit in the control field for the account is set.

The interdomain trust account is used only by the primary domain controller and is invisible in User Manager for Domains. The password is randomly generated and is maintained by User Manager for Domains.

Even NT has to validate itself. When this trust relationship is established, the NetLogon service on the trusting (or resource) domain attempts discovery on the trusted (accounts) domain. The interdomain trust account is authenticated (by the same processes described earlier) by a domain controller on the trusted domain.

Similar accounts and procedures are used in the trust relationships between a PDC and a BDC and between a domain controller running Windows NT and a computer running Windows NT Workstation in that domain. This is the implicit trust relationship mentioned back in step 4 of the NT access process.

Summary

In this chapter, we looked in depth at the Windows NT security model and its major components: the Local Security Authority (LSA), Security Reference Monitor (SRM), directory database, and logon authentication process. Each of these items plays a significant role in the Windows NT security subsystem.

We have examined the logon validation process of NT and found that it's not easy to slip in the back door. In fact, there is no back door. NT ensures system integrity from the start by restricting access to validated users only.

At this point in the book, you should understand the statement that "NT is inherently secure." From objects and file systems, to the architecture and kernel, to logon and access validation, NT is tightly integrated with its security subsystem. All the security components are vital to the health and security of your NT domain. Although we did not include the NetLogon service as a component of the security subsystem, we have shown you the key role it plays in allowing access to domains. The NetLogon service provides users with a single access point to a domain's PDC and all BDCs.

In Chapter 6 you will see how the user validation result, which is your access token, is applied to objects (file access rights). Building on your knowledge of users and groups, SIDs and access tokens, you will learn how the system uses discretionary access control.

- *The Security of Objects in Windows NT*
- *SID Definition and Format*
- *Discretionary Access Control*
- *Permissions*
- *The NT Security Process*
- *Tools for Managing Local Resources*
- *Creating and Managing Folders and Subfolders*

CHAPTER

Local Resource Security

IN THIS CHAPTER, WE ARE GOING TO TAKE AN IN-DEPTH LOOK AT managing security for your local resources. You've learned in the preceding chapters about the creation of users, deployment of access tokens, and other topics concerning how the network user is affected by the NT security subsystem. In this chapter's study of security for the local resources, you'll learn about the process of designating who may have access to an object and what kind of access is allowed.

NOTE. *Having access to an object, or setting the access rights to an object, is directly related to the permissions one can obtain on said object. Although not identical, permissions and access rights/access controls have a symbiotic relationship—or at least some synchronicity. When reading about one, you must be thinking also about the other.*

The Security of Objects in Windows NT

Under Windows NT, objects fall into many categories, including folders, files, processes, threads, shares, and devices. Essentially, all resources are represented by objects, and only Windows NT can directly access an object. When an object is accessed under Windows NT, the security subsystem performs a security check on that object. Since every object is treated individually under NT, this provides enhanced security.

All objects in Windows NT can be protected by means of a *security descriptor.* Figure 6.1 illustrates the elements of this descriptor, which describes the security attributes for an object. An object's security descriptor includes the following:

- An *owner SID (security ID),* which indicates the user or group who owns the object. The owner of an object is allowed to change the access permissions for the object.
- A *group SID,* which is used only by the POSIX subsystem and ignored by the rest of Windows NT.
- A *discretionary ACL (access control list)*, which identifies the users and groups who are granted or denied specific access permissions. The discretionary ACL is controlled by the owner of the object.
- A *system ACL,* which controls the auditing messages the system will generate. System ACLs are controlled by the network security administrators.

NOTE. Permissions *are inserted into an ACL when the owner sets discretionary access controls for the object. If the object's owner does not set discretionary access controls for the object, a default ACL is created. We'll explore permissions in an upcoming section.*

SID Definition and Format

A SID (security identifier) is used to uniquely identify a user or group. The Windows NT security model relies heavily on these identifiers. According to Microsoft, a SID should never occur twice. Anywhere. It is a statistically unique number.

Figure 6.1

The components of an object's security descriptor

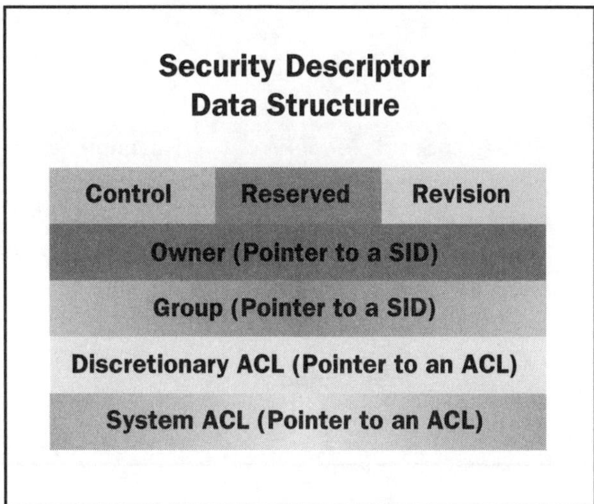

A combination of user information, time, date, and domain information is used to create a SID. To make it easier to visualize and understand the SID's components, we'll use the following standardized shorthand notation:

```
S-R-I-S-S
```

where

```
S identifies the series of digits as a SID
R is the revision level of the SID
I is the identifier authority value
S is the first subauthority value
S is another subauthority value, and so forth
```

According to this format, here is an example of a SID that represents the local Administrators group:

S-1-5-32-544

The components of this identifier represent that the SID has a revision level of 1; an identifier authority value of 5; a first subauthority value of 32; and a second subauthority value of 544. Figure 6.2 illustrates the SID data structure.

The identifier authority value is probably the most important information contained in a SID. This value identifies the issuing agency, typically a corporation or large organization.

Figure 6.2

The structure of data in a SID

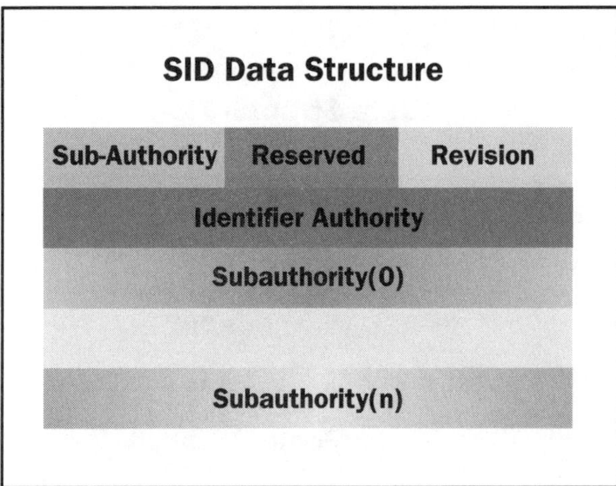

Well-Known SIDs

A Windows NT system contains some predefined, or "well-known" SIDs. A well-known SID is a SID whose value is constant across all Windows NT systems. In addition, there are some well-known SIDs that are universal across all systems. Table 6.1 is a listing of well-known SIDs.

Table 6.1

NT Well-Known SIDs

TYPE	SID
NT Authority	S-1-5
Dial-up	S-1-5-1
Network	S-1-5-2
Batch	S-1-5-3
Interactive	S-1-5-4
Service	S-1-5-6
Anonymous Logon (aka null logon session)	S-1-5-7
Proxy	S-1-5-8
Server Logon (aka domain controller account)	S-1-5-8
Logon IDs	S-1-5-5-X-Y

Table 6.1 (Continued)

NT Well-Known SIDs

TYPE	SID
NT nonunique IDs	S-1-5-0x15
Built-in domain	S-1-5-0x20
Null SID	S-1-0-0
World	S-1-1-0
Local	S-1-2-0
Creator Owner ID	S-1-3-0
Creator Group ID	S-1-3-1
Creator Owner Server ID	S-1-3-2
Creator Group Server ID	S-1-3-3
Nonunique IDs	S-1-4

Discretionary Access Control

Discretionary access control (DAC) is one of the requirements needed to meet the U.S. government's C2 security rating. DAC is the ability of a resource's owner to specify which users and/or groups are allowed to access the resource, and what types of access they're allowed. DAC is the method of the action allowed and/or taken to set security.

Access types include read, write, delete, and others. Every object in Windows NT has a list of users and groups who are authorized and not authorized to access that object; these lists are called discretionary access control lists (ACLs or DACLs). Any owner, administrator, or account that has the proper permissions may change this list as they please ("at their discretion"). The ACL and its entries are critical components for implementing DAC in Windows NT.

Access Control Lists (ACLs)

The primary means of discretionary access control is the use of *access control lists* (ACLs). ACLs offer versatility in controlling access to objects. They work with the file systems to protect files from unauthorized access. ACLs allow users to specify and control access to the objects they own, or the explicit denial of access to those objects. The ACL data structure is illustrated in Figure 6.3.

Figure 6.3

Structure of data in an access control list (ACL)

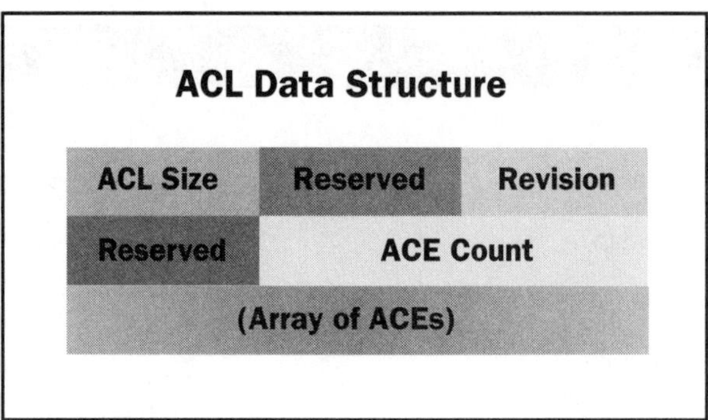

You can see in Figure 6.3 that ACEs (access control entries) are a part of ACLs. For each object, the ACL contains ACEs that define specific access permissions to the object. ACEs contain the SIDs for each user or group and the specific access given to these users/groups on the object. In addition to users and groups, Windows NT allows applications and services to be given access to objects.

There are actually two types of access control lists: discretionary and system. The discretionary access control list (DACL) is used to specify discretionary protection information, and user/group access permissions. System Security ACLs are used to specify system-level security information. Frequently DACLs and ACLs are used interchangeably, as they are more commonly referenced than System Security ACLs.

NOTE. *There is an important distinction between a DACL that is empty (one with no ACEs) and an object without a DACL. When a DACL is empty, no accesses are explicitly granted, so access is denied. When an object has no DACL, the object has no protection, so any access request is granted.*

As stated earlier and as seen in Figure 6.3, access control lists have entries: ACEs. Think of ACLs as tables, and ACEs as rows of data in the table. There are three defined ACE types. The following table lists these ACEs and the type of security they support. Figure 6.4 illustrates the data structure of ACEs.

Access Masks

An *access mask* is a component of an ACE; it contains a list of access types possible for the object. As an example: A file on an NTFS drive is an object. This object has an ACL; the ACL has an ACE; the ACE has an access mask; and the access mask has a list of access types.

Let's use an analogy. Girl Scout cookies! Have you seen that list of cookies? You get this *big* sheet, and across the top are all the types of cookies.

Figure 6.4

Structure of data in an ACE

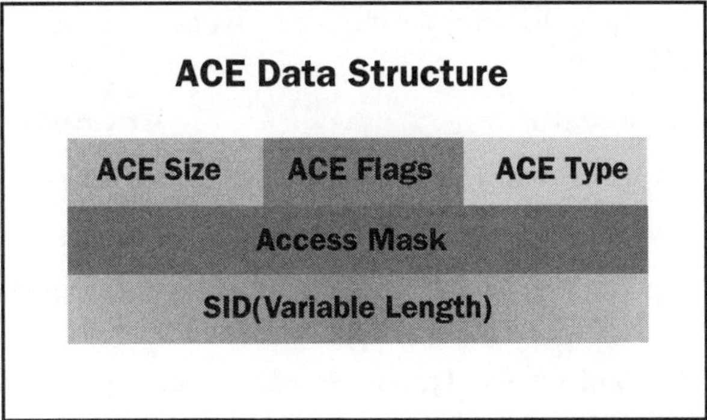

ACE Type	Type of Security	Function
Access-Allowed	Discretionary access control	Used to grant access to a user or group of users. The ACE contains a SID for the user or group, and the access to be granted by the ACE. Used in DACL only.
Access-Denied	Discretionary access control	Used to explicitly deny access to a user or group. The ACE contains a SID for the user or group, and the access to be denied by the ACE. Used in DACL only.
System-Audit	System security and auditing	Used to generate a log of significant security events. Used in System ACL only.

Along the left-hand side you enter your name in one row, and check off the type of cookies you want. I don't usually order them all (no matter what my wife thinks); I just choose the ones I like. But I also don't delete any of the other columns of cookie types, because other people may order those. The access mask is like the columns of cookie types: It's a list of the types of controls or access that you can grant to the object.

There are three sets of access types within the access mask, specific types, standard types, and generic types that define the access a user or a group has to an object.

Specific Access Types Specific types of access contain the access mask information specific to the object type. A file object, for instance, will have different specific access types than a service object, such as Replication. When an object is defined, the specific access types must be defined as well. There may be up to 16 specific access types per object type, and, as such, they provide a precise level of control.

The following specific access types are available for file objects on NTFS drives:

ReadData	**WriteData**
AppendData	ReadEA (Extended Attribute)
WriteEA (Extended Attribute)	Execute
ReadAttributes	WriteAttributes

Standard Access Types Standard access types apply to all objects, and control the following types of access to an object:

- SYNCHRONIZE is used to synchronize access (more than one user); and to allow a process to wait for an object to enter the signaled state.
- WRITE_OWNER is used to assign a write owner.
- WRITE_DAC is used to grant or deny write access to the discretionary ACL.
- READ_CONTROL is used to grant or deny read access to the security descriptor and owner.
- DELETE is used to grant or deny delete access.

These are very interesting controls. Have you ever wondered why an administrator can still gain control of an object when you have denied access to that object for the administrator? It has to do with standard access. Notice the WRITE_DAC entry in the list of access types: To what is it granting or denying access? The ACL itself.

You see, although the administrator might be denied access to the object from the AccessDenied ACE, the administrator still maintains access to the ACL. So, should administrator MaPatel be stopped from access to a file object, he can always change the security and grant himself access to the object, because he has the rights to change the ACL, apart from the rest of the object.

Generic Access Types Generic access types comprise a broad category of access used mostly by programmers to group the specific and standard access types. The generic types are mapped to the specific and standard types when access to an object is requested. Following are some examples of this mapping.

NOTE. *When conducting auditing, only specific and standard accesses will appear in the details of the Security Log (see Chapter 12). Generic access types do not appear in the Security Log; the corresponding (mapped) specific and standard types are listed instead.*

This Generic Access Type	Is Mapped to These Specific/Standard Types
FILE_GENERIC_READ	STANDARD_RIGHTS_READ FILE_READ_DATA FILE_READ_ATTRIBUTES FILE_READ_EA SYNCHRONIZE
FILE_GENERIC_WRITE	STANDARD_RIGHTS_WRITE FILE_WRITE_DATA FILE_WRITE_ATTRIBUTES FILE_WRITE_EA FILE_APPEND_DATA SYNCHRONIZE
FILE_GENERIC_EXECUTE	STANDARD_RIGHTS_EXECUTE FILE_READ_ATTRIBUTES FILE_EXECUTE SYNCHRONIZE

How It Works

When a user attempts to access an object, their SID or the SID of one of the groups to which they belong is matched to the list of ACEs, and the user's desired activity is compared to the access permission defined in the ACL. If a user's SID and access request match an ACE's SID and permission, the user is granted access. This process occurs on NTFS drives only.

Here's an example: MaPatel is the owner of printer resource HPColorJet. From the Printers folder, MaPatel selects Printer/Properties and in the Security Tab sets up Print permission for user KyTrenton to resource HPColorJet. KyTrenton sends a document to HPColorJet and requests HPColorJet's ACL for permission. KyTrenton's SID is matched with the ACE containing the same SID. Since HPColorJet's ACE contains Print permission, KyTrenton's document is printed.

ACL Representation

ACEs in an ACL are prioritized by type of access; these types are Deny access and Grant access. Windows NT first checks ACEs with a Deny access, and then it checks ACEs with a Grant access. Deny access always overrides Grant access.

If any group to which a user belongs is denied access to an object, that user will be denied access regardless of any access rights the user is granted in either their personal user account or the accounts of other groups to which they belong. Therefore, if the No Access permission is given to the Everyone group, all users in Everyone will be denied access, including the owner of the object. No Access permission does not, however, prevent the owner from changing permissions on the file and restoring access.

Permissions

Permissions that are placed on an object determine the type of access to it that a user will have. Let's take a closer look at permissions and what they mean.

In order for you to set permissions on an object, one of several conditions must be met:

- You must be running a secure file system (NTFS).
- You must be the owner/creator of the object.
- You must be given explicit permission to change permissions on the object.
- You must have full control of the object. (Full control permission is defined in Table 6.2.)

Windows NT comes with several predefined combinations of permissions that allow a user to set various common access levels for files (see Table 6.2) and folders (see Table 6.3).

NOTE. *The letters R, X, W, D, P, and O represent permissions as described beneath the tables.*

Table 6.2

Predefined Permissions on Files

PERMISSION	R	X	W	D	P	O
No Access Read	x	x				
Change	x	x	x	x		
Full Control	x	x	x	x	x	x
Special Access (any combo)	?	?	?	?	?	?

R = Read Access. User can display data and attributes and copy the file.
X = Execute. User can run the file but not copy it.
W = Write. User can write to the file or change the file's attribute.
D = Delete. User can delete the file.
P = Permission. User can change permissions on the file.
O = Ownership. User can take ownership of the file.
Special Access is any combination of R, X, W, D, P, and/or O.

Table 6.3

Predefined Permissions on Folders

PERMISSIONS	R	X	W	D	P	O
No Access						
List	x	x				
Read	x	x				
Add		x	x			
Add & Read	x	x	x			
Change	x	x	x	x		
Full Control	x	x	x	x	x	
Special Access (any Combo)	?	?	?	?	?	?

R = Read. User can see files, their attributes and permissions, and ownership of the folder.
X = Execute. User can run files in folder and can change to subfolders.
W = Write. User can write to and create new files and subfolders in the folder, or change the folder's attribute.
D = Delete. User can delete files in the folder or delete the folder itself.
P = Permission. User can change permissions of the folder.
O = Ownership. User can take ownership of the folder.
Special Access is any combination of R, X, W, D, P, and/or O.

The default permission on any newly created object is *Everyone: Full Control.* This means any user who has a valid username and password on the system has unlimited access to the object. If the object is created within another object (as in a file within a folder) then the "inner" object (the file) will inherit the permissions of the parent object (the folder).

All permissions are cumulative except No Access. If any user or group is assigned No Access permission, access to the object is explicitly denied no matter what other permissions the user or group has.

The NT Security Process

Now that you've learned about discretionary access control and ownership of objects, let's take a look at how Windows NT handles the overall process of security management for the network. There are many components in the Windows NT security process. The Security Reference Monitor (SRM), the Local Security Authority (LSA), the Security Account Manager (SAM), the Object Manager, and the Process Manager all work together to provide tight security for all objects in Windows NT 4.0.

The Security Reference Monitor (SRM) is responsible for enforcing the access token and any audit policies that are currently active. The SRM is the component that actually validates a user's access token against the object's ACL. The same routines are run, no matter which object is being accessed. This gives Window NT a uniform security system.

The SRM is used only when an object has an ACL, however. If the object does not have an ACL—for example, a file on a FAT partition—then no reference is made to the SRM and security is not checked.

The Local Security Authority (LSA) is also called the *security subsystem.* This component ensures that the user has the correct permissions to access the resource. As explained in Chapter 5, the LSA is responsible for generating the user's access token. The LSA also controls the audit policy and account policy, and provides interactive user validations with third-party services.

The Security Account Manager (SAM) contains all the user and group accounts on the system. This is a flat file database. When users require validation, the LSA queries the SAM. Every Windows NT machine contains a SAM, no matter which network model is being implemented. If an NT machine is not a member of a domain, that machine may only query its own database. On NT machines that are part of a domain, the LSA can forward the query to a domain controller via the NetLogon service.

Object Manager

Object Manager is the Windows NT component that provides uniform rules for retention, naming, and security of objects. Before a process is allowed to manipulate a Windows NT object, the process must first acquire a *handle* to the object. An object handle includes access control information and a pointer to the object itself. All object handles are created through the Object Manager, which works with the SRM to obtain the access control information. When Windows NT grants access to an object, it is actually giving the user's process a pointer or handle to the object.

As illustrated in Figure 6.5, following are the steps in the process of gaining access to a resource:

1. User's process asks for type of access to resource (such as Read/Write access).
2. SRM validates the access by comparing the user's access token to the ACL on the object.
3. User's process is given a handle ID along with current access rights to the object.
4. Object handle is checked against type of access requested. See Figure 6.5.

Figure 6.5

The Windows NT handle process

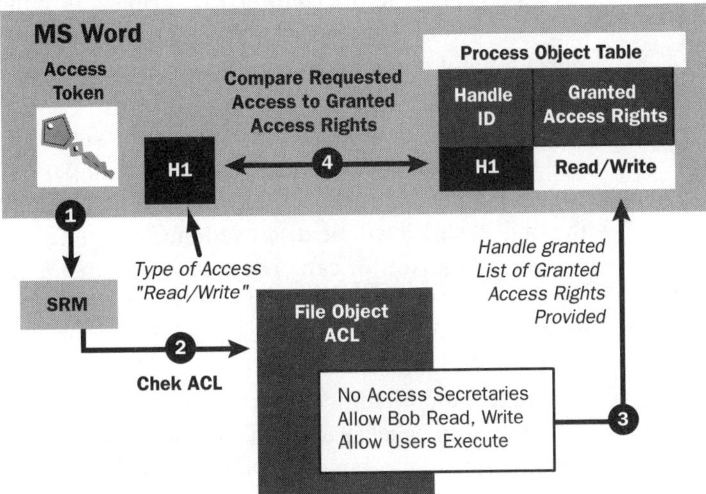

This handle process is only done once, when the object is initially accessed from a program such as MS Word. All subsequent requests are checked against the current handle. If the type of access to the resource changes, then the process is completed again for the new type of access.

For example, suppose JaHunter opens the Word file she has been working on and she is given Read/Write permissions on the document. As long as those permissions are enough for JaHunter to finish up her work, Windows NT does not check security again. However, if JaHunter decides she no longer needs the Word file and wants to delete it, then Windows NT needs to create a new handle that includes the Delete permission on the file. Security is rechecked at this point.

Process Manager

The Process Manager is the Windows NT component that manages the creation and deletion of processes and threads.

- A *process* is defined as the combination of an address space, a set of objects (resources) visible to the process, and a set of threads that run in the context of the process.
- A *thread* is the system's most basic entity that can be scheduled.

The Process Manager provides interprocess protection. When threads reference objects, the access token of the user running the process is taken by the SRM and compared to the object's ACL.

Object Ownership

As stated earlier in the chapter, every object in Windows NT 4.0 has one and only one owner. This owner may be a component of Windows NT or it may be a user, but it cannot be a group of users. *The only group that can be an owner is the Administrators group.*

The owner of an object gets to decide who is allowed to access the object and the type of access that's allowed—it's all part of discretionary access control, as mentioned earlier. The owner of the object can also set auditing on the object, which will be discussed in Chapter 12.

An administrator can always take ownership of any object. When this occurs, the user will no longer be the owner of the object and will no longer be able to modify the ACL of the object. Furthermore, if proper Windows NT auditing is enabled, a footprint will be left by the administrator that can later be tracked and identified.

One of the checks and balances in Windows NT security is the prohibiting of a user's granting ownership to another user. A user may only be given the ability to take ownership; the user must then *take* ownership in order to be the owner. You cannot *give* ownership.

For example, MaPatel, who is responsible for product inventory, is currently working on the end-of-year report. He will work on the report and then will need to give the YearEnd folder to KyTrenton to complete the report. MaPatel wants to make sure that he is the only person who has access to the folder until he passes it on.

The Take Ownership right on the YearEnd folder has been given to MaPatel by an Administrator. MaPatel, through Windows NT Explorer, takes ownership of the folder and modifies the ACL, removing all users except himself. When he finishes his section of the report, he sets the Take Ownership permission on the folder for KyTrenton. KyTrenton then takes ownership. Once MaPatel has done this, he is free of the end-of-year report and KyTrenton is responsible for it.

Tools for Managing Local Resources

Table 6.4 summarizes management vehicles under Windows NT used for setting or changing ACLs.

Windows NT Explorer

Windows NT Explorer is most typically employed to set file- and folder-level permissions on local and remote resources. Any user can use this efficient, graphical tool.

Table 6.4

ACL Management

NETWORK RESOURCE	ACL MANAGEMENT VEHICLE
Files/Folders	NT Explorer
Printers	Printers folder
Users	User Manager (Windows NT Workstations/Servers) User Manager for Domains (Windows NT domains)
Shares	NT Explorer Server Manager

The CACLS Utility

Another tool that you can use to set permissions is the CACLS.EXE program, a command-line utility included with Windows NT 4.0. CACLS allows administrators to set permissions in batch mode or through a remote shell.

There is a catch with CACLS.EXE: You can only grant Read, Change, and Full Control permission, or you can deny access. You can also remove the user or group with no specified access. Figure 6.6 shows what you see when you type the following command at the command prompt:

```
CACLS.EXE /?
```

File Manager Lives On

File Manager was our mainstay in previous versions of NT. With NT 4.0, Explorer has of course become the main tool for accessing disk resources; File Manager is no longer represented by an icon in NT 4.0. But that does not mean it is gone. The executable for File Manager is winfile.exe, located in the System32 folder off the root of your NT installation. If you like, you can create a shortcut to it on your desktop.

NOTE. *In this book we will demonstrate all graphical disk access through Explorer.*

■ Creating and Managing Folders and Subfolders

This section describes the procedure for creating and managing local resources: specifically, folders and subfolders. These procedures include the steps for giving or taking ownership of a folder or subfolder.

Figure 6.6

The CACLS utility for setting permissions

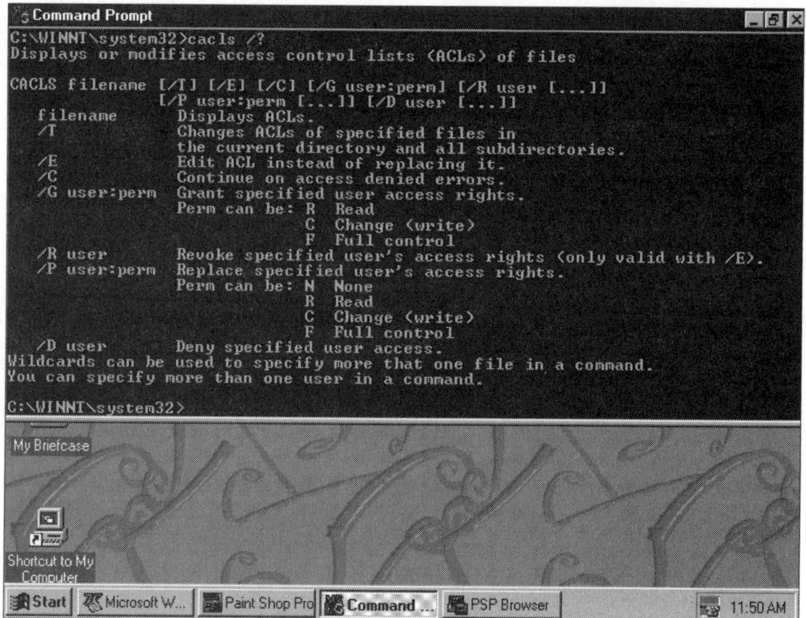

Creating a Folder

Let's start with creating the folder.

1. From the desktop, click the Start button to open the Windows taskbar.
2. Go to Programs, and click on Windows NT Explorer.
3. In Windows NT Explorer, double-click on your NTFS drive.
4. Select File/New and choose Folder (see Figure 6.7).
5. On the right side of the screen, type **YearEnd** as the name for the new folder. The new YearEnd folder now appears in the tree on the left side of the Explorer window, on your NTFS drive.
6. To create sub-folders, you highlight an existing folder, and go through the same process described in steps 4 and 5.

Taking Ownership of a Folder

Next we'll take on the task of assigning permissions. For your new folder and subfolders, you'll start by assigning ownership rights. Here are the steps to transferring and taking ownership of folders.

Figure 6.7

Using the NT Explorer File menu to create a new folder

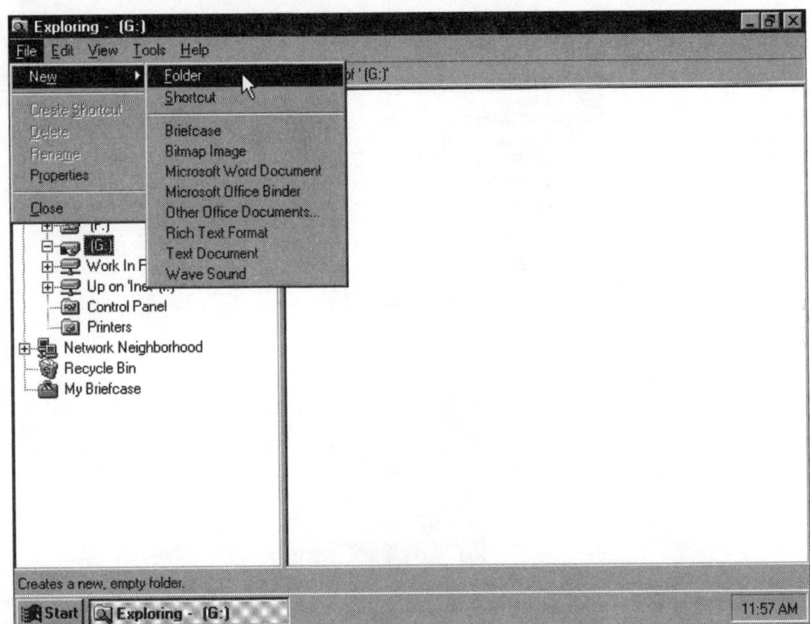

1. In Explorer, right-click the YearEnd folder on the NTFS drive, and select Properties from the submenu (see Figure 6.8).
2. In the YearEnd Properties dialog, click to open the Security tab (see Figure 6.9).
3. In the Security tab, click the Ownership button and note the folder's ownership (see Figure 6.10). Close the Owner dialog.
4. Click the Permissions button. In the Directory Permissions dialog (see Figure 6.11), Everyone is highlighted. Click the Add button.
5. In the Add Users and Groups dialog (see Figure 6.12), click the Show Users button.
6. Scroll through the Names window and highlight MaPatel.
7. Open the Type of Access list and select Full Control (see Figure 6.13). Click OK.
8. Highlight MaPatel again, and in the Type of Access list box select Special Directory Access (see Figure 6.14).
9. In the Special Directory Access dialog, check the Take Ownership option under Other (see Figure 6.15).

Figure 6.8

Opening the Properties dialog

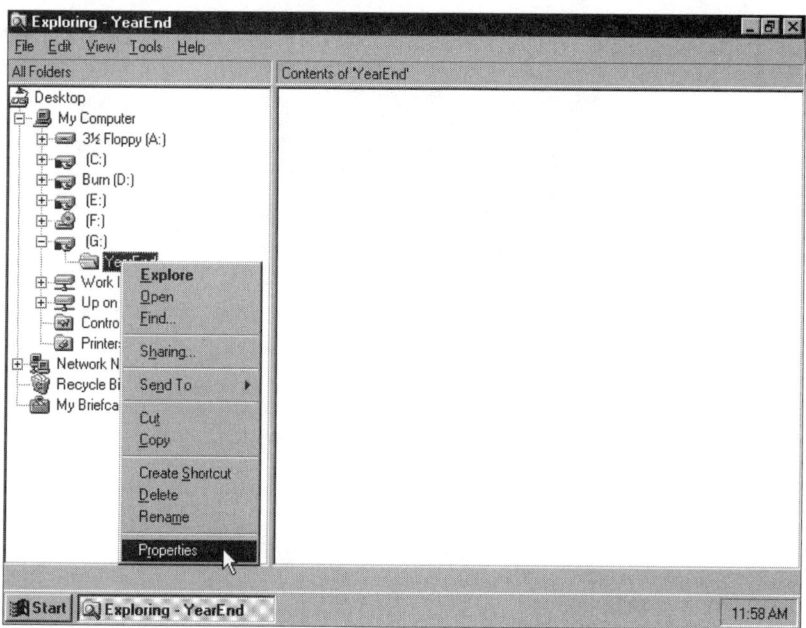

Figure 6.9

Security properties for YearEnd folder

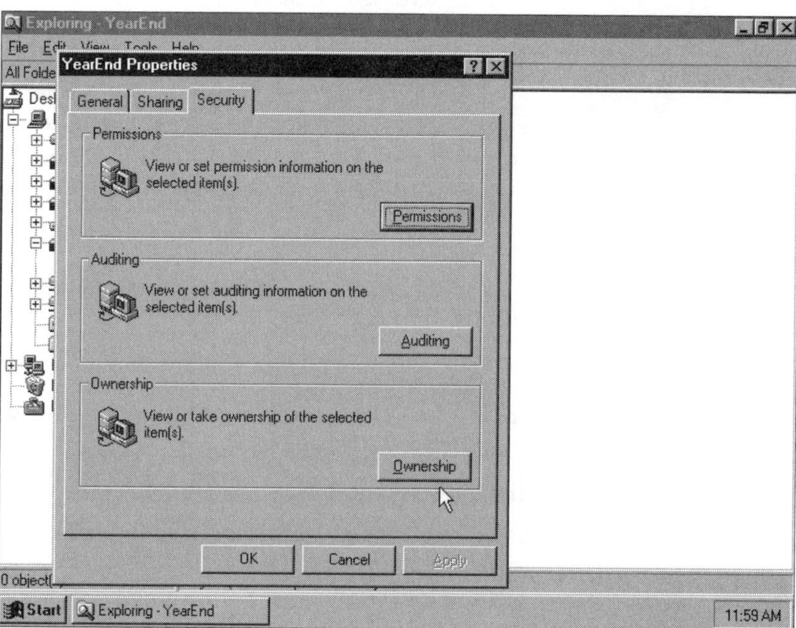

Figure 6.10

Owner dialog for the YearEnd folder

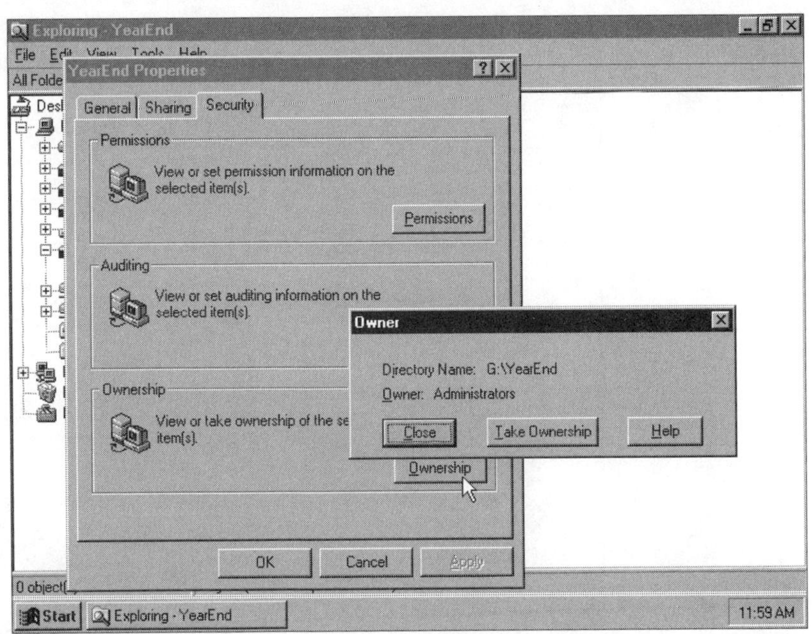

Figure 6.11

Permissions dialog for the YearEnd folder

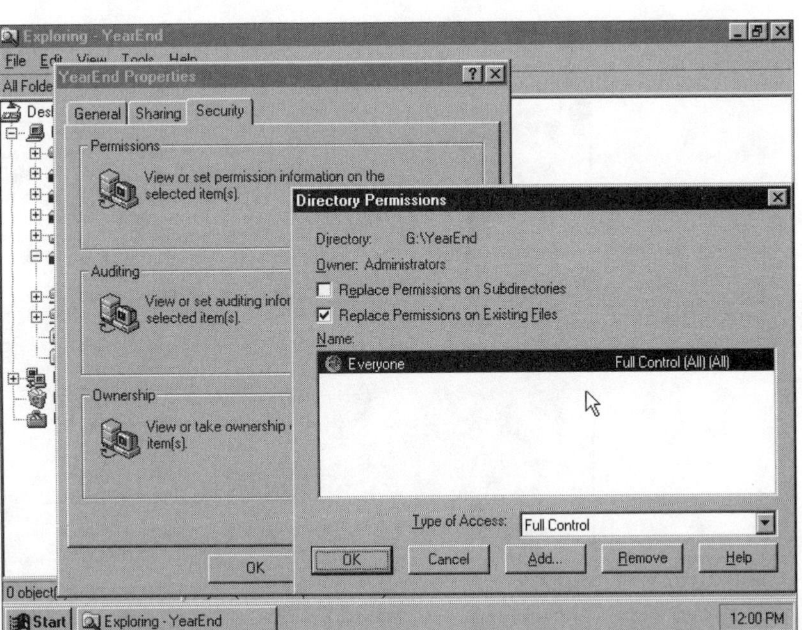

Figure 6.12

Add Users and Groups dialog

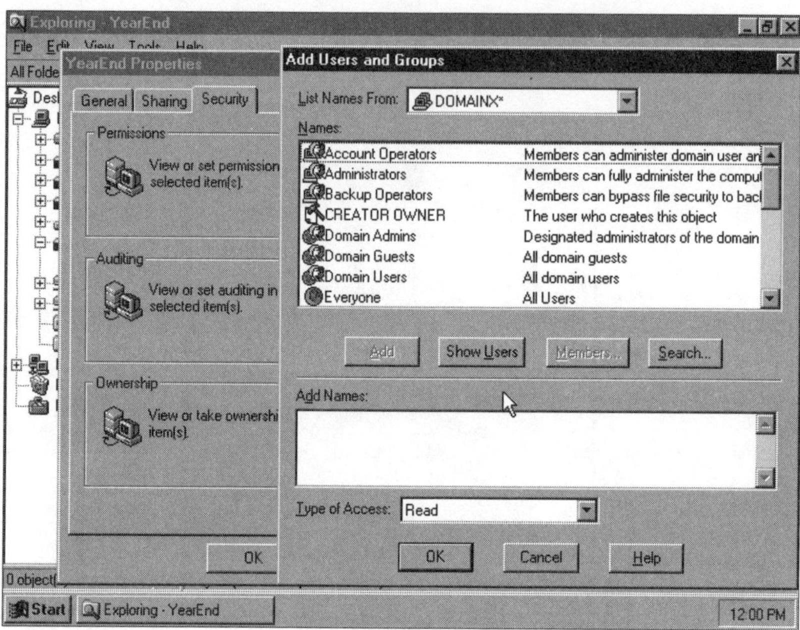

Figure 6.13

Choosing Full Control permission for MaPatel

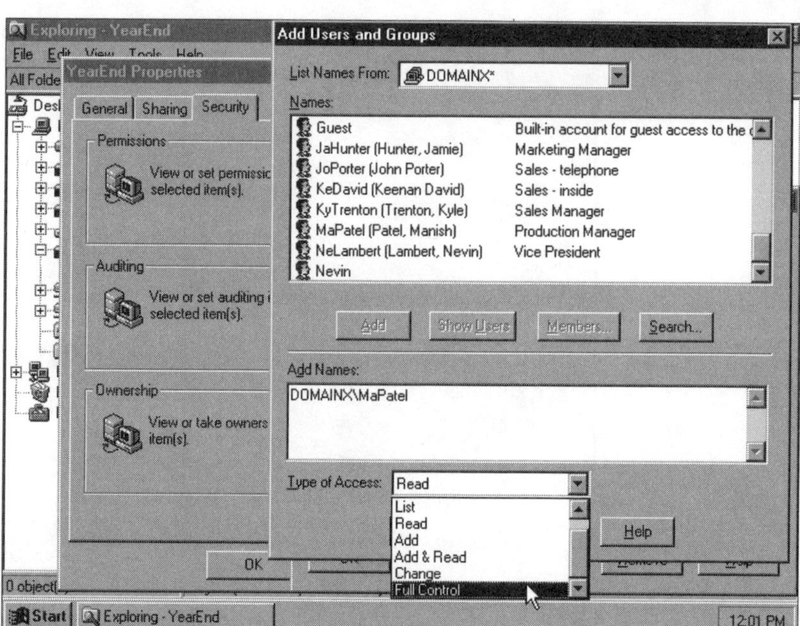

Figure 6.14

Choosing Special Directory Access permission for MaPatel

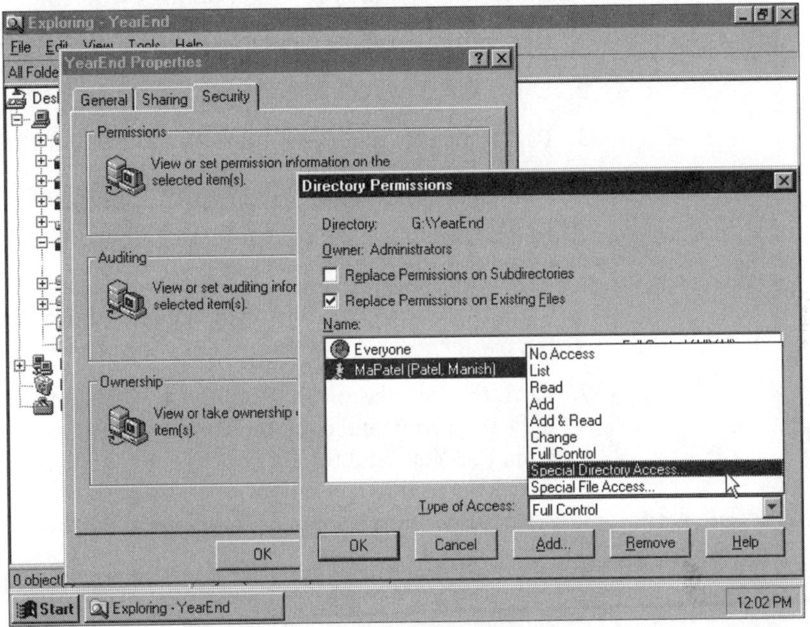

Figure 6.15

Turning on the Take Ownership option for MaPatel's access to YearEnd

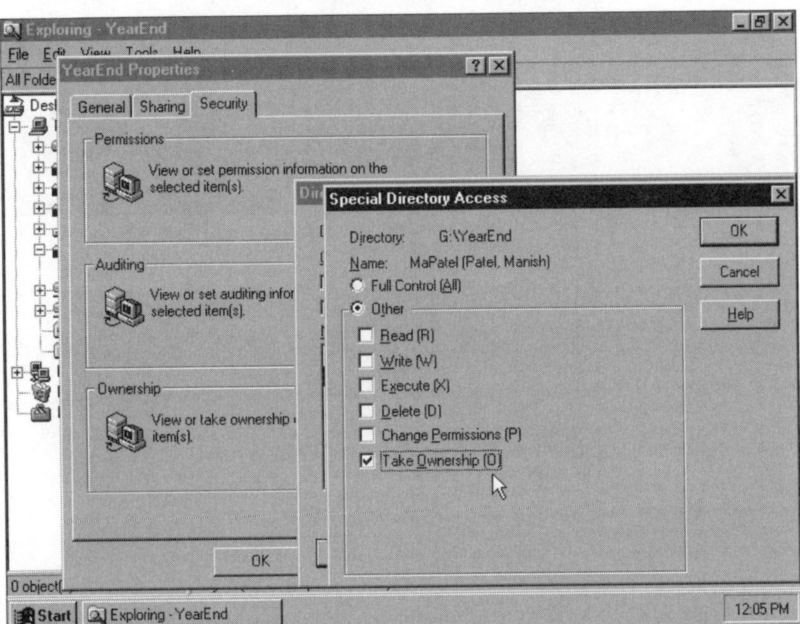

MaPatel now has the right to take ownership of the YearEnd folder. Next, step through the process of taking ownership.

1. Log off the computer and log on again as MaPatel.
2. Open Windows NT Explorer.
3. Right-click on the YearEnd folder and select Properties.
4. Open the Security tab and click the Ownership button.
5. In the Owner dialog, click the Take Ownership button and click Yes in the pop-up box.
6. Click the Ownership button again, and notice that MaPatel is now the owner.
7. Click the Permissions button. In the Directory Permissions dialog, highlight Everyone and click the Remove button. This removes Everyone from the YearEnd folder's permissions (see Figure 6.16).

Figure 6.16

Everyone removed from folder permissions

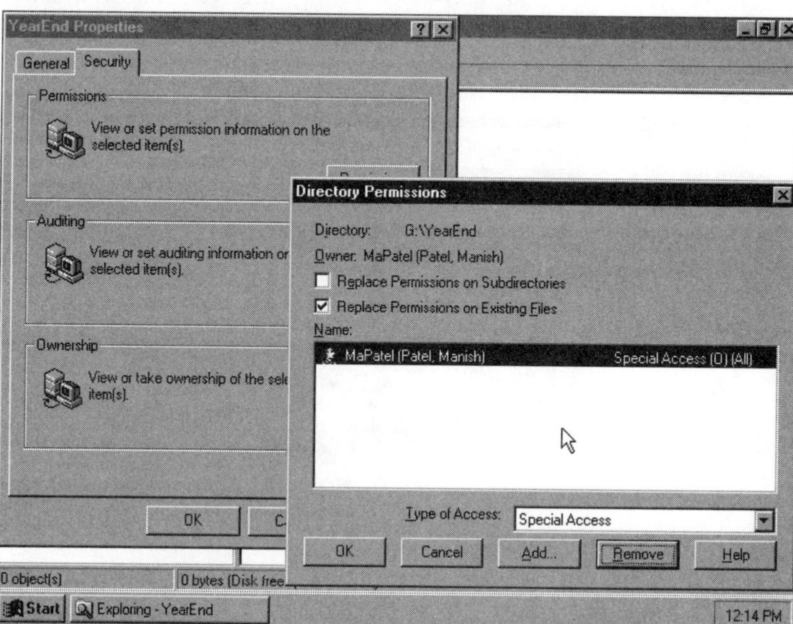

Now, let's say that MaPatel has finished his report and is ready to pass it over to KyTrenton. As the owner of the document, MaPatel must take the following steps to give KyTrenton permission to take ownership.

1. In Explorer, right-click the YearEnd folder and select Properties.
2. Open the Security tab and click the Permissions button.
3. In the Permissions dialog, highlight KyTrenton and click the Add button.
4. Under Type of Access, select Full Control. Click OK.
5. Under Type of Access, select Special Directory access.
6. In the Special Directory Access dialog, click the Take Ownership check box.
7. Click OK to close all three dialogs and return to the Explorer window.

Now KyTrenton can take ownership of the file in the same manner that MaPatel took ownership. KyTrenton has all responsibility for this document.

Summary

In this chapter, we examined the management of security for local resources. "Local resource security" is defined as the ability of Windows NT to protect network resources from interactive users.

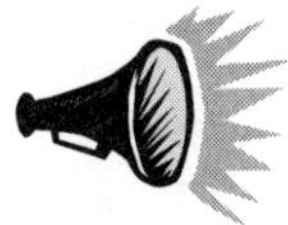

NOTE. *As you learned in Chapter 4, the only file system that supports this local resource security is NTFS.*

Every object has an Access Control List (ACL). This list is then checked against the access token created by the Local Security Authority (LSA). The Security Reference Monitor (SRM) is responsible for these actions. All of these integral processes working together provide Windows NT with its tight security model. In Chapter 7 we shall examine networking and the security of the network as a whole. Chapter 8 covers the Remote Access Server, and Chapter 9 describes printing services and how to secure them.

- *Windows NT Network Architecture*
- *Protocols*
- *TCP/IP and NT*
- *Network Security*
- *How Windows NT Handles Network Security*

CHAPTER

7

Networking and Network Security

WINDOWS NT SERVER 4.0 HAS BEEN DESIGNED FROM THE GROUND up with connectivity and networking in mind. It provides robust, built-in, 32-bit integrated networking components. Microsoft began a quest to provide a powerful, reliable network operating system that was at the same time easy to use and helpful to developers. NT 4.0 accomplishes this by having a modularized, open architecture. With this approach, Microsoft has encouraged third-party development of drivers and add-on products; all together, that has made Windows NT a very appealing enterprise solution.

To understand the hows and whys of networking security, you need to know the fundamentals of the Windows NT networking architecture. In the first part of this chapter, we will discuss the NT 4.0 network model, Network Driver Interface Specification (NDIS), common supported protocols, and implementation of protocols. In the second part of the chapter we will cover the implementation and functionality of networking security.

Windows NT Network Architecture

Microsoft has tried to make Windows NT 4.0 meet a variety of de facto industry standards. The definition of these standards has been left up to certain recognized bodies: the Internet Engineering Task Force (IETF), International Standards Organization (ISO), and the Institute of Electrical and Electronics Engineers (IEEE). Your network operating system's ability to interconnect is dependent on which of these standards it supports.

The ISO/OSI Model

ISO introduced a set of standards that allowed various manufacturers to create network operating systems that could communicate regardless of the equipment they were using. This model was called the Open Systems Interconnect (OSI) model. The OSI model consists of seven layers, each of which provides a specific network function. Each layer has defined standards and specifications for various protocols; any vendor can provide connectivity to other network operating systems that also meet these specifications.

Figure 7.1 shows the ISO/OSI model. Bear in mind that the model is viewed from the bottom up, since that is the flow of network data. This approach also clearly represents the lower layers' importance to the upper layers. The following paragraphs provide short descriptions of each layer and its functionality.

Physical Layer

The Physical layer specifies the characteristics of the "wire" that is used to connect the machines in a network. It also designates the way in which the bits are encoded, which defines the standards required for physical interconnections (the wire). Here is where the cable, connector, and signaling specifications are defined.

Data Link Layer

The Data Link layer defines the protocols for exchanging data frames over a "wire." This layer deals with getting data packets on and off the wire, error detection and correction, and retransmission.

Figure 7.1

The ISO Open Systems Interconnect (OSI) model

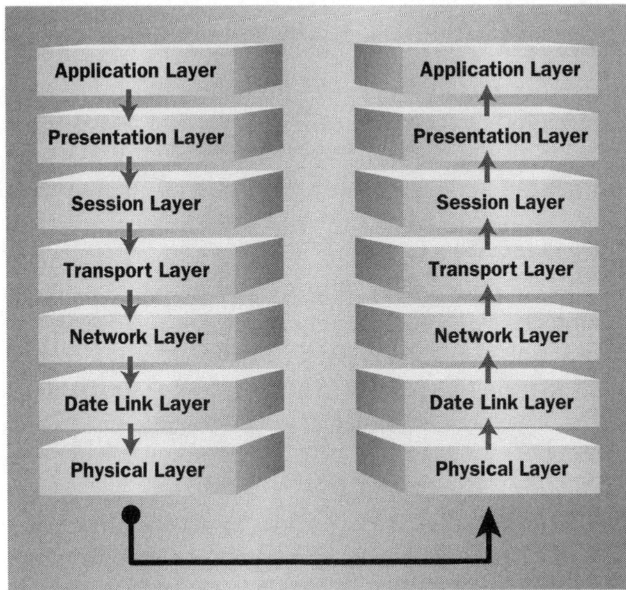

The Data Link layer generally comprises two sublayers:

- The LLC (Logical Link Control), which does the error checking and handles frame transmission. Each frame is a packet of data with a sequence number that is used to ensure delivery, and a checksum to track corrupted frames. Several algorithms are available for acknowledging delivery of packages.
- The MAC (Medium Access Control), which deals with getting the data on and off the wire. It defines protocols for access to the shared wire of a LAN. Examples of such protocols are IEEE 802.2 and 802.3. This Medium Access layer was made necessary by systems that share a common communications medium.

Network Layer

The Network layer has the responsibility for routing packets to the correct destination. Routing and flow controls are performed here. This is the lowest layer of the OSI model that can remain independent of the physical network.

Transport Layer

The Transport layer provides for end-to-end connection between machines. It makes sure the lower three layers are doing their jobs correctly and provides a transparent, logical data stream between the end-user and its chosen network service. This is the layer that provides local user services.

The Transport layer is also responsible for creating frames, taking them apart, and putting them back together.

Session Layer

The Session layer provides for dialog control among processes. Virtual circuit sessions between applications across a network are controlled at the Session layer. Testing for out-of-sequence packets and the handling of two-way communication are done here, as well as user authentication and security.

Presentation Layer

The Presentation layer does translation of data structures among various architectures. Differences in data representation are managed at this level. For example, UNIX-style line endings (CR only) might be converted to MS-DOS style (CRLF), or EBCIDIC to ASCII character sets.

Data compression and data encryption are also handled at this level.

Application Layer

The Application layer provides application-level access to the network, file transfer, remote terminals, and other elements of the network. Here is where the user applications live. Such issues as file access and transfer, virtual terminal emulation, interprocess communication, and the like are managed here.

OSI vs. NT Layer Model

In Windows NT 4.0, certain functions at each of the various OSI levels are implemented, as illustrated in Figure 7.2. The various NT layers provide functionality similar to that of the OSI model.

NOTE. *The scope of this book does not permit in-depth coverage of each of these subjects. If you are interested in more detailed information on the layers and functions within the NT model, refer to the Microsoft Windows NT Server Networking Guide in the Windows NT Resource Kit 4.0.*

Network Driver Interface Specification (NDIS)

The NDIS specification was created to allow any Windows NT 4.0 transport protocol to communicate with any third-party network interface card driver.

The primary function accomplished by the NDIS specification is communication between the network interface card itself and the driver program. The NDIS *wrapper*, which is a small piece of code surrounding all of the NDIS device drivers, controls the communication between the various compatible protocols and the network card driver. This allows multiple network cards and protocols to bind to a single adapter card. Without NDIS support, each protocol would have to know specific information about each and every

Figure 7.2

Windows NT model vs. OSI model

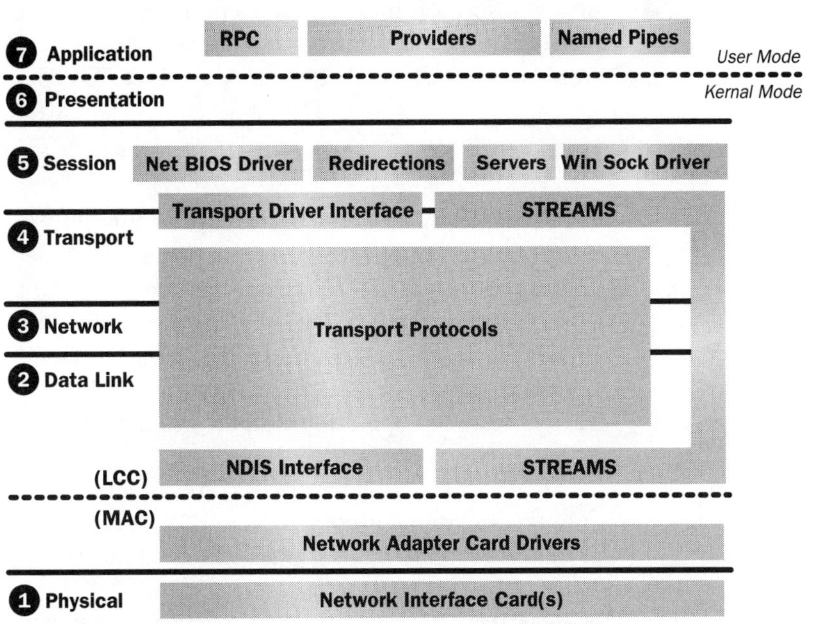

adapter card. Instead, each protocol can address the NDIS layer, which passes the information to the appropriate network card. NDIS is the go-between the two networking components.

By using the NDIS layer, Microsoft simplifies the complex issues involved in creating network-card drivers. Hardware vendors do not have to be concerned with the specific protocol that will be used, since the network card won't be talking to the protocols directly. They simply make the card NDIS compatible, and let NDIS communicate with the protocols. The reverse is also true. Microsoft can add new or update existing protocols in the NT model, without forcing hardware vendors to rewrite drivers for every change.

Transport Driver Interface (TDI)

The TDI was created to provide a communication link between the various file-system drivers and transport protocols. This layer allows the independent development of network redirectors, without requiring explicit knowledge of the protocols they are going to use. TDI simply passes messages back and forth between the protocols and the network redirectors, the server driver, and network API drivers (NetBIOS and Winsock).

For example, if Novell wanted to create a client redirector for Windows NT, developers would simply have to make the redirector understand the TDI. The protocol to be used is immaterial. The redirector communicates with the TDI, and the TDI communicates with the protocol. At the same time, if Microsoft implemented a new protocol or updated an existing one, developers would not need to address redirector compatibility. All they would have to do is make the new product TDI compatible.

■ Protocols

Transport protocols allow two or more computers to communicate in a common language. Many protocols have been developed by various manufacturers over the years, and Microsoft has chosen to implement three common ones in the Windows NT networking model: NetBEUI, NWLink, and TCP/IP. Each protocol has its own strengths and weaknesses. Microsoft has positioned Windows NT as an ideal solution to a heterogeneous environment. Various network operating systems will use various protocols, and NT can install as many as are needed.

This section provides discussions of these three transport protocols, plus another commonly used one: NetBIOS. This is followed by the related topics of bindings, subnet masks, and default gateways.

NetBEUI

NetBEUI Frame Protocol (NBF) is a modified version of NetBEUI (NetBIOS Extended User Interface). Developed in 1985 by IBM, NetBEUI—a sleek little protocol for use in small, nonrouted local area networks (LANs)—was the default protocol in Microsoft's earlier network products.

The current specification of NBF is v3.0. It is fully compatible with earlier Windows NT implementations as well as LAN Manager and Windows 3.*x*-based products. (Note that the updated NBF protocol is generally still referred to as NetBEUI.) From a network perspective, the packets produced by both protocols are identical. The differences are in how Windows NT implements the NetBIOS interface.

One of the major benefits in the NBF stack is that the 254-session limit in NetBEUI has been removed. The NBF protocol also provides automatic memory allocation when needed. This process is dynamic, so no preconfiguration is necessary. Automatic memory allocation decreases the total memory needed by the protocol stack. NetBEUI has a very small header and thus less overhead. All of this makes it one of the fastest protocols supported by Windows NT.

There are two major drawbacks to NBF: The first one is the protocol's inability to be routed. This means it is virtually useless in wide area networks. The second drawback is the NBF's reliance on broadcast messages to communicate among machines on the network.

Microsoft has addressed both of these problems and has alternate solutions available if either issue is a concern. If you require routing, TCP/IP is your clear choice. If the broadcasting is taking up too much of your valuable bandwidth, then the installation of Windows Internet Name Service (WINS) Server can alleviate the problem.

NetBIOS

NetBIOS (Network Basic Input/Output System) is an interface and an upper-level protocol developed by IBM. This protocol's functionality ranges over the top three layers (Session, Presentation, and Application) in the OSI model and provides a standard interface to the lower networking layers. NetBIOS can also serve as an API (Application Program Interface) for data exchange. It provides programmers with access to resources for establishing a connection between two machines or between two applications on the same machine.

NetBIOS serves three networking functions:

- **Naming Service.** Used for broadcasting group, user, and computer names on the network. This ensures that duplicate names do not occur. These unique names are referred to as *NetBIOS names.*
- **Datagram Support.** Provides connectionless transmissions that do not guarantee successful packet delivery. Packets in this mode are usually no larger than 512 bytes. The datagram method is used by the Naming Service.
- **Session Support.** Allows transmissions in which a virtual circuit session is established so that delivery of packets can be monitored and acknowledged. In this reliable connection-oriented mode, NetBIOS will guarantee delivery of messages of up to 64K. The session method is used when making network connections in Network Neighborhood or through the use of the NET USE command-line statement.

Regardless of what protocol you decide to use, Microsoft networking currently requires a protocol capable of handling NetBIOS. NetBEUI would be a natural choice, since it was created for this purpose; however, TCP/IP and NWLink both handle NetBIOS at a slighter overhead to the network.

NWLink

NWLink is a 32-bit Microsoft implementation of the IPX/SPX-compatible protocol stack. It can be used to establish connections between Windows NT computers and MS-DOS, OS/2, Windows, or other NT computers; this is accomplished through a variety of communication mechanisms. NWLink was the default protocol in Windows NT 3.5; Microsoft wanted to provide a routable protocol for enterprise-wide solutions. However, although NWLINK has a large acceptance on the Intel platform, it has virtually no support on other platforms.

Internetwork Packet Exchange (IPX) and Sequenced Packet Exchange (SPX) are separate protocols that are implemented in Novell NetWare networks. IPX is responsible for the routing and delivery of packets, and SPX creates the connections and provides acknowledgment of delivery. Windows NT-based networks can use these protocols to create reliable, routed internetworks.

NWLink as a protocol does not allow an NT computer to access files or printers on NetWare servers. Nor does it allow NetWare clients to gain access to NT machines emulating NetWare servers. The upper layers of NetWare's networking model use NetWare Core Protocol (NCP) to provide network services. Microsoft did not, however, build this into the NWLink protocol. For a Windows NT client to access files or printers on a NetWare server, a redirector must be used—such as Microsoft's Client Services for NetWare (CSNW), Microsoft's Gateway Services for NetWare (GSNW), or Novell's 32-bit NetWare Client for Windows NT.

NWLink is appropriate when you have client-server applications that use one of two supporting network APIs: Sockets Interface or NetBIOS Interface. NetBIOS over the IPX/SPX (NWNBLink) protocol can be run on an NT computer that is accessing the server portion on a NetWare server, or vice versa. The NWNBLink component contains Microsoft enhancements to Novell's NetBIOS. It is used to format NetBIOS-level messages and pass them to the NWLink component for transmission on the network.

With Windows NT 4.0, NWLink will generally be installed only when interoperating with Novell NetWare networks. NWLink will also be used where a routed network is required, but the complexity of TCP/IP is overwhelming to set up.

TCP/IP

TCP/IP stands for Transmission Control Protocol/Internet Protocol. TCP/IP is not a single protocol, but a suite of protocols and utilities. Each protocol in the suite has a specific role. It is the combination of these protocols that gives TCP/IP its strength.

Microsoft has made TCP/IP its default protocol in Windows NT. Developed for the U.S. Department of Defense in 1969 by the Advanced Research Projects Agency (ARPA), TCP/IP was created to support three clear objectives. ARPA wanted a protocol that was

- Capable of connecting different operating systems
- Reliable and able to deliver high-speed communications
- Routable and scalable to meet the needs of large, vast networks

As networks connected up, the ARPAnet grew into what is now called the Internet.

Advantages of the Microsoft TCP/IP protocol include the following:

- A 32-bit, industry-compliant protocol that supports many Request For Comment (RFC) specifications
- Internet access
- Dynamic routing support
- Simple Network Management Protocol (SNMP) support
- Dynamic Host Configuration Protocol (DHCP) support
- Windows Internet Name Service (WINS) support
- Domain Name Service (DNS) support

TCP/IP has several disadvantages, as well. Its setup and administration are much more complex. It requires strict compliance with certain numbering schemes. Operation is much slower than the other protocols available under Windows NT.

TCP/IP and NT

As mentioned, TCP/IP is the default protocol in Windows NT. It was chosen by Microsoft to provide a routable, scalable, and common protocol as an enterprise solution. In addition, TCP/IP is the choice protocol on the Internet and the growing number of networks joining that realm.

Many of TCP/IP's features are implemented as services under Windows NT. Features such as DHCP, WINS, DNS, and SNMP (described earlier) are all installed as background applications that can work while users are not logged on.

Addresses

A TCP/IP address is a 32-bit binary value that is assigned to each host on a network. This value is used to identify the network on which the host is attached and identify the host's unique number on that particular network. Every host/interface connected together on an internetwork must have a unique TCP/IP address.

The concept of assigning a unique number is similar to the way the Postal Service routes mail. Every house on a single street shares the same street name (the network) while having an individual house number (the host number). When a machine wants to send data to another machine, the sender must address the data with the appropriate "address" of the recipient or the network won't know where the data is going. This is the responsibility of the sending computer.

TCP/IP addresses are generally distributed in one of two ways: manual or automatic. In a manual distribution, an administrator is given the responsibility of walking around and entering the exact values for each machine. This administrator also must make sure that each machine has indeed been given a unique address.

In an automatic distribution, a Windows NT service such as DHCP is used to assign TCP/IP address to each host as it comes on line from a database or address. The Windows NT machine will be responsible for maintaining the uniqueness of the TCP/IP addresses. Many companies are finding automatic distribution a much more desirable option because it reduces administration costs, human error, and allows the allocation of TCP/IP addresses based on who is on line and who is not.

Each address is made up of two components:

- *Network ID.* This is a piece of the IP address that represents the user's physical network. Each machine on a particular network segment will have the same network ID.
- *Node ID.* This represents the individual portion of the address. If the machines on your network segment have the same addresses, the network needs to know to whom the packet belongs.

The IP addresses, as mentioned earlier, are 32-bit binary values that are separated into four sets of 8-bit numbers called octets. Here's an example of a TCP/IP address:

```
10.221.14.112
```

Using this example, let's say the administrator sets up a network with all machines having the following as common values:

```
10.221.14.x
This is the Network ID. The number at x would be the Node ID:
xxx.xxx.xxx.112
```

Each set of TCP/IP addresses fall into a *class* of address. The class represents a group of addresses that can be quickly identified by software components as being associated with a physical network. For example, take the following TCP/IP address and its equivalent binary value:

```
10.221.14.112
00001010 11011101 00001110 01110000
```

By examining the first three binary values, we determine that this address is a Class A. Any software component looking at this bit will recognize this address as belonging to a specific Class A network (10.0.0.0 network in this case) and will route any packets destined for this network there.

Shortly, we will discuss another value—the subnet mask—that can be used to determine if another machine is on the same subnet or not.

Table 7.1 describes the three primary classes of IP address, the number of hosts each class can support, and the possible values of the first octet.

Table 7.1

TCP/IP Class Addresses

CLASS	NO. HOSTS ON EACH NETWORK	RANGE OF FIRST OCTET
A	16,777,216	1-126
B	16,536	128-191
C	256	192-223

Subnet Mask

Each machine on a network generally wants to send a piece of data directly to another machine. The sending machine must determine if the recipient is on the same network or on another. The *subnet mask* is used by the TCP/IP protocol stack to determine if the host you are trying to communicate with is on your local network or on a remote network. This is a very important part of the TCP/IP configuration. If you give an incorrect subnet mask, you may not be able to communicate with other hosts properly. Table 7.2 shows the typical subnet mask for each of the address classes.

Table 7.2

TCP/IP Subnet Masks

CLASS	SUBNET MASK
A	255.0.0.0
B	255.255.0.0
C	255.255.255.0

Essentially, the subnet mask "masks" out the network ID portion of the IP address from the node ID. For example, in a class B address, the binary output of the subnet would look like this:

```
10000011 01101011 00000010 11001000 (131.107.2.200)
11111111 11111111 00000000 00000000 (255.255.0.0)
10000011 01101011 00000000 00000000 (Network ID)
Compare this to another machine in a Class B:
10011001 01101011 00011001 11001101 (153.107.25.205)
11111111 11111111 00000000 00000000 (255.255.0.0)
10011001 01101011 00000000 00000000 (Network ID)
```

As you can see, the two Network IDs do not match, and therefore the two machines are on different networks. The TCP/IP stack performs this quick calculation each time data goes out to the network. If the numbers are the same, the host simply places the data on the local network. If the numbers do not match, as in our scenario, then the data is forwarded to and handled by a default gateway. (We will talk more about default gateways in the next section.)

So, the calculation to determine the Network ID is done by multiplying the top number by the bottom number, as follows:

```
Top value x Bottom value = Subnet mask
1 x 1 = 1
1 x Ø = Ø
Ø x 1 = Ø
Ø x Ø = Ø
```

The subnet mask also allows network administrators to break large class addresses down into more manageable and efficient smaller network representations. Let's say you have a class A address such as 10.0.0.0 (which is reserved for private networks that may be connected to the Internet). You would have to have the 16.7 million hosts on a single physical network, and there aren't many of those around. You can apply a class B subnet mask (255.255.0.0) instead of the class A (255.0.0.0), and this will allow 254 segments with 16,536 hosts each.

What's a Default Gateway?

The default gateway, also known as a router, is where a host sends all of its remote-bound datagrams. The gateway will have a table of possible routes to where the remote network may exist and will route it to the location. The gateway sends the data via the shortest possible path based on information contained in the routing table. Windows NT 4.0 machines can have multiple default gateways for fault tolerance. If one of the gateways goes down, your machine can try the next one on the list.

The default gateway is an optional parameter. It is only needed if you have more than one network segment and you are going to be communicating between them.

Windows NT 4.0 can also act has a default gateway. This is accomplished by placing two or more network cards into the machine and selecting the IP Routing option in the Routing tab of the Microsoft TCP/IP Properties dialog.

TCP/IP Security

The TCP/IP protocol has no inherent security, but Windows NT 4.0 has included a new TCP/IP Security feature. Administrators now have the ability to designate allowed TCP ports, UDP ports, and IP protocols. With this enhanced security option, NT administrators can control what type of information passes through the protocol stack, and thus the type of network traffic allowed on the computer.

Here are the steps to set up this security:

1. Select the property sheet for Network Neighborhood.
2. Open the Protocols tab, click on TCP/IP Protocol, and choose Properties.
3. Open the IP Address tab and click the Advanced button. The Advanced IP Addressing dialog appears (Figure 7.3).
4. Click the Configure button under the Enable Security check box in the bottom-left corner.
5. Use the TCP/IP Security dialog (Figure 7.4) to configure the TCP/IP security by adapter. You can choose to allow access to all TCP ports, all UDP ports, or all IP protocols. The other option is to permit only certain ports and protocols to be accessible. If you choose this setup, all nonpermitted packets to UDP and IP are dropped. For TCP, all connection requests are sent an acknowledgment reset.

Figure 7.3

Advanced IP Addressing dialog

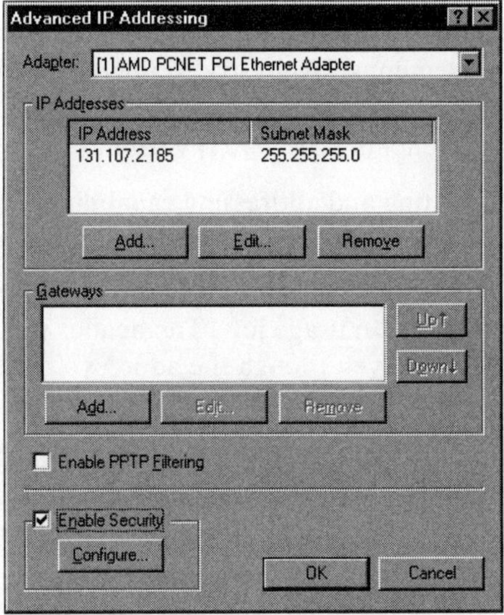

Figure 7.4

Setting up TCP/IP security

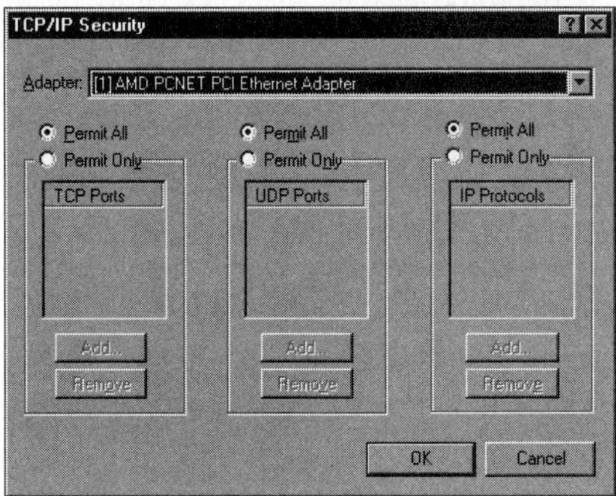

IPv6: The Future of TCP/IP

Among the current growing pains of the Internet, as well as many private and public networks that are getting into 'nets and the Net, is the problem of scalability—issues that arise when a network grows or changes. Ipng, also known as IPv6, is a new implementation of the Internet Protocol. IPv6 has been designed to meet the needs of high-performance networks of the future, while fitting the current bandwidth capabilities of the present.

IPv6's new 128-bit address scheme will replace the current 32-bit address scheme used by IPv4. Although this will be considered a new implementation, it will be fully compatible with the existing functionality of IPv4. Most vendors will implement software-based upgrades to current TCP/IP stacks, allowing a smooth integration.

Some of the benefits added by IPv6 are as follows:

- Expanded routing and addressing capabilities, which will support more levels of addressing and will be easier to configure automatically.
- A simplified header format to reduce the overhead of packet handling and keep bandwidth usage low. The header will be only twice the size of the IPv4 header, even though the address size is four times as large.
- Improved support for options, allowing for more efficient forwarding, fewer restrictions on the length of options, and greater flexibility for expanding options in the future.
- Authentication and privacy capabilities that support authentication, data integrity, and confidentiality. This is included as a basic element of Ipng and will be included in all implementations.

This new version of IP has been enumerated in a series of Request for Comments (RFCs) published on the Internet. These RFCs will be implemented over the next five to seven years into the mainstream Internet. Ease of transition is a key point in the design of Ipng; it is not something added in at the end. Ipng is designed to interoperate with IPv4. Several mechanisms (embedded IPv4 addresses, checksum rules, and more) are built into IPv6 to support the transition and compatibility with the existing IP. The new protocol was designed to allow a gradual deployment with a minimum of dependencies.

Time will tell how well the industry adjusts to the new IPv6, and whether it will indeed meet the demands of the growing Internet.

Bindings

A *binding* lets the network know which protocols to use and with which network card. When bindings are created, Windows NT has a logical link for all network communications. NT can then determine your preferred method of transmitting data across the network using various combinations of network services, protocols, and adapters. All the administrator has to do is draw it out—or, more appropriately, bind them together.

Bindings are set up using the settings in the Bindings tab of the Network Properties dialog (see Figure 7.5). You can highlight the binding and use the Move Up and Move Down buttons to adjust the binding order. You can also use the Enable and Disable buttons to turn on/off the bindings of any communication links you choose not to use, so that resources can be conserved.

Figure 7.5

Bindings tab of the Network Properties dialog

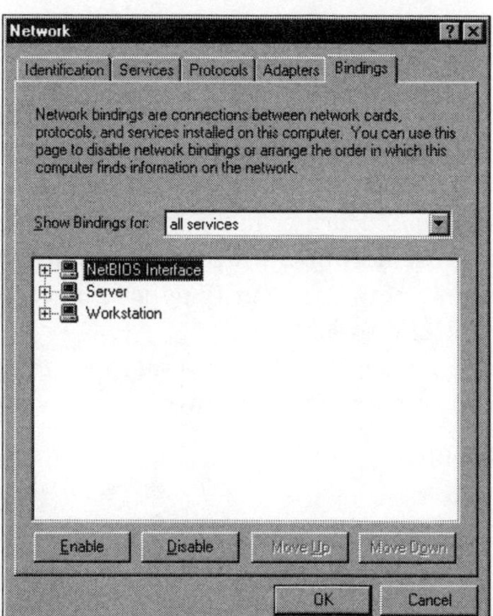

Binding priorities help Windows NT to determine which protocol to use. The network components will simultaneously submit connection requests to the various protocols, and NT will wait to see which of the protocols can establish a successful connection. If more than one can satisfy the request, NT will choose the one with the highest binding order. Thus, it is suggested that you bind your most used protocols first.

Registry Parameters

The following is a list of the Registry locations for each of the three common protocols in Windows NT. For detailed Registry entries, refer to the Windows NT 4.0 Resource Kits. A registry.hlp file lists all the entries with their possible values.

Windows NT Protocol	Registry Location
NWLink parameters	HKEY_LOCAL_MACHINE\System\CurrentControlSet\Services\NwlnkIpx HKEY_LOCAL_MACHINE\Software\Microsoft\NwlnkIpx
TCP/IP parameters	HKEY_LOCAL_MACHINE\Software\Microsoft\Tcpip
NetBIOS over TCP/IP	HKEY_LOCAL_MACHINE\System\CurrentControlSet\Services\NetBT HKEY_LOCAL_MACHINE\Software\Microsoft\NetBT
NetBEUI parameters	HKEY_LOCAL_MACHINE\System\CurrentControlSet\Services\Nbf

■ Network Security

Network security is a very important topic that warrants serious attention. Allowing users access via a network connection incurs risk that does not exist when users sit down at a terminal and log on. When a user logs on at the terminal, physical security can be implemented on that machine. When a user connects via the network, however, the identity of the user cannot be presumed. A strong network security policy is necessary to provide adequate protection for the enterprise.

In this chapter, we will look at several topics of concern to an administrator who wants to create a proper network security policy:

- Sharing resources
- User rights
- LAN/WAN or remote access
- Effective network permissions

Two Types of Network Security

A *share* is a mechanism that allows users to exchange information and resources with other users. Shares allow directories and printers to be accessed via the network. There are two types of network security when determining how users can access these shares: user-level and share-level.

A user-level security model is much more secured than a share-level security model. The ability to determine whether a specific user is allowed to access resources based on a user account or group account provides flexibility as well as security. Share-level security models have their place in small LANs that elect to use small deterrents against intrusion rather than strict security polices.

User-Level Security

User-level security is the model used by Windows NT and optionally under Windows 95. With user-level security, user accounts are given access to shares.

Under Windows NT, any member of the Administrators, Power Users, and Server Operators groups can create shares on directories or printers. Print operators can also create shares on printers. The creator of the share has discretionary access control on it (the ability to control who has access to the share and what type of access is allowed).

On a Windows 95 machine, in order for user-level security to be implemented, a security provider such as a Windows NT or Novell NetWare machine is required to validate users. Windows 95 can't maintain a user database from which it can validate access to resources.

The biggest advantage of user-level security is the ability to assign specific users access to a share and then determine what kind of access is given. For example, assuming KeDavid has sufficient rights, he can assign JoPorter the ability to print to KeDavid's color printer. JoPorter must be the user account used to gain access to the resource. Furthermore, with user-level security, auditing can be implemented so that JoPorter will be recognized as the account used to access the resource. Auditing allows administrators to hold individuals accountable for their respective accounts.

The disadvantages of user-level security include a complex setup process. Administrators need to provide users with accounts and maintain proper security policies. Not only must administrators provide a list of prospective users, but they must also teach users the implications of giving access to other users. If shared access is not properly set up, network security may be compromised. A database and a security provider must be made available to each machine that requires shared resources.

Share-Level Security

Share-level security was first introduced in Windows for Workgroups and is supported in Windows 95. This type of security model is referred to as a *peer-to-peer network.* Share-level security allows any user to share a resource and to decide if a password will be required for such access. Shares are created to allow access to any folder or printer on the machine.

There are some advantages to this type of network security. The first is its simplicity. Share-level security does not require user accounts for permitting access. Instead, the person sharing the resource simply chooses whether or not a password will be required. If no password is required, then anyone can access the resource.

In addition to determining user access, the creator of the share can also specify the user's level of permitted access: read-only or full control. To share resources, no special rights are required on either Windows for Workgroups or Windows 95.

See Figure 7.6 for an example of Windows 95 share-level security.

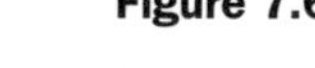

Figure 7.6

Share-level security

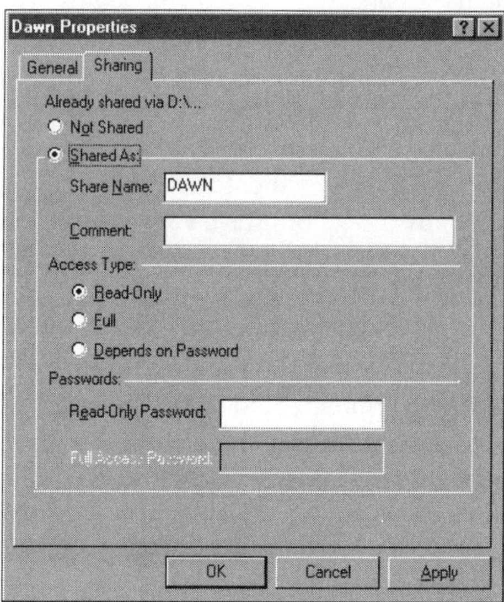

The major disadvantage of share-level security is that once the password is given out, there is no control over who will access the resource. For example, once KeDavid gives a password to JoPorter for a share on the KeDavid machine that will allow access to a color printer, KeDavid has lost total control. If JoPorter decides to give the password to someone else, KeDavid has no control other than to stop sharing the resource or to change the password. In the meantime, security has been compromised. Because accounts are not used under this model, there is no way to determine who actually used the resource. There is no audit trail and no proof of which user compromised security.

Methods to Create Shares

Creating shares requires three specific bits of information.

- What information needs to be shared? This can be a printer or folder or an entire hierarchical structure of a hard drive.
- Who are the users? Does JoPorter need access to the resource or does the entire Sales group need access to it, or perhaps some combination of users?
- What kind of access needs to be given? Do users need to be able to read, delete, and/or change information within these shares?

Shares can be created on either the FAT or NTFS file system. On a FAT file system, shares are the only way to govern network access. Whatever rights are given to the share are the effective permissions given throughout the hierarchy of the share. For example, in Figure 7.7, there is a share on the folder E:\badstuff. Because this folder is on a FAT file system, whatever access given to the badstuff share is given throughout the badstuff subdirectories. Users given read permissions on the share get read permission on the Backup and Data subdirectories, as well.

Figure 7.7

On a FAT partition, the share on E:\badstuff extends to badstuff's subdirectories.

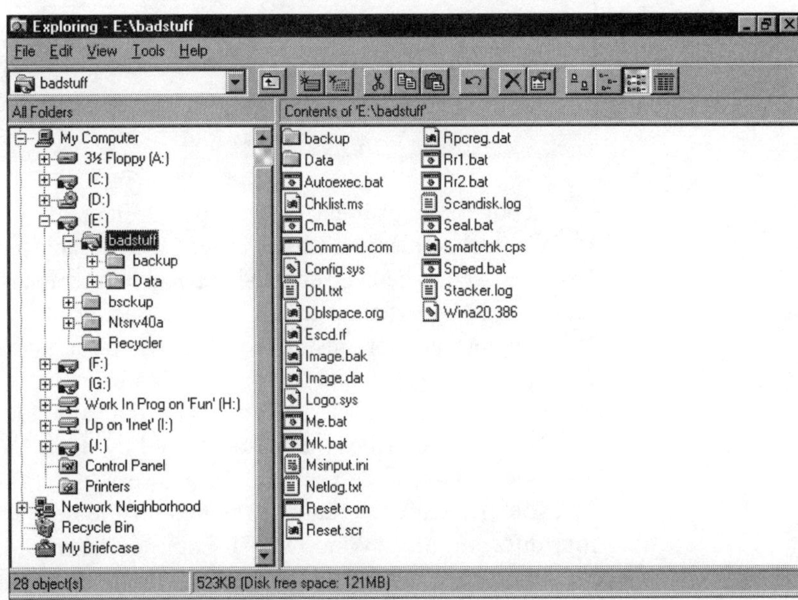

On the other hand, permissions on an NTFS partition can be placed at both the share and the file/folder levels. This provides maximum security as well as flexibility. Let's say we have a C:\Collwin folder on an NTFS partition. Once this folder is shared as read only, all users accessing this share via the network get this permission (see Figure 7.8). Next, Windows NT looks at local security (see Figure 7.9), checking the access control lists (ACLs) of each file and folder as it is accessed. In determining the effective permissions, NT takes the most restrictive of the two (cumulative share vs. cumulative local).

Figure 7.8

Setting share permissions on NTFS partition

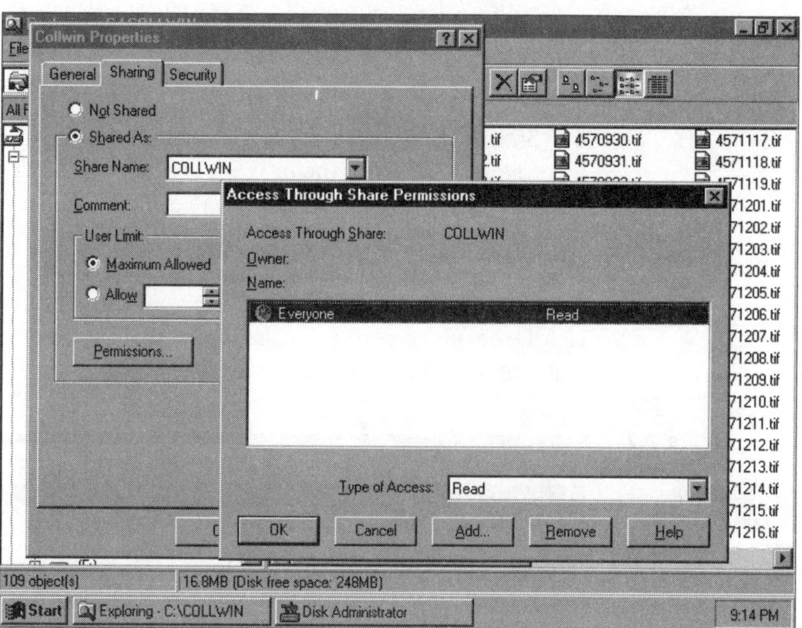

In our earlier example of the badstuff share, JoPorter has been given the Full Control permission. This gives him considerable access to the file system. However, he has been given explicit Read permission on the badstuff\Data subfolder, and Not Specified on the badstuff\Backup subfolder. In this situation, JoPorter gets the more restrictive of the two permissions. So Data gives JoPorter Read permission; and badstuff gives him Full Control over the Backup subfolder because no explicit permissions for that subfolder were given to JoPorter.

Table 7.3 describes the tasks allowed by shared folder permissions.

Once you have determined the answers to the three questions listed earlier, you are ready to create the shares for the network. You can do this with four different tools: Windows NT Explorer, Server Manager, the Printers Folder, and the command line. Let's take a look at each of these methods.

Figure 7.9

Setting local permissions on NTFS partition

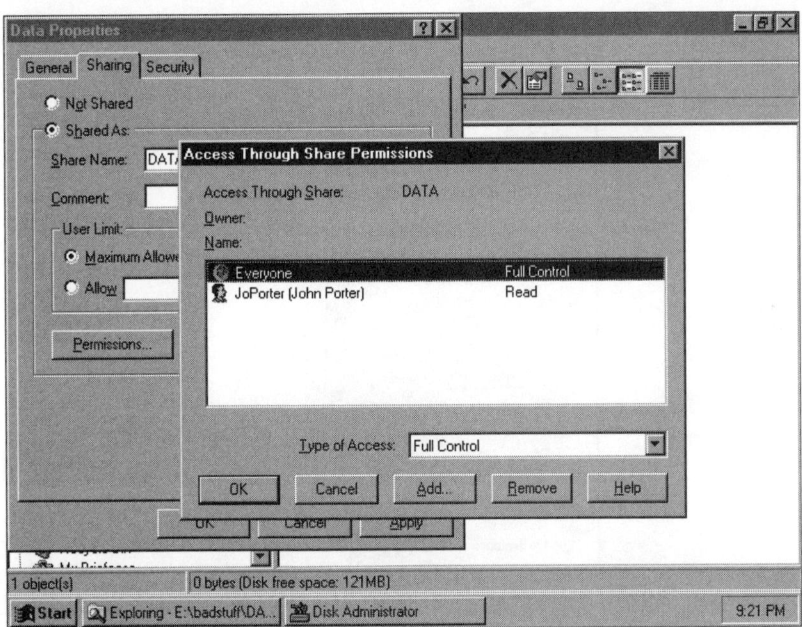

Table 7.3

Shared Folder Permissions

TYPE OF ACCESS	ALLOWED TASKS
No Access	Denies complete access to share hierarchy.
Read	Allows user to view filenames and directories, and allows changing directories. In addition, users can run applications in the share.
Change	All tasks allowed for Read permission, plus add, change, and delete files and directories in the structure.
Full Control	Allows complete access to hierarchy.

Creating Shares with NT Explorer

Using Windows NT Explorer is by far the easiest approach to creating shares. With this tool and the proper user rights, shares can be created quickly and easily.

1. Right-click the folder you want to share, to pop up the context menu. Click Sharing (see Figure 7.10).
2. In the property sheet, open the Sharing tab (see Figure 7.11).

Figure 7.10

Creating shares for the YearEnd folder

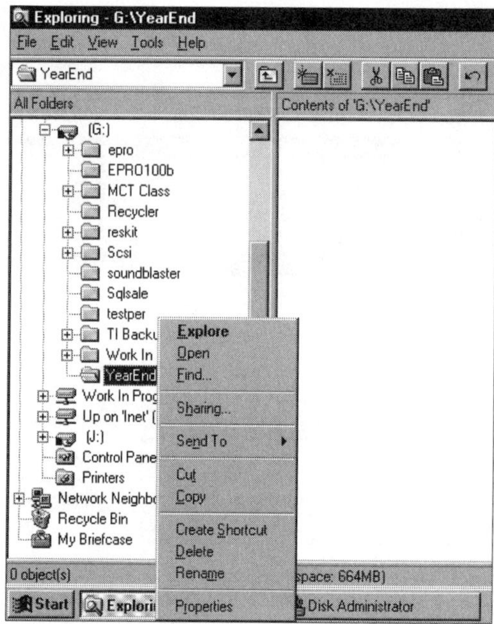

Figure 7.11

Share properties for the YearEnd folder

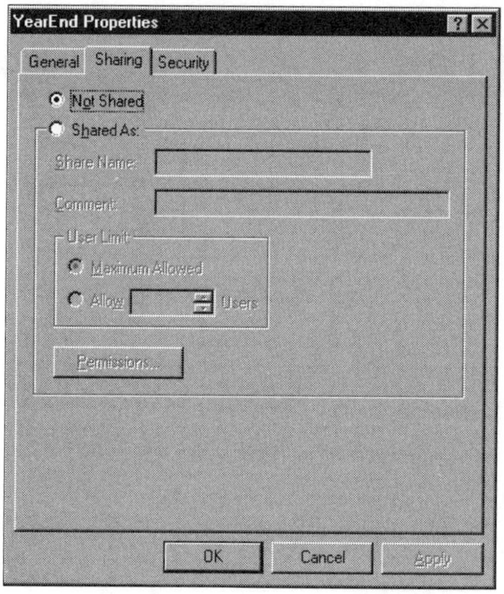

3. Click the Shared As radio button.
4. Fill in the Share Name, up to 12 characters. The folder name will appear here by default.

Helpful Tip

You can place a $ at the end of the share name to hide it in Network Neighborhood.

5. In the Comment field, type in a comment that will be seen in the Network Neighborhood of any client that is browsing the network.
6. In the User Limit box, you can designate a User Limit if you wish to control the number of concurrent connections to the share.
7. Click the Permissions button to get the Access Through Share Permissions dialog (see Figure 7.12).
8. In the Name list, designate the users who can access the share. For each user, pick an access type from the Type of Access list box at the bottom. (See Table 7.3 for definitions of the access types.)

Figure 7.12

Specifying access and permissions for the YearEnd folder

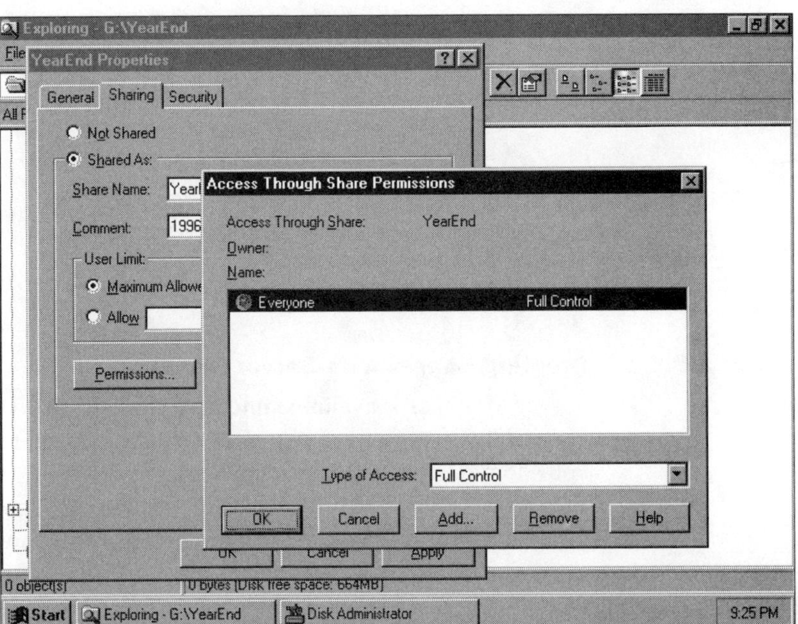

9. Click OK twice to close the dialogs and process your entries.

To view network shares, Windows NT users can use Network Neighborhood to see a list of servers that are available on the network. When you double-click the Network Neighborhood icon, you get a view similar to that shown in Figure 7.13. The machines listed in the right-hand pane are machines that are part of either your immediate workgroup or your domain. Double-click Entire Network to see all the available domains. If you have a valid domain account on the domain, you can double-click a domain and see a list of available servers. Double-clicking a server shows the shares available on that machine.

Figure 7.13

Using Network Neighborhood to view network shares

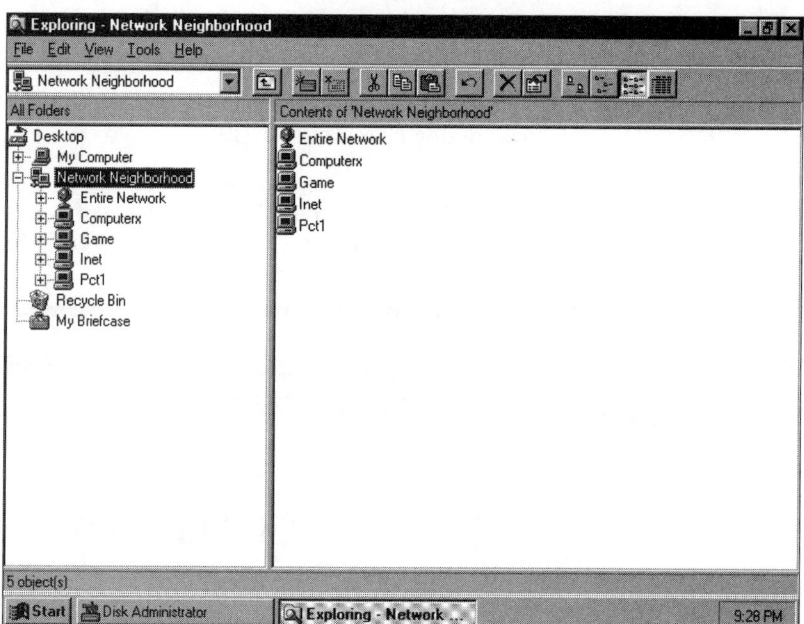

Creating Shares with Server Manager

Server Manager is available under Administrative Tools. You can use this graphical interface to view, manage, and create shares on any machine in your domain or any domain for which you have the proper permissions. When you're using this tool to set up shares, Windows NT still checks security and requires you to be an administrator or proper operator.

Here are the steps to use Server Manager for creating shares:

1. In Server Manager, highlight the Windows NT machine you wish to manage.
2. Open the Computer menu and choose Shared Directories (see Figure 7.14).

Figure 7.14

Using Server Manager to create shares

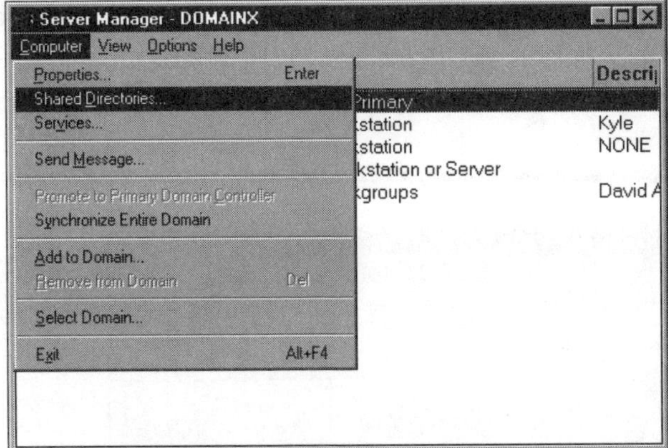

3. In the Shared Directories dialog (Figure 7.15), you'll see a list of available shares for the selected computer, with scroll bars to help you move up and down in the list. Each share is listed with its corresponding folder.

Caution

Do not change any system shares (the ones with $ at the end of the share name) or you may cause a system component to fail. See the sidebar, "Watch Out for System Shares."

Figure 7.15

Shared Directories dialog

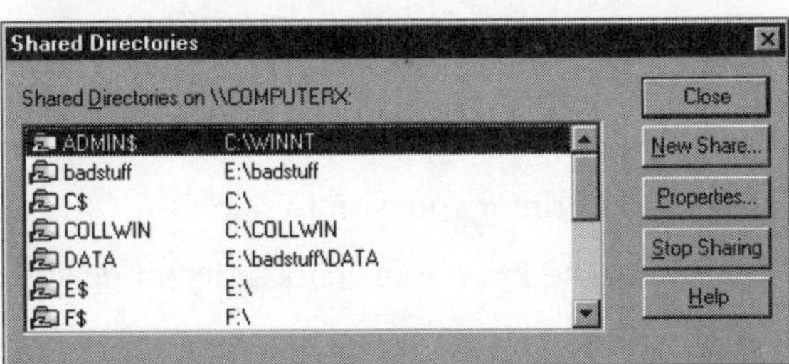

4. Use the buttons on the right side of the window to create and modify shares as follows:
   - To create a new share, click New Share. In the New Share dialog (see Figure 7.16), enter a share name, a local path (which must already exist) and a comment. Choose the User Limits if desired, and click the Permissions button to set permissions on the share.
   - To modify an existing share, highlight it and click the Properties button, and make your modifications.
   - To delete an existing share, highlight the share and choose Stop Sharing.

Figure 7.16

New Share dialog for creating a new share in the Server manager

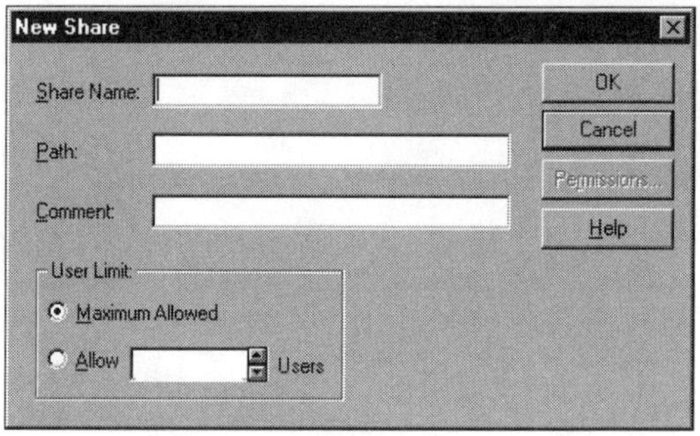

Creating Shares from the Printers Folder

The simplest method to create shares is through the Printers Folder under My Computer. Sharing printers involves choosing which one of the printers you wish to share, not sharing the entire folder.

Windows NT 4.0 supports the ability to store print drivers from other versions of Windows NT and Windows 95. This feature allows any of those operating system users to connect and print to the printer. The administrator has the option of which drivers to load and which ones not to load on the system. One word of warning: you will need the original source files of any of the versions you choose to install drivers for.

To share the printer:

1. Double-click the Printers Folder.
2. Choose the Printer you wish to share.
3. Right-click the Printer and choose its properties.
4. Click the Sharing tab.
5. Choose the Shared radio button and pick the drivers you want to install.

Watch Out for System Shares

Notice in Figure 7.15 that several shares have a $ character at the end of the share name. These are hidden administrative shares that are automatically created each time Windows NT is booted up. Do not stop sharing these system shares or you may cause a system component to fail. The following table describes these shares and the system processes that use them. In addition, you'll find more information about administrative shares later in the chapter, in the section on Windows NT's handling of network security.

System Shares

Share Name	Path	Used By
A$...Zx$	Root of local directories	Administrators, to access the root directories of any NT machine over which they have administrative rights via the network.
Admin$	d:\win_root	System components, to locate the NT system files.
IPC$		InterProcess Communications
Netlogon	d:\win_root\system32\repl\import\scripts	Logon process uses this share to run logon scripts and parse through system policies.
Print$	d:\win_root\system32\spool\drivers	Client spooler services, to connect to a printer server and download print drivers.
REPL$	d:\win_root\system32\repl\export	Replication service on import computers, to connect up to the export computer.

Creating Shares from the Command Line

Windows NT also allows administrators to view and create network shares through the age-old command line.

Use the NET SHARE command from a DOS prompt to create shares. As with the other methods described in this chapter, you must have proper administrative permissions for creating network shares.

The following NET SHARE command will share the C:\public folder:

```
C:\net share public=c:\public
```

NET SHARE makes a server's resources available to network users. When used without options, it lists information about all resources being shared on the computer. For each resource, Windows NT reports the device names or pathnames and a descriptive comment associated with it.

Additional parameters can be used with the NET SHARE command. The following listing of NET SHARE parameters is the result of typing the command

C:\net help share

and these parameters are defined in Table 7.4.

```
NET SHARE sharename
          sharename=drive:path [/USERS:number | /UNLIMITED]
                               [/REMARK:"text"]
          sharename [/USERS:number | /UNLIMITED]
                    [/REMARK:"text"]
          {sharename | devicename | drive:path} /DELETE
```

Table 7.4

Parameters for the NET SHARE Command

PARAMETER	USAGE
sharename	The network name of the shared resource. To display information about a share, type NET SHARE with that sharename only. NOTE: If there are any spaces in *sharename* names, you must use quotes around the arguments.
drive:*path*	Specifies the absolute path of the folder to be shared.
/USERS:*number*	Sets the maximum number of users who can simultaneously access the shared resource.
/UNLIMITED	Specifies that an unlimited number of users can simultaneously access the shared resource.
/REMARK:"*text*"	Adds a descriptive comment about the resource. Encloses the *text* in quotation marks.
Devicename	Specifies one or more printers (LPT1: through LPT9:) shared by *sharename*.
/DELETE	Stops sharing the resource.

NOTE. *There is no way to set permissions on the share through the command line. Shares set with NET SHARE will be given the default permissions of EVERYONE: Full Control.*

Viewing Shares from the Command Line You can also take a look at network shares from the command line using the NET VIEW command. There are two steps in looking for resources on the network via the command line.

First, type the comand

```
c:\net view
```

This allows you to view all the servers in your workgroup/domain. If you have multiple domains or workgroups on your network, then use the following statement:

```
C:\net view /domain:{domain_name}
```

This will return a list of servers on the network similar to that in Figure 7.17.

Figure 7.17

Network browsing via the command line

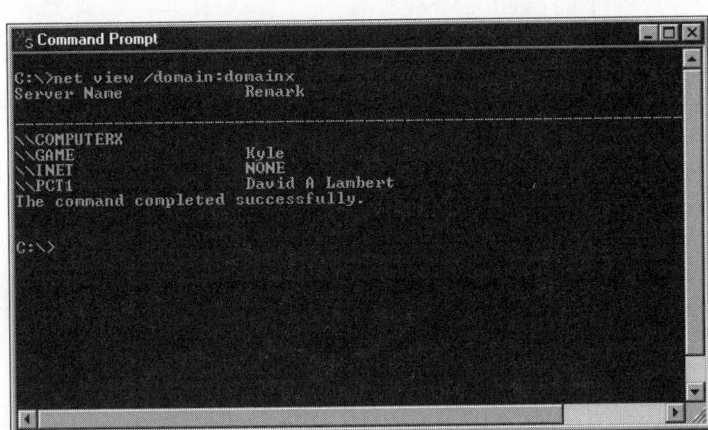

The second step—to view the shares on a specific server—is to enter the following command:

```
C:\net view \\server_name
```

With this list of available shares on the server, you can execute the NET USE statement to make a network redirection to a network share.

An alternate way to make a connection via the command line is to click the Start button and choose the Run command. In the Run dialog from the

START menu, type in the UNC path (\\servername\sharename), as shown in Figure 7.18. In this figure, we are opening a network connection and running the Registry Editor from a network share.

Figure 7.18

Opening a network connection with the Run command

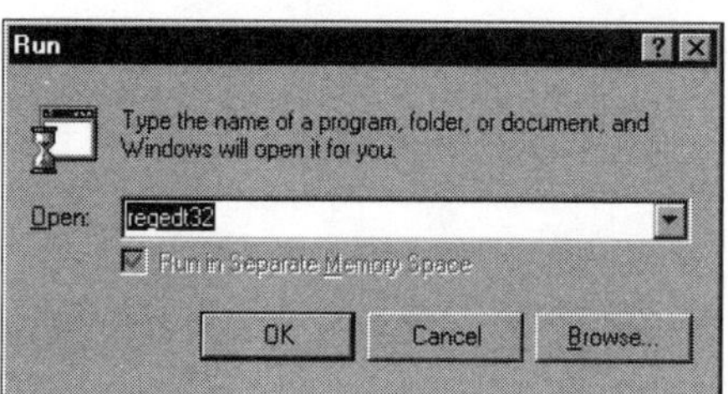

The foregoing sections about network security have presented several ways for you to consider in setting up users to have access to network resources. Next, we will look at how to prevent users from accessing *all* these methods when you want users to be prevented from accessing network shares altogether.

■ How Windows NT Handles Network Security

In this section of the chapter, we are going to take a more detailed look at the following subjects:

- Security from Windows NT's viewpoint
- Assigning permissions
- RAS security
- Internet security
- Administrative shares

Our first topic is network security from an internal architectural viewpoint. We are going to look at how Windows NT uses security and the network to send and receive data between client and server, from start to finish.

Let's assume that KeDavid is going to make a connection to a share called PUBLIC, on a machine called INSTRUCTOR.

1. KeDavid begins by trying to establish the initial network connection. Windows NT creates a Server Message Block (SMB) session that sends the username, password, and domain name over a secured named-pipe connection.

2. The machine INSTRUCTOR receives the request and checks the username and password against its local SAM (Security Account Manager) database if it is a stand-alone server, or against the domain SAM database if INSTRUCTOR is part of a domain. One of the following occurs:

   - When a successful match occurs, the machine generates a security identifier (SID) and access token for the user, maps the SID to the access token, and sends the SID back to KeDavid's computer. KeDavid's computer then uses this SID for all further communications in the current session. If the session gets disconnected, the same process will have to occur again.
   - If the username is found in the database but the passwords don't match, the user is prompted to enter a valid password. If the password still does not match, then a system error 1326 is generated: "Logon failure: unknown username or bad password."
   - If the account is not found in the database at all, then Local Security Authority (LSA) will try to grant the user Guest access if the Guest account is enabled. If the Guest account is disabled, the user is prompted for an alternate username and password. If the user still cannot provide adequate credentials, access is denied.

3. If the user requesting access is from a trusted domain, the request gets passed along to a domain controller in that domain via the NetLogon Service. If the user is not found in this SAM database, then the original domain's SAM is checked for Guest access.

Regardless of how the user is authenticated, several constants are in place.

First, all network communication occurs using secured, name-piped connections. This guarantees that the passwords will not be intercepted and compromised.

Second, since there are several places a Windows NT machine can check for user account information, network administrators have the flexibility to create a user folder wherever it will provide centralized administration; the same kind of authentication will take place.

Third, the access token is never passed over the network. The LSA on each machine maintains the security. This again provides added levels of security in the network.

The last constant is that the security is not checked again if the user makes additional connections during the current session. Should the user need to map additional drives or make additional printer connections, the same security context is used for all connections. Should the user want to give a different set of credentials for use of an existing connection, then that user must first break all current connections to the machine and reestablish the connection.

For example, suppose KeDavid has access to PUBLIC and he makes the connection using his current username and password. Later, he wishes to connect to the PRIVATE share on INSTRUCTOR. However, only the Administrator account has been given access to the PRIVATE share. For KeDavid to use the Administrator's security context, he will have to first break the PUBLIC connection. Otherwise, he'll get the error message, "The credentials supplied conflict with an existing set of credentials."

Assigning Permissions

Windows NT allows administrators to assign each share a set of permissions that are checked each time a user attempts to access the resource, as just described above. These permissions are similar to local NTFS permissions that are applied on a folder or file basis. Permissions on shares are applicable to all resources that are accessed through the entire hierarchy of the share. For example, if a user is granted Read privilege on a share, that user will not be permitted to delete any file within the share.

NTFS local permissions are still used by NT, as well. They are applied individually each time a user tries to gain access to a protected resource. The NT security subsystem then applies the more restrictive of the two (NTFS local vs. share).

RAS Security for Remote Users

Windows NT uses the Remote Access Service (RAS) to allow remote users access to a network via a dial-up connection. In terms of risk, dial-in access has the most potential for breaking security. There is no guarantee the user who is calling in is the same person who has been allowed network access. Windows NT implements many security measures to assure network administrators of tighter security when remote dial-in is being used.

The first line of defense is the requirement to enter a valid domain user name. This allows NT to apply the same secured access to remote network users as it applies to local network users. A user must be authenticated by a domain controller, or by the RAS server that the user is calling. Next, the user must also have been granted Dial-in permissions through User Manager. All the usernames and passwords transferred can be encrypted. This encryption can be required, as can the level of encryption. All transferred data can be encrypted, as well. Chapter 8 discusses encryption.

For environments requiring even more security for remote access, several third-party security solutions can be appended to RAS. These security hosts can provide levels of security that are typically more advanced and elaborate than Windows NT's.

Windows NT can also provide callback security. The user is required to enter a valid phone number, which the RAS server calls back and the client answers. The numbers then can be logged. Alternatively, the administrator can designate a phone number that the user is required to answer in order for the RAS session to continue.

The last form of remote-access security comes in the form of auditing. Throughout the RAS connection you can set audit trails to track whom, when, and from where users have accessed your RAS server. Additionally, the auditing functions allow administrators to determine what resource has been accessed. Auditing is discussed in greater detail in Chapter 12.

An administrator can choose any, all, or none of the above methods for remote-access security, based on your organization's security standards and the cost trade-off of the various measures.

Internet Services Security

The first word that comes up in most discussions of Internet security is *firewalls.* A firewall gives a network the ability to filter out network traffic. Either routes or machines can be specifically set up to block messaging between machines. These machines can be on your private network, or perhaps between your network and the Internet.

Microsoft provides limited firewall capabilities with its Internet Information Server (IIS). This product allows certain IP addresses or ranges to be blocked. If you require more sophisticated protection, you may need to install something like the Microsoft Proxy Server. The proxy server is a go-between; users communicate with the proxy server machine, and the machine then communicates with the Internet. Proxy servers can shield your network from unwanted access from the Internet.

Along with the "standard" Internet security measures just described, Windows NT also throws its own security model in the way of intruders from the Internet. Users who would like to access resources on NT-based Web servers must first be authenticated by the server. Then, both share permissions and local NTFS permissions are applied to the user.

There is more on Internet security in Chapter 13. For now, just keep in mind that Internet security is fully integrated into Windows NT.

Administrative Shares

Computer users have traditionally worried about the "back door" in their operating systems. The closest thing to a "back door" in Windows NT is the designation of administrative shares. Administrative shares allow any administrator to gain access to any Windows NT server or workstation via the network.

Before branding this feature of Windows NT as a "risk," let's consider the purpose of administrative shares. First of all, for any user to gain access to a machine, a share must exist. In addition, shares prevent "upward" access—that is, access to any folders higher in the hierarchy of the disk structure. For example, say Admix wants access to maple's C:\DOS folder. maple's machine already has a share called PUBLIC that points to C:\public. When Admix connects to the share, he only has access to the \Public folder and its subfolders, but he cannot change folders to C:\DOS.

As described earlier in the chapter (see the sidebar, "Watch Out for System Shares"), administrative shares show up as C$ or D$. They are automatically set up each time Windows NT boots up. The Server service is responsible for creating these shares. When that service is started, it looks to the Registry to see if administrative shares have been turned on; if so, the Server service creates them.

Administrative shares are enabled by default; if you want to disable them, there are two ways to do it. The first is to edit the following Registry setting:

```
HKEY_LOCAL_MACHINE\System\CurrentControlSet\Services\
LanmanServer\Parameters AutoShareServer

Value Name: AutoShareServer  {For Windows NT Server 4.0}
Data Type: Reg_DWORD
Values: 1 or 0  (default=1)

Value Name: AutoShareWks  {For Windows NT Workstation 4.0}
Data Type: Reg_DWORD
Values: 1 or 0  (Default=1)
```

The second method of disabling administrative shares is through the use of System Policies. Figure 7.19 shows a dialog for System Polices. You simply need to check the Create Hidden Drive Shares check box for each of the appropriate values. This will essentially change the Registry values for you automatically when users log on.

Normal Shares in the Registry

In addition to checking administrative shares, the Server service looks at the following Registry entry regarding "manually created" shares. This Registry entry tells the Server service which shares to create "manually" and the type of security to set on each of them.

```
HKEY_LOCAL_MACHINE\System\CurrentControlSet\Services\LanmanServer\Shares
```

Helpful Tip

If you have problems with shares being created, stop the Server service in Control Panel/Services and then start it up again. This will first remove existing shares and then re-create them when the service is restarted.

Figure 7.19

System Policies dialog

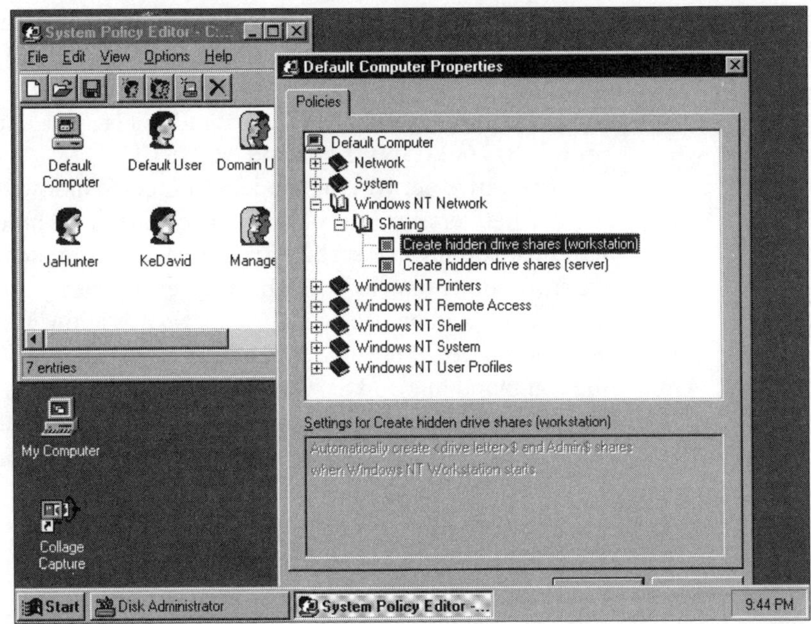

There is one more Registry setting to be aware of when working with shares. Each user can potentially store *persistent network connections* in the Registry. This type of setting is stored as part of the user profile (ntuser.dat). When the user logs on again, NT will automatically reconnect them to these shares.

```
HKEY_CURRENT_USER\SOFTWARE\Microsoft\Windows NT\
CurrentVersion\Network\Persistent Connections

Value Name: DriveMappingLetter
Data Type: REG_SZ
Values: UNC  Sharename to connect to

Value Name: SaveConnections     REG_SZ
Data Type: REG_SZ
Value: Yes or No (Default=Yes)
```

Summary

Windows NT 4.0 was created from the ground up with networking in mind; it includes all the software needed to integrate itself into any mixed network. Microsoft has made strides to create a modularized, open system platform for its network operating system. Windows NT has a full set of feature-rich protocols: TCP/IP, NWLink, and NetBEEUI.

The entire networking model leverages Windows NT's security model.

NT delivers a robust networking client/server model, as well. This model has the flexibility and scalability to meet the demands of small networks and enterprise networks as well. The user-level security model protects all of its resources based on users and groups. Shares allow users to gain access to network resources; these shares can be created through Windows NT Explorer, the command line and Server Manager. Security is also extended across remote network users via RAS, and for Internet applications as well.

- *The RAS Configuration*
- *Remote Access Clients*
- *Network Servers*
- *LAN Protocols*
- *The RAS Server*
- *Remote Access Protocols*
- *Wide Area Network (WAN) Connectivity*

- *Security for Remote Access Clients*

CHAPTER

8

Remote Access Service (RAS)

IN THE WINDOWS NT ENVIRONMENT, REMOTE OR MOBILE WORKERS are connected by the Remote Access Service (RAS, pronounced like "jazz") to RAS servers. This is usually for the purpose of giving these workers access to a corporate network. The Remote Access Service gives an enterprise network the capability of growing by extending itself across the Internet, Public Switched Telephone Networks (PSTN), and Integrated Services Digital Networks (ISDN).

Making Windows NT secure in today's "on the move" world requires knowledge of the Remote Access Service. RAS works with protocols, and across both WANs and LANs, while operating within the Windows NT security model. With RAS, remote access simulates physical connection to the network. RAS on Windows NT appears as a Dial-Up Networking icon in My Computer.

Although it includes a lot of hardware and setup options, RAS is not very complicated. Once you figure out what hardware you want to use and what type of connections you'll be making, the choices are clear and simple. (Most of the hardware issues are beyond the scope of the book and are detailed in the Microsoft Windows online administration manuals.)

RAS benefits from the robustness of NT and NT Security, making Windows NT overall one of the most secure WAN and Internet servers on the market today. Although RAS adds several new features, they are primarily hardware related—such as Multilink aggregation (the grouping of multiple physical links into a single logical link with higher bandwidth). The key to the enhanced power of RAS plus the NT security model is that Microsoft has extended the LAN to the Internet, while maintaining LAN-like security.

This chapter offers a synopsis of the basic operation of Windows NT Remote Access Service, and describes how to implement specific security components in a Windows NT Server network.

The RAS Configuration

Simply put, RAS allows remote users to work as if they were connected directly to the network. The process begins when a user runs the RAS graphical Phonebook (Dial-up Networking) on a remote computer and initiates a connection to the RAS server. The RAS server authenticates the user and services the session until terminated by the user or network administrator. All services typically available to a LAN-connected user (including file- and print-sharing, database access, and messaging) are enabled by means of the RAS connection.

The architecture that underlies this process is illustrated in Figure 8.1.

Clients needing remote access are the first component in this discussion of the RAS configuration. Next, we'll look at the server and connectivity components, which include network servers and LAN protocols; then the WAN connectivity options; and, of course, the RAS server itself and the remote access protocols. Security options, including special security hosts and encryption, form the final component.

Figure 8.2 illustrates all RAS components and possible configurations. Of course, actual implementations and configurations will vary.

Figure 8.1

The RAS architecture

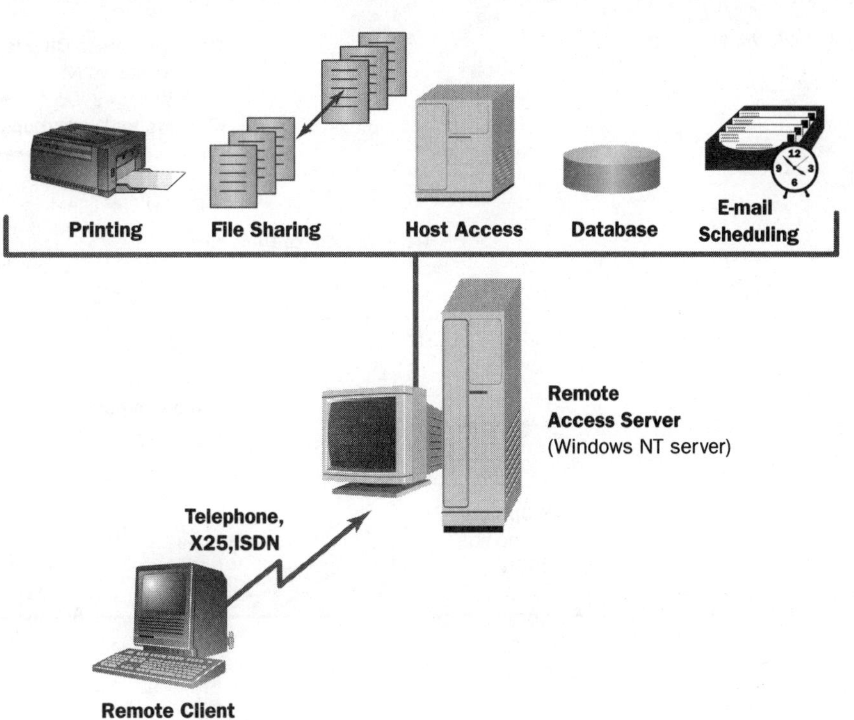

Remote Access Clients

Clients connecting to RAS servers can be Windows NT, Windows 95, Windows for Workgroups, MS-DOS, LAN Manager, or any PPP client. The client must have a modem (at least 9600 baud is recommended for acceptable performance), an analog telephone line or other WAN connection, and remote access software installed.

Connecting is automatic with the new RAS AutoDial feature. AutoDial learns every connection made over the RAS link and automatically reconnects you when you access a resource for the second time. For more information, see the Microsoft Windows NT 4.0 Workstation Resource Kit.

Connecting can also be automated for any Microsoft client. This is accomplished by means of a simple batch file and the RASDIAL command, or with a custom, RAS-aware application using the appropriate API for RAS. You can also schedule automatic backups to or from remote computers by using RAS and the AT command.

Figure 8.2

RAS configuration options

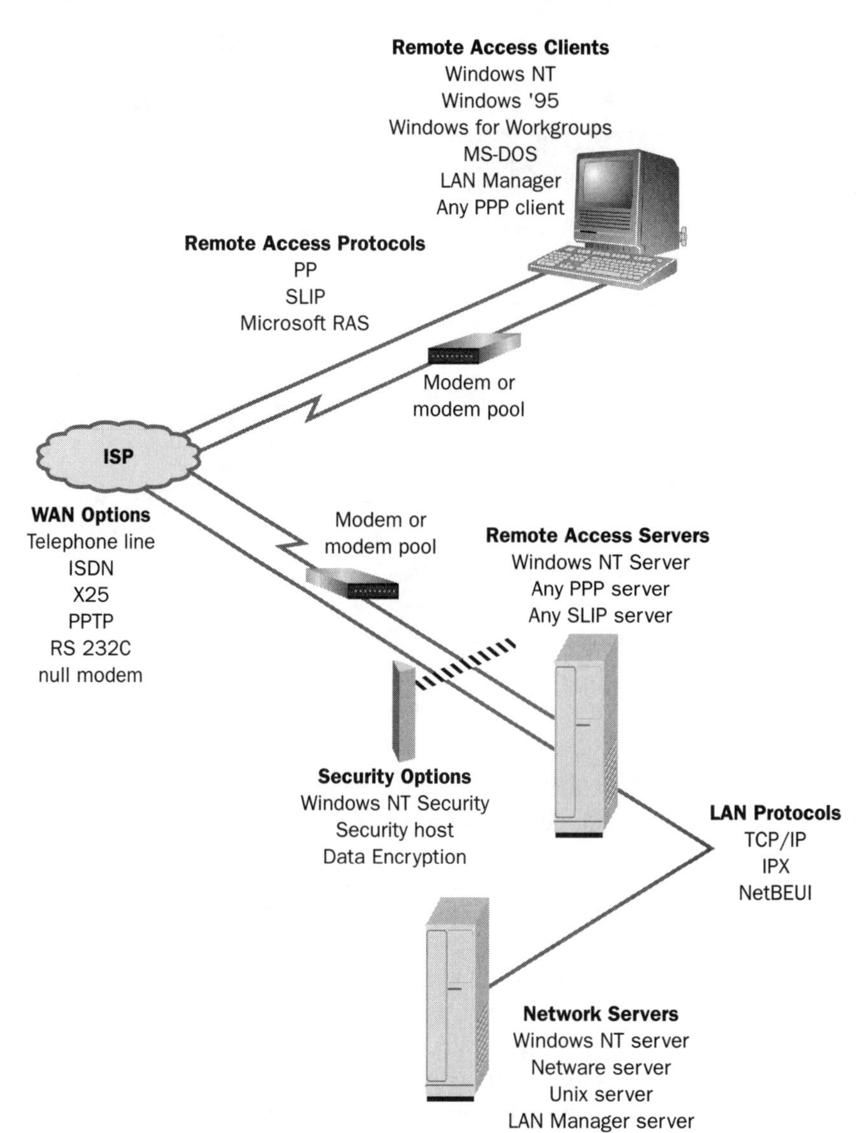

Once they're connected, remote clients use standard tools to access resources. For example, the Windows Explorer is used to make drive connections and to connect printers. You have the option of making connections persistent, which means users do not need to reconnect to network resources during their remote sessions.

Let's take a closer look at the remote setup for each of these types of clients.

Windows NT 3.5, 3.51, and Windows 95 Clients

Windows NT 3.5*x* and Windows 95 clients can take full advantage of Windows NT 4.0 RAS features, except for Multilink functionality. These clients can also connect to any non-Microsoft remote access PPP server or SLIP server.

NT 3.5*x* and Windows 95 clients negotiate logon and authentication with the server, whether the server is a Microsoft RAS server, a PPP server, or a SLIP server. You can also configure RAS Phonebook entries to use scripts that can completely automate logon.

Windows NT 3.1 Clients

Windows NT 3.1 clients use the Microsoft RAS protocol and are fully compatible with all versions of Microsoft RAS. These clients do not support the PPP protocol introduced in Windows NT 3.5. Only NT 3.5*x* or other PPP clients provide the support necessary to run TCP/IP or IPX (Internet Packet Exchange) applications on clients that directly communicate with servers on the LAN using TCP/IP or IPX.

Windows for Workgroups, MS-DOS, and LAN Manager Clients

Windows NT Server provides a Microsoft Network Client version 3.0 for MS-DOS, and a Windows for Workgroups client that both provide remote access. Separately purchased Windows for Workgroups and LAN Manager RAS clients can also connect to Windows NT 3.5 or later RAS servers. These clients are fully (3.5*x*) compatible with all versions of Microsoft RAS protocol.

The Microsoft Network Client version 3.0 for MS-DOS must be set up to use the full redirector (the default setting). If the basic redirector is used, the Remote Access program (RASPHONE) will not start.

The Windows for Workgroups, MS-DOS, and LAN Manager clients can use the RAS NetBIOS gateway to access NetBIOS servers running TCP/IP, IPX, or NetBEUI, but these clients cannot run applications that must use TCP/IP or IPX on the client. These clients also do not support the PPP protocol introduced in Windows NT 3.5.

PPP Clients

Non-Microsoft PPP clients using TCP/IP, IPX, or NetBEUI can access a Windows NT version 3.5 or later RAS server. The RAS server will automatically negotiate authentication with PPP clients; the Windows NT RAS software needs no special configuration for non-Microsoft PPP clients.

Network Servers

The RAS client component is a complete communications package. It will allow connections to heterogeneous environments and provide full Internet access. You are not limited to using a RAS client to connect only to RAS servers. Specifically, RAS can provide remote access to NetWare communication servers, UNIX servers, LAN Manager servers, and other systems.

LAN Protocols

LAN protocols transport packets across a local area network, whereas remote access protocols control the transmission of data over the wide area network (WAN). Windows NT supports LAN protocols such as TCP/IP, IPX, and NetBEUI, which enable access to the Internet and to NetWare and UNIX servers. The protocols used in an existing network affect how you plan, integrate, and configure RAS. Because Windows NT RAS supports these LAN protocols, you can integrate RAS into existing Microsoft, UNIX, or NetWare networks using PPP or SLIP.

When you install and configure RAS, any protocols already installed on the computer (TCP/IP, IPX, and NetBEUI) are automatically enabled for RAS on inbound and outbound calls. You must also specify if you want users to have access to the entire LAN; otherwise, users will be able to access only the RAS server. If you provide access to the entire LAN using TCP/IP or IPX, you must also configure how the server will provide IP addresses or IPX net numbers. If you provide access to the entire LAN using NetBEUI, no additional configuration is needed.

TCP/IP and RAS

The routing capabilities of TCP/IP provide maximum flexibility in an enterprise-wide network. On a TCP/IP network, you must provide IP addresses to clients. Clients might also require a naming service or method for name resolution. This section explains IP addressing and name resolution for Windows NT RAS servers and clients on TCP/IP networks.

Assigning IP Addresses to RAS Clients

In Windows NT, each remote computer connecting to a RAS server through PPP on a Microsoft TCP/IP network is automatically provided an IP address. This address is assigned from a static range assigned to the RAS server by the administrator during setup.

Windows NT RAS clients can also use an assigned IP address specified in their Phonebook. In this case, the RAS server must be configured to permit users' requests for a specific address.

Name Resolution for RAS Servers and Clients

In addition to an IP address, RAS servers and clients on a TCP/IP network might require a mechanism to map computer names to IP addresses. Four name-resolution options are available on an NT network: Windows Internet Name Service (WINS), broadcast name resolution, Domain Name System (DNS), and the HOSTS and LMHOSTS files. RAS servers can use all these name-resolution methods for operations performed on the server.

NOTE. *RAS clients are assigned the same WINS and DNS servers that are assigned to the RAS server. You must use the Registry to override this automatic assignment.*

RAS clients in small networks where IP addresses do not change can use a HOSTS or LMHOSTS file for name resolution. By using these files on the local drive, you avoid the requirement of transmitting name-resolution requests to a WINS server and waiting for the response over the modem.

IPX and RAS

IPX is the native NetWare protocol used on many Novell networks. Because it is a routable protocol, IPX is suitable for enterprise-wide networks. This section explains how to integrate Windows NT RAS clients and servers into a NetWare IPX network.

If Windows NT RAS computers must see a NetWare network, the client computer must run a NetWare redirector. In NT Workstation computers this redirector is called the Client Service for NetWare; in NT Server computers this is called the Gateway Service for NetWare.

An NT RAS server is also an IPX router and Service Advertising Protocol (SAP) agent for RAS clients only. To configure the remote access line for IPX, RAS servers and their clients use the PPP protocol IPXCP (IPX Configuration Protocol) defined in RFC 1552. Once configured, RAS servers enable file and print services and the use of Windows Sockets applications over IPX on the NetWare network for RAS clients.

IPX Addressing for Remote Clients

RAS servers provide an IPX network number to clients connecting to an IPX network, and act as their SAP agent as well. The IPX net number is either generated automatically by the RAS server, or a static pool of network numbers is given to the RAS server for assignment to RAS clients.

Connecting to Third-Party RAS Servers Using IP

The Windows NT RAS server enables remote clients to share subnet addresses with computers on the LAN, thereby conserving IP addresses. Remote access servers from other vendors might require that remote clients have a different subnet address than clients on the LAN. If remote clients dial into another vendor's remote access server and cannot connect to resources on the LAN, check the following configuration on your remote access server:

- If your third-party remote access server does not support proxy-ARP (Address Resolution Protocol), your remote clients must be assigned a different subnet address than that for LAN clients. Be sure your server is configured to assign remote clients a unique subnet address.
- Ensure that your network routers are configured so that remote access clients can use ping on target hosts, and vice versa. Use ping in the following order:
    1. Remote client to target server, then remote client to remote access server, then remote access server to target server.
    2. Target server to remote client, then target server to remote access server, then remote access server to remote client.

For automatically generated IPX net numbers, the RAS server uses the NetWare Router Information Protocol (RIP) to determine a number that is not in use in the IPX network.

You can override the automatic assignments of network numbers. Manual assignments can be useful if you want more control of network number assignments for security or monitoring. You can also assign the same network number to all clients to minimize RIP announcements from the RAS server. When assigning IPX net numbers to a RAS server, ensure that duplicate numbers are not assigned and that other NetWare services cannot assign the RAS IPX addresses.

NetBEUI and RAS

NetBEUI is suited for use in small workgroups or LANs. A NetBIOS gateway and the NetBEUI client protocol are installed by default on all Windows NT RAS servers and on most Windows networking clients. NetBEUI is required for Windows NT 3.1 RAS clients, LAN Manager RAS clients, MS-DOS RAS clients, and Windows for Workgroups RAS clients.

The RAS Server

The Windows NT RAS server permits up to 256 remote clients to dial in. Actually, NT can support more than 256 through other third-party products, but Microsoft will only support NT with up to 256 connections. The RAS server can be configured to provide access to an entire network, or you can restrict access to the RAS server only.

RAS enables NT to provide complete services to the Internet. A Windows NT Server computer can be configured as an Internet service provider, offering dial-up Internet connections to a PPP client. A computer running Windows NT Workstation can dial into an Internet-connected computer running Windows NT Server 3.5 or later, or to any one of many industry-standard PPP or SLIP-based Internet servers. (For more information see the *Windows NT Resource Kit Internet Guide.*)

Windows NT Server administrators use the Remote Access Admin program to control the RAS server, as well as to view users, grant permissions, and monitor RAS traffic. For more information about using the Remote Access Admin program, see the RAS online help.

The RAS server must have a multiport adapter or modems (at least 9600 baud is recommended for acceptable performance), analog telephone lines or other WAN connections, and the RAS software installed. If this server will provide network access, a separate network adapter card must be installed and connected for each network to which the server provides access.

RAS servers are configured during initial RAS setup. You must specify whether access will be to the entire network or to the RAS server only. You must also select the protocols to use on the LAN (IPX, TCP/IP, and NetBEUI), and an authentication encryption option. Other sections in this chapter provide additional information about remote access protocols and LAN protocols.

Ports on RAS servers are configured individually. Each port can be set to Dial Out Only, Receive Calls Only, or Dial Out And Receive Calls, and these settings affect only the port specified. For example, your RAS server can be configured to provide access to the entire network, COM1 to receive calls, and COM2 for dial-out and receive. A remote user can call in on either COM port, but a local user can use only COM2 for outbound RAS calls.

Events and errors are recorded in Event Viewer on Windows NT RAS clients and servers. Evaluating the log in Event Viewer can help you determine the source of problems.

Use the Control Panel/Network option to install and configure RAS. Use the Control Panel/Services option to specify startup options.

Remote Access versus Remote Control

There are important distinctions between RAS and remote control solutions such as pcANYWHERE:

- RAS is a software-based multiprotocol router. The RAS server's CPU is dedicated to communications, not to running applications.
- In a remote control solution, users share a CPU or multiple CPUs on the server. Remote control solutions work by sharing screen, keyboard, and mouse over the remote link.

Remote Access Protocols

Remote access protocols can be confusing because of the similarity of many acronyms, significant differences between server and client support, and interoperability (or not) between the remote protocols and those of the LANs. RAS supports several modem protocols, as described in the sections that follow:

- Serial Line Internet Protocol (SLIP)
- Point-to-Point Protocol (PPP)
- PPP Multi-link Protocol (MP)
- Point-to-Point Tunneling Protocol (PPTP)
- RAS protocol

RAS must support many protocols and service options to support today's demanding WAN and remote-access needs. Mobile clients need access to corporate data, and their needs differ greatly from the WAN functionality of high-speed network communications that bind corporate offices together. Add the necessity of working with legacy systems, and trying to pave the superhighway of the future using new technologies and improving on the old ones, and you have one heck of a challenge.

Serial Line Internet Protocol

Support for Serial Line Internet Protocol (SLIP) allows Windows NT RAS clients to connect to third-party remote access servers that use the SLIP remote communication standard. Clients can use SLIP only if the port for the Phonebook entry is a serial COM port.

When a user connects to a SLIP server, a Windows Terminal dialog box pops up for an interactive logon session with the UNIX SLIP server. The UNIX logon overrides and prevents the RAS logon from appearing. After a connection is established, remote network access becomes transparent to the user.

RAS supports SLIP only for dialing out. SLIP is an older remote-access standard that addresses TCP/IP connections made over serial lines (that is, the type of connection typically used by UNIX remote access servers). Windows NT RAS clients support SLIP and can connect to any remote access server using the SLIP standard. This permits Windows NT 3.5 clients to connect to the large installed base of UNIX servers. The Windows NT RAS server, however, does not support SLIP clients. And SLIP, please note, does not support IPX/SPX or Net BEUI.

The RFCs supported in this version of Windows NT RAS are

- RFC 1144, Compressing TCP/IP Headers for Low-Speed Serial Links
- RFC 1055, A Nonstandard for Transmission of IP Datagrams Over Serial Lines: SLIP

Point-to-Point Protocol

Windows NT supports the Point-to-Point Protocol (PPP) in RAS. This is a set of industry-standard framing and authentication protocols that enable remote-access solutions to interoperate in a multivendor network. Microsoft recommends that you use PPP because of its flexibility and its role as an industry standard; in addition, it offers future flexibility with client and server hardware and software.

With PPP support, computers running Windows NT can dial in to remote networks through any server that complies with the PPP standard. PPP compliance also enables a Windows NT Server computer to receive calls from and provide network access to other vendors' remote-access software.

PPP replaces SLIP by supplying a process of data transmission over a point-to-point link. PPP also supports TCP/IP, and several other protocols as well: IPX, NetBEUI, and OSI (Open Systems Interconnection) to name a few. The PPP architecture allows clients to load any combination of IPX, TCP/IP, and NetBEUI. Applications written to the Windows Sockets, NetBIOS, or IPX interface can be run on a remote Windows NT Workstation computer. Figure 8.3 illustrates the PPP architecture of RAS.

Remote Access protocol standards are defined in RFCs published by the Internet Engineering Task Force and other working groups. The RFCs supported in this version of Windows NT RAS are

- RFC 1549, PPP in HDLC Framing
- RFC 1552, The PPP Internetwork Packet Exchange Control Protocol (IPXCP)
- RFC 1334, PPP Authentication Protocols
- RFC 1332, The PPP Internet Protocol Control Protocol (IPCP)

Figure 8.3

PPP architecture of RAS

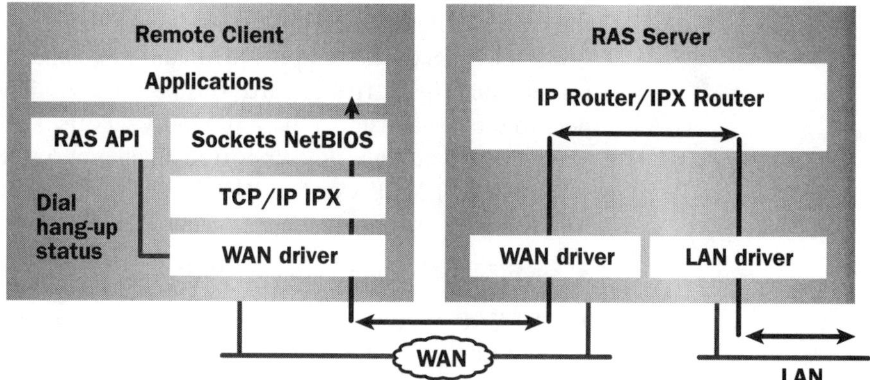

- RFC 1661, Link Control Protocol (LCP)
- RFC 1717, PPP Multilink Protocol

NOTE. *If your remote clients connect to third-party PPP servers, they might need to enable a post-connect terminal script to log on to the PPP server. After the server informs them it is switching to PPP framing mode, the user must start Terminal to complete logon.*

Windows NT Protocol Support over PPP Windows NT support of TCP/IP gives remote clients access to the Internet through Windows Sockets (WinSock) applications. IPX support allows remote clients to access NetWare servers. Supporting PPP makes it possible for RAS servers to give access to third-party remote-access client software. TCP/IP, IPX, and NetBEUI will automatically be bound to RAS upon installation, if they have previously been installed on the machine.

Upon connecting to a remote computer, PPP negotiation proceeds as follows:

1. Framing rules are established between the remote computer and server. This allows continued communication (frame transfer) to occur.
2. The RAS server then authenticates the remote user using the PPP authentication protocols (PAP, CHAP, and SPAP, covered later in the "Encrypted Authentication and Logon Process" section). The protocols invoked depend on the security configurations of the remote client and server.
3. Once authenticated, the Network Control Protocols (NCPs) enable and configure the server for the LAN protocol used on the remote client.

When the PPP connection sequence is successfully completed, the remote client and RAS server can begin to transfer data using Windows Sockets, RPC, NetBIOS, or another supported protocol.

NOTE. *If your remote client is configured to use the NetBIOS gateway or SLIP, this sequence is invalid.*

Figure 8.4 illustrates the position of the PPP protocol on the ISO/OSI model.

Figure 8.4

The PPP protocol in the ISO/OSI model

Remote Computing Applications
Win 32 RAS API
Win Sockets, NetBIOS
PPP Control Protocols
PAP
CHAP
SPAP
IPCP
IPXCP
NBFCP
7 Application
User Mode
RAS Connection Manager
Kernal Mode
6 Presentation
5 Session
Redirector
Server
4 Transport
TCP/IP, IPX, NetBEUI
3 Network
2 Data Link
TAPI Wrapper
WAN Miniport Wrapper
Compression
Encryption
Simple HDLC Framing
NDIS Wrapper
Simple HDLC Framing
1 Physical

PPP Multilink Protocol

The PPP Multilink Protocol (MP) is available on computers that have more than one modem or ISDN. The unique MP technology allows for the aggregation of communications channels. It combines multiple physical links to increase bandwidth.

NOTE. *In other words, you can use two PSTN 28.8 modems, aggregate them, and voila! you have a 56K line. This works with more than two lines and with ISDN, as well—a feature I have deemed VC (very cool).*

Point-to-Point Tunneling Protocol

PPTP has a method called *tunneling* to route PPP packets over a TCP/IP network—including, of course, the Internet. This tunneling allows multiprotocol encapsulation of any type of PPP packet, TCP/IP, IPX, or NetBEUI to be routed over a TCP/IP network. PPTP just treats the existing network as a PSTN, ISDN, or X.25 connection and assumes it is being accessed through a public carrier (such as the Internet).

You normally access a RAS server directly through a modem, ISDN card, or X.25 PAD. Now you can securely access these servers indirectly via the Internet by using PPTP. It's the new technology that brings virtual private networks (VPNs) to life at low cost while maintaining high levels of security. PPTP also supports multiple protocols. This breakthrough technology enables remote users to access corporate networks securely across the Internet.

Users and clients, including you, can use PPTP to access a corporate LAN by dialing an ISP or by connecting directly through the Internet. PPTP connections are encrypted, secure, and work with any NT protocol including TCP/IP, IPX, and NetBEUI.

PPTP offers the following advantages:

- Lower transmission costs
- Lower hardware costs
- Lower administrative overhead
- Enhanced security

Security Benefits of PPTP

Data sent across the PPTP tunnel is encapsulated in PPP packets. Because RAS supports encryption, the data will be encrypted. RAS supports bulk data encryption using RSA RC4 and a 40-bit session key that is negotiated at PPP connect time between the RAS client and the Windows NT RAS server. PPTP uses the Password Authentication Protocol and the Challenge Handshake Authentication Protocol encryption algorithms.

In addition to supporting encrypted PPP links across the Internet, a PPTP-based solution also enables the Internet to become a network backbone for carrying IPX and NetBEUI remote-access traffic. PPTP can transfer IPX traffic because it encapsulates and encrypts PPP packets so that they can ride TCP/IP. Thus, a solution does not depend only on TCP/IP LANs.

Installing the PPTP Protocol

You must have the PPTP protocol installed on the RAS server—and on the client or communications server—for PPTP tunneling to succeed. Following are the steps to install PPTP on the RAS server.

1. In Control Panel, double-click the Network icon. In the Network dialog box, open the Protocols tab.
2. Click Add and select Point to Point Tunneling Protocol. When prompted for the path to the distribution files, provide the path and click OK.
3. Enter the number of connections you want available to PPTP (e.g., Virtual Private Networks, VPN).
4. RAS setup starts and the PPTP protocol is added to RAS. Choose the port on which you want to install the PPTP protocol and click OK.
5. Restart your computer to have the PPTP configuration take effect.

Now, with PPTP installed on the RAS server, let's look at the alternatives for installing it on either the client or the communications server.

Using PPTP via the Internet and Virtual Private Networks

In this scenario, we need to have PPTP on the client. So in this case, RAS on the client uses PPTP as its WAN driver and can access resources on a remote LAN, by connecting to a Windows NT RAS server through the Internet. There are two ways to do this: by connecting directly to the Internet or by dialing an ISP. Following are examples of both. Remember that PPTP must be installed on the server.

- A client directly connected on the Internet dials the number for the RAS server. PPTP on the client makes a tunnel through the Internet and connects to the PPTP-enabled RAS server. After authentication, the client can access the corporate network, as shown in Figure 8.5.

NOTE. *Connecting directly to the Internet means direct IP access without going through an ISP. (For example, some hotels allow you to use an Ethernet cable to gain a direct connection to the Internet.)*

- The same functionality is achieved by calling an ISP instead of being directly connected to the Internet. The client first makes a call to the ISP. After that connection is established, the client makes another call to the RAS server that establishes the PPTP tunnel. See Figure 8.6.

Using PPTP for Simple Client-Outsourced Communications Service

When the corporation wants to outsource its remote communications, PPTP is installed on the communications server and the client is unaware of PPTP

Figure 8.5

RAS client connected directly to the Internet

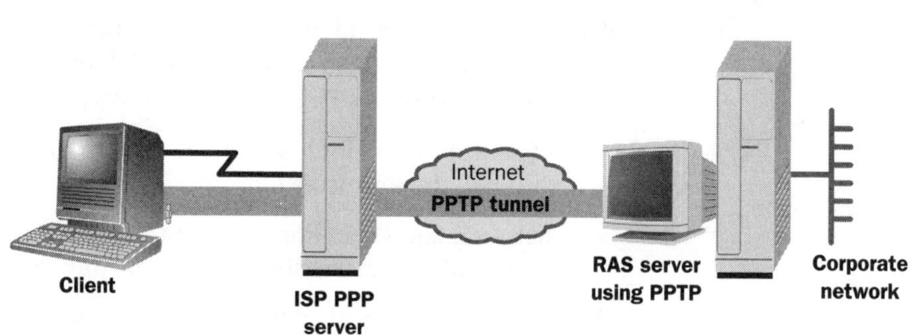

Figure 8.6

RAS client dialing into an ISP

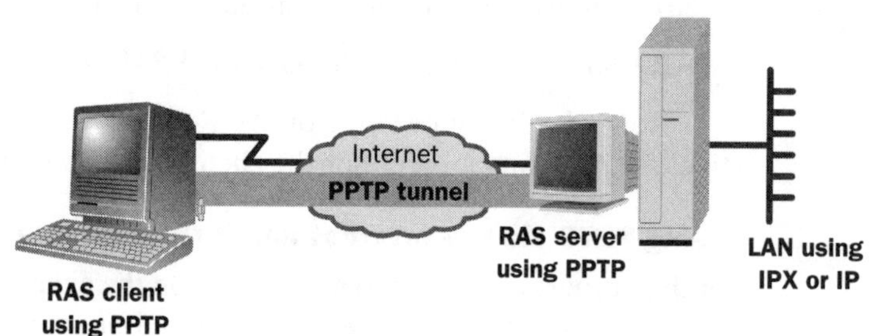

or any special operations. For example, a mobile user with a laptop dials up to a PPTP-enabled RAS server, which is connected to the corporate network. This type of solution leverages existing, proven PPP authentication, encryption, and compression technologies on the client. It also maintains high levels of security through the corporate communications (WAN) backbone. As stated, the RAS client does not need to have PPTP; the client simply makes a PPP connection to the outsourced communication system. See Figure 8.7.

Figure 8.7

An outsourced dial-up network using PPTP

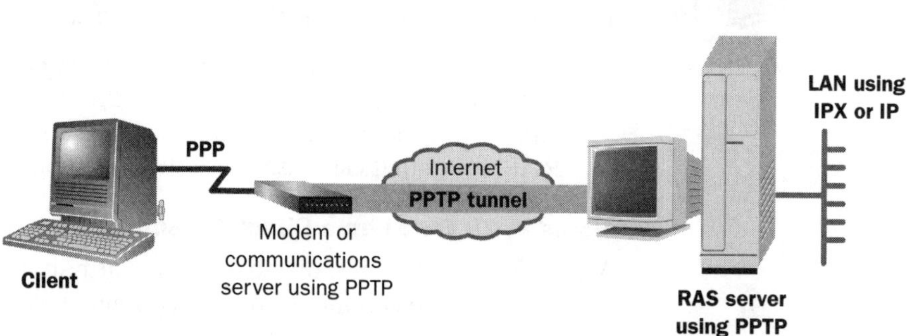

PPTP Filtering

PPTP filtering is a key security feature. You can apply a filter that gives access to the network from outside sources (Internet) to only users using PPTP. This ensures that connections coming in for the Internet are secure. Through normal user, group, and file management techniques, the administrator can still control who accesses networking resources. By filtering out non-PPTP packets, you avoid the risk of unauthorized users slipping in and attacking your network through your Internet gateway server.

Protecting a RAS Server from Internet Attacks

If you select PPTP filtering, you effectively disable the selected network adapter for all other protocols. Only PPTP packets will be allowed in. You might want to do this when you have a multihomed computer with one network adapter (with PPTP filtering enabled) connected to the Internet, and another network adapter connected to the internal corporate network. Clients outside the corporate network can use PPTP to connect to the computer from across the Internet and gain secure access to the corporate network. Thus, access to the corporate network is limited to PPTP packets from clients who have been authenticated using RAS authentication. Figure 8.8 illustrates this concept.

NOTE. *The RAS client can either be connected to the Internet directly or to a service provider. It is not necessary to be connected to both to use PPTP.*

Figure 8.8

PPTP filtering between the Internet and the corporate network

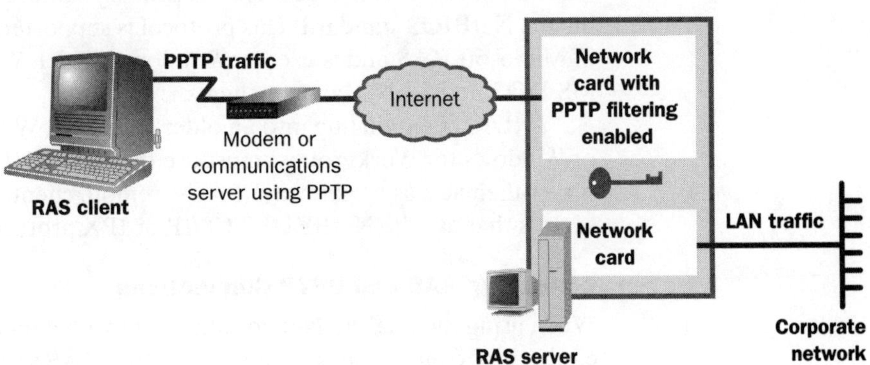

Enabling PPTP Filtering

Following are steps for setting up PPTP filtering:

1. In Control Panel, double-click the Network icon. In the Network dialog box, open the Protocols tab.
2. Select TCP/IP Protocol, and click Properties.
3. In the IP Address tab, click Advanced.
4. In the Adapter box, select the network adapter for which you want to specify PPTP filtering. The settings displayed are for the adapter listed.

Caution

> *If you have more than one adapter, this is an easy place to make a mistake. For example, you may have one adapter servicing the Internet and one for your intranet. You want to set PPTP filtering for the Internet adapter, but the intranet adapter is listed first. Be sure to specifically choose the right adapter in the pull-down menu, or you'll wind up changing the settings for the wrong adapter.*

5. Select Enable PPTP Filtering.
6. Restart the computer to make the settings take effect.

Microsoft RAS Protocol

The Microsoft RAS protocol is a proprietary remote-access protocol supporting the NetBIOS standard. This protocol is supported in all previous versions of Microsoft RAS and is used on Windows NT 3.1, Windows for Workgroups, MS-DOS, and LAN Manager clients.

A RAS client dialing into an older version of Windows (Windows NT 3.1 or Windows for Workgroups) must use the NetBEUI protocol. The RAS server then acts as a "gateway" for the remote client, providing access to servers that use the NetBEUI, TCP/IP, or IPX protocols.

Comparing RAS and PPTP Connections

When using the Dial-up Networking client with a modem, ISDN, or X.25 card, a PPP connection is established with a RAS server, which routes the packets to the destination network. Contrast this with PPTP, for example, which allows direct connection to a RAS server. The PPTP connection uses a protocol such as TCP/IP for the connection. Once that connection is established to the RAS server, PPP packets are sent by means of TCP/IP to the RAS server.

■ Wide Area Network (WAN) Connectivity

WAN options for remote access include client dial-in using standard telephone lines and a modem or modem pool. Faster links are possible using ISDN. You can also connect RAS clients to RAS servers using X.25, an RS-232C null modem, or using the new PPTP (see the earlier section).

Modem Pool Access

The most common WAN connection is a standard analog telephone line and a modem. Standard analog phone lines are available worldwide and will meet most RAS needs for mobile users.

NOTE. *Standard analog phone lines are also called PSTN (Public Switched Telephone Network) or POTS (Plain-Old Telephone Service).*

Third-party modem pools can be used on either the client side or the server side. Modem pools are made available to RAS through the Network icon in Control Panel. Consult your modem pool documentation for more information.

Modems are automatically detected. Automatic modem detection is especially useful for users who are not sure what modem is installed (for example, an internal modem).

Modem data compression and error control are available, but built-in software compression offers better performance.

Access via Dial-up Networking

In addition to TAPI configuration (discussed later in this section on WAN connections), there are several other configuration options that can be set in Dial-Up Networking. Some of these additional configuration options include configuring Phonebook entries, logging on using a dial-in entry, and the Auto-Dial feature. Once Dial-up Networking is installed, clients can use the Phonebook feature to record telephone numbers that are needed to connect and disconnect from remote networks.

Calling an Internet Service Provider

When using an ISP with PPTP, the only difference is that the client must first call the ISP to gain access to the Internet. In addition, PPTP must be supported at the ISP's point of presence. The client first calls the ISP, and after establishing a connection calls the Windows NT RAS server through that connection to establish the PPTP tunnel.

NetBIOS Gateway

Windows NT continues to support NetBIOS gateways—the architecture used in previous versions of NT and LAN Manager. Remote users connect using NetBEUI, and the RAS server translates packets, if necessary, to IPX or TCP/IP. This enables users to share network resources in a multiprotocol LAN but prevents them from running applications that rely on IPX or on client-supported TCP/IP. The NetBIOS gateway is used by default when remote clients are using NetBEUI. Figure 8.9 illustrates the NetBIOS gateway architecture of RAS.

Figure 8.9

NetBIOS gateway architecture of RAS

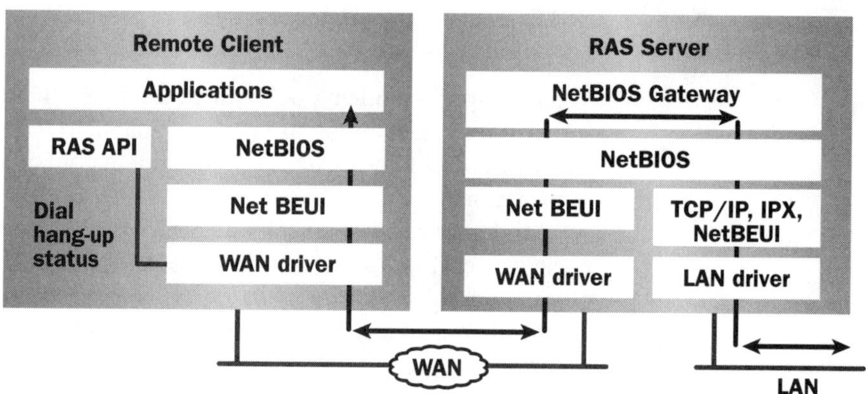

An example of the NetBIOS gateway capability is remote network access for Lotus Notes users. Although Lotus Notes does offer dial-up connectivity, the dial-up is limited to the Notes application. RAS complements this connectivity by providing a low-cost, high-performance, remote network connection that not only connects Notes, but offers file and print services as well as access to other network resources.

Virtual Private Network

A virtual private network (VPN) allows "tunneling" through the Internet and still provides the same security and other features available on your LAN. A user on a RAS client machine with a PPTP driver as its WAN driver will be able to access resources across the Internet on a remote LAN, through a Windows NT RAS server via tunneled and encrypted PPP packets. (RAS supports bulk data encryption using RSA RC4 and a 40-bit session key negotiated at the time of PPP connection between the RAS client and the Windows NT RAS server.)

Using Phonebook Entries

The Dial-Up Networking remote access client stores all of its configuration data for a single connection in a Phonebook file. A Phonebook entry stores all the settings needed to connect to a particular remote network. Phonebooks can be specific to an individual user or shared among all users on the computer.

You access Dial-Up Networking through the Accessories menu. To create a new Phonebook entry, click New in the Dial-Up Networking dialog box.

AutoDial

The AutoDial feature maps network connections to Phonebook entries. In this way the Phonebook entry can be automatically dialed when an attempt is made to access a network connection that has been mapped. This feature is available from applications, as well as from the command prompt for Internet host names, IP addresses, and NetBIOS names.

NOTE. *AutoDial does not support IPX connections.*

AutoDial also keeps track of all connections made over a Dial-up Networking connection so that clients can be automatically reconnected.

AutoDial is enabled by default. A user can disable the feature in the User Preferences dialog for a Phonebook entry.

ISDN Access

To enhance WAN speeds at a stationary remote site or at sites that will use RAS, use an Integrated Services Digital Network (ISDN) line. Whereas standard phone lines typically transmit at 9600 bits per second (bps), ISDN lines can transmit at speeds of 64 or 128 kilobits per second (kbps).

An ISDN line must be installed by the phone company at both the server and at the remote site. In addition, an ISDN card must be installed in place of a modem in both the server and remote client. Costs for ISDN equipment and lines can be higher than standard modems and phone lines. The resulting faster communication speed, however, reduces the duration of connections and may save toll charges.

X.25 Access

X.25 is a standard packet-switching communication protocol (or transport) designed for WAN connectivity. Windows NT RAS supports connections based on the X.25 standard using Packet Assemblers/Disassemblers (PADs) and X.25 smart cards. In place of a PAD or smart card on RAS clients, you can use a modem and special dial-up X.25 carriers (such as Sprintnet and Infonet). For more information about RAS and X.25, see the RAS online help.

Figure 8.10 shows how a client connects to the RAS server through a dial-up PAD and the X.25 network.

Figure 8.10

Connection to RAS server through a dial-up PAD

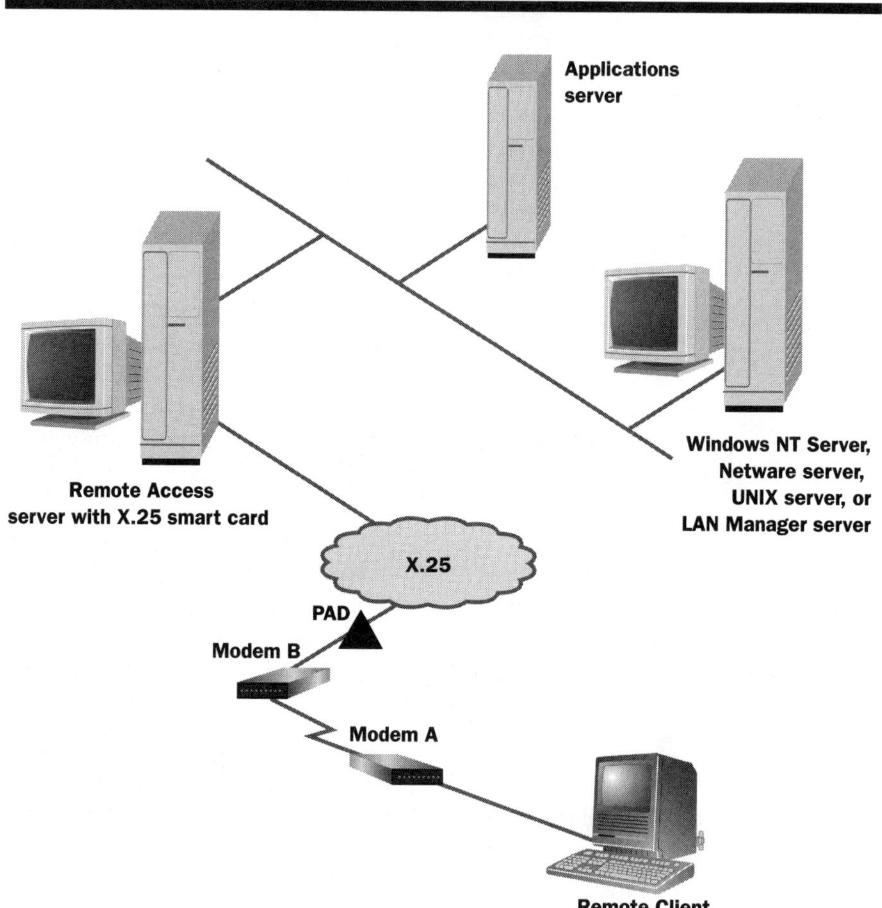

RS-232C Null Modem Connection

Suppose two or more networks are in the same location but are not physically connected. To access resources on both networks from one computer, use an RS-232C null modem. The client connects an RS-232C cable from a COM port to a COM port on the RAS server. RAS is used to create network access.

An RS-232C null modem can also be used as a substitute for a network card in a computer located physically near (less than 50 feet of cable) a RAS server.

Telephony API (TAPI) Connection

Windows NT Telephony API (TAPI) provides a standard way for communications applications to control telephony functions for data, fax, and voice calls. TAPI manages all signaling between a PC and a telephone network, including such basic functions as establishing, answering, and terminating calls. TAPI can also include additional functions such as hold, transfer, and conference call, found in PBXs, ISDN, and other phone systems.

The basic TAPI settings for a system are set up through the Dial-up Networking icon or when an TAPI-aware program is run for the first time. Any program that uses TAPI has access to the Dialing Properties dialog.

TAPI uses *calling cards* to create the sequence of numbers to be dialed for a particular card. The number is stored in scrambled form and will not be displayed once it is entered. This security feature protects the number from being stolen and used for fraudulent calls. Multiple calling cards may be defined.

Security for Remote Access Clients

A number of security configuration options together offer secure network access for remote clients. Windows NT logon and domain security are fundamental elements in that they provide encrypted authentication for users. Windows NT RAS implements a number of special security measures to validate remote client access to a network, including data encryption and callback. For yet more protection, RAS supports intermediary security hosts, to prevent unauthorized access to your LAN. In some ways, connecting to a network through RAS is more secure than accessing a network through a local connection.

The Windows NT operating environment, designed to meet the requirements of C-2 level (U.S. Department of Defense) security, provides the following checks:

- Access to system resources can be discretely controlled.
- All system access can be recorded and audited.
- Access to the system requires a password and leaves an audit trail.

Windows NT Server uses a *trusted domain, single-network logon* model. Users and groups of one domain can be granted access to resources in a trusting domain. After being authenticated, users carry access credentials that are presented whenever access to a resource is requested on the network. A Windows NT Server computer—provided it is secured physically—can be locked down using software.

This single-network logon model extends to RAS users. RAS access is granted from the pool of all Windows NT user accounts. An administrator grants the right to dial in to the network, and users then enter their domain login to connect via RAS. After being authenticated by RAS, users can access resources throughout the domain and in any trusted domains.

Finally, Windows NT provides the Event Viewer for auditing. All system, application, and security events are recorded to a central secure database which, with proper privileges, can be viewed from anywhere on the network. Attempts to violate system security, to start or stop services without authorization, or to gain access to protected resources are recorded in the Event Log and can be viewed by the administrator.

Auditing

RAS also generates audit trails of remote connections. With this feature, you can audit all remote access activity using Windows NT Server Event Viewer. You can also monitor servers and users with RAS Administrator With auditing enabled, RAS generates audit information on all remote connections, including processes such as authentication and logging on.

For more information about audits and logging, see Chapter 12.

Integrated Domain Security

Windows NT Server provides for enterprise-wide security using a trusted domain, single-network logon model. RAS, being fully integrated with NT, also uses the single-network logon model. The RAS server uses the same user-account database as the Windows NT-based computer. This allows easier administration because clients can log on with the same user accounts that they use at the office. They have the same privileges and permissions, as well. Clients must be authenticated by RAS before they are allowed to log on to Windows NT.

Centralized Servers

For the simplest administration, centralize all RAS servers in a single domain. Only one user account database will need to be maintained, and the system administrator will be able to monitor all RAS servers and users at one time. Because the domain is logical rather than physical, centralized servers can be in different locations and still be part of the same domain.

Distributed Servers

Smaller organizations that value flexibility and local control, or organizations that have no clear need for centralized security, might prefer a *distributed server system,* in which individual departments or workgroups set up and maintain their own RAS domains.

Encrypted Authentication and Logon Process

Authentication is an important concern for many corporations. This section shows how RAS helps ensure password privacy.

All authentication and logon information is encrypted when transmitted over RAS. It is also possible to configure Dial-Up Networking and RAS so that all data that passes between a client and server is encrypted. Table 8.1 defines various encryption methods and their uses.

Table 8.1

Security Levels and RAS Encryption Protocols

LEVEL OF SECURITY	TYPE OF ENCRYPTION	RAS ENCRYPTION PROTOCOL
High	One-way	CHAP, MD5
Medium	Two-way	SPAP
Low	Clear-text	PAP

RAS uses the Challenge Handshake Authentication Protocol (CHAP) to negotiate the most secure form of encrypted authentication supported by both server and client. CHAP uses a challenge/response mechanism with one-way encryption on the response. This protocol allows the RAS server to negotiate from the most secure to the least secure encryption mechanism, and it protects passwords transmitted in the process.

CHAP allows different types of encryption algorithms to be used. Specifically, RAS uses DES (the U.S. government standard) and RSA Security Inc.'s MD5. Microsoft RAS uses DES encryption when both the client and the server are using RAS. Windows NT 3.5 and later, Windows for Workgroups, and Windows 95 *always* negotiate DES-encrypted authentication when intercommunicating. When connecting to third-party remote access servers or client software, RAS can negotiate SPAP or cleartext authentication if the third-party product does not support encrypted authentication.

MD5, an encryption scheme used by various PPP vendors for encrypted authentication, can be negotiated by the Microsoft RAS client when connecting to other vendors' remote access servers. MD5 is not available in the RAS server.

The Shiva Password Authentication Protocol (SPAP) is a two-way (reversible) encryption mechanism employed by Shiva. Windows NT Workstation, when connecting to a Shiva LAN Rover, uses SPAP, as does a Shiva client when connecting to a Windows NT Server. This form of authentication is more secure than clear-text but less secure than CHAP.

Password Authentication Protocol (PAP) uses clear-text passwords and is the least sophisticated authentication protocol. It is typically negotiated if the remote workstation and server cannot negotiate a more secure form of validation.

NOTE. *The Microsoft RAS server has an option that prevents cleartext passwords from being negotiated. This option enables system administrators to enforce a high level of security.*

RAS Security

The security features of Remote Access Service include

- Password encryption
- Callback security
- Data encryption

Applying RAS security to clients involves three steps: setting up RAS in a Windows NT domain, granting RAS permission to Windows NT user accounts, and then setting RAS security on these accounts. This section explains Windows NT user accounts and approaches for implementing domain-based security for RAS. It is assumed you have a domain structure established. RAS servers can be centralized in a single domain or distributed among several domains.

Granting RAS Access and Permissions

After a RAS server is installed, you must specify who can dial in to it. To accomplish this, use the Remote Access Admin utility or User Manager to select a computer's or domain's user accounts. Then grant RAS permission to the user accounts, as shown in the following procedures. Once they have passed RAS authentication and connected to the LAN, remote users can access resources on the application server for which they have permission.

NOTE. *Remember, you grant or revoke remote access privileges on a user-by-user basis. So although RAS is running on a Windows NT Server computer, access to the network must be explicitly granted to each user who needs it. Remote users are subject to Windows NT Server security, just as they are at the office. In other words, they cannot do anything for which they lack sufficient privilege, nor can they access resources for which they do not have permission.*

You do not need to create user accounts just for RAS users. RAS servers apply the user accounts of any trusted domain or computer on the Windows NT network.

Setting Up RAS Security on Accounts

Remote users must be authenticated by a RAS server before they can access or generate traffic on the network. This authentication is a separate step from logging on to Windows NT. User passwords and the authentication procedure are encrypted when transmitted over phone lines.

You can restrict remote users' access to the network and to the RAS server. This allows an administrator to tightly control what information is available to remote users, and to limit their exposure in the event of a security breach.

Sets of protocols and adapters called *bindings* help you to dictate network access by remote users. You enable bindings to grant user access to resources, and disable the bindings to prevent access. Bindings are discussed in detail in the Windows NT 4.0 Resource Kits.

Even if the RAS server is connected to a network, you can restrict remote users to just the server they dial in to, as shown in Figure 8.11. For more information, see "Network Configuration" in the RAS online help.

Figure 8.11

Remote users restricted to the dial-in server

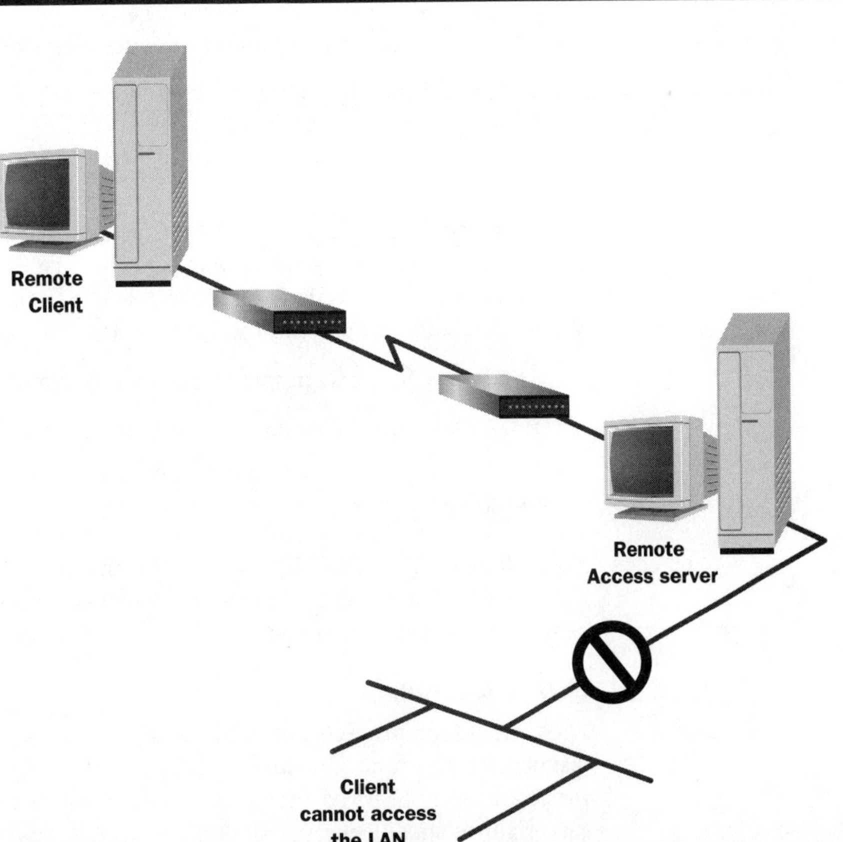

Callback Security

The RAS server can be configured to provide callbacks as a means of increasing security. When callback security is enabled, the server receives the call from the client computer, disconnects, and then calls the client back at either a preset phone number or a number that was provided during the initial call. This deploys another level of security by guaranteeing that the connection to the local network was made from a trusted site, such as a branch office. It also saves toll charges for the user. Until the user has been authenticated and called back, no data from the remote client or the RAS server are transferred.

You configure each user's callback privilege when granting remote access permission. In Remote Access Admin, the Remote Access Permissions dialog box contains three callback options: Preset To, Set By Caller, and No Callback.

Preset To For maximum security, select the Preset To callback option, and type in the number of the phone to which the user's modem is connected. Set this option for stationary remote computers, such as those in home offices. When the user's call reaches the RAS server

1. The server determines whether the username and password are correct.
2. If they are correct, the server responds with a message announcing that the user will be called back.
3. The server disconnects and calls the user back at the preset number.

Set By Caller Although the Set By Caller callback option is not really a security feature, it is useful for mobile users who call from various locations and phone numbers. It also minimizes telephone charges for these users. When the user's call reaches the RAS server, the following events occur:

1. The server first determines if the username and password are correct.
2. If they are, the Callback dialog box appears on the user's computer.
3. The user types the current callback number in the dialog and waits for the server to return the call.

No Callback The No Callback option is the default callback option. When the user account is configured for no callback, RAS establishes a connection as soon as the user's name and password are authenticated.

Data Encryption

Data encryption protects data and ensures secure dial-up communications. For installations where total security is required, the RAS administrator can set the RAS server to force encrypted communications. Users connecting to that server automatically encrypt all data sent. RAS provides data encryption in addition to password encryption (as described earlier in the section "Encrypted Authentication and Logon Process").

How Security Works at Connection

The following steps show what happens during a call from a client to a RAS server:

1. Through Dial-Up Networking, a client dials the RAS server.
2. The server sends a challenge to the client.
3. The client sends an encrypted response to the server.
4. The server checks the response against the user database.
5. If the account is valid, the server checks for Remote Access permission.
6. If Remote Access permission has been granted, the server connects the client.

If callback is enabled, the server calls the client back and repeats steps 2 through 6.

NOTE. *When using RAS in a domain environment, changes in Remote Access permission do not take effect immediately on all servers. It can take up to 15 minutes for replication of the change to be registered in other servers in the domain. If necessary, you can resynchronize the domain to ensure that a user with revoked permissions cannot gain access to the network before the change is automatically replicated.*

Intermediary Security Hosts

It is possible to add another level of security to a RAS configuration by connecting a third-party intermediary security host between the RAS client or clients and the RAS server or servers. A *security host* is a third-party authentication device that verifies whether a caller from a remote client is authorized to connect to the RAS server.

When an intermediary security host is used, clients must type a password or code to get past the security device before a connection is established with the RAS server. Security devices include

- Modem-pool switch
- Security host
- X.25 network

Figure 8.12 shows a sample configuration incorporating a modem pool and a security host.

Figure 8.12

Sample configuration with modem pool and security host

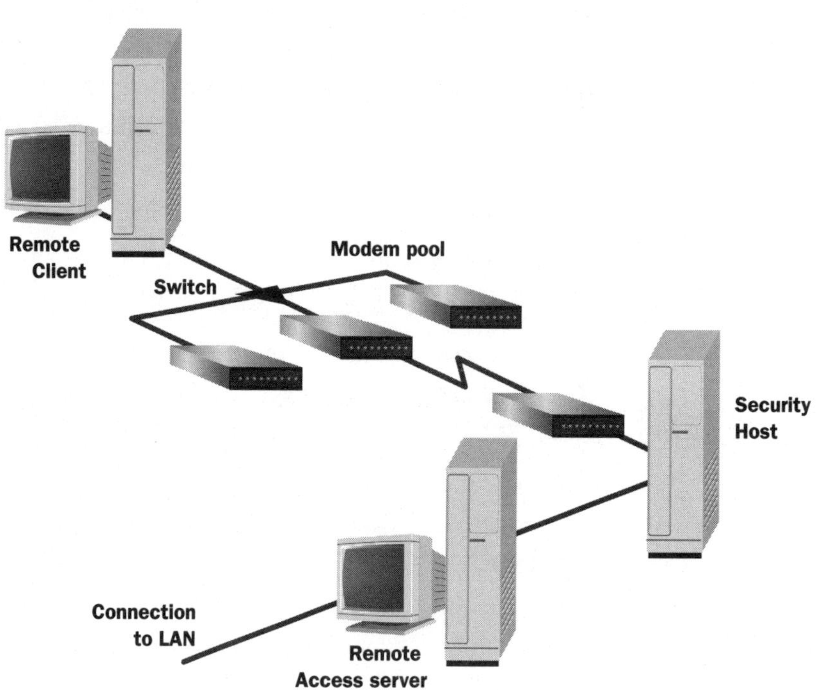

The security host, sitting between the remote user and the RAS server, generally provides an extra layer of security by requiring a hardware key of some sort in order to provide authentication. Verification that the remote user is in physical possession of the key takes place before access to the RAS server is granted. This open architecture allows customers to choose from a variety of security hosts to augment the security in RAS.

For example, one kind of system consists of two hardware devices: the security host and the security card. The security host is installed between the RAS server and its modem. The security card is a small unit that generates a different access number every minute. This number is synchronized with the same number calculated every minute in the security host. When connecting, the remote user sends the number on the security card to the host. If the number is correct, the security host connects the remote user with the RAS server.

Another kind of security host setup prompts the remote user to type in a username (which may or may not be the same as the RAS username) and a password (which differs from the RAS password).

The security host must be configured to allow the RAS server to initialize the modem before the security functions take effect. The RAS server must also be able to directly initialize the modem connected to the security host without security checks from that host. (The security host might interpret the RAS server's attempt to initialize the modem as an attempt to dial out.)

For more information on security hosts, refer to the Windows NT 4.0 Administration guides, Resource Kits, and the Security Hosts product documentation.

■ Summary

Security does not end with the LAN. WAN and dial-in access provide users and companies with attractive communication capabilities. For security administrators, remote communications can be frightening. NT provides ease of use and integrated security options to ease the administrative burden yet maintain reliability and flexibility for the user and the enterprise. In this chapter we discussed many of the RAS options and examples of their uses. We then covered security aspects relating to those options. By no means is this chapter an exhaustive coverage of RAS implementation, however; before you do implement RAS, we suggest you make good use of the Windows NT Resource Kits.

- *The Printing Process*
- *Configuring Security for Print Operations*
- *Connecting to and Creating Printers*

CHAPTER

9

Printer Services and Security

PRINTING FROM WINDOWS NT INVOLVES A COMBINATION OF components, configurations, and network options. Printers can very easily become the weak link in your security plan. No matter how secure your system is, without securing your various printers and setting permissions on who can use them and when, you could have night-shift employees printing signed payroll checks at their leisure.

This chapter explains how you, the system administrator, can control and secure the printers in your network. At the end of the chapter are some step-by-step instructions on how to establish "connected-to" printers and "created" printers. You'll also see how and where to select your security options.

The Printing Process

Having an understanding of the printing process will help you manage the printers in your network. Figure 9.1 illustrates the printing process on Windows NT and Windows 95 clients.

Figure 9.1

Printing process for Windows NT and 95 clients

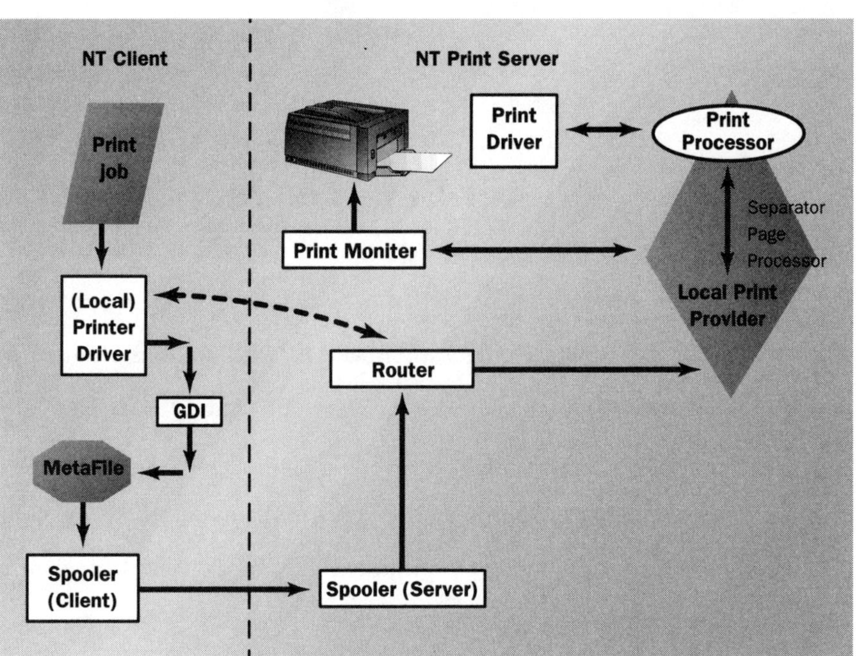

The printing process starts when a user tries to print a document, report, or other file. As shown in Figure 9.1, the user's computer will connect to a printer and receive, from the print server, a download of the print driver program into memory.

A copy of the appropriate print driver is downloaded to the client's memory every time a printer is added or a print job is sent to the print server. The Graphical Device Interface (GDI) works with the print driver to change the print job to a rendered MetaFile. Then the spooler on the client side makes a remote procedure call (RPC) to the print spooler on the server.

On the server side, the spooler receives the print job and passes to the router, which determines the format of the print job. The job is passed to the appropriate print processor via the local print provider. The print processor checks the print job format and changes the file to a format usable by the printing device; then the document is returned to the local print provider. Next, the separator page processor is called; it creates the separator page and attaches it to the beginning of the print job. The print monitor then routes the job to the printing device, which prints the file.

Print Servers

One computer in the network creates the printer and shares it with other computers, becoming the print server. Printer driver settings are controlled by the print server. The queue listing will appear on all connected machines, so that the users know where their print job is in the queue. Therefore, all error messages will appear on all the machines, so that problems such as paper jams, empty paper trays, or a printer off line can be fixed quickly. With this setup, you have only one auditing log for the printing events on a particular printing device.

NOTE. *For instructions on setting up auditing mechanisms for printers, you can jump to Chapter 12 "Auditing and Logging."*

Creating vs. Connecting to a Printer

How users connect to printers will be decided by the structure of your network. There are two methods of setting up printers in Windows NT: connecting to the printer, and creating the printer. Generally, you *create* printers on print servers, and *connect to* print servers from client machines. There are advantages and disadvantages to both options.

Connecting to a remote printer is easy and fast. If the client machine is connected to a remote printer, however, the client will have little control over that printer—just a front-end tool, the Printer dialog. It allows users to change only their own print jobs, unless they have additional permissions that allow them to control the printer remotely.

Creating a printer gives users more control over the print jobs. By creating a printer on the local machine, users are, in a sense, creating a mini-print server that forwards the print jobs to the print server. The users thus have full, independent control of their print jobs. This independent control also allows users to set printing security on a particular machine.

This chapter explains the procedure for both connecting to and creating printers, and how security is implemented.

Bidirectional Printing

Bidirectional printing requires a printer that understands how to use bidirectional input and output, has a special cable, and a compatible port on the computer. With bidirectional communication, your applications can examine the print device to ascertain its capabilities. The printer driver will automatically determine memory capacity, available fonts, and so on. The bidirectional print device itself can send messages to Windows NT giving detailed status reports on a variety of information, including maintenance needs, toner replacement, paper jams.

Although it is better, faster, and delivers more information, the bidirectional printer does not in and of itself effect printing security.

Forwarding Print Jobs

To forward a print job from one print server to another, Windows NT uses a null session. You enable job forwarding by editing the following Registry subkey:

```
\HKEY_LOCAL_MACHINE\SYSTEM\CurrentControlSet\Services\LanmanServer\Parameters
```

NullSessionShares is a value in this subkey. You need to create a new line with the printer's share name. The Spooler service must be stopped and restarted before the change is complete. (This process is described in the "Spooling" section.) The null session is then disabled, to prevent job forwarding, by default.

NOTE. *You must be an Administrator to access the Registry and be able to make any changes to it. See Chapter 10 for more information on the Registry.*

Taking Ownership of a Printer

By default, the user who installed the printer, owns the printer. The owner can enable other users to administer the printer by giving them Manage Documents or Full Control permissions. If you do not want the owner/user to have these ownership permissions on the printer (or if this person leaves the company), you can take ownership just as you can with a file or document.

As stated earlier, to take ownership you must be an Administrator, Print Operator, Server Operator, Power User, or member of a group that has been granted Full Control permissions on the printer.

Pausing, Resuming, Purging, and Redirecting

In the Printer window for a particular printer, the Printer menu contains options for Pause Printing and Purge Print Documents.

- Select Pause Printing to interrupt the printing of all documents to the print device. A check mark appears beside the option when it is enabled. To resume printing, click again on Pause Printing to disable it and remove the check mark.
- Purge Print Documents removes all print jobs currently queued to the print device. This is a helpful command in the event that the same document has been sent multiple times, or that the queue contains old jobs that are no longer needed.
- To redirect documents from the print device, select Properties in the Printer menu and click on Ports. You can only add an existing port. (Ports must be created and configured locally; this cannot be done with a connected-to printer.) Redirecting documents is helpful when a printer goes off line for repairs or is no longer a part of the network.

Anyone with Full Control over a printer, such as Administrators and Print Operators, can delete a document before it prints. Any document can be deleted from the print queue by its owner.

Configuring Security for Print Operations

Security can be set up on a printer when it is initially installed using the Add Printer Wizard, or on an existing printer using the printer's Properties dialog. Both the Add Printer Wizard and the Properties dialog give you the same options for setting permissions and access for the printers.

NOTE. *There are many ways you can limit users' access to printers and the Spool directory. To do this, you need Full Control Print permission. Administrators, Print Operators, Server Operators, and Power Users have this permission by default. This allows them to create and remove printers, share printers, and take ownership of a printer, among other things.*

Setting Properties

Printer properties can be configured in two places in Windows NT:

- The Add Printer Wizard, available by clicking Start and choosing Settings/Printers. We will see this in action later in the chapter.
- The Properties dialog for a particular printer (see Figure 9.2), reached by clicking that printer's icon in the Settings/Printers window. The Properties dialog for a printer consists of six tabs: General, Ports, Scheduling, Sharing, Security, and Device Settings. We will access these tabs and set some properties later in the chapter.

Figure 9.2

Properties dialog for an HP Color LaserJet

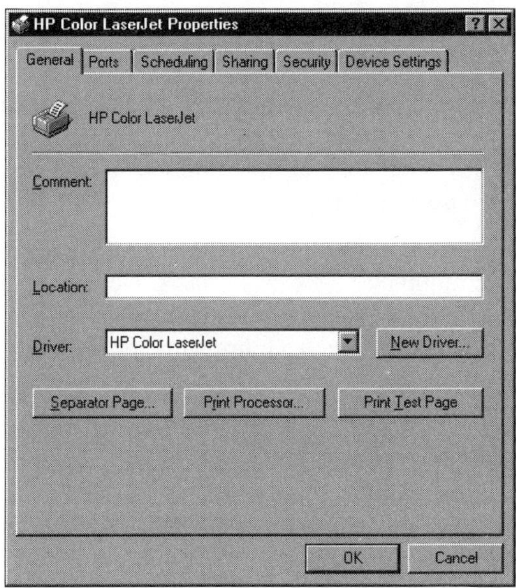

Establishing Permissions

To apply permissions on individual printers, use the Security tab in the Properties dialog. The most efficient way to set security permissions is to assign permission levels to different users and groups. For example, you could give all nonadministrative users in a department the Print level of permission, and all managers Full Control permission.

Printer permissions can be managed by the owner of the printer or by users who have Full Control permission. Four permissions are available for assignment to users and groups for printer access: No Access, Full Control, Manage Documents, Print. Users with the Manage Documents permissions can control all document settings on all documents: pause, resume, and delete. Users with Full Control permissions can do all that, as well as change document printing order; pause, resume, and purge printers; change printer properties and permissions; and delete printers. The owner of a document can perform Manage Documents operations on that document. No Access means just that; and Print permission allows the user/group merely to send print jobs to be printed, period.

Default Permissions

Windows NT Workstations have the following permissions set by default:

- Administrators—Full Control
- Owner—Manage Documents
- All users—Print

Windows NT Servers acting as a member server have the following default permissions:

- Creator Owner—Manage Documents
- Everyone—Print
- Local Administrators group—Full Control
- Local Power Users group—Full Control

And Windows NT Server as a domain controller has the following default permissions:

- Local Administrators group—Full Control
- Creator Owner—Manage Documents
- Everyone—Print
- Print Operators—Full Control
- Server Operators—Full Control

Controlling Print Jobs

You control a specific print job by setting the printing hours, priority, and person to be notified. You do this in the print job's Properties dialog, available from the Document menu (an example is shown in Figure 9.3).

- In the Notify box, type the Logon name of the user who needs to be notified that the job has been printed.
- In the Priority field, drag the slide bar to set a print priority between 1 and 99, with 99 carrying the highest priority. Your selection will be displayed on the Current Priority line.
- In the Schedule field, you can select No Time Restriction, or select Only From and then specify the timing for the printing of your document. You may want to schedule it for after-hours if it is long or highly graphical and will take a long time.

Figure 9.3

The Properties dialog for the "Introduction" document

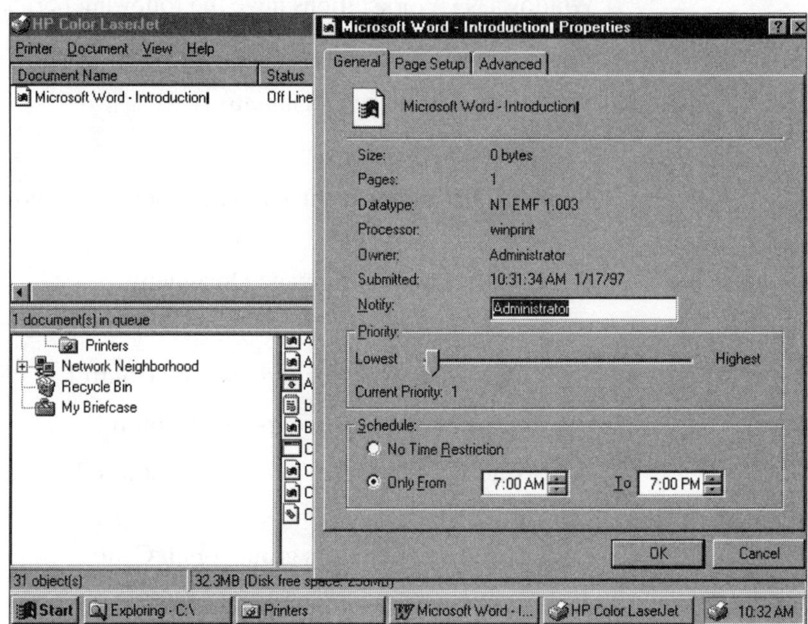

Spooling

By default, the Everyone group is given Change permission in the default Spool directory, %Winnt\System32\Spool\Printers. For spool file security, you will need to change the default Spool directory to an NTFS partition and a directory where permissions can be limited on an individual or group basis.

To change the default Spool location for a specific printer, you need to add a new Spool directory and assign that path to the printer to use. Open the Registry and find this line:

```
HKEY_LOCAL_MACHINE\SYSTEM\CurrentControlSet\Control\Print\printers\printername
```

Then edit the SpoolDirectory value to change it from the default location to the location of the new Spool directory. See Figure 9.4. The new SpoolDirectory location must already have been created. (You cannot spool to a root directory.)

When you've finished changing the value, you must stop and restart the Spooler Service for the change to take effect. To do this from Control Panel, Click the Services icon, and highlight the Spooler Service in the Services dialog (see Figure 9.5). Choose Stop, and then Start again after the Service has successfully stopped.

Figure 9.4

Registry location of the SpoolDirectory

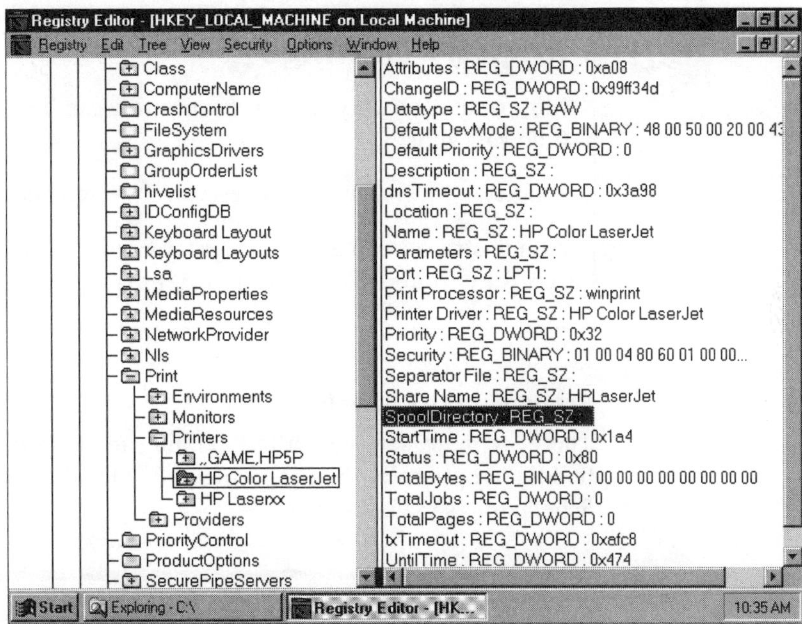

Figure 9.5

Restarting the Spooler Service after changing the Spool directory

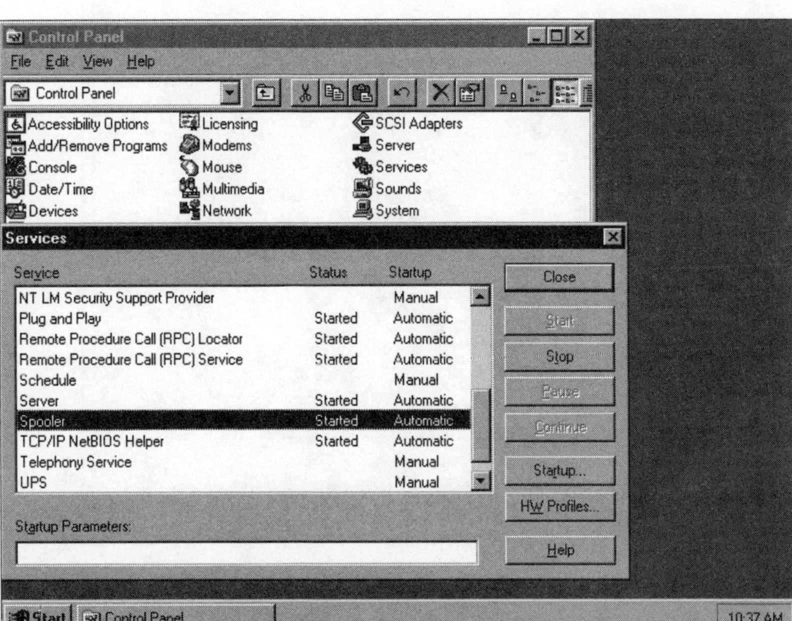

Registry Settings

Most of the Registry settings for printing can be found in the following subkey

```
HKEY_LOCAL_MACHINE\SYSTEM\CurrentControlSet\Control\Print
```

Administrators can use the Registry Editor to provide different access to printers. The Registry Editor is fully covered in Chapter 10.

Scheduling the Spooler

There are many settings for the spooling and operation of the printer. You'll find these options in the Properties dialog for the specific printer, under Scheduling (see Figure 9.6).

Figure 9.6

Scheduling the spooler for the HP Color LaserJet

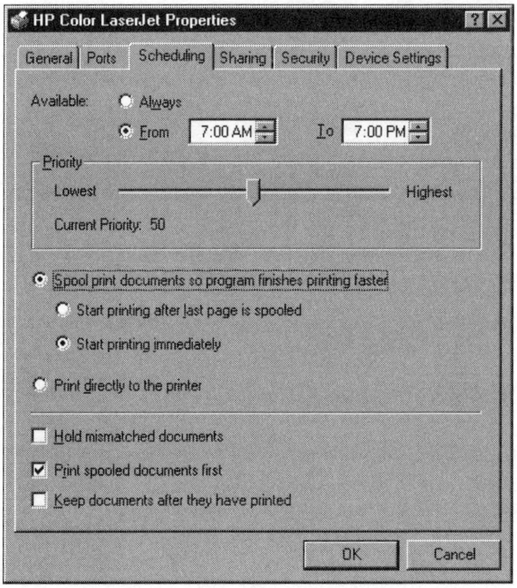

The first two settings in the Scheduling tab also appeared in the print job's Properties dialog. They control this printer's availability and its priority. Availability is by default set to Always, but you can limit the hours of operation. The Priority slide bar sets priority for the printer queues. As mentioned earlier for controlling print jobs, the choices are from 1 to 99, with 99 being the highest priority.

Let's take a look at other settings for print spooling that can help you control the printer's operation.

Spool Print Documents So Program Finishes Printing Faster The option to "Start printing after the last page is spooled" ensures that printing cannot begin until the entire job has been spooled. With this setting on, if a user sends a 500-page job that's full of graphics to the printer, it won't start printing when the first page arrives and clog up the printer for other users. Instead, the entire job must have arrived before the first page is printed, allowing other jobs to come in and jump ahead in line and get printed first.

The option to "Start printing immediately" is selected by default. With this setting, jobs start printing as soon as the first page of the job has been spooled.

Print Directly to the Printer When this option is enabled, print jobs bypass local spooling; this reduces the server's work as much as possible.

Hold Mismatched Documents This option allows Administrators to see if a person is sending print jobs to a "mismatched" printer. For example, if you create a file and it is rendered for PostScript printing, but it gets routed to the HP, Windows NT will recognize the mismatch. It will discard the job unless the Hold Mismatched Documents option is selected.

Print Spooled Documents First This option allows documents that are still spooling to go ahead and start printing as long as there are no other documents in the queue that are already spooled and ready to go.

Keep Documents After They Have Printed In a secure environment, you may need to keep track of all items printed. Enabling this option allows you to have more than a record of printing jobs; you have the actual jobs themselves.

Caution

This is a dangerous setting, in that print jobs quickly start taking up large chunks of disk space. Usually the spooler deletes jobs after printing, but with this setting turned on the spooler continues to store all jobs until administrative action is taken. Use this setting with caution and allocate plenty of disk space to the drive that will hold the Spool directory.

Connecting to and Creating Printers

This section is dedicated to walking you, step by step, through the setup of a *connected-to* or *created* printer. It will show you how and where to designate the security parameters needed for your company's printing operations.

Connecting to a Printer

The following steps are for connecting to a network printer—in this case, in a trusted domain.

1. In the Start menu, select Settings and then Printers.
2. Double-click on Add Printer. The Add Printer Wizard appears.
3. Select Network Printer Server to connect to a printer on another machine (see Figure 9.7). Click the Next button.

Figure 9.7

Using the Add Printer Wizard to connect to a printer on another machine

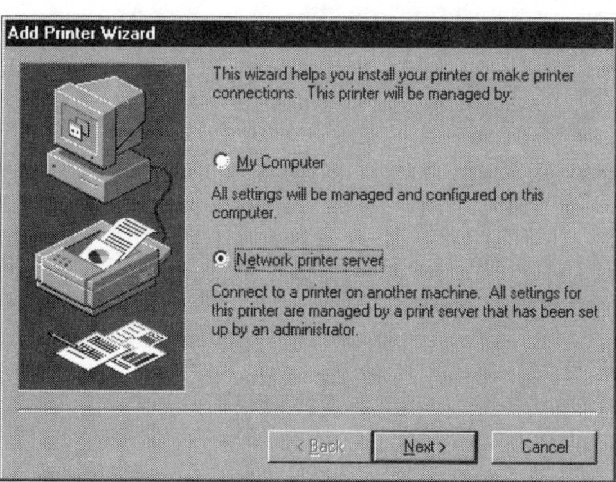

4. In the Connect to Printer dialog, highlight the printer you are going to connect to, and click OK. In Figure 9.8, we are connecting to a different domain, Test, and a Windows 95 server, Game, and the printer HP5P.
5. A message box appears, stating that the server does not have the correct drivers and asking if you want to install them. Click Yes, and your NT machine will prompt you to choose the type of printer you are connecting to and load the files for you.
6. Now the Wizard asks if you want to use this printer as the default. Select No and click Next.

Figure 9.8

Connecting to the HP5P printer on the Game server

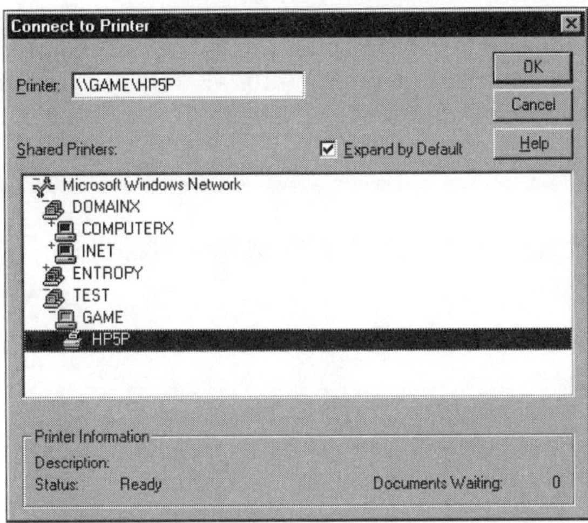

7. In the next window, you are notified that the printer has been successfully installed. Click Finish.
8. The new printer now is in the Printers window, as shown in Figure 9.9.

Figure 9.9

After connecting to the HP5P printer, it appears in the Printers window.

Connecting to a Print Server

Here are the steps for connecting to a print server in your domain. The beginning of the procedure is the same as the preceding one for "Connecting to a Printer"; only a few steps within the Add Printer Wizard are different.

1. In the Start menu, select Settings and then Printers.
2. Double-click on Add Printer to get the Add Printer Wizard window.

3. Select Network Printer Server to connect to a printer on another machine. Click the Next button.
4. In the Connect to Printer dialog, highlight a print server in your domain and click OK. In Figure 9.10, we have selected the HPLaserJet on our Member Server print server.

Figure 9.10

Connecting to a print server

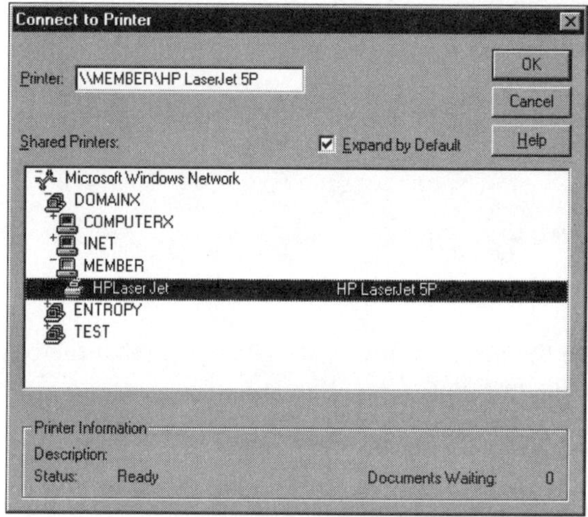

5. The next Printer Wizard dialog asks if you want this printer to be the default printer. Answer this question appropriately and click Next. In Figure 9.11, we've selected No.

Figure 9.11

Print server is not to be the default printer.

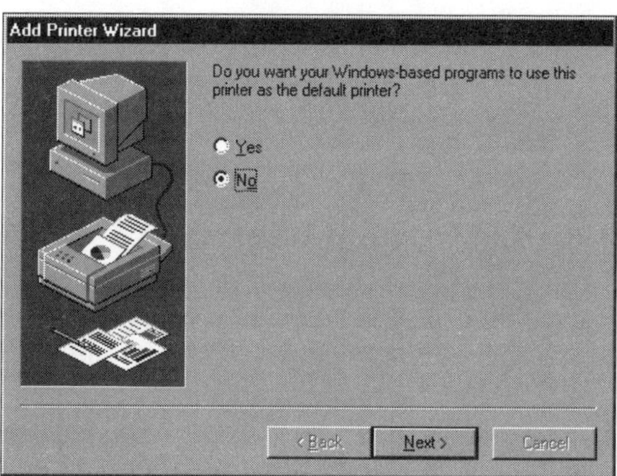

6. In the next window, click Finish. The new printer appears in the Printers window.

Creating a Printer

In this procedure you'll again be using the Add Printer Wizard, but the steps are different.

1. In the Start menu, select Settings and then Printers.
2. Double-click the Add Printer to get the Add Printer Wizard.
3. Select My Computer to manage all settings for this printer locally (see Figure 9.12). Click the Next button.

Figure 9.12

Creating a local printer

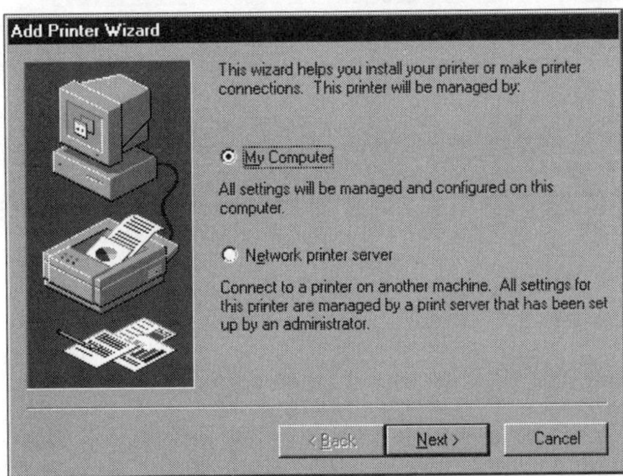

4. In the next Wizard window (see Figure 9.13), select LPT1 (or whichever port you want to use) as the port for this printer. Click Next.
5. In the next window, scroll through the Printers window and find the printer you are adding, and highlight it. Click Next. (In Figure 9.14, we have selected the HP Color LaserJet.)
6. When prompted, as shown Figure 9.15, click Yes to use this printer as your default. Click Next.
7. Note that the setting for By Default Not Shared is selected (see Figure 9.16); leave it as is for now. We'll get into printer sharing and other security properties later. Click Next.

Figure 9.13

Designating a port for the printer you are creating

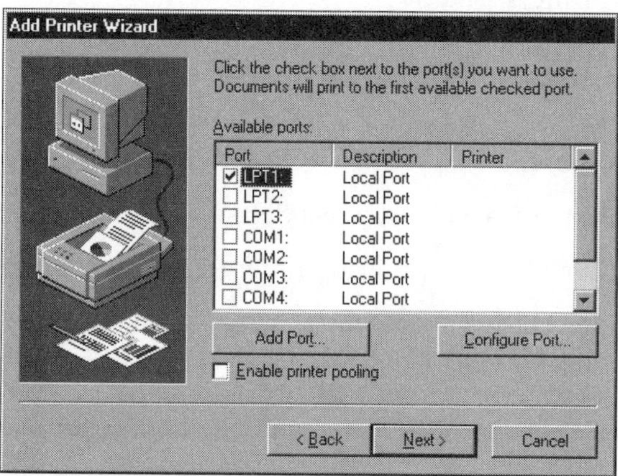

Figure 9.14

Selecting the printer you are creating

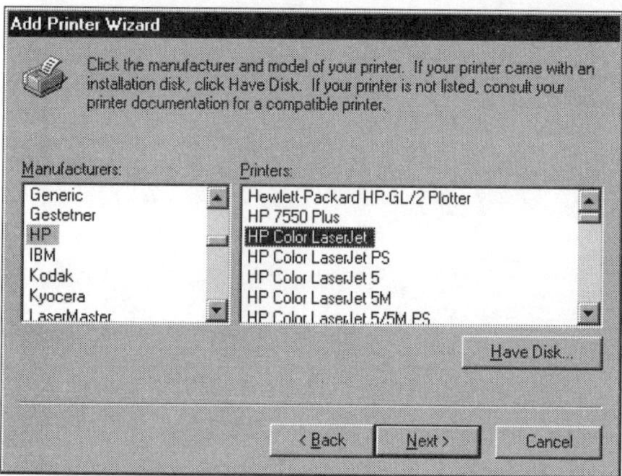

8. Want to print a test page? In this window (see Figure 9.17) you can elect to do it or not. (In ordinary circumstances, you would probably say Yes.) It's your call.
9. After you've printed any needed test pages, click Finish.
10. The Files Needed dialog appears (see Figure 9.18). Here you must indicate the location of the printer driver. Type the disk or CD drive letter. Manually install the printer driver disks or the Windows NT Server CD.
11. Click OK. As shown in Figure 9.19, now all three printers are in your Printers window: the client printer, the print server, and the printer you created.

Figure 9.15

Use this printer as the default.

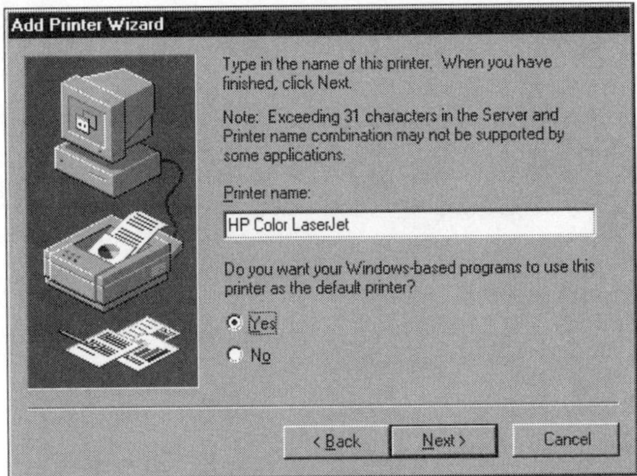

Figure 9.16

Setting sharing permissions in the Add Printer Wizard

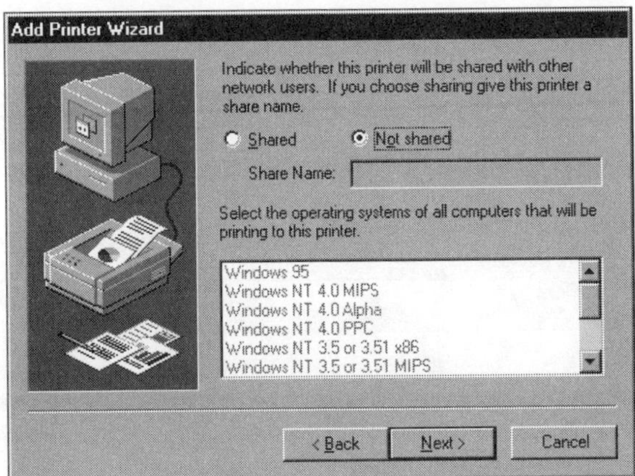

Printer Properties and Permissions

In this section we will examine each tab of a printer's Properties dialog and explain the security options you can apply to your printers.

1. Open the Printer you created. (In our previous example, it was the HP Color LaserJet.)
2. Pull down the Printer menu and choose Properties (see Figure 9.20).
3. From the General tab of the Properties dialog (shown earlier in Figure 9.2), you can set up separator pages, change the print processor, and print your test page.

Figure 9.17

Test page prompt

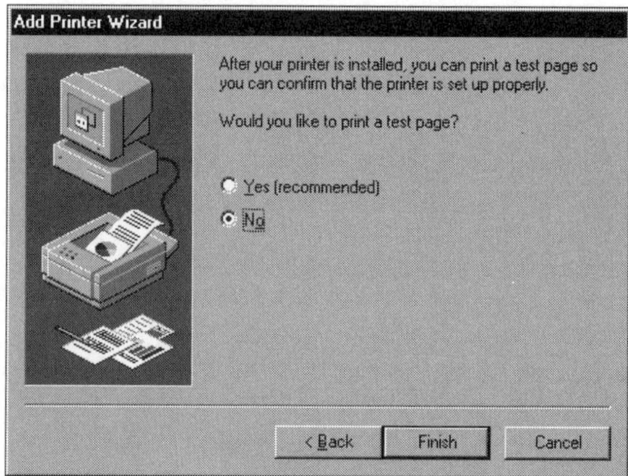

Figure 9.18

Specify the printer driver path

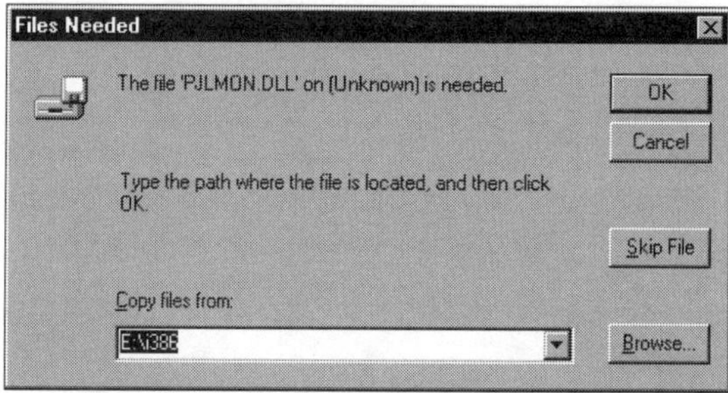

Figure 9.19

Printers window with the connected-to client printer and print server, and your created printer

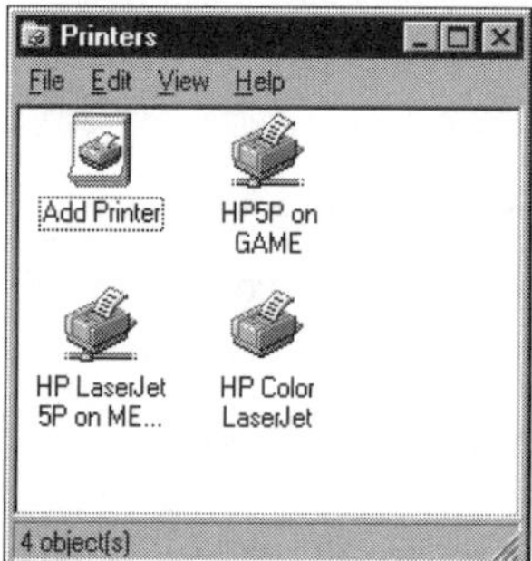

Figure 9.20

Setting properties for the HP Color LaserJet

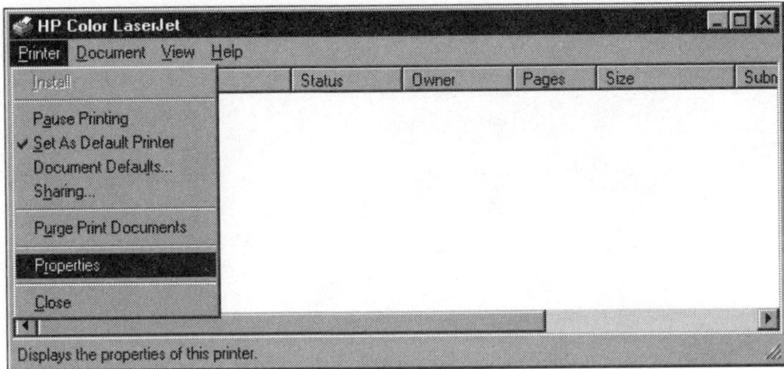

4. The Ports tab (see Figure 9.21) allows you to add, delete, and configure the port for this printer, and to enable bidirectional support and printer pooling if desired.

Figure 9.21

Ports tab of the printer's Properties dialog

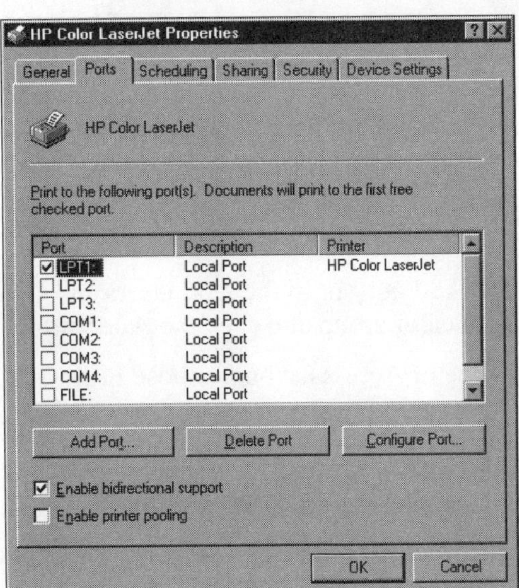

5. The Scheduling tab was shown earlier in Figure 9.6. in the print job's Properties dialog. Here in the printer's properties is where you can set hours of availability, the priority level, and the spooling options for the printer.

6. Next, on the Sharing tab, you can set up the share arrangement for this printer. In Figure 9.22, we are going to specify that our printer will be shared, under the name HPLaserJet.

Figure 9.22

Sharing the HP LaserJet printer

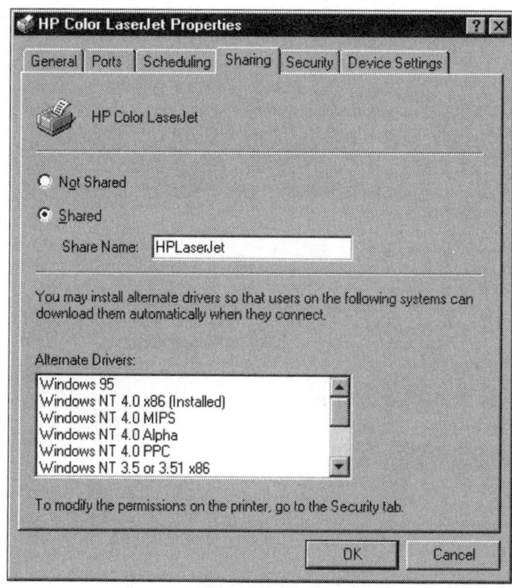

7. The next tab, for Security, will look familiar (see Figure 9.23). As with directories and files, we have to set the permissions, auditing requirements, and ownership for this printer. Start by clicking the Permissions button.
8. In the Printer Permissions dialog (see Figure 9.24), highlight Everyone and click the Remove button.
9. Click the Add button. In the Add Users and Groups dialog, highlight the HPColerJet group and click the Add button.
10. In the Type of Access list box, choose Print (see Figure 9.25).
11. Click OK twice to return to the Properties dialog.
12. The last tab, Device Settings, lets us set up the hardware structure of our printer. You can designate paper tray assignments, memory, fonts, and more.
13. Click OK when you're done, and your printer properties are set.

Redirecting a Printer

When you want to redirect print jobs to a different printer, follow these steps. This procedure is helpful in the event that a particular printer will be off line for any length of time, to do maintenance, toner changes, and so on.

Figure 9.23

Security tab for HP LaserJet

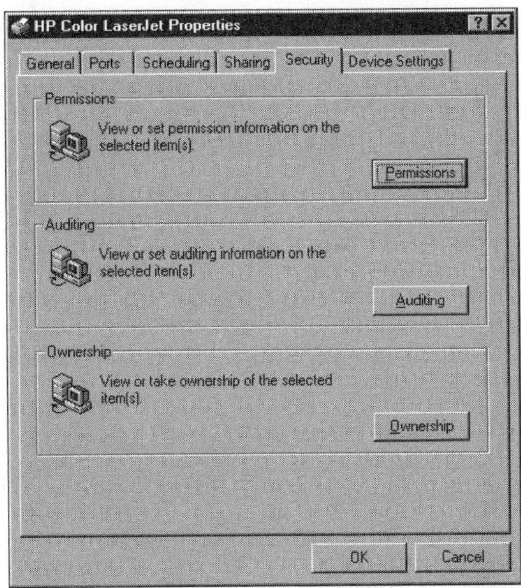

Figure 9.24

Setting Printer permissions

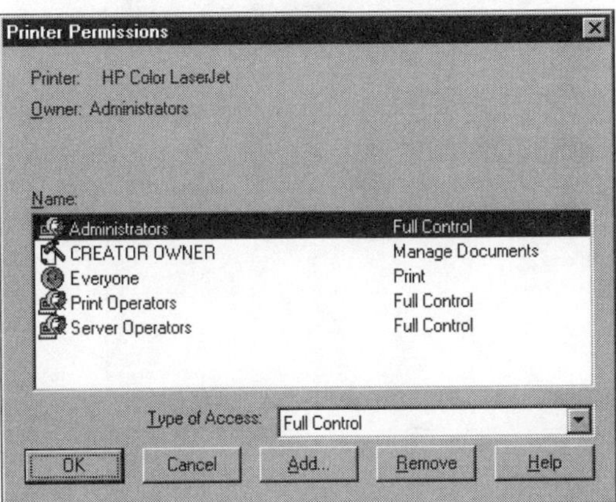

1. Starting from the Printers window, double-click to open the printer window for the HP Color LaserJet.
2. From the Printer menu, select Properties and open the Ports tab (see Figure 9.27).
3. Select the connected-to printer, in our case, the printer on Game, and click OK.

Figure 9.25

Adding the HPColorJet group, with Print access

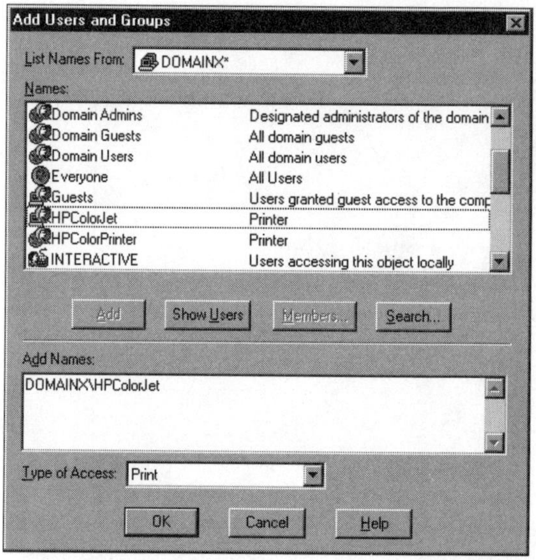

Add Users and Groups

List Names From: DOMAINX*

Names:

Domain Admins	Designated administrators of the domain
Domain Guests	All domain guests
Domain Users	All domain users
Everyone	All Users
Guests	Users granted guest access to the comp
HPColorJet	Printer
HPColorPrinter	Printer
INTERACTIVE	Users accessing this object locally

Add | Show Users | Members... | Search...

Add Names:

DOMAINX\HPColorJet

Type of Access: Print

OK | Cancel | Help

Figure 9.26

Device Settings for the HP Color LaserJet

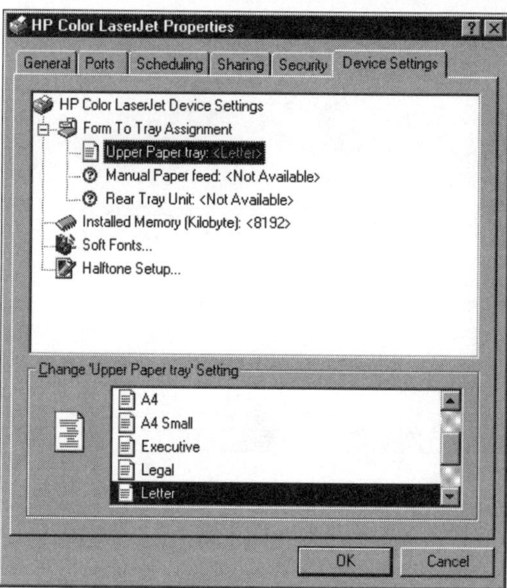

Figure 9.27

Ports tab, with new port selected for redirection of print jobs

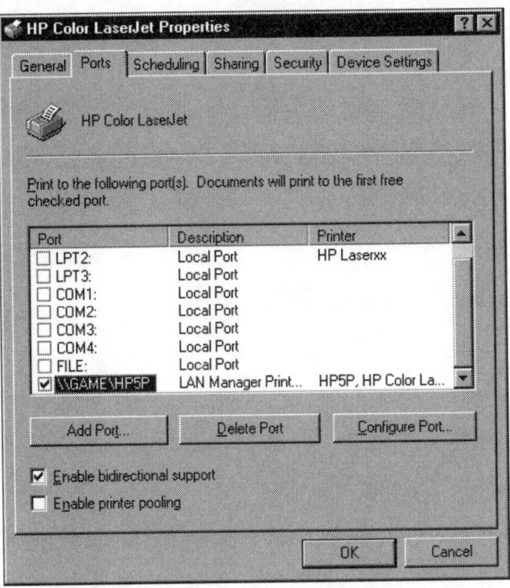

Helpful Tip

When you choose a printer on your own network, you'll want to reroute to a printer that is not a high-level security risk. Also, it should be physically located in a convenient area for your users.

The printer, HP Color LaserJet, has thus been redirected to the connected-to network printer, and all print jobs sent to the default HP Color LaserJet printer will be printed at the \\GAME\HP5P printer until you redirect again. HP Color LaserJet is still set as the default printer, so users using this printer will not have to change any print settings on their local machines.

Summary

Printer security, although not hard to implement, is an important part of overall network security. It is also one of the most overlooked security elements and therefore most open for violation and intrusion. Consider a work environment that has established a fairly high level of security. Permissions on files and folders are strictly controlled. Auditing is in place to ensure protection of sensitive data from unauthorized users. All it takes, however, is for one user to print a report or copy of a document and give it to anyone who's not supposed to see it—and there goes all that hard work. If you secure your documents, you need to secure your printers.

- *The Windows NT Registry*
- *Working with the Registry Editor*
- *The NT Registry Files*
- *Registry Security*
- *Backing Up the Registry*
- *Procedures for Changing the Registry*
- *Maximum Protection of the Registry*

CHAPTER

10

The NT Registry

IN WINDOWS NT, ALL CONFIGURATION INFORMATION IS HOUSED IN A central database called the Registry. The configuration data for previous Windows environments was handled by .INI, .SYS, and .COM files, all of which are now replaced by the Registry in NT. In this chapter we find out what the NT Registry is, how it works, and also what can be done to protect the integrity of the data it holds.

The Registry is a centralized database and therefore simply holds the configuration information that is entered by programs and administrators. Clearly, protection of Registry data is very important to NT security. In this chapter we will see how it protects itself, and learn some of the pitfalls to avoid to keep the Registry secure.

The Windows NT Registry

Every system has a central location for its configuration information, and Windows NT uses the Registry. The Registry is accessed through the Registry Editor (as well as Windows NT Diagnostics tools), System Policies, and Win32-based applications. It is the central database for all configuration information of a computer using NT. Access to this information could compromise security and must be strictly controlled and monitored. Furthermore, if invalid information is entered, it could cause the system to halt.

Though this chapter covers the Registry from a security perspective, it is important for administrators to understand the structure and controls of the Registry. An excellent source of detailed information regarding all issues involving the Registry and Registry Editor is the *Windows NT Workstation 4.0 Resource Kit* (Microsoft Press).

The Hierarchy

The NT Registry is organized in a hierarchical structure. There are four main areas, called *subtrees*, each with its own *key* (which can contain subkeys), *hive*, and *value entry.* Keys may also house subkeys. These structures will be explained as we work through this discussion.

Subtrees

Each subtree in the Registry is divided into *per-computer* and *per-user* databases. Per-computer data include information about the hardware and software installed on the computer in question. The information in the per-computer *key* is specific to the computer and remains the same no matter which user is logged on. Consider the example of a video driver with an ATI video card and the proper drivers; these elements will be the same no matter who logs on.

Per-user data are all the user-specific configuration settings, including desktop settings, network connections, bookmarks, and personal program groups. The per-user data is referred to as a *user profile.* Profiles can be stored on the local workstation or on a server. This location is determined by the administrator, as well as whether to allow users to change the profile information.

Table 10.1 describes each subtree in the Registry. Each of these subtrees begins with the prefix HKey_ to signal that the name is a handle. (Handles are values that are used by processes to identify resources; they are discussed in Chapter 6.) Registry subtrees or root keys can be used by programs.

Table 10.1

Registry Subtrees

SUBTREE ROOT KEY NAME	CONTENTS
HKey_Local_Machine	Information about the local computer system, including hardware and operating system. Examples are bus type, system memory, device drivers, and startup control data.
HKey_Classes_Root	Houses object linking and embedding (OLE) and file-class association information. This subtree is similar to the Registry in MS-DOS (reg.dat).
HKey_Current_User	User profile that belongs to the user currently logged on. Includes environmental variables, desktop settings, network connections, printers, and application preferences.
HKey_Users	All the active, loaded user profiles. Includes the HKey_Current_User, which always refers to a child of HKey_Users, as well as the default profile. Remote users accessing the server will not have profiles under this key on that server, because their profiles are loaded into the Registry on their own computers.
HKey_Current_Config	Current hardware configuration profile as chosen during the boot process.

Hives and Files

The subtree HKey_Local_Machine is divided into segments called *hives.* Each hive is a discrete body of keys, subkeys, and values that are rooted at the top of the Registry hierarchy. The five hives are SAM (Security Account Manager), Security, Software, System, and Hardware.

The first four of these hives are stored physically in the %SystemRoot%\system32\config folder. This folder contains two files for each hive: one file of the actual data and the other file containing a log of all changes to be made to the hive. For example, for the SAM hive, the two files would be SAM and SAM.log (see Table 10.2). The fifth hive, for hardware, is stored in physical RAM and is dynamically created upon boot-up by ntdetect.com.

The subtree HKey_Users has two hives associated with it: default and ntuser.dat. These hives are stored in %SystemRoot%\profiles directory.

The standard NT hives are listed in Table 10.2, along with their usual file and companion .log file.

Table 10.2

Standard NT Hives

REGISTRY HIVE	COMPANION FILES
HKey_Local_Machine\SAM	SAM and SAM.log
HKey_Local_Machine\Security	Security and security.log
HKey_Local_Machine\Software	Software and software.log
HKey_Local_Machine\System	System and system.log
HKey_Local_Machine\Hardware	In RAM
HKey_Current_User	NTUser.dat and NTUser.log
HKey_Users\Default	Default and default.log

Registry Key Value Entries

Value entries are information that may also be housed in a Registry key. Think of value entries as files, whereas keys are like directories.

There are three parts to a value entry: the name of the value, the data type of the value, and the value itself. The value itself can be data of any size. A value entry might look like this:

```
DependOnService: REG_MUTLI_SZ: Tcpip Ntbsys Streams
```

where *DependOnService* is the value name, *REG_MULTI_SZ* is the data type, and the *Tcpip Ntbsys Streams* is the actual value.

NOTE. *Registry values are case sensitive, and you must be careful when entering new values.*

Data Types

The data types available to the Registry begin with REG_ they are listed in Table 10.3. Data types can be as large as 1MB. Types from 0 to 0x7fffffff are reserved for use by the system and are not to be used by applications. The data entries from 0x80000000 to 0xffffffff are reserved for applications to use.

Registry Use by Windows NT

With a basic knowledge of how the Registry is designed and structured, your next step in securing Registry data is understanding how Windows NT uses the Registry.

The majority of NT's components, and the third-party applications designed for Windows NT, use the Registry's information to read and write

Table 10.3T

Data Types for Registry Value Entries

DATA TYPE	DEFINITION	EXAMPLE
REG_BINARY	Binary data, including that for most hardware components, are shown in the Registry in hexadecimal. Use NT Diagnostics (WINMSD.EXE) to display values in readable format.	Component Information : REG_BINARY : 00 01 B1 C0 40
REG_DWORD	Information shown as a number 4 bytes long. Device drivers and services parameters are often this type and can be viewed in binary, hexadecimal, or decimal using the Registry Editor.	Instructions : REG_DWORD : 0x1
REG_EXPAND_SZ	An expandable string, which would be text that houses a variable that is replaced when the string is called by an application.	File : REG_EXPAND_SZ : %SystemRoot%\ system32\config
REG_MULTI_SZ	A multiple string. Typically human-readable text in the form of lists or multiple values. Each entry is separated by null characters.	class : REG_MULTI_SZ : smc8000basic smc8000advanced
REG_SZ	A sequence of characters; human-readable.	Title : REG_SZ : Computer Browser

data. Key components using the Registry include Setup, NTDetect.com, the NT Kernel, device drivers, and administrative tools, as shown in Figure 10.1.

The term *Setup* in this case comprises both the Windows NT's Setup program and other setup programs, whether they are for new hardware or for software. Win32-based setup programs can read valuable information from the Registry during installation. When you install MS Office, for example, it searches the Registry to find out if you have already installed components of MS Office. It can also get information such as your name and company information. (In the past, users had to retype this information each time they loaded applications.) A setup program can also write information to the Registry, such as what the program has installed and where.

Windows NT's own Setup program does similar things when it installs hardware or software components for NT. One example is the data added when a network interface card (NIC) is installed, including IRQ, and I/O or Bus type, so that the machine can use the card.

NTDetect occurs during the boot process and again whenever the Setup program is run. NTDetect goes through and enumerates the hardware on the system and places this information in physical RAM. This is referred to as the *hardware hive,* as mentioned earlier in the chapter. With *x*86-based computers, this hardware detection is done by both NTDetect.com and NT kernel

Figure 10.1

Windows NT components using the Registry

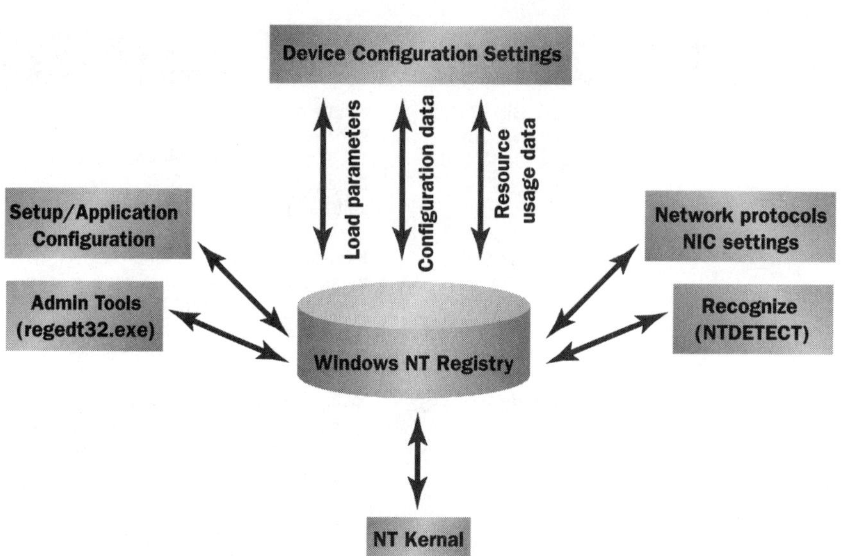

(ntoskrnl.exe). With RISC-based computers, the data are found using the ARC firmware.

The NT Kernel reads data from the Registry during start-up. This information includes the device drivers to load and in what order. The Kernel uses information obtained by NTDetect.com to load specific drivers. The types of driver loaded are the ones required for the boot process to complete, and the ones needed for the Kernel to initialize. The ntoskrnl.exe program also writes into the Registry information such as the Kernel version and NT build number.

Device drivers send and receive information from the Registry in the form of load parameters and configuration data. Information here is similar to that found in the DOS config.SYS file under the DEVICE= entries. System resources used by the device drivers, such as direct memory access (DMA) and hardware interrupts, are reported so that this data is updated to the Registry. This information can then be used by applications and device drivers to provide users with informed installation and configuration programs.

The Registry provides its own form of fault tolerance. It records changes in any key or value in transaction log (*.log) files. Windows NT uses these files to make sure the change is guaranteed. Any change made to the Registry either works or does not work: You will not have to deal with a change that was not fully implemented (that is, if half the data is old and half the data is new). A change may not work if the system stops unexpectedly because of power failure, hardware failure, or software problems and Windows NT isn't able to flush the cache buffer in time. For example, suppose you are setting up Microsoft Office10 and it sets a value for an entry, but the system shuts down while this change is being made. When the system restarts, the entry will have *either* the old value *or* the new value. Either way, you do not end up with partial changes.

Windows NT includes a variety of administrative tools that can affect the Registry and must be used by someone who has the proper administrative rights. These tools are generally placed in the Administrative Tools folder, but they may also be located in other folders at the discretion of the application you are installing.

The tools that can be used to view and modify Registry contents are summarized just below and discussed in detail later in this chapter.

- Registry Editor is used to directly edit and view the Registry. The Registry Editor has a read-only mode and also has an associated access control list (ACL).
- System Policy Editor presents Registry data in a GUI. This Editor is capable of changing any Registry information and is used for viewing certain predefined settings.
- Windows NT Diagnostics (WinMSD) allows viewing of Registry information in a graphical interface. The information presented is frequently viewed by users and administrators. It's easier to use WinMSD than to search the Registry.

Caution

Directly editing the Registry can cause problems, and you make these changes at your own risk. Because most of NT's configuration is received from the Registry, any person who modifies it needs to make sure that the changes are proper. The Registry is a database, a storage mechanism for data, and so it will accept anything you give it; this can lead to security problems. Check the entries properly before entering data. As you would for most system configuration changes, you should always back up critical information before making changes. Backing up the Registry will be discussed later in the chapter.

Working with the Registry Editor

The Registry Editor allows a user to view and modify the Registry by directly editing it. There are actually two Registry Editors with Windows NT 4.0: REGEDIT.EXE and REGEDT32.EXE. They are similar, except that REGEDIT.EXE has an Explorer look and feel. It also has an enhanced search engine. But the REGEDIT.EXE editor does not have the capability of changing security permissions. For our discussion here, then, we will use REGEDT32.EXE. See Figure 10.2.

Figure 10.2

Registry Editor (REGEDT32.EXE)

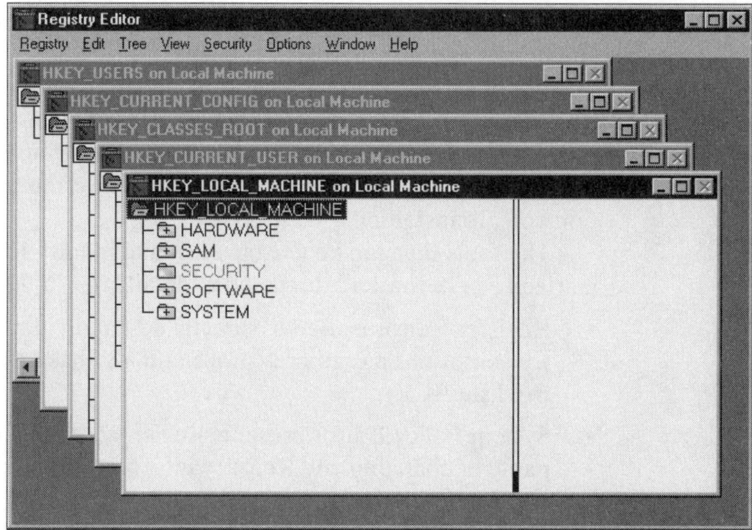

It is always much safer to make changes to the Registry using the designated Control Panel dialog than it is using any other editing tool. These dialogs, available by clicking the icons in the Control Panel for Network, Devices, Desktop, Display, Services, and so forth have built-in safeguards that prevent damage to the system because of Registry modifications. The Registry Editor is typically used with certain configuration settings that cannot be set through a graphical tool. Remember, you always use Registry Editor at your own risk.

The Registry Editor (in this case, REGEDT32.EXE) is not located in any default folder. You'll find it in the \%YourSystemRoot%\system32 directory.

To run the Registry Editor, click Start, choose Run, and type **regedt32.exe.**

Helpful Tip

You could also add the Registry Editor to the Administrator Tools group or create a shortcut on the desktop.

Viewing of the Registry

The five Registry subtrees are the first windows presented by Registry Editor when it starts, as shown in Figure 10.2. The hierarchical directory structure of the Registry is similar to that of NT Explorer.

Before any changes can be made using Registry Editor, the user's access token is checked immediately to see what permissions have been granted to the user, and which Registry entries the user can modify. By default, common users can only view information in the Registry. Only administrators and the Windows NT System itself can make changes to the Registry directly. This list of users (ACL) can be altered at the request of any administrator.

The window for each subtree is divided into two panes, the left pane containing the keys, and the right pane holding the value entries associated with the keys. The panes for HKey_Local_Machine are shown in Figure 10.3.

Figure 10.3

Registry subtree panes

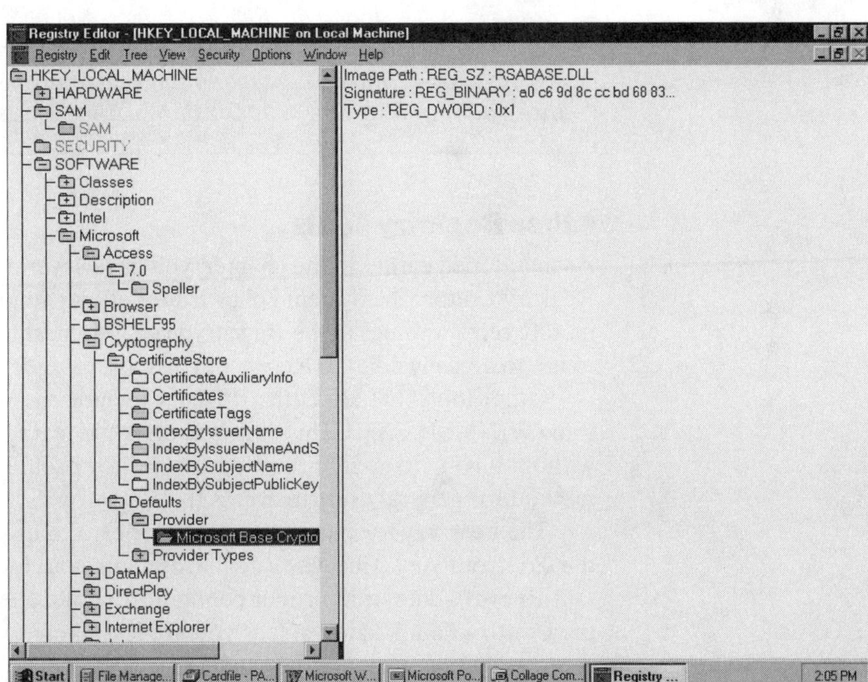

As stated, there are actually two versions of Registry Editor available on NT. REGEDT32.EXE works only on NT systems; REGEDIT.EXE will work on NT *and* either Windows 3.1 or 3.11 or Windows 95, depending on what NT detected during installation.

The NT version is found in the \%YourSystemRoot%\system32 folder. The Windows 3.*x* and 95 Registry Editor is located in the \%YourSystem-Root%\ folder. The version of Registry Editor installed depends on whether the NT Setup program detects either Windows 3.*x* or 95 present on the system where NT is being installed. If Windows 3.*x* is found in the same directory where the NT installation/upgrade is being placed, then the 3.*x* version of Registry Editor is loaded in. If not, then the Windows 95 version of Registry Editor is loaded in by default.

To simplify matters, it is advised that you use the 32-bit version of Registry Editor that comes standard for NT 4.0. The Windows 95 version can be used to perform advanced searches on the Registry, such as searches on data or value fields. The Windows 3.*x* version is simply included for backward compatibility with Windows 3.*x* so that 16-bit applications can read/write to reg.dat.

Caution

One word of warning: Do not make changes to the Registry with the Windows 95 version of the Registry Editor. Not all data types are supported by this Editor version, including Reg_Expand_SZ and Reg_Multi_SZ, and that limitation can lead to invalid entries. In addition, the Windows 95 version does not allow editing of security on any keys.

Other Registry Tools

As mentioned earlier in the chapter, you have several alternatives to using the Registry Editor. The System Policy Editor allows administrators to edit and modify certain values in the Registry via a graphical tool. This is the best tool to use to actually edit the Registry in an easy-to-understand interface.

Other tools that affect the Registry include the Windows NT Diagnostics tool (WINMSD.EXE). This allows users to view Registry settings and values without having to go into the Registry Editor itself. This is a much safer method for general users to access the Registry.

The best way to change Registry entries is to use the appropriate icon in the Control Panel. This way safeguards against accidental deletion of important Registry data or improper configuration of a Registry value entry. Using the Control Panel dialog means you are less likely to do something that causes a conflict with another value entry.

System Policy Editor

There are two components of the Registry that can be manipulated using the System Policy Editor: the local computer settings (under HKey_Local_Machine) and the user's profile (NTUser.dat). Each of these can be independently manipulated.

The System Policy Editor is the NT tool for creating and controlling a System Policy, which is a way to manage user work environments and events, as well as enforce the system's configuration settings. System Policies are supported under both Windows NT 4.0 and Windows 95; however, each environment implements Policies in a different file. (Creation and maintenance of system policies will be discussed in detail in Chapter 11.)

The System Policy Editor cannot be used to set binary values in the Registry. Hardware component information is often stored as binary data. If you view a Windows NT Registry using REGEDT32.EXE, you will see binary value entries marked with data type REG_BINARY. (See Figure 10.3 for an example.)

You can use the System Policy Editor to edit the HKey_Current_User portions of the interface. If you need to access a different part of the Registry, such as HKey_Dyn_Data, use the Registry Editor.

The System Policy Editor can edit only entries that are predefined through administrative templates. These templates provide for the Editor the exact Registry paths and possible values and their limits. There are three default templates supplied with Windows NT 4.0, stored in the %SystemRoot%\System32\Inf directory. These templates are as follows:

- The Windows.adm file presents possible Windows 95 Registry entries. They are specific to Windows 95.
- The Winnt.adm file presents possible Windows NT Registry entries. They are specific to Windows NT.
- The common.adm file contains Registry entries common to Windows 95 and Windows NT.

For more information on *.adm files, see Chapter 11.

Windows NT Diagnostics

The Windows NT Diagnostics (WINMSD.EXE) utility is a graphical tool for viewing and troubleshooting the Registry (see Figure 10.4). This tool provides a safe way to view the Registry data, and the information is centralized and easier to view.

The tabs allow users and administrators to access and work with the following types of information:

- Current version, build number, and hardware settings
- Information on disk drives and partitions
- NT services and their state
- The computer's memory usage
- Network settings and statistics
- Environmental settings

Figure 10.4

Windows NT Diagnostics

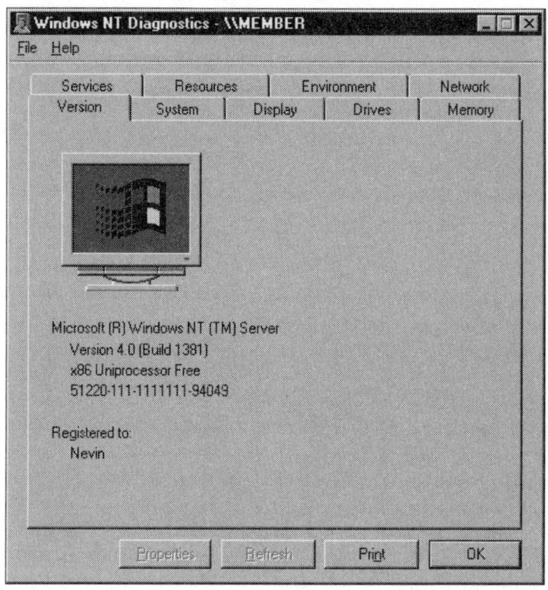

The Diagnostics utility has been improved in Windows NT 4.0; it is much more intuitive and easier to read than the tool provided in NT 3.51. Diagnostics under NT 4.0 can also be used to view remote registries; this is a new feature.

To run Windows NT Diagnostics, click Start and choose Programs, and select Administrative Tools (Common). Then double-click Windows NT Diagnostics.

Although you cannot make changes to the Registry using NT Diagnostics, you can easily view the results of changes made using the Control Panel or the various Registry editors. There is also an option to print the contents of the Registry to a file, the Clipboard, or a specific printer, which can be helpful in keeping track of each system's hardware and settings.

Registry Editing Tools from the Server Resource Kit

The following tools are included in the Windows NT 4.0 Server Resource Kit. For documentation on command-line parameters and usage, see the rktools.hlp file in the CD-ROM included with the products. Table 10.4 is a summary.

Table 10.4

NT 4.0 Resource Kit Tools for Working with the Registry

UTILITY NAME	PROGRAM	DESCRIPTION
Delete Service	delsrv.exe	Command-line utility that unregisters a service with the Service Control Manager.
Registry Change	regchg.exe	Command-line utility that adds or changes Registry values on the local or a remote computer.
Registry Delete	regdel.exe	Command-line and batch utility that removes Registry keys remotely or on the local computer. Can be used in batch files to delete Registry settings on multiple servers.
Registry Read	regread.exe	Command-line utility that reads the Registry, parses out values, and outputs them to the screen.
Registry Save	regsave.exe	Command-line utility that saves a Registry key to a file.
Registry Secure	regsec.exe	Command-line utility that removes the Everyone group from a Registry key.
Remote Registry Change	rregchg.exe	Command-line and batch utility that creates or changes Registry settings on a remote computer (across networks).
Restore Key	restkey.exe	Command-line utility that restores a Registry key from a file.
Security Add	secadd.exe	Command-line utility that adds user permissions to a Registry key.
Registry Backup	regback.exe	Command-line utility that creates backups of Registry files.
Registry Entries	regentry.hlp	Windows Help file that documents Windows NT Registry entries.
Registry Init	regini.exe	Command-line utility that makes Registry changes by using script files.
Registry Restore	regrest.exe	Command-line utility that restores Registry hives that were saved.
Scan Registry	scanreg.exe	Win32 character-based/command-line "Registry GREP" that searches for any string in key names, value names, and/or value data in local or remote Registry's keys in both Windows NT and Windows 95.
Compare Registry	compreg.exe	Win32 character-based command-line "Registry DIFF" that compares any two local and/or remote Registry keys in both Windows NT and Windows 95.
Registry Key Editor	regkey.exe	Windows-based tool that sets new Registry logon and FAT file system settings without actually editing the Registry.

The NT Registry Files

There are a substantial number of files used by the Registry, including the .INI and .SYS file types. Each type of file has its own characteristics, but the most challenging in terms of security maintenance are the .INI files, which are profiled in depth in this section. By understanding their behavior in the NT Registry, you will be better prepared to face any threats you may encounter.

Initialization (.INI) Files

The .INI files used in MS-DOS are very similar to the Registry and its database of keys and value entries. The keys in the Registry are similar to the bracketed headings of the DOS .INI files. The Registry's value entries are comparable to the .INI file headings.

Where the similarity ends is that the NT Registry can store subkeys for all its keys; DOS, however, was unable to support nested headings in its .INI files. Another difference is that Registry values may contain executable code, whereas .INI files have only simple strings representing values. Lastly, the .INI files are unable to contain individual user preferences, but the NT Registry can.

Although the Registry does replace the DOS .INI files, some .INI files can be found in NT (in the NT system folder). Any 16-bit applications being run on NT need to also read and write .INI file initialization data that may have been previously kept in the WIN.INI or SYSTEM.INI files.

Mapping of .INI Files to the Registry

If NT 4.0 is installed as an upgrade on top of Windows 3.1, then all the past settings from the numerous initialization files, such as CONTROL.INI, PROGMAN.INI, SYSTEM.INI, WIN.INI, and WINFILE.INI, will be copied to the Registry. To find these Windows .INI files in the Registry, look for them under the subkey HKey_Local_Machine with the path

```
SOFTWARE\Microsoft\Windows NT\CurrentVersion\IniFileMapping
```

Any 16-bit executables loaded into NT have a setup routine that can read/write configuration information to both the WIN.INI and SYSTEM.INI files. The entries in the Registry for these applications cannot be updated, because 16-bit programs do not have the ability to update the Registry, to which both WIN.INI and SYSTEM.INI have migrated. To solve this problem, basic versions of the WIN.INI, SYSTEM.INI, and WINFILE.INI files are kept by NT in the \%YourSystemRoot%\ folder.

The only way a Windows-based application can place its data into the Registry is if it uses the Registry's APIs to write to the WIN.INI, SYSTEM.INI, or any of the other sections found in the IniFileMapping key in the Registry. If the application cannot use the Registry's APIs, then its information is not saved in the Registry but rather in the appropriate .INI file.

The system finds data concerning mapping information in the HKey_Local_Machine\Software key by locating the initialization file with this filename format:

```
filename.extension
```

If the system finds the .INI file in the HKey_Local_Machine\Software key, the next step for the system is to search for the application name connected to the .INI file and a variable name, all located under the mapped key. If necessary, the system will continue through the Registry keys looking up value entries that are the designated variable name. When no mapping data for the application or filename can be located in the Registry, the system locates an .INI file for the application and reads and writes the file contents to the key.

Various symbols are used in the IniFileMapping key to accomplish different tasks in the mapping process. These symbols, listed in Table 10.5, function in both the IniFileMapping key and other areas of the Registry, which are discussed in upcoming next sections.

Table 10.5

IniFileMapping Keys' Special Symbols

SYMBOL	ACTION
!	Forces all writes to go to both the Registry and to the .INI file on disk.
#	Makes the Registry value be set to the value in the Windows 3.1 .INI file whenever a new user logs on for the first time after setup, if NT is installed over Windows 3.1.
@	Disallows any reads to the .INI file on the disk if the requested data are not found in the Registry.
USR	Represents HKey_Current_User, where the text after the prefix is relative to that key.
SYS	Represents HKey_Local_Machine\Software, where the text after the prefix is relative to that key.

The Win.INI Registry Settings

Finding the Registry information equivalent to that of the WIN.INI file can be challenging. To help you, Table 10.6 lists the WIN.INI setting, the path it has in the Registry, and a brief description of that setting.

NOTE. *Remember—The individual dialogs accessed through the Control Panel do control a lot of the system's configuration data. These individual dialogs help you interact with and modify the Registry much more safely than direct modification of the Registry.*

Table 10.6

Win.INI Settings and Their Registry Equivalents

WIN.INI SETTING	REGISTRY PATH	DEFINITION
[colors]	#USR\Control Panel\ Colors	Defines display colors as set by Control Panel/Display.
[compatibility]	#SYS...\Compatibility	N/A
[desktop]	#USR\Control Panel\ Desktop	Specifies desktop appearance as set with Control Panel/ Display.
[embedding]	#SYS...\Embedding	Lists server objects used in object linking and embedding (OLE), which are created during software startup.
[extensions]	#USR...\Extensions	Associates types of files with applications as set by double-clicking the program in NT Explorer.
[fonts] and [fontSubstitutes]	#SYS...\Fonts and #SYS...\FontSubstitutes	Describes screen font files loaded by Windows as set using Control Panel/ Display.
[intl]	#USR\Control Panel\ International	Describes items for languages and locales as set using Control Panel/ Regional Settings.
[mci extensions]	SYS...\MCI Extensions	Associates file types with Media Control Interface (MCI) devices as set by double-clicking the file in NT Explorer.
[network]	USR...\Network\ Persistent Connections and network printers in HKey_Local_Machine\ SYSTEM\Control\Print	Describes network printer port settings as set using under the Printer settings; and persistent network connections as set using Network Drive Connections.
[ports]	SYS...\Ports	Lists all available printer and communication ports as set by using the Control Panel/Ports.
[printerPorts] and [devices]	SYS...\PrinterPorts and SYS...\Devices	Lists active and inactive output devices to be accessed by Windows as set using the Printer settings.
[sounds]	#USR\Control Panel\ Sounds	Lists the sound files assigned to system events as set using Control Panel/Sounds.
[TrueType]	#USR...\TrueType	Describes options for using TrueType fonts as set using the Control Panel/Fonts.

Table 10.6 (Continued)

Win.INI Settings and Their Registry Equivalents

WIN.INI SETTING	REGISTRY PATH	DEFINITION
[Windows Help]	USR\Software\Microsoft\Windows Help	Lists settings for Help window as set using mouse or menus in any Help window.
[Windows]	#SYS...\Winlogon	Specifies Windows environment and user startup options as set using Control Panel/Display, Keyboard, and Mouse.

The SYSTEM.INI Registry Settings

Similar to Table 10.6 in the preceding section, Table 10.7 contains the Registry paths for SYSTEM.INI settings equivalents.

When NT is installed, the entries from a Windows for MS-DOS SYSTEM.INI file are preserved along the following path:

```
HKey_Local_Machine\Software\Microsoft\Windows NT\CurrentVersion\WOW
```

Table 10.7

SYSTEM.INI Settings and Their Registry Equivalents

SYSTEM.INI SETTING	REGISTRY PATH	DEFINITION
[boot] and [boot description]	#SYS...\WOW\Boot and \Boot description, replaced by CurrentControlSet\Control	Lists drivers and Windows components as set using Control Panel/System.
[drivers]	Replaced by #SYS...\Drivers32	Houses a list of aliases assigned to installable driver files as set using Control Panel/ Multimedia and /Devices.
[keyboard]	#SYS...\WOW\Keyboard and #USR\Keyboard Layout	Houses data about the keyboard as set by Control Panel/Regional Settings or identified by the Hardware Detector.
[mci] and [mci32]	Replaced by #SYS... MCI and \MCI32 and #SYS...\Drivers.desc	Lists all Media Control Interface (MCI) drivers as set by Control Panel/Multimedia.
[NonWindows App]	#SYS...\WOW\NonWindowsApp	Contains information used by non-Windows applications as defined in PIFs for specific applications, or in config.nt.
[standard]	Standard in #SYS...\WOW	Contains data used by Windows for MS-DOS in Standard and 386 Enhanced mode. All memory management is handled automatically by Windows NT.

Miscellaneous Initialization Files and Registry Settings

There are three other initialization files—CONTROL.INI, PROGMAN.INI, and WINFILE.INI—that have Registry equivalents, and these are defined in Table 10.8.

Table 10.8

Miscellaneous Initialization File and Registry Equivalents

MISCELLANEOUS .INI SETTING	REGISTRY PATH	DEFINITION
control.INI [Current], [Color Schemes], [Custom Colors]	Color Schemes, Current, and Custom Colors subkeys are in #USR\Control Panel	Describes the color schemes and custom colors as set using Control Panel/Display.
control.INI [Patterns] and [Screen Saver]	Patterns and Screen Saver x subkeys I n#USR\Control Panel	Describes elements of desktop appearance and behavior as set using Control Panel/Display.
control.INI [MMCPL], [Drivers.Desc], [Userinstallable.drivers]	#USR\Control Panel\ MMCPL and #SYS...\ Drivers.Desc and #SYS...\ Userinstallable.drivers	Houses values for installable drivers and devices used for multimedia as set using Control Panel/Multimedia.
progman.INI [groups], [restrictions], [settings]	Groups, Restrictions, and Settings subkeys in #USR...\Program Manager	Describes window appearance, folders and icons in folders, and restrictions on Taskbar operations. Restrictions are set with User Manager for Domains, which can do this on the server only.
winfile.INI [settings]	#USR...\File Manager	Describes the appearance and behavior of items in NT Explorer.

MS-DOS Configuration Files

MS-DOS applications run in a process called *virtual DOS machine* (VDM). Windows 3.*x* applications run in a modified VDM called *Win16 on Win32* (WOW). The WOW loads up a copy of Windows 3.*x* to run these programs. You can think of VDM/WOW as a "separate" computer with its own resources running within Windows NT. The brief explanation of how NT does this is that it translates the 16-bit program's application calls using the Win16 VDM, and then runs the program on *x*86-based machines in 386 Enhanced mode, or in standard mode on the RISC-based machines.

The control parameters to initiate WOW and the WOW application environment are located in the Registry in

```
HKey_Local_Machine\SYSTEM\CurrentControlSet\Control\WOW
```

Each setting in this key is automatically maintained by the system, requiring no manual changes.

The Windows 3.*x* system.INI equivalent environment settings are found along this Registry path:

```
HKey_Local_Machine\SOFTWARE\Microsoft\Windows NT\CurrentVersion\WOW
```

Here each of the WOW subkeys has the same name as the headings in the SYSTEM.INI file.

Virtual MS-DOS Machine Sessions (VDM)

Under Windows NT, all of the 16-bit MS-DOS applications are run in the VDM. This includes the virtual device drivers (VDDs) for the mouse, keyboard, printer, and COM ports, and the network support necessary for use on NT.

The VDDs are loaded into every VDM, as determined by the values stored in the Registry. Data concerning VDDs are found in the Registry along this path:

```
HKey_Local_Machine\SYSTEM\CurrentControlSet\Control\VirtualDeviceDrivers
```

When any device driver is added to the system through the Control Panel, VDD entries are automatically updated.

Registry Security

The Registry must be protected from user tampering, whether accidental or intentional. As usual, there is no substitute for backing up the Registry, and this process is discussed later in the chapter.

Preventive Measures

There are several actions that system administrators can take as preemptive measures against intrusion.

- Make sure that no one except an administrator is able to access the %SystemRoot%\system32\config directory, where the Registry files are stored. This is achieved through an NTFS partition.
- Consider removing or renaming the NT Registry Editor, the Windows 95 Editor/Windows 3.*x* Editor, and the System Policy Editor programs to prevent users from running these programs.
- Always protect the Administrator accounts from unauthorized usage.
- Provide NTFS-level protection to each user's profile directory (%SystemRoot%\Profiles\%*username*%). These files can also be relocated to a central server.

Registry Auditing

Keeping track of what is going on in the Registry can help you determine who has made or attempted to make changes to the various hives of the Registry. Put Windows NT 4.0's internal auditing capabilities to work on these tasks.

There are three steps to setting up a Registry audit. Only administrators are allowed to do any of these procedures.

1. With User Manager or User Manager for Domains, enable auditing and set auditing policies. This entails selecting the particular Registry activities you wish to monitor.
2. Indicate which Registry keys you want to monitor, and for which users and groups. Do this using the Audit command on the Security menu in the Registry Editor.
3. On the computer being audited, use the Security log in Event Viewer. It contains the results of all Registry activity you selected for auditing in steps 1 and 2.

Auditing and its implementation are discussed in Chapter 12.

Backing Up the Registry

In view of the Registry's significance to the Windows NT environment, the necessity of backing up the Registry becomes paramount. The following factors are at issue:

- First of all, all the Registry files are kept open while Windows NT is running. Because they are kept open, a simple Copy command will not work to back up the files.
- Another issue is who can do this backup. The user performing backup procedures must be a member of the Backup Operators group, Server Operators group, or Administrators group. No one else can perform the backup.
- When a backup is performed, a proper Win32-based application must be used and must provide the proper API calls to perform the backup. Thus, a backup program intended for Windows NT must be used.

The following sections discuss several methods of backing up the Registry, taking into account these factors.

Windows NT Backup (NTBACKUP.EXE)

The NTBACKUP.EXE program works only with tape devices. The program offers you an option to automatically include a copy of the local Registry files in the backup set.

NOTE. *This is the fastest and best method for backing up the Registry.*

Emergency Repair Disk (RDISK.EXE)

The Emergency Repair Disk (ERD) program, RDISK.EXE, should be run whenever changes are made to the Registry. In fact, when you execute certain activities in Windows NT, you will be notified that running this program is strongly recommended; you should follow the suggestion.

By default, the ERD backs up only the System and Software hives. These hives are first backed up to the %SystemRoot%\Repair directory on your hard drive; then the information is copied to a floppy disk. This backup information is in a compressed format and will have a name such as System.lo_.

You can back up the remaining hives, as well, by using the /s parameter when executing the ERD program.

NOTE. *When you use the* /s *parameter, the entire Registry may not fit onto a single floppy disk if your system has a lot of users and you have made a significant number of updates to the Registry. If this occurs, you can back up the* %SystemRoot%\repair *directory to a tape device or a network drive.*

Here are the steps to run the ERD program, RDISK.EXE:

1. Click Start and choose Run.
2. Type **rdisk.exe** to back up just the System and Software hives. Or, type **rdisk.exe /s** to back up all the other hives.
3. Choose Create Repair Disk.

Registry Backup (REGBACK.EXE)

The REGBACK.EXE program is included on the Windows NT Workstation Resource Kit CD. You can use this tool from a command line or a remote session to back up the Registry. REGBACK.EXE lets you back up the contents of the Registry to a network drive or to any location other than a tape device.

Helpful Tip

The program also can be used in conjunction with Windows NT's Scheduler Service (AT.EXE) to create a regular Registry Back Schedule.

Using an Alternate Operating System

Another way to back up the Registry is to use a different operating system to start the computer, and then copy all files in the %SystemRoot%\System32\config directory to a safe backup location. For example, you might use another installed copy of Windows NT as the alternate if the Registry is stored on an NTFS partition, or use MS-DOS if the Registry is stored on a FAT partition.

NOTE. *This method of Registry backup is the least preferred.*

Registry Editor (REGEDT32.EXE)

In the Registry Editor, the Save Key command on the Registry menu backs up Registry keys manually. For each key immediately below HKey_Local_Machine and HKey_Users, you click to highlight the key, and then select the Save Key command. For the saved keys, choose filenames that match the key names; for example, save the Software key to a file named \regBack\Software.

Restoring the Registry from Backups

To restore the Registry in the event of corruption or other problems, you can use the same tools described in the preceding sections to restore each part of the Registry.

Users must have the Restore Files/Dir right in order to restore the Registry.

■ Procedures for Changing the Registry

This section describes step by step how to make changes in the Registry. We'll use two examples in these procedures. The first entails changing the security access permissions to a subkey, and the second example adds and changes keys and values. In both, we'll use the Registry Editor (REGEDT32.EXE).

Controlling Access to the Registry

To change the access permissions (ACL) on a hive, follow these steps:

1. As previously described, run REGEDIT32.EXE (from the Start/Run dialog or from a shortcut on the desktop).
2. Choose the HKEY_LOCAL_MACHINE on Local Machine subtree.
3. Go to the subkey \Software\Microsoft\RPC (see Figure 10.5).
4. In the Security menu, choose Permissions.

Figure 10.5

Selecting the RPC subkey

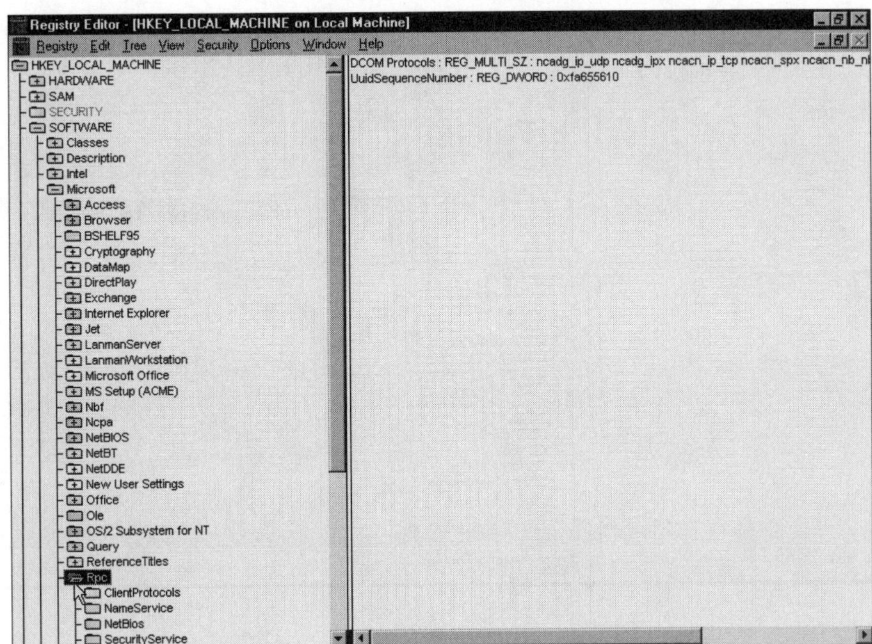

5. In the Registry Key Permissions dialog, select Replace Permission on Existing Subkeys.
6. Select the Everyone group, and for Type of Access choose Special Access.
7. In the Special Access dialog (see Figure 10.6), select Other, and check the check boxes for Query Value, Enumerate Subkeys, Notify, and Read Control permissions. Click OK.
8. In the Registry Key Permissions dialog, click OK, and choose Yes to confirm your wish to change permissions on subkeys.

Displaying a Legal Notice Before Logon

In Chapter 1, we suggested the use of a warning message displayed before logon, as a security measure against unauthorized access. Or perhaps just a helpful dialog to instruct users on what to do next. The procedure that follows changes the Registry to accomplish this message.

Figure 10.6

Assigning Special Access permissions for the Registry

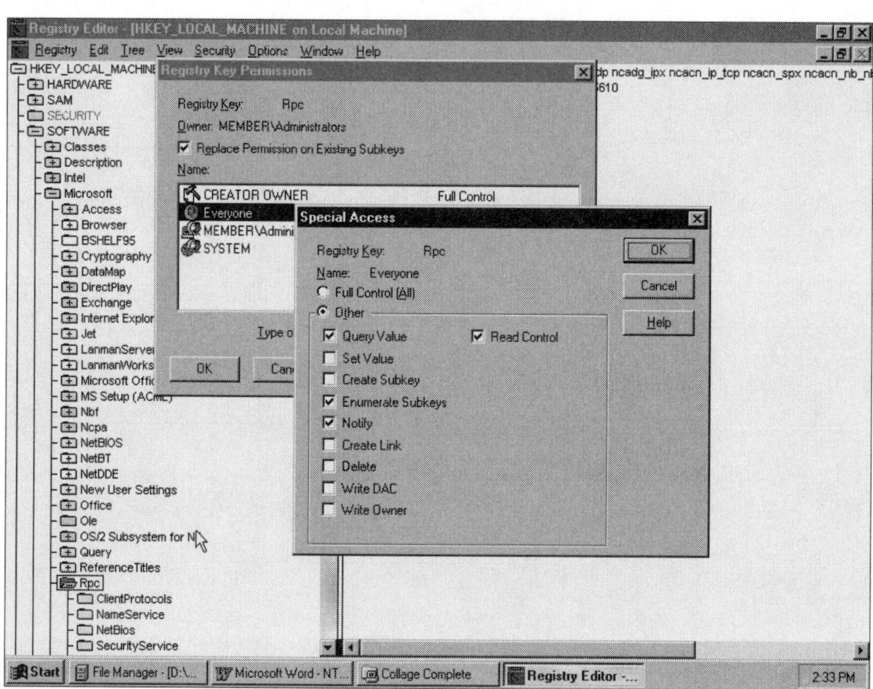

Following are the Registry Locations and values we will be changing or adding:

Hive	HKEY_LOCAL_MACHINE\SOFTWARE
Key	\Microsoft\Windows NT\Current Version\Winlogon
Name	LegalNoticeCaption
Type	REG_SZ
Value	Enter title of message box here

Hive	HKEY_LOCAL_MACHINE\SOFTWARE
Key	Microsoft\Windows NT\Current Version\Winlogon
Name	LegalNoticeText
Type	REG_SZ
Value	Enter text of message box here

Here are the steps for the Registry changes:

1. From the Registry Editor, make the HKEY_LOCAL_MACHINE on Local Machine subtree the active window.
2. Scroll down to Microsoft\Windows NT\Current Version\Winlogon. See Figure 10.7.

Figure 10.7

Winlogon Registry entries

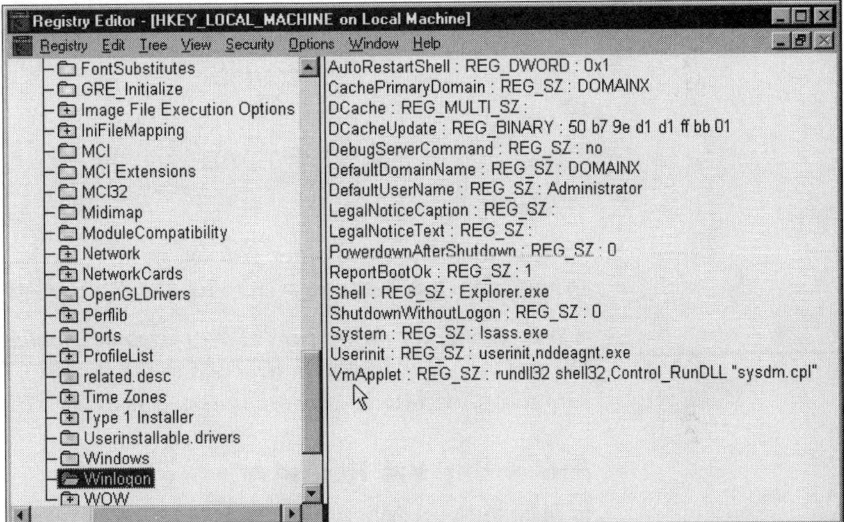

3. In the list of values on the right, double-click on the LegalNoticeCaption value. You are now editing the Title Box.
4. Type in **Warning! Protected System** for the Title Box. Then choose OK.
5. Double-click the LegalNoticeText value. You are now editing the Text Message Box.
6. Type **This System has Restricted Access to Authorized users only! Any and all unauthorized attempts to access this system will be prosecuted to the fullest extent of the law.** Click OK.
7. Exit the Registry Editor and log off the system. When you log on again, you will see your new message box.

Maximum Protection of the Registry

The following are Registry modifications recommended to accomplish a higher level of security for your Registry.

Restricting Remote Access

To restrict remote access to the Registry use the Registry Editor to create the following Registry key:

Hive	HKEY_LOCAL_MACHINE
Key	\CurrentcontrolSet\Control\SecurePipeServers
Name	\winreg
Type	REG_DWORD
Value	1

The security permissions you set on this key define which users or groups can connect to the system for remote Registry access.

NOTE. *By default, Windows NT Workstation installations do not define this key and do not restrict remote access to the Registry. Windows NT Server permits only Administrators remote access to the Registry.*

Protecting the Registry

In maximum-security installations, there are several keys and values that merit more protection than in the default installation. You might want to change the access permissions of the following keys so that the group Everyone is only allowed QueryValue, Enumerate Subkeys, Notify, and Read Control accesses: In the HKEY_LOCAL_MACHINE on Local Machine dialog:

```
\Software\Microsoft\RPC (and its subkeys)
\Software\Microsoft\Windows NT\CurrentVersion
```

Under the \Software\Microsoft\Windows NT\CurrentVersion\ subtree:

Profile List	AeDebug
Compatibility	Drivers
Embedding	Fonts
FontSubstitutes	GRE_Initialize
MCI	FontSubstitutes

In the HKEY_CLASSES_ROOT on Local Machine dialog:

```
\HKEY_CLASSES_ROOT (and all subkeys)
```

The Schedule Service (AT Command)

The Schedule task is run in the context run by the Schedule Service (typically the operating system's context, or, as set, the Services dialog). This service should not be used in a highly secure environment.

Only Administrators can submit AT commands in a default installation. To allow the group System Operators to also submit AT commands, use the Registry Editor to create or change the following Registry key value:

Hive	HKEY_LOCAL_MACHINE\SYSTEM
Key	\CurrentControlSet\Control\Lsa
Name	Submit Control
Type	REG_DWORD
Value	1

There is no way to allow anyone else to submit AT commands. The changes will take effect the next time the computer is started.

Hiding the Last Username

By default, Windows NT places the username of the last user to log on the computer in the Username text box of the Logon dialog. Although this makes it more convenient for the most frequent user to log on, it is also an invitation to hackers, who would know one of the two items needed to log on. You can prevent Windows NT from displaying the username from the last logon.

NOTE. *It's a good idea to do this on all computers accessed by Administrators.*

Use the Registry Editor to create or assign the following Registry key value:

Hive	HKEY_LOCAL_MACHINE\SOFTWARE
Key	\Microsoft\Windows NT\Current Version\Winlogon
Name	DontDisplayLastUserName
Type	REG_SZ
Value	1

Allowing Only Logged-On Users to Shut Down the Computer

Normally, you can shut down a computer running Windows NT Workstation without logging on, by choosing Shutdown in the Logon dialog. This step is not required for Windows NT Server, because it is configured this way by default. (If desired, however, you can set the value to 1 on NT Server and have the capability to shut down the computer from the Logon dialog.)

To require users to log on before shutting down the computer, use the Registry Editor to create or assign the following Registry key value:

Hive	HKEY_LOCAL_MACHINE\SOFTWARE
Key	\Microsoft\Windows NT\Current Version\Winlogon
Name	ShutdownWithoutLogon
Type	REG_SZ
Value	0

The changes will take effect the next time the computer is started.

Controlling Access to Removable Media

Windows NT allows any program to access files on floppy disks and CDs. In a maximum security environment, you might want to allow only users who are interactively logged on to access those devices. This security measure protects the operation for the interactive user.

In this operating condition, the floppy disks and/or CDs on your system are allocated to a user as part of the interactive logon process. When that user logs off, these devices are freed for general use or for reallocation.

To Allocate Floppy Drives During Logon

Use the Registry Editor to create or assign the following Registry key value:

Hive	HKEY_LOCAL_MACHINE\SOFTWARE
Key	\Microsoft\WindowsNT\CurrentVersion\Winlogon
Name	AllocateFloppies
Type	REG_SZ
Value	1

If the value does not exist, or is set to any other value, then floppy devices will be available for shared use by all processes on the system. This value will take effect at the next logon.

To Allocate CD-ROMs During Logon

Use the Registry Editor to create or assign the following Registry key value:

Hive	HKEY_LOCAL_MACHINE\SOFTWARE
Key	\Microsoft\WindowsNT\CurrentVersion\Winlogon
Name	AllocateCDRoms
Type	REG_SZ
Value	1

If the value does not exist or is set to any other value, then CD-ROM devices will be available for shared use by all processes on the system.

This value assignment will take effect at the next logon.

Summary

The Registry is a logical configuration database that is used by virtually everything in Windows NT. The tools we have examined in this chapter are used to modify the Registry. With the variety of ways and tools available to do this, it is important to secure not only the Registry itself by following the security measures outlined in this chapter (such as configuring each Registry file's ACL), but also the tools necessary to modify it. Keep the dangerous toys away from the kids, and it is less likely they will hurt themselves and others.

It's also important to keep a current backup of the Registry files. Using the proper tool is a must. The user who backs up the system will also require proper rights. In the next chapter we shall look at implementing system policies on the Windows NT Registry.

- *Types of Profiles*
- *System Policies*
- *Creating Profiles and Policies*

CHAPTER

11

User Profiles and System Policies

WINDOWS NT 4.0 PROVIDES TWO IMPORTANT SECURITY MANAGEMENT tools for users and administrators to control their NT environments: *user profiles* and *system policies.* This chapter explains these tools and gives suggestions for their management.

User profiles contain all the user-specific settings on a system running Windows NT. The profiles make up one portion of the Windows NT Registry (HKey_Current_User). The default arrangement is for users to have the ability to change their profile; you can dictate this arrangement based on your own system security policy.

System policies, created and implemented by administrators, are a security mechanism new to Windows NT in version 4.0. The policies alone are not meant to provide for all your security needs; implemented correctly, however, they help to effect security in the Windows NT environment. A system policy is a set of Registry entries designated for use by a user, group, or machine. These entries are written to the local Registry of a machine when a member of the designated set is detected using the machine.

Types of Profiles

Windows NT employs four types of profiles: local, default, system, and server-based. Each type of profile has its role in the environment.

- The *local profile* is stored on the local workstation and can only be accessed from that workstation.
- Another locally stored profile is the *default profile.* This profile is used as a template (or as a default setup) for each new user profile when no other profile is defined. The default profile is copied to the folder name of the logged-on user shown as %*username*% folder.
- The *system profile* is used by the System account and Windows NT when no user is logged on. It is stored in %SystemRoot%\System32\config\default.
- Server-based profiles are stored on a central server and can be accessed from any Windows NT machine. These profiles are also known as "roaming" profiles because users get the same profile downloaded to them wherever they roam in the network.

The user-specific settings for each user are stored in one of these profiles. The contents of a user's profile are listed in Table 11.1.

Each user gets a default group of settings when logging on to a system for the first time. Within the %SystemRoot%\profiles folder is a \Default User folder that contains the default profile. This folder is copied into another folder in the ..\Profiles folder, with the username as the folder name. See Figure 11.1 for a view of MaPatel's profile.

Within the ..\profiles\MaPatel folder is another structure of folders; these make up MaPatel's desktop environment (Figure 11.2). See Table 11.2 for a list of user profile folders and their contents.

Figure 11.1

MaPatel's profile in the Profiles folder

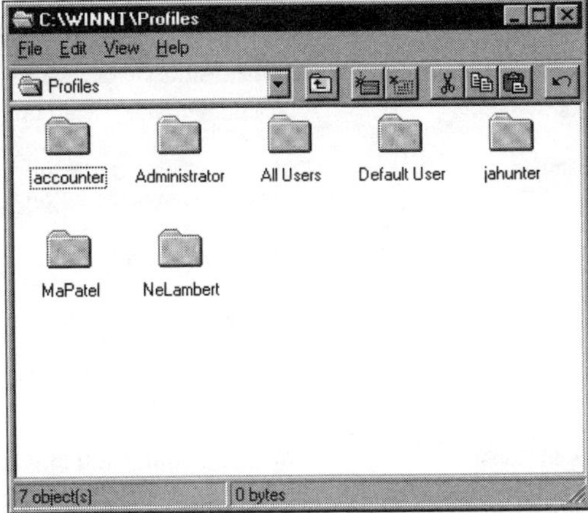

Figure 11.2

MaPatel's desktop environment

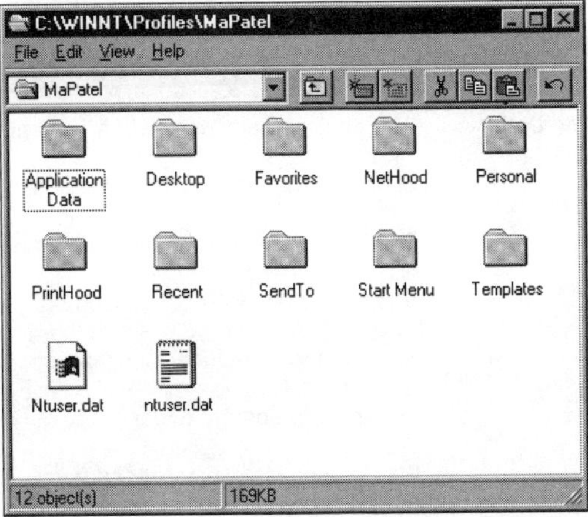

The last component of the profile is NTuser.dat. This file contains all the entries in HKey_Current_User. All of these components are then combined with the ones under the ..\profiles\All Users folder, and all of these components together comprise the entire desktop environment. The All Users folder has the common settings that each user gets automatically. Obviously, these settings are stored separately.

The folders listed in Table 11.2, when installed on NTFS partitions, have rights assigned to them when they are created. The Everyone group has Read rights on the All Users folder, and each user is given explicit Full Control over his or her own folder. These rights should not be changed, else the

Table 11.1

User Profile Contents

WINDOWS NT COMPONENT	INFORMATION STORED IN PROFILE
Bookmarks	Any bookmarks placed on Help system.
Control Panel	The color, sound, desktop, display, cursor, and all other user-specific settings.
Network	All the persistent network connections.
Printers	Network printer connections.
Taskbar	All the personal program groups and their properties (stored as shortcuts).
Win32-based Apps	All user settings within Windows NT/95 applications.
Windows NT Explorer	All option settings.

Table 11.2

User Profile Folders

PROFILE FOLDER	CONTENTS
Application Data	Specific third-party application settings.
Desktop	Shortcuts that are placed in the desktop.
Favorites	Shortcuts to program items and favorite locations.
NetHood	Shortcuts in Network Neighborhood.
Personal	Shortcuts to communal files/folders accessed by users.
PrintHood	Shortcuts to Printers folder.
Recent	Shortcuts to last 15 accessed items. (These are what make up the Documents list accessed from the Start menu.)
SendTo	Shortcuts to locations to which a document can be sent (3_" disk, fax, any folder, etc.).
Start Menu	Shortcuts here make up Start menu items.
Templates	Shortcuts to templates.

system or user applications may not be able to update settings. If you make the rights any less restrictive or leave the Profiles folder on a FAT drive, users will be able to alter not only their own profile settings but those of other users as well.

Figures 11.3 and 11.4 show the default permissions.

Figure 11.3

Permissions on user MaPatel folder

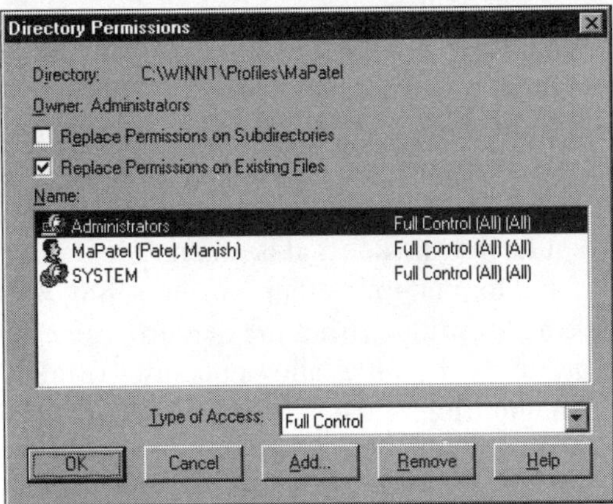

Figure 11.4

Permissions on All Users folder

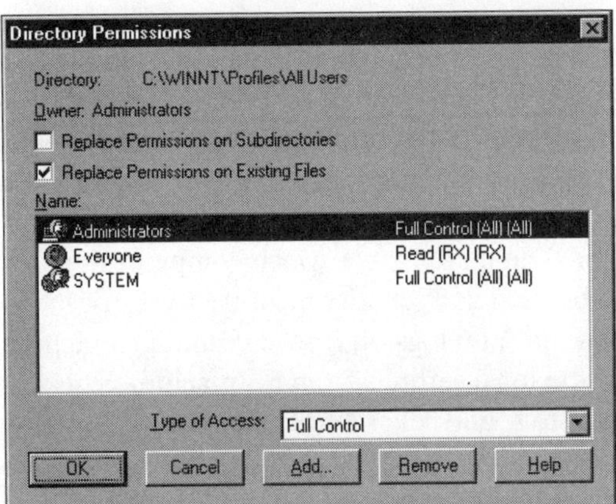

Local Profiles

The local profile is by default stored locally—that is, on the machine where the user logs on—in the \Winnt_root\profiles*username* directory. This profile is only available when the user logs on to (is validated by) the local machine, or when the user does not have a server-based profile defined.

A local profile is created for each individual user at logon, and it contains user-specific Registry settings in a Windows NT environment. Every user who logs on to a Windows NT machine will have a local profile, and the Registry settings it contains are loaded into the system Registry after successful logon.

NOTE. *The server-based profile has the same content as a local profile, except that the server-based profile can be accessed from and downloaded to any Windows NT machine.*

Let's examine an example of local profiles in use. MaPatel logs on from his NT Workstation, as a local user to the workstation. After validation, a profile stored on his machine in %SystemRoot%\profiles\%*username*% is loaded. This profile contains all his personal settings and will retain any changes that he may make (that is, changes to items listed in Table 11.1).

If MaPatel logs on to another machine—say JaHunter's—then MaPatel will receive a new profile (from the default profile) on that machine. The practical use of local profiles allows one user (MaPatel) to maintain his own desktop configuration, while allowing other users (JaHunter) to keep their own separate and unique desktop configuration on the same computer.

Server Profiles

Server-based profiles come in two types: the *personal user profile* and the *mandatory user profile.* A user can have *either* a personal profile *or* a mandatory profile, but not both at the same time. We'll take a closer look at the roles of personal and mandatory profiles shortly.

A server profile sets up a user's environment when the user logs on to a domain from any Windows NT computer. Information contained in server profiles typically includes settings that you want to be the same (such as printer connections) no matter from which computer the user logs on. These profiles may also be used as a security measure to restrict the user's desktop access.

When MaPatel logs on from JaHunter's machine, MaPatel does not have access to the local settings from his machine. This does not mean, however, that he has to spend several hours trying to re-create his network settings, printer connections, desktop settings, and application settings for Microsoft Office 95 and other programs. Under Windows NT, administrators can place user profiles on a central server and have the profile information copied down to and updated from a local computer. In addition to saving time for users, this also allows administrators to easily back up and maintain all the user accounts without a great deal of overhead.

Personal User Profile

A personal user profile allows the user to change his or her own profile or configuration choices, such as drive mappings and printer connections. (The specific components of personal profiles are listed in Tables 11.1 and 11.2.) When a user makes a change to these settings, they are saved to the user's personal user profile when the user logs off. At the next logon, the user's profile is loaded just as it was last saved.

Because users can modify the personal profile, it is essential (but not required) that each personal profile be assigned to only one user. In the event a personal profile is assigned to more than one user, the profile settings are always set to the configuration of the user who last used the profile. Thus the next user cannot accurately anticipate what desktop will be available at the next logon.

Mandatory User Profile

The mandatory user profile is used to permanently set a desktop environment. This profile allows users to make temporary, session-only changes to their settings. The revised settings are discarded when the user logs off. Thus when a user logs off and on again, the environment settings created while last working under the mandatory profile are discarded, and the original mandatory environment is restored. Because users cannot change mandatory profiles, these profiles can be assigned to any number of users. Mandatory profiles have the filename extension .MAN.

A major security benefit of mandatory profiles is that if an assigned mandatory profile is not available when a user tries to log on, the user is denied logon access and not allowed to access the computer. Let's see what happens when MaPatel is assigned a mandatory profile.

When MaPatel logs on from his workstation, a mandatory profile stored on a server to his machine in %SystemRoot%\profiles\%*username*% is downloaded. This profile dictates all his settings. If MaPatel logs on to another machine—say NeLambert's—NT notes that MaPatel's user profile specifies a mandatory profile and attempts to download the profile from the appropriate server. If the profile is unavailable, then MaPatel is denied access.

Creating Server-Based Profiles

To create a server-based profile, you have several choices: setting a profile path in User Manager for Domains; copying a profile to another location; and creating a mandatory profile.

The first method is to go into User Manager for Domains and set a profile path, as shown in the User Profiles box in Figure 11.5. Once the path is established, Windows NT can go to work creating server-based profiles as each user logs on. NT uses a default profile, creates a local profile for the user, and copies it to the centralized location. When the user logs off, both the local and server-based profiles are updated.

If the user logs on at another machine, the newly created server-based profile is downloaded and used. Once again, when the user logs off, both the local and server profiles are updated. Thus, Windows NT takes care of the burden of making sure the user has the most up-to-date profile.

Figure 11.5

Establishing the user profile path

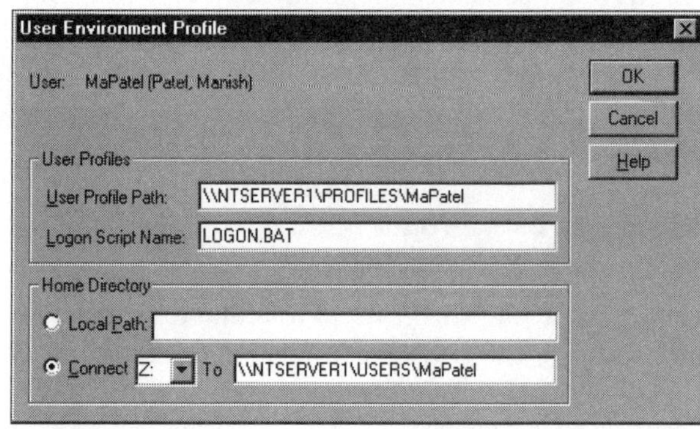

If a profile is already on the machine, as would be the case if MaPatel logged on again to his own machine, then the most recent profile copy is used—in this case, the one on the server. If the server containing the profile is down, or the path typed in is invalid, then Windows NT will create a local profile using the default settings for the local workstation.

A second method of creating a server-based profile is to set a path with User Manager for Domains, and then copy a default profile to the location specified. This allows an administrator to create, in advance, a profile with the exact desktop settings the user needs. After the user logs on, this is the profile used. When copying the default profile to the server, it is easiest to use Control Panel/System and the User Profiles tab (Figure 11.6). By using the Copy To button for this task, you ensure that the entire profile is copied.

Caution

A different problem may occur when using Windows NT Explorer to copy profiles. If any of the profiles are opened when you execute your copy operation (especially if you are copying to or from the one you are using currently), the copy procedure will not copy all components correctly. This is not a bug. Several of the properties of a profile cannot be changed or copied while in use. So stick to the built-in tools and you'll be fine.

Another method of creating a profile is to create a mandatory profile. This profile has a special designation that prevents users from making changes to it. In effect, you are creating a restricted profile. Since permanent changes to it cannot be made, this profile can be shared by multiple users. When a user does make a change to profile settings—say JaHunter changes her color scheme to Rose—the setting will be valid only for the session.

Figure 11.6

In Control Panel, use the Copy To button to copy entire user profiles.

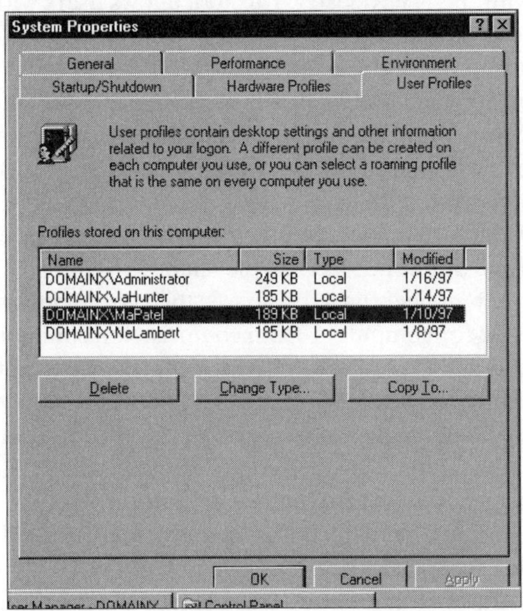

Once JaHunter logs off, her changes are discarded. When she logs on the next time, she will again have the original settings.

To create a mandatory profile, select one of the two ways described just above for creating the initial user profile. Then, in any profile that you want to make read-only, rename the NTuser.dat file to NTuser.man. If a user has been assigned a mandatory profile and the profile path is either not valid or cannot be found, the user logon will be denied. This security measure assumes that you are using mandatory profiles as a restriction.

In Windows NT 3.51, user profiles were the only option for administrators wanting to restrict access to the desktop. We will now look at system policies and how they help in controlling/restricting the Windows NT environment.

System Policies

Absolute control over users' desktop environment is not possible with just the user profile structure. When you add Windows NT system policies to the mix, however, you can restrict the desktop environment with sufficient control to handle most of the system's users. This kind of user control includes designating certain Control Panel options, customizing desktop options, and configuring network settings.

In Chapter 10, we showed you how to use the System Policy Editor to work with the NT Registry. This tool allows users with proper authentication to directly edit the Registry in a real-time situation. The System Policy Editor is useful in editing a single Registry at a time, but making the same alteration on 500 machines would involve considerably more time and tedious effort. Enter system policies, which allow the automatic updating of several machines with the same configuration settings, or different settings for each computer. System policies work the same in both Windows NT 4.0 and Windows 95 but are implemented differently in the two environments. We will look at the difference later in the chapter.

System policies have two parts: the system policy for users and the system policy for computers. Both comprise the configuration options that can be placed in a user profile, plus logon settings and network access settings.

System policies for both users and computers overwrite the data in the Registry database, in the subkeys for the current user and the subkeys for the local machine. The overwriting of data in these Registry areas by the system policy allows control of user actions through the user profiles, and control of computer actions for users and groups using the System Policy Editor.

The user settings are controlled by means of the Default User settings; administrators can modify such things as the user's desktop settings. The computer settings are controlled by means of the Default Computer settings, with modifications to such things as logon and network settings.

System Policy Templates

The system policy template contains all the possible settings and their values that are available through the System Registry Editor. If a setting is not defined in the template, then the Editor cannot change that setting. Template settings must be valid Registry settings, either predefined by Windows NT or installed by other applications. These are the rules that define the Policy and its scope.

Three system policy template files, described in the following table, are included with Windows NT 4.0. They are stored in the %SystemRoot%\Inf folder. These templates can be loaded in any combination you want. Administrators can also design their own templates to accommodate Registry restrictions needed in a particular environment, as in Figure 11.7.

System Policy Template	Content
Common.adm	Registry entries that are common to both Windows NT and Windows 95
Winnt.adm	Registry entries specific to Windows NT 4.0
Windows.adm	Registry entries specific to Windows 95

Figure 11.7

Policy Template Options dialog

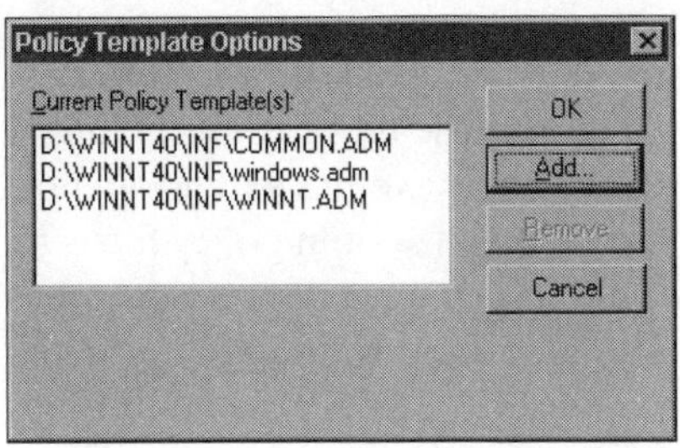

If you want to control Registry settings that are not included in the predefined templates, you can create your own template file. This file then can be used by the System Policy Editor to add new Registry settings as part of the system policy. Essentially, system policies manipulate the entries in the Registry, so administrators must be careful when designing their own templates.

The system policy templates have a structured format. Template files use a scripting language that is outlined in Windows NT 4.0 Workstation Resource Kit. Any text-based editor, such as Notepad, can be used. Figure 11.8 is an example of a template file (winnt.adm) open in Notepad.

Figure 11.8

The winnt.adm template open in Notepad

winnt.adm - Notepad

File Edit Search Help

```
CLASS MACHINE

CATEGORY  !!Network
        CATEGORY !!Sharing
                KEYNAME
System\CurrentControlSet\Services\LanManServer\Parameters

                POLICY !!WorkstationShareAutoCreate
                        VALUENAME "AutoShareWks"
                        VALUEOFF NUMERIC 0
                        PART !!ShareWks_Tip1            TEXT    END PART
                        PART !!ShareWks_Tip2            TEXT    END PART
                END POLICY

                POLICY !!ServerShareAutoCreate
                        VALUENAME "AutoShareServer"
                        VALUEOFF NUMERIC 0
                        PART !!ShareServer_Tip1         TEXT    END PART
                        PART !!ShareServer_Tip2         TEXT    END PART
                END POLICY

        END CATEGORY    ; Sharing

END CATEGORY    ; Network
```

Your System Policy File

The System Policy file is created to enforce a System Policy on users. This Policy contains Registry settings on a per user, per computer and by group basis. You can only have one of these files at a time, and it must be named *NTconfig.pol*; all system policy files have the extension .pol.

The first step in creating a system policy file is to Start the System Policy Editor. Then make sure the appropriate template files are loaded, as described in the preceding section and illustrated in Figure 11.7.

After the Policy Editor is loaded, the main Editor window presents two icons: Default Computer and Default User (see Figure 11.9).

Figure 11.9

System Policy Editor

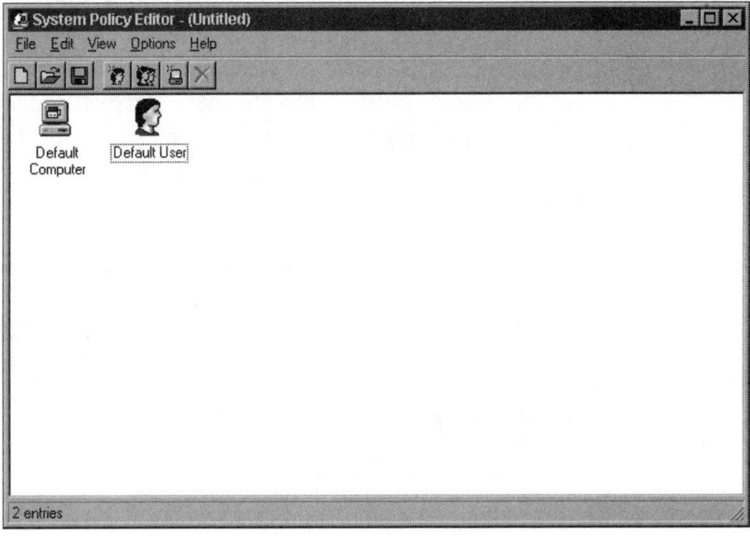

The Default User icon takes you to the desktop settings you can modify for a new account (or, as they are known to NT, the Default User). These modifications affect the HKey_Current_User key of the Registry. The Default User values define the data in the user profile that are in effect on the computer.

The Default Computer icon takes you to the logon and network access settings that you can modify for all computers (AKA Default Computer). This affects the HKey_Local_Machine key of the Registry. These values control hardware settings at all computers to which this Policy is downloaded.

After it's created, the System Policy file must be placed in the %SystemRoot%\System32\Repl\Import\Scripts folder of each domain controller. This folder is also shared as the NetLogon share. The best way to accomplish this is by using Directory Replication to replicate the Ntconfig.pol to each domain controller, in the same way you replicate logon scripts.

How Policies Work

Every time a user logs on from an NT system and is validated by a domain controller, the logon process checks to see if there is an NTconfig.pol file in the Netlogon share of the validating computer. If this file is present, NT copies the appropriate user, group, or computer policy data to the local computer's Registry, overwriting the current user and local machine parts of the Registry.

When Windows NT finds the NTconfig.pol file, the steps that take place depend on what options you have chosen for the policy. The following numbered steps describe the flow of this implementation.

Step 1. The user performs a successful logon.

Step 2. A user profile—either the server-based or local cached profile—is loaded and applied. This profile contains NTuser.dat, which will be modified by the system policy.

Step 3. Windows NT checks the NetLogon share of the domain controller for NTconfig.pol.

Step 4. Assuming the NetLogon share is found, Windows NT checks the policy file for any explicit user settings. For instance, if JaHunter were logging on, NT would look for a profile assigned to JaHunter. Assuming her profile is found, the system will use her settings.

Step 5. If no user policy is found, NT searches the policy for any groups the user may belong to. If no groups are found, then the Default User settings are applied to the Registry. If groups are found, then their settings are applied one at a time based on the priority of the group. See Figure 11.10.

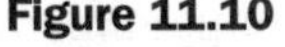

Figure 11.10

Group Order determines which settings are applied for a user who doesn't have a profile.

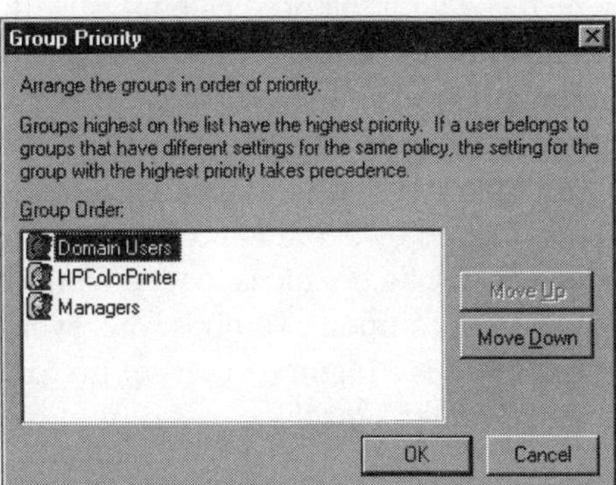

For example, say a user is a member of both the Managers and Domain Users groups. Managers has a higher priority then Domain Users; so the Domain Users settings get applied first, followed by the Managers policy settings, which *overwrite* the Domain Users settings. So in Figure 11.10 the

Group Order from top to bottom is the order in which the group settings are applied. HPColorPrinters will overwrite Domain Users, and Managers will overwrite HPColorPrinter. Managers, at the bottom, has the highest priority; and Domain Users, at the top, has the lowest.

Step 6. The next process involves looking for an explicit policy for the computer at which the user is being validated. If the name is found, then the specific settings are implemented. If no computer name is found, then the Default Computer settings are applied. Thus, if MaPatel logs on from his computer called Member and there is a setting for it in the policy, then it would be applied.

System Policy Pitfalls and Bugs

For some time, there has been a saying among Windows NT system users and administrators that "whoever controls (understands) the Registry, controls (understands) Windows NT." This power when utilized properly can be a productive and beneficial factor in system management; however, improperly implemented system policies can cause confusion or even damage to an environment.

NT system policies give an administrator substantial control over certain aspects of the Registry, and before sitting down to implement these policies, it's important to decide exactly what users do and do not need access to. If you put your policies into action without thinking them through, you may run into some unpleasant situations.

The Default Computer settings will overwrite all local settings of computers that have no settings defined. If you're careless about implementation, you may be faced with the predicament of getting settings that you didn't want on a certain computer. These settings are permanent until they are changed manually or through a different policy.

A situation like this can definitely happen in a trusted environment. For example, suppose MaPatel's account resides in the Master/Accounts domain. Thus, he will be validated by a domain controller from that domain. As mentioned earlier, the NTconfig.pol file is loaded from this domain controller and applied to the user and computer settings wherever MaPatel is logging on.

Now suppose there is a logon banner set up for the Sales domain. MaPatel walks over to JaHunter's machine in Accounting and logs on. JaHunter's machine is a member of the Accounting Resource domain, which maintains trust relationships with the Sales domain that allow users to log on from any machine. When MaPatel logs on, his system policy will be downloaded. MaPatel's policy requires a logon banner. Later, when JaHunter logs on to her machine, she will get a logon banner welcoming her to the Sales domain—which was not the case before MaPatel used her machine.

To understand what has happened, remember that the System Policy is downloaded from the domain that validates you, and that's not necessarily the same as the machine's domain. To prevent this problem, it is strongly advised that if you are going to use system policies you should employ them on *all* domains of your network. Had this been done in our example, JaHunter would have a policy that is downloaded to her machine and posts a logon banner for her domain, as well—thus avoiding confusion.

System policies provide a manual update mode, as well, for environments that need to use more than one system policy file. You must set the Network System Policy switch in the policy file for each computer that is going to receive its policies from another policy file. This switch is called the Remote Update setting, as seen in Figure 11.11. With the Remote Update setting enabled, you can choose Manual as the Update mode at the bottom of the window, and enter an alternate path (other than the default, Netlogon) for the system policy file.

Figure 11.11

Turning on manual mode for remote updating

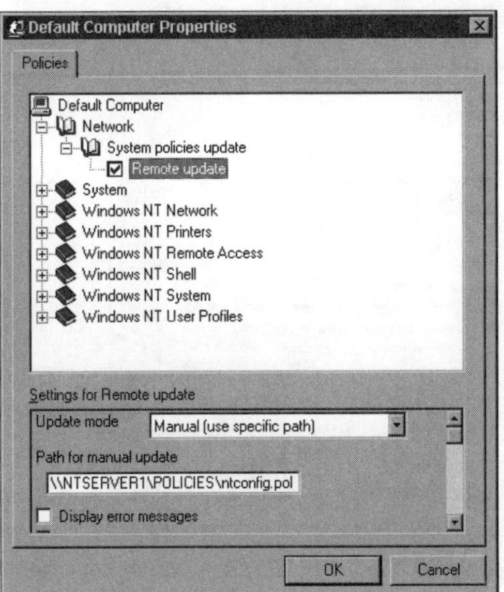

For example, say we wanted a separate policy for all the computers in the Accounting department and another for the machines in Sales. We could have one policy on an NT Server in each domain. Then, by means of the Remote Update settings, each machine in each domain would know to look for the policy in the new location. In this case, using the manual update mode ensures that the system policy stays consistent regardless of the machine on which a user is logging on.

Another pitfall to avoid: The Default User and Default Computer profile settings are applicable to *every* user and computer that does not have a policy specifically defined. These settings should be kept generic. Any specific settings needed should be explicitly placed in a particular user, group, or computer policy.

Working with the Policy's Settings

Let's see how to make changes to various settings in the system policy. First, open the policy by double-clicking it in the Policy Editor. You'll see a graphical tree representation of the Registry in the main Policies window. See Figure 11.12. Each of the major categories (such as Windows NT Shell) is further divided into subcategories (such as Custom Shared Folders). The options you can modify for computer and user operation are presented as either check boxes or text boxes.

Figure 11.12

View of settings for Default Computer in system policy file

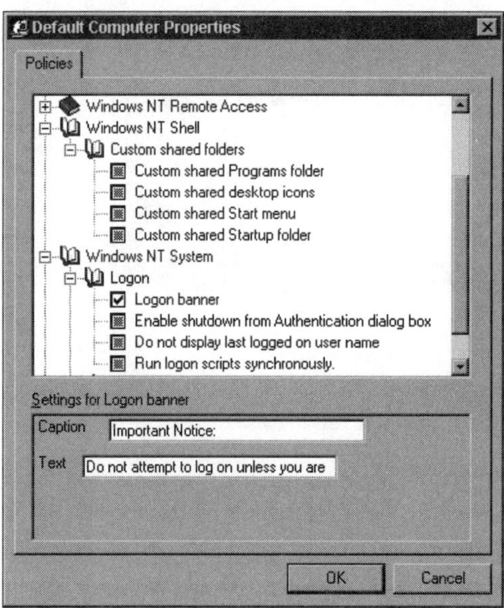

The check box options in the tree can have one of three states:

- Clear indicates that the entry is to be turned off. This will be applied no matter what the current setting is.
- Checkmarked indicates that the entry is to be turned on. This will be applied no matter what the current setting is.

- Shaded indicates no change in current settings. It leaves the setting alone, whether it's on or off.

The following table defines terms used in some of the policy settings. The table explains how the setting you choose will manifest itself to the user in on-screen command choices.

Term Used in Setting	Displayed Result
"Disable"	When you disable a setting, user sees a dimmed ("grayed out") command item—on the menu.
"Remove"	When you remove an item, user does not see the command item at all.
"Hide"	When you hide a command item, it is invisible to the logged-on user only.

Default User Settings

In the Default User Properties window are the list of policies and the settings that can be modified. (Remember, to get here you double-click the Default User icon in the System Policy Editor main window.) The categories of settings for Default User include the Control Panel, Desktop, Shell, System, NT Shell, and NT System. The most important of these options from a security standpoint are the Shell and System options.

Under the Shell options, you can restrict the user's access to the Run, Find, and Shutdown commands available from the Program Manager. You can also customize the entire Start menu. See Figure 11.13.

In the System settings, you can restrict the ability to use Registry tools (NT Registry Editor and Windows 95 Registry Editor) by disabling the user's access to these applications. This is an important option; Registry editing should be disabled for the Default User and enabled on specific users such as administrators, who need access to these tools. See Figure 11.14.

Default Computer Settings

As mentioned, you control logons and network access through the Default Computer settings. These settings are used to prevent users from changing either the hardware or environment settings for the operating system. Figure 11.15 shows the areas available for modification.

In terms of security, the critical categories for Default Computer are System, Windows NT Remote Access, and Windows NT System.

The System settings are used to control the applications that are launched at start-up: They can be designated Run or Run Once. You can also control Simple Network Management Protocol (SNMP) configuration settings.

Figure 11.13

Restrictions available in the Shell category

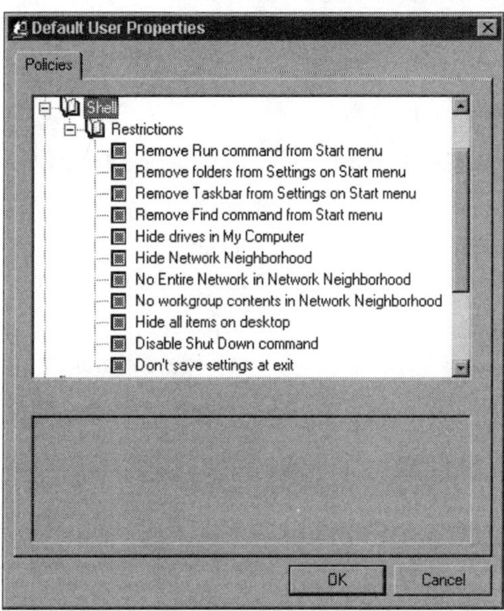

Figure 11.14

Restrictions available in the System category

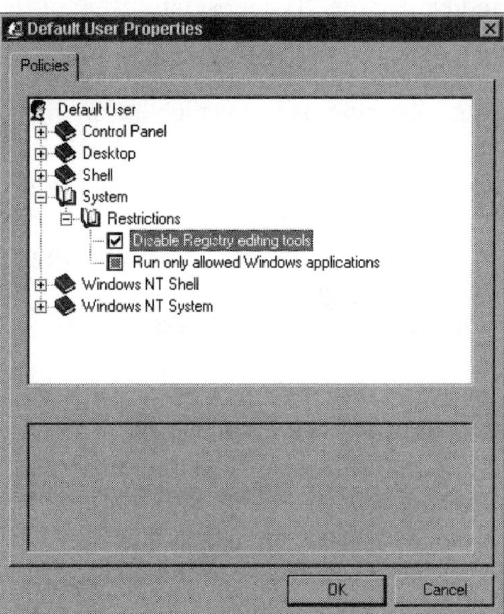

Figure 11.15

Policy settings for Default Computer

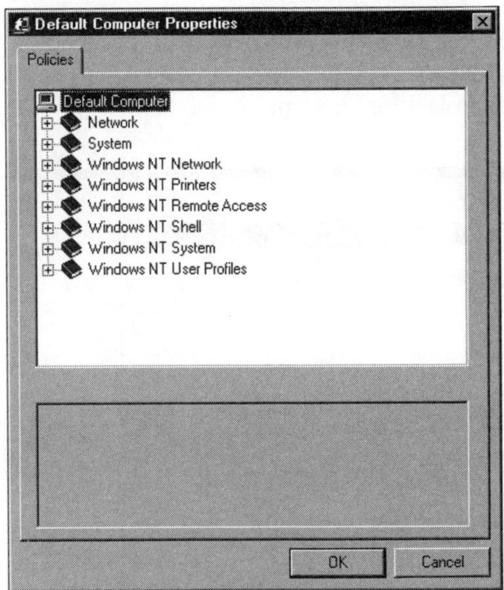

Windows NT Remote Access contains settings having to do with the Remote Access Service (RAS). For the RAS server, you can set maximum authentication retries, intervals on call-back security, and automatic disconnection times.

In the Windows NT System settings, two elements can be modified: File System and Logon settings. Only the Logon settings have any important security implications; these settings are shown in Figure 11.16. You can configure the Logon policy for user accounts, which includes

- Creation of a logon banner. (Take a look back at Figure 11.12 to see the related settings for the banner.)
- Enabling or disabling automatic logon.

NOTE. *Enabling the automatic logon settings does not bypass NT security per se. You are simply providing a username, password, and domain name ahead of time. The information is stored in the Registry and is used each time the system is started or when a user logs off. An access token is created as usual, but the user is saved the effort of providing any credentials to use the system. It boots up and logs on as the "automatic logon" user. It is recommended that you only enable automatic logon for computers that pose no risk to data integrity should unauthorized users operate that machine. The automatic logon option is provided as a convenience for individuals and groups that have no real need for security.*

- Disabling shutdown from logon prevents unauthorized users from shutting down the machine.
- Preventing the display of the last user logged on helps keep logon names secret. (See Chapter 10 for more about maximum security elements and display of last logon name.)

Figure 11.16

Preventing the display of the last logon name

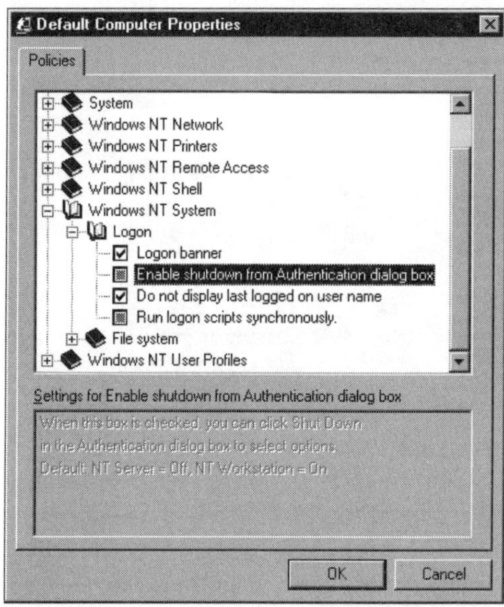

■ Creating Profiles and Policies

Now that you understand the use of policies and profiles, here are the step-by-step instructions to implement them.

Creating a Server-Based User Profile

1. From the Start menu, select Settings/Control Panel.
2. Double-click the System icon, and click on the User Profiles tab.
3. Highlight the profile you want to use, and click the Copy To button.
4. Type in the Network Path for the profile.
5. Under Permitted to Use, click on Change.
6. Choose the username for this profile and select Add.

7. Click OK three times to close all windows and finalize the copy process.
8. Load User Manager for Domains, and double-click the user for whom you just copied the profile. Click the Profile button.
9. Enter the UNC path name for the profile you just created.

Viewing or Adding Policy Templates

Here are the steps to add or choose a policy template in the Systems Policy Editor.

1. From the Start menu, choose Programs/Administrative Tools. Click System Policy Editor.
2. In the Options menu, choose Policy Templates.
3. Select the template of your choice, or choose Add/Remove template files.

Creating a System Policy

Here are the steps to create a system policy for user MaPatel on a machine called Member.

1. Run System Policy Editor (see step 1 of procedure just above).
2. Select File/New Policy.
3. Select Edit/Add User.
4. For the username, type in MaPatel (or choose Browse and select MaPatel or another user).
5. Select Edit/Add Computer.
6. Type in **Member** as the computer name, or click Browse and select a computer.
7. Select Edit/Add Group.
8. Type in the name of the group or groups, or select Browse and pick from the list. (We selected Managers.)
9. As you add groups, you will want to set Group Priority for use in assignment of settings (see "How Policies Work" earlier in this chapter). To do this, select Options/Group Priority, and set the—priority desired.

Summary

This chapter covers user profiles and system policies—important security elements in the Windows NT environment. User profiles are a vital component; NT can store user-specific settings in a separate file for each user. The file can also be used to give roaming users a consistent desktop environment. System policies are used to enforce computer-specific and user-specific settings in the Registry. These settings allow administrators to control what parts of the system a user can access. The System Policy Editor is the graphical tool used to create and modify these Policies.

In Windows NT, the implementation of profiles and policies allow tighter security, with ease of administration.

- *Whom Should You Audit?*
- *What Should You Audit?*
- *Setting Up Your Audit Policy*
- *The Event Viewer Security Log*
- *Events in Detail*

CHAPTER

12

Auditing and Logging

ALL SECURITY POLICIES INCLUDE A SET OF AUDITING CRITERIA and audit logs. These tools are what allow you to watch and learn, once you have put all your security mechanisms on line. As users access and work on the system, auditing allows you to find areas where you may have overlooked necessary controls, or areas you may have actually overprotected. In addition, when someone attempts unauthorized access, auditing helps you discover where security is breached, the extent to which the system is penetrated, and by whom.

If you use auditing as a deterrent to vandalism or illegal usage of your system, then advertise that fact. Let users know periodically that they are subject to auditing. Consider putting this reminder in a logon banner, for instance—but don't tell too much. If you specify exactly what you are auditing and when, users will relax their vigilance when they are not working on those areas or during those times. Keep them on their toes!

Caution

Don't make the mistake of overauditing (for example, auditing the Read accesses on all files), or you'll create huge audit logs that may in fact hide the event that indicates a real problem.

Ultimately, our most important advice to system administrators is LEARN! Know what you are auditing. Review your audit results and understand what they tell you. Useful auditing requires time, planning, and continual tweaking.

Whom Should You Audit?

This chapter discusses the elements within your NT system that should be audited:

- Any and all users and groups who have access to sensitive data
- The data itself
- Logon and logoff events
- Failed attempts to log on and to access data without the correct permissions

And there's one more element that, unfortunately, most people forget—but it's one of the most important groups for auditing: administrators. Auditing administrators is like questioning your priest—you hate to do it but it's got to be done. Although NT administrators can basically do anything, they should not necessarily be doing everything. For example, should they be able to browse users' personal directories? Change a domain's audit policy? Administrator rights should be controlled and audited just as other users' are.

NOTE. *An administrator out to do real malice could alter the Security Log itself. Preventing this action is critical, and you can do it by having more than one person responsible for the reviewing of the system's security policy and the auditing logs. For instance, you might arrange for the CFO to have the responsibility of auditing the IS group's auditing policy.*

What Should You Audit?

Many administrators believe that their file system layout does not affect security. They are wrong. Concentrate your sensitive material in specific locations and audit those locations. Do not allow extraneous directories to be created within these structures. Do not allow, through directory propagation, the useless auditing of files and folders.

With your file system structure at work assisting your auditing game plan, the fundamental element to be audited in your Windows NT environment is *events*. You should particularly audit events that can be threats to system security. Construct your auditing policy and strategies to find and counter these threats.

Events cover a wide range of activities, including user actions, changes of rights, and system shutdowns. Most events fall into the categories indicated in Table 12.1. In this table, the left-hand column lists the event categories as defined in the audit policy, and the right-hand column lists the corresponding categories of audited events that you'll see in the Security Log.

Table 12.1

Comparison of Event Categories

AUDIT POLICY EVENT CATEGORY	SECURITY LOG CATEGORIES OF AUDITED EVENTS
Logon and Logoff	Logon/Logoff
File and Object Access	Object Access
Use of User Rights	Privilege Use
User and Group Management	Account Management
Security Policy Changes	Policy Change
Restart, Shutdown, and System	System Event
Process Tracking	Detailed Tracking

NOTE. *We'll look at this table again in a later section when we examine the Security Log itself.*

Setting Up Your Audit Policy

Events are not audited by default. To specify what types of system events are audited, you must have Administrator permission.

The audit policy is the system component that determines the type and range of security event-logging performed by Windows NT. You can specify that audit entries are to be written to the Security Log in the Event Viewer (described shortly) whenever certain actions are performed or files are accessed.

To set up the audit policy, open the User Manager application. In the Policies menu, select Audit to display the Audit Policy dialog (see Figure 12.1). This is where you first enable auditing for a particular domain.

Figure 12.1

Audit Policy dialog

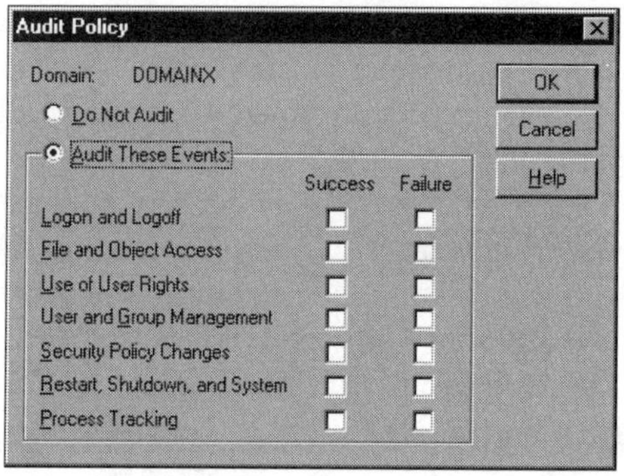

When you select the Audit These Events radio button, auditing is enabled. Nothing is logged in the Security Log, however, until you select one of the check boxes (Success or Failure) for each of the event categories that you want to audit. If you leave Do Not Audit selected, no auditing occurs and of course nothing is logged.

Once auditing is enabled and one or more of the seven event categories are selected, Windows NT will log these events into the Security Log.

Auditing Categories for Windows NT Events

Each entry in the Security Log shows the action performed, the user who performed it, and the date and time of the action. You can audit for either the failed attempt of an action or the successful completion of an action, or both. This lets you specifically track who performed certain tasks across the network and who attempted to take actions that are not allowed.

■ The Event Viewer Security Log

The Windows NT Event Viewer is your window to the events that you audit. To get to the Event Viewer, click on the Event Viewer icon in the Administrative Tools group.

Event Viewer provides three logs: the Application, System, and Security event logs. Our focus in this chapter is the Security Log (see Figure 12.2).

Should You Audit Success or Failure?

Successful events or failed attempts—which is the bigger threat? Auditing for successful operations helps you trace and reconstruct events. The downside is that all successful operations have passed NT security checks, and this type of auditing can create a significant number of events. Auditing for failures can help you identify and arrest someone's attempt to penetrate your network, before they actually succeed. There is no right answer here. It is a matter of what works better for you.

Figure 12.2

A page from the Event Viewer's Security Log

Event Viewer - Security Log on \\COMPUTERX

Log View Options Help

Date	Time	Source	Category	Event	User	Computer
2/11/97	2:20:57 PM	Security	Detailed Tracking	592	Administrator	COMPU
2/11/97	2:20:54 PM	Security	Detailed Tracking	593	Administrator	COMPU
2/11/97	2:20:49 PM	Security	Detailed Tracking	593	Administrator	COMPU
2/11/97	2:20:49 PM	Security	Detailed Tracking	593	Administrator	COMPU
2/11/97	2:20:49 PM	Security	Detailed Tracking	593	Administrator	COMPU
2/11/97	2:20:48 PM	Security	Detailed Tracking	593	Administrator	COMPU
2/11/97	2:20:48 PM	Security	Detailed Tracking	592	Administrator	COMPU
2/11/97	2:20:48 PM	Security	Detailed Tracking	592	Administrator	COMPU
2/11/97	2:20:47 PM	Security	Detailed Tracking	593	Administrator	COMPU
2/11/97	2:20:47 PM	Security	Detailed Tracking	592	Administrator	COMPU
2/11/97	2:20:45 PM	Security	Detailed Tracking	592	Administrator	COMPU
2/11/97	2:20:44 PM	Security	Detailed Tracking	592	Administrator	COMPU
2/11/97	2:20:44 PM	Security	Detailed Tracking	592	Administrator	COMPU
2/11/97	2:20:43 PM	Security	Detailed Tracking	592	SYSTEM	COMPU
2/11/97	2:20:43 PM	Security	Detailed Tracking	592	SYSTEM	COMPU
2/11/97	2:20:42 PM	Security	Privilege Use	576	Administrator	COMPU
2/11/97	2:20:42 PM	Security	Logon/Logoff	528	Administrator	COMPU
2/11/97	2:20:42 PM	Security	Privilege Use	576	Administrator	COMPU
2/11/97	2:20:42 PM	Security	Logon/Logoff	528	Administrator	COMPU
2/11/97	2:20:35 PM	Security	Logon/Logoff	538	Administrator	COMPU
2/11/97	2:20:33 PM	Security	Detailed Tracking	593	Administrator	COMPU
2/11/97	2:20:33 PM	Security	Detailed Tracking	593	Administrator	COMPU
2/11/97	2:20:32 PM	Security	Detailed Tracking	593	Administrator	COMPU
2/11/97	2:20:31 PM	Security	Privilege Use	578	Administrator	COMPU

The first item to look at in Figure 12.2 is the Category column. Note that the categories listed in the Security Log do not match the event categories you saw in the Audit Policy dialog. This is just one of Microsoft's ways of keeping us all on our toes. For help, take another look at Table 12.1, which cross-references the two sets of categories.

Working with the Security Log

You can view the Security Log for other NT machines (workstations or servers), as long as you have the rights. To switch to another machine's Security Log, choose Select Computer from the Security Log's Log menu. In the Select Computer dialog (see Figure 12.3), simply highlight the computer you want to view and click OK.

Figure 12.3

Selecting another computer's Security Log

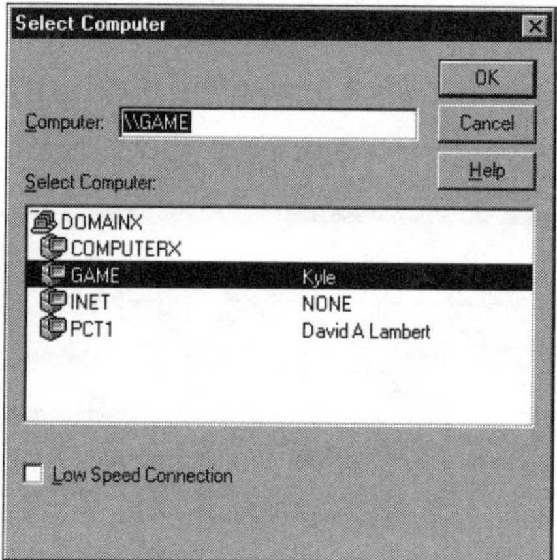

You can also save the Security Log to a file. This is important when you are trying to keep a nonstop log. Just periodically save the Log to file, and then clear the Security Log itself. You have several choices of file formats for saving the Log: text file, comma-delimited file, or Event Log file. The comma-delimited file allows for easy import into a database or spreadsheet for better analysis. This is particularly good for complex searches and trend analysis. The Event Log file format allows you to open the saved Log file within the Event Viewer, with the same look and feel of the "live" Log.

One of the commands in the Log menu is for Log Settings; this is where you find disk space usage controls. It is very important to understand how this works. If you do not allow overwrites as needed, then you stand the chance of locking your entire system if the Security Log fills up. On high-security systems, that is probably what you want. But in lower-security environments it can create substantial difficulty. Many Administrators choose to set the Overwrite Events as Needed option, and adjust the size of the log file up far enough to keep it from getting full in between file save-and-clear operations.

Of course, you may need to have very tight security in your environment. Indeed, you may not only want to have your Security Log file overwritten, but also for the system to shut down when the Log file is full. You can set this up by adding a new entry in the Registry. This setting causes system shutdown when an audit event tries to write to a full Security Log. The Registry entry is as follows:

```
HKEY_LOCAL_Machine:
SYSTEM\CurrentControlSet\Control\LSA
```

Then create a value named CrashOnAuditFail with REG_WORD value of 1.

You must restart for this to take effect. The system will actually crash. Upon recovery, immediately go in as an administrator and save and clear the Security Log. The value will be reset to zero after a crash, so after the recovery you may want to set the CrashOnAuditFail value back to 1.

You can change the location of the Security Log in the Registry at

```
HKEY_LOCAL_Machine:
SYSTEM\CurrentControlSet\Services\EventLog\Security
```

Events in Detail

The following sections describe the details of events to audit. Events of concern include logon and logoff, file and object access, use of user rights and privileges, user and group management, security policy changes, and system and process tracking events.

Logon and Logoff Events

The Logon/Logoff category includes both primary and secondary logon and logoff attempts. A primary attempt is a user logging on or off the domain; a secondary attempt is a user making a network connection. Since logon authentication is a fundamental part of security, it is recommended that you always audit for both successful and failed logon attempts.

The details of this event category indicate what type of logon was attempted/performed interactive, network, or service. In creating the Log in Figure 12.4, we have set the audit policy in User Manager to audit only Logon and Logoff for both Successful and Failed attempts. No other audit policy item was selected. Then we cleared the Security Log and logged on to the domain controller (domain name DOMAINX; and computer name COMPUTERX) as NeLambert, MaPatel, and Administrator; and as JaHunter we did a remote logon from a Windows 95 workstation.

If we double-click on the 12:49:23PM entry for NeLambert (see Figure 12.5), the event details appear in the Event Detail dialog shown in Figure 12.6. The type of event is specified by the number in the Event ID field. Event 528 is a successful logon, and event 538 is a successful logoff.

Figure 12.4

Logon/Logoff events in the Security Log

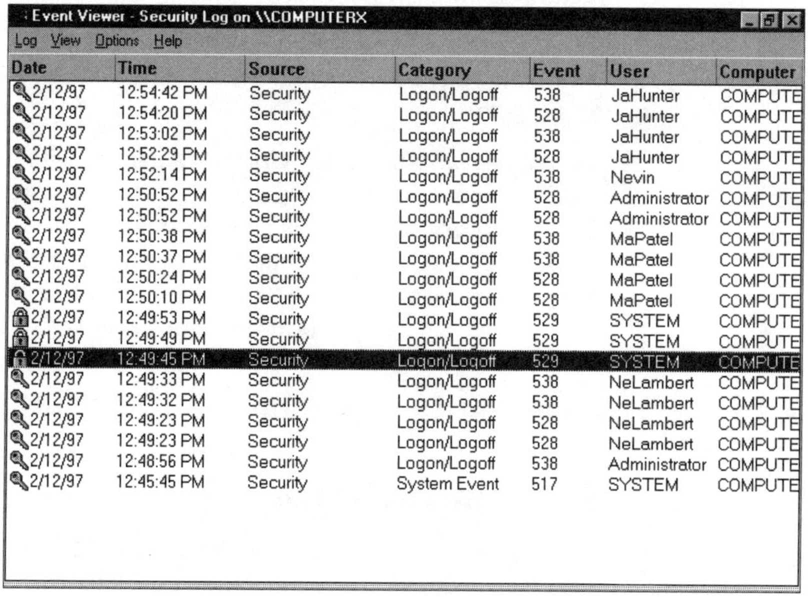

Event Viewer - Security Log on \\COMPUTERX

Log View Options Help

Date	Time	Source	Category	Event	User	Computer
2/12/97	12:54:42 PM	Security	Logon/Logoff	538	JaHunter	COMPUTE
2/12/97	12:54:20 PM	Security	Logon/Logoff	528	JaHunter	COMPUTE
2/12/97	12:53:02 PM	Security	Logon/Logoff	538	JaHunter	COMPUTE
2/12/97	12:52:29 PM	Security	Logon/Logoff	528	JaHunter	COMPUTE
2/12/97	12:52:14 PM	Security	Logon/Logoff	538	Nevin	COMPUTE
2/12/97	12:50:52 PM	Security	Logon/Logoff	528	Administrator	COMPUTE
2/12/97	12:50:52 PM	Security	Logon/Logoff	528	Administrator	COMPUTE
2/12/97	12:50:38 PM	Security	Logon/Logoff	538	MaPatel	COMPUTE
2/12/97	12:50:37 PM	Security	Logon/Logoff	538	MaPatel	COMPUTE
2/12/97	12:50:24 PM	Security	Logon/Logoff	528	MaPatel	COMPUTE
2/12/97	12:50:10 PM	Security	Logon/Logoff	528	MaPatel	COMPUTE
2/12/97	12:49:53 PM	Security	Logon/Logoff	529	SYSTEM	COMPUTE
2/12/97	12:49:49 PM	Security	Logon/Logoff	529	SYSTEM	COMPUTE
2/12/97	12:49:45 PM	Security	Logon/Logoff	529	SYSTEM	COMPUTE
2/12/97	12:49:33 PM	Security	Logon/Logoff	538	NeLambert	COMPUTE
2/12/97	12:49:32 PM	Security	Logon/Logoff	538	NeLambert	COMPUTE
2/12/97	12:49:23 PM	Security	Logon/Logoff	528	NeLambert	COMPUTE
2/12/97	12:49:23 PM	Security	Logon/Logoff	528	NeLambert	COMPUTE
2/12/97	12:48:56 PM	Security	Logon/Logoff	538	Administrator	COMPUTE
2/12/97	12:45:45 PM	Security	System Event	517	SYSTEM	COMPUTE

Figure 12.5

NeLambert's logon entry in the Security Log

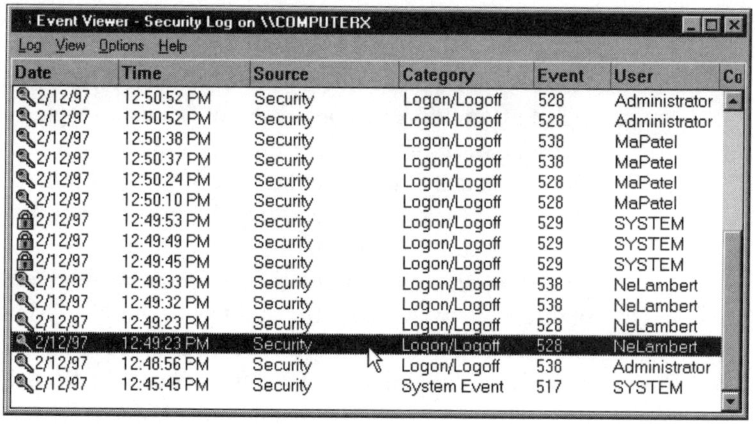

Event Viewer - Security Log on \\COMPUTERX

Log View Options Help

Date	Time	Source	Category	Event	User	Co
2/12/97	12:50:52 PM	Security	Logon/Logoff	528	Administrator	
2/12/97	12:50:52 PM	Security	Logon/Logoff	528	Administrator	
2/12/97	12:50:38 PM	Security	Logon/Logoff	538	MaPatel	
2/12/97	12:50:37 PM	Security	Logon/Logoff	538	MaPatel	
2/12/97	12:50:24 PM	Security	Logon/Logoff	528	MaPatel	
2/12/97	12:50:10 PM	Security	Logon/Logoff	528	MaPatel	
2/12/97	12:49:53 PM	Security	Logon/Logoff	529	SYSTEM	
2/12/97	12:49:49 PM	Security	Logon/Logoff	529	SYSTEM	
2/12/97	12:49:45 PM	Security	Logon/Logoff	529	SYSTEM	
2/12/97	12:49:33 PM	Security	Logon/Logoff	538	NeLambert	
2/12/97	12:49:32 PM	Security	Logon/Logoff	538	NeLambert	
2/12/97	12:49:23 PM	Security	Logon/Logoff	528	NeLambert	
2/12/97	12:49:23 PM	Security	Logon/Logoff	528	NeLambert	
2/12/97	12:48:56 PM	Security	Logon/Logoff	538	Administrator	
2/12/97	12:45:45 PM	Security	System Event	517	SYSTEM	

Figure 12.6

Details of NeLambert's logon event

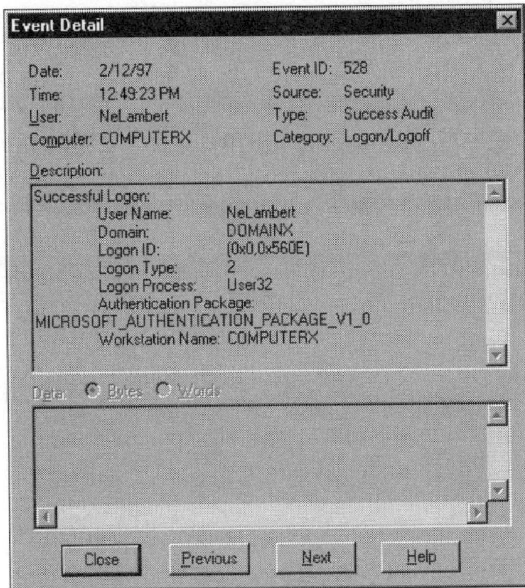

Logon/Logoff Event Details

Let's examine the details of the Security Log's entries in the Logon/Logoff category.

Authentication Package Remember the MSV1_0 authentication package (MSV1_0.DLL) discussed in Chapter 5? It shows up here as MICROSOFT_AUTHENTICATION_PACKAGE_V1_0.

Domain This is the name of the computer or domain from which the account is validated.

Logon ID This is a unique identifier given to the user's process on logon; it can be used to pair up with corresponding logoffs. The Logon ID will appear in other audited events generated from this logon session; therefore, the event can be associated with a user via this ID.

Logon Process This is the process that generates the logon request. Interactive logons are requested by User32, and a network logon may be generated by KSecDD or NTLanMan.

Logon Type This is the type of logon or logon process. Type 2 is an interactive logon, and Type 3 is a remote or network logon.

Reason This detail is only seen on failed logon attempts. It states the system's reason for the failure of the attempt.

User Name This is the name of the user attempting to log on.

Multiple Logon Entries

On most NT Servers, you will see two logon events in the Security Log when a user successfully logs on. In Figure 12.7, note the multiple entries for the users named test, MaPatel, NeLambert, and Administrator.

Figure 12.7

Multiple logon entries

Event Viewer - Security Log on \\COMPUTERX

Log View Options Help

Date	Time	Source	Category	Event	User	Computer
2/12/97	10:03:56 PM	Security	Logon/Logoff	538	test	COMPU
2/12/97	10:03:55 PM	Security	Logon/Logoff	538	test	COMPU
2/12/97	10:03:19 PM	Security	Logon/Logoff	528	test	COMPU
2/12/97	10:03:19 PM	Security	Logon/Logoff	528	test	COMPU
2/12/97	10:02:15 PM	Security	Logon/Logoff	538	NeLambert	COMPU
2/12/97	10:02:13 PM	Security	Logon/Logoff	538	NeLambert	COMPU
2/12/97	7:28:50 PM	Security	Logon/Logoff	528	Dalambert	COMPU
2/12/97	4:15:14 PM	Security	Logon/Logoff	528	NeLambert	COMPU
2/12/97	4:15:14 PM	Security	Logon/Logoff	528	NeLambert	COMPU
2/12/97	4:15:02 PM	Security	Logon/Logoff	538	Administrator	COMPU
2/12/97	4:13:39 PM	Security	Logon/Logoff	538	Administrator	COMPU
2/12/97	4:03:37 PM	Security	Logon/Logoff	528	Administrator	COMPU
2/12/97	4:03:37 PM	Security	Logon/Logoff	528	Administrator	COMPU
2/12/97	4:03:22 PM	Security	Logon/Logoff	529	SYSTEM	COMPU
2/12/97	4:03:11 PM	Security	Logon/Logoff	538	MaPatel	COMPU
2/12/97	4:03:10 PM	Security	Logon/Logoff	538	MaPatel	COMPU
2/12/97	4:02:48 PM	Security	Logon/Logoff	528	MaPatel	COMPU
2/12/97	4:02:36 PM	Security	Logon/Logoff	528	MaPatel	COMPU
2/12/97	4:02:19 PM	Security	Logon/Logoff	538	Administrator	COMPU
2/12/97	2:58:35 PM	Security	Logon/Logoff	528	Nevin	COMPU
2/12/97	2:31:00 PM	Security	Logon/Logoff	538	Nevin	COMPU
2/12/97	2:15:29 PM	Security	Logon/Logoff	528	Nevin	COMPU
2/12/97	1:50:23 PM	Security	Logon/Logoff	538	Nevin	COMPU
2/12/97	1:41:50 PM	Security	Logon/Logoff	528	Nevin	COMPU

Look at the details of the first MaPatel entry at 4:02:36PM (see Figure 12.8); this is an interactive logon (Type 2).

Now look at the previous entry just seconds later at 4:02:48PM (see Figure 12.9). Note the logon type is 3, and the process is KSecDD. This tells us that MaPatel has a successful network logon.

And when MaPatel logs off, we get two more entries at 4:03:11PM and 4:03:10PM (refer back to Figure 12.7). The details of these entries are shown in Figures 12.10 and 12.11.

Now we have two logoffs. This is easy to explain. When you log off, NT automatically logs you off *all* sessions started from the original logon. Since the first interactive logon spawned the second network logon when MaPatel logged off NT, the system automatically closed all network logons first and then carried out the interactive logoff. But why was there a network logon in the first place?

Figure 12.8

Successful interactive logon

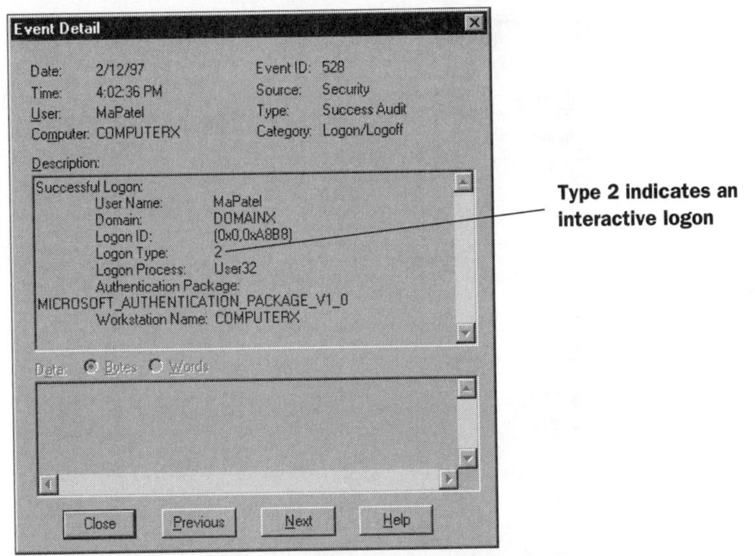

Figure 12.9

Network logon

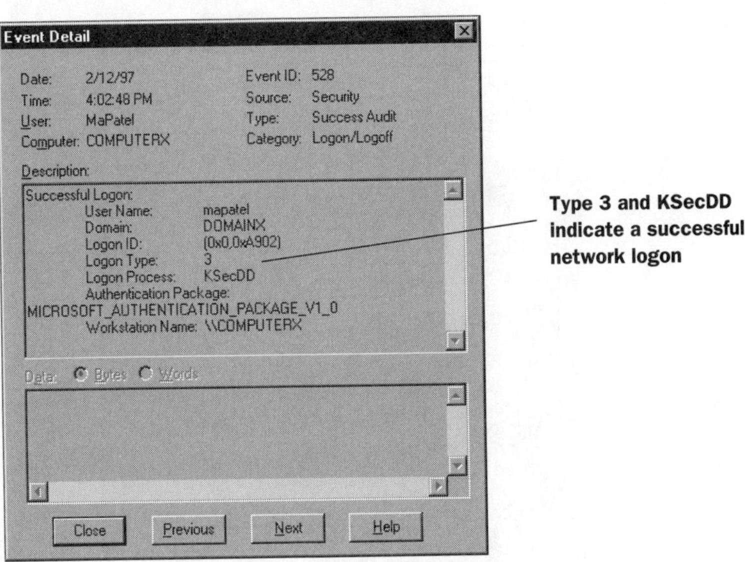

Figure 12.10

Entry 4:03:11, interactive logoff (Type 2)

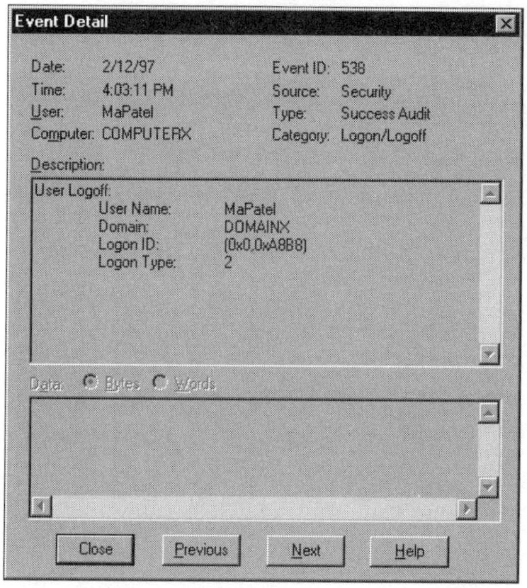

Event Detail

Date: 2/12/97
Time: 4:03:11 PM
User: MaPatel
Computer: COMPUTERX
Event ID: 538
Source: Security
Type: Success Audit
Category: Logon/Logoff

Description:
User Logoff:
User Name: MaPatel
Domain: DOMAINX
Logon ID: (0x0,0xA8B8)
Logon Type: 2

Data: Bytes Words

Close Previous Next Help

Figure 12.11

Entry 4:03:10, network logoff (Type 3)

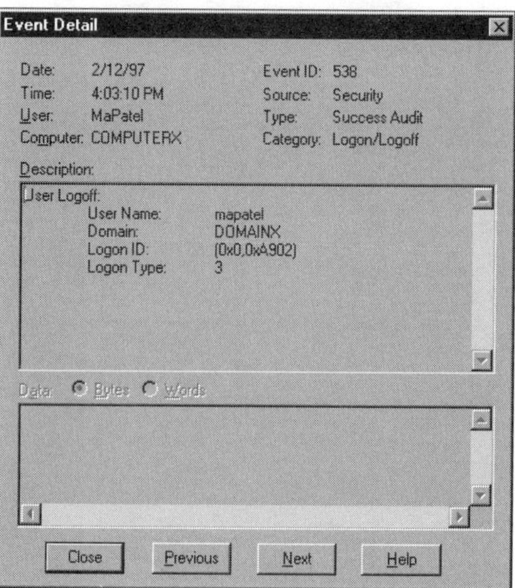

With a little background knowledge, this is fairly easy to understand. Let's recall some of what has been covered in previous chapters. First, remember NT's physical and network architecture, as described in Chapters 2 and 7. NT is a client/server operating system, even to the point of the interactive logon at an NT system. As a user on an NT machine, you frequently access resources exactly as if you were connecting to that same resource across a network.

Second, recall the different logon processes and options. Frequently NT must connect to the NetLogon share to carry out certain actions, such as logon scripts or profiles. If you log on to a domain controller interactively, the system may have to connect to its own NetLogon share. You can do this yourself; you probably have. In Explorer, go to Network Neighborhood and connect to your own machine. As long as you have shares available, you can access your machine just as if it were miles away. See Figure 12.12.

Figure 12.12

ComputerX connecting to ComputerX

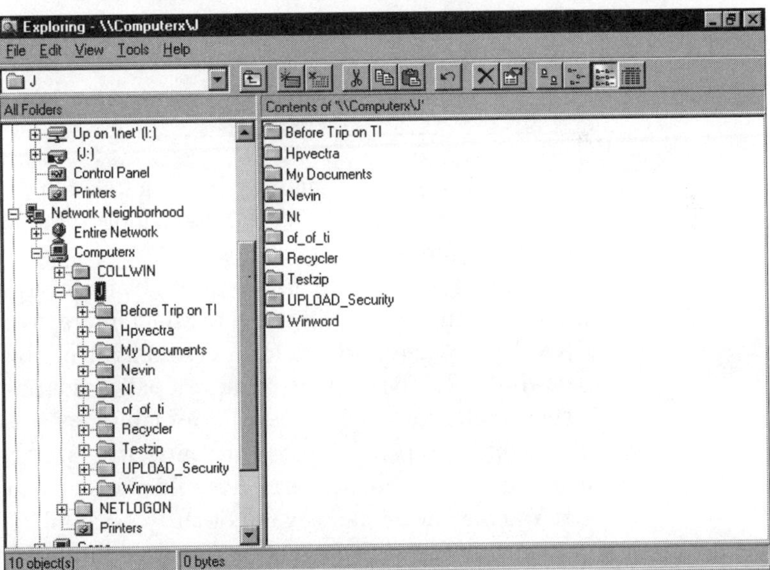

At logon, NT frequently establishes both the primary (Type 2) interactive logon and the secondary (Type 3) network logon. When might this not happen? On a member server or workstation that is not operating as a part of a domain or has no need to directly access itself during the logon process.

Failed Logon Attempts

In Figure 12.13 you can see several entries with lock icons at the left margin. These represent failed logon/logoff attempts (You'll see these locks on any failed events you have designated to be audited.)

Figure 12.13

Failed logons

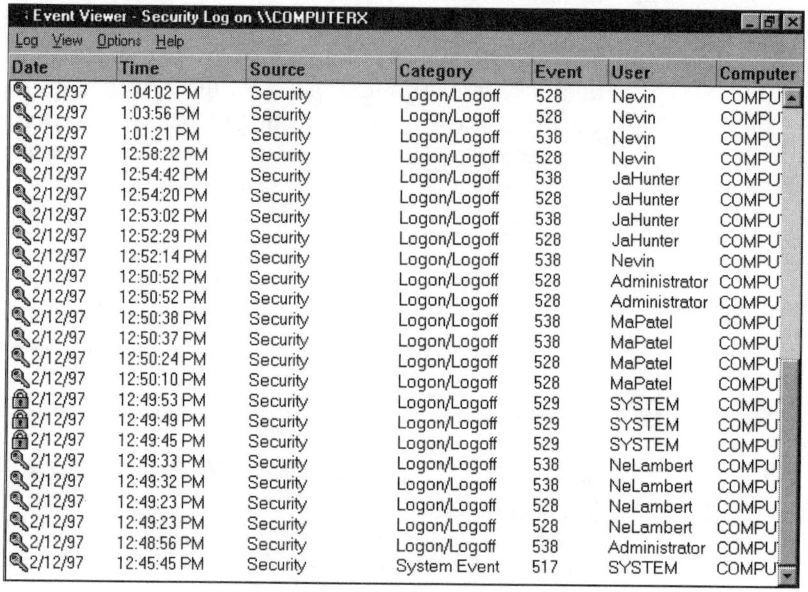

Event Viewer - Security Log on \\COMPUTERX

Log View Options Help

Date	Time	Source	Category	Event	User	Computer
2/12/97	1:04:02 PM	Security	Logon/Logoff	528	Nevin	COMPU
2/12/97	1:03:56 PM	Security	Logon/Logoff	528	Nevin	COMPU
2/12/97	1:01:21 PM	Security	Logon/Logoff	538	Nevin	COMPU
2/12/97	12:58:22 PM	Security	Logon/Logoff	528	Nevin	COMPU
2/12/97	12:54:42 PM	Security	Logon/Logoff	538	JaHunter	COMPU
2/12/97	12:54:20 PM	Security	Logon/Logoff	528	JaHunter	COMPU
2/12/97	12:53:02 PM	Security	Logon/Logoff	538	JaHunter	COMPU
2/12/97	12:52:29 PM	Security	Logon/Logoff	528	JaHunter	COMPU
2/12/97	12:52:14 PM	Security	Logon/Logoff	538	Nevin	COMPU
2/12/97	12:50:52 PM	Security	Logon/Logoff	528	Administrator	COMPU
2/12/97	12:50:52 PM	Security	Logon/Logoff	528	Administrator	COMPU
2/12/97	12:50:38 PM	Security	Logon/Logoff	538	MaPatel	COMPU
2/12/97	12:50:37 PM	Security	Logon/Logoff	538	MaPatel	COMPU
2/12/97	12:50:24 PM	Security	Logon/Logoff	528	MaPatel	COMPU
2/12/97	12:50:10 PM	Security	Logon/Logoff	528	MaPatel	COMPU
2/12/97	12:49:53 PM	Security	Logon/Logoff	529	SYSTEM	COMPU
2/12/97	12:49:49 PM	Security	Logon/Logoff	529	SYSTEM	COMPU
2/12/97	12:49:45 PM	Security	Logon/Logoff	529	SYSTEM	COMPU
2/12/97	12:49:33 PM	Security	Logon/Logoff	538	NeLambert	COMPU
2/12/97	12:49:32 PM	Security	Logon/Logoff	538	NeLambert	COMPU
2/12/97	12:49:23 PM	Security	Logon/Logoff	528	NeLambert	COMPU
2/12/97	12:49:23 PM	Security	Logon/Logoff	528	NeLambert	COMPU
2/12/97	12:48:56 PM	Security	Logon/Logoff	538	Administrator	COMPU
2/12/97	12:45:45 PM	Security	System Event	517	SYSTEM	COMPU

Note that the event number is 529, a failed logon attempt, and also that the user is listed as the SYSTEM. Let's look at the details of one of these entries (see Figure 12.14).

Here we have an attempt to log on by a user using MaPatel for a username. We can see that they tried to do an interactive logon on COMPUTERX. The reason for the failure is given as "Unknown user name or bad password." NT does not keep track of passwords and certainly would never display them. Although these kinds of failure events are often caused by simple spelling errors in the password entry, they are one of your first signs of unauthorized system access and should always be audited.

You may encounter several other types of failed logon events that are self-explanatory, such as password expired (event 535), account restricted (event 534), and account disabled (event 531).

File and Object Access Events

File and object access events occur when a user or program accesses a file, folder, printer, or other ACL-controlled object. This category is special in that it requires other action before actual logging of events takes place. You must specify the object that you want tracked, and what actions you want to audit. This is done through the *auditing controls* of the object.

Figure 12.14

Failed logon details

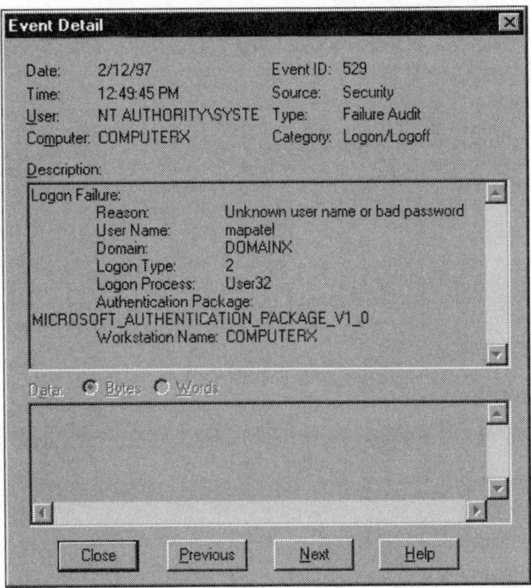

The auditing controls for files and folders are found in Explorer, much like setting file and folder permissions. You open the Properties dialog of the folder, choose Security, and select Auditing. (More on this later.)

Determining the auditing of objects is the most challenging category for setting up auditing in Windows NT. Here you can specify files and folders to be audited and thus keep very good track of what is happening to your sensitive material. On the other hand, it is very easy to get out of control and audit too much. "Too much" auditing is apparent when you wind up with an overwhelming number of entries in the log, and thus the chances of spotting anomalies are significantly reduced.

Auditing of Files and Folders

To enable file and folder auditing, you need to have checked the Success and Failure boxes for File and Object Access in the Audit Policy dialog (see Figure 12.15).

Now you are ready to specify objects to audit. Using Explorer, select a file or folder on an NTFS partition to audit. In Figure 12.16, we have selected the Yearend Folder on drive F.

We select all the files in Yearend and choose File/Properties, click on the Security tab, and then on the Auditing button. This displays the File Auditing dialog (see Figure 12.17).

Take a look at the Events to Audit section: It is grayed out because we have not yet selected anyone to audit. If we click on Add, we get the list of

Figure 12.15

Adding File and Object Access auditing to the audit policy

Audit Policy
Domain: DOMAINX
Do Not Audit
Audit These Events:

	Success	Failure
Logon and Logoff	☑	☑
File and Object Access	☑	☑
Use of User Rights	☐	☐
User and Group Management	☐	☐
Security Policy Changes	☐	☐
Restart, Shutdown, and System	☐	☐
Process Tracking	☐	☐

OK
Cancel
Help

Figure 12.16

Auditing the Yearend folder

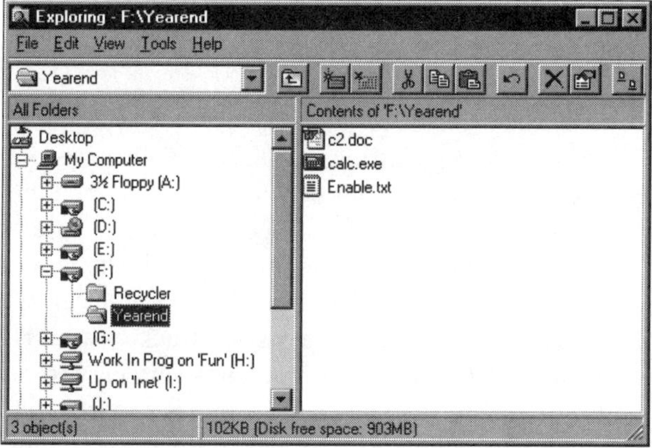

groups and users from our domain, much like setting file and folder security permissions (see Figure 12.18). For this example we will select Everyone and audit for Write events, as shown in Figure 12.19.

Suppose MaPatel logs on and accesses the enable.txt file with notepad.exe, without making any changes. Then he closes the file and reopens it, this time editing the file. And finally he logs off. Let's look at Figure 12.20.

Look down the list of events at MaPatel's logon entries (primary and secondary). Bring up the Event Detail dialog that shows the details of the first object-access entry after MaPatel's logon—the entry at 10:46:49AM (see Figure 12.21a). Event 560 is important in that it shows you what level of access was granted for the user. In Figure 12.21b you see that several types of read access were granted. The next event in the Log is also at 10:46:49AM; bring up the Detail dialog (see Figure 12.22) and it shows the handle-closed event. Since MaPatel hasn't done anything to the file yet, this is as we expected.

Figure 12.17

File Auditing dialog

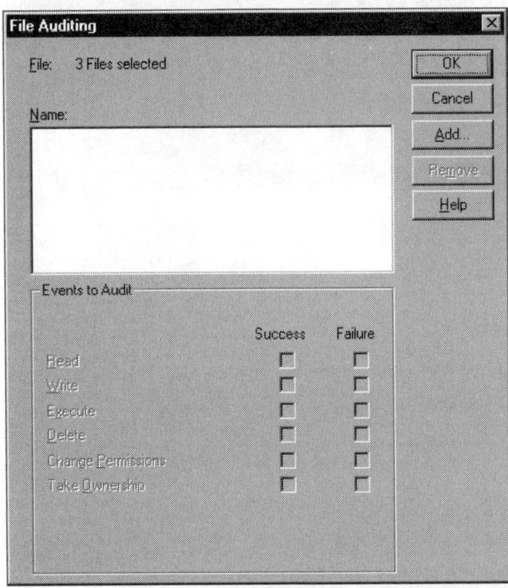

Figure 12.18

The Add Users and Groups dialog helps us specify whom to audit.

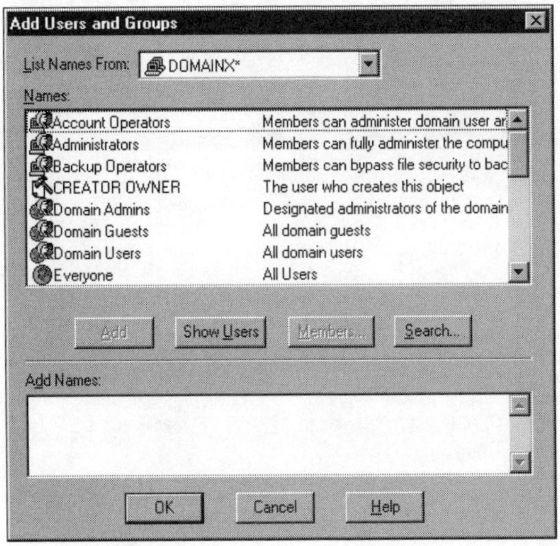

Add Users and Groups

List Names From: DOMAINX*

Names:

Account Operators — Members can administer domain user ar
Administrators — Members can fully administer the compu
Backup Operators — Members can bypass file security to bac
CREATOR OWNER — The user who creates this object
Domain Admins — Designated administrators of the domain
Domain Guests — All domain guests
Domain Users — All domain users
Everyone — All Users

Add | Show Users | Members... | Search...

Add Names:

OK | Cancel | Help

Figure 12.19

Setting up to audit Write events for Everyone

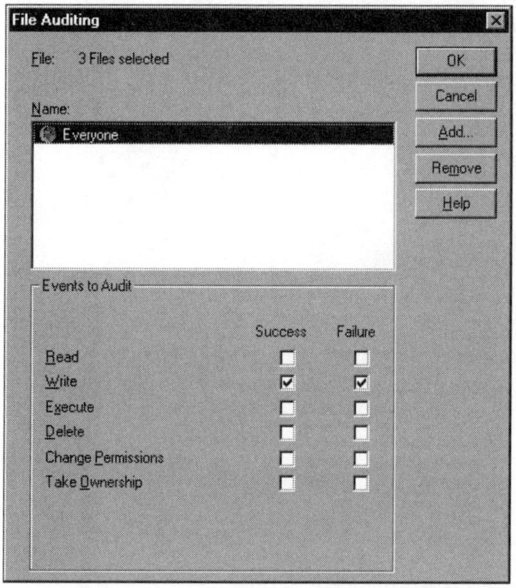

File Auditing

File: 3 Files selected

Name: Everyone

OK | Cancel | Add... | Remove | Help

Events to Audit

	Success	Failure
Read	☐	☐
Write	☑	☑
Execute	☐	☐
Delete	☐	☐
Change Permissions	☐	☐
Take Ownership	☐	☐

Figure 12.20

Event log

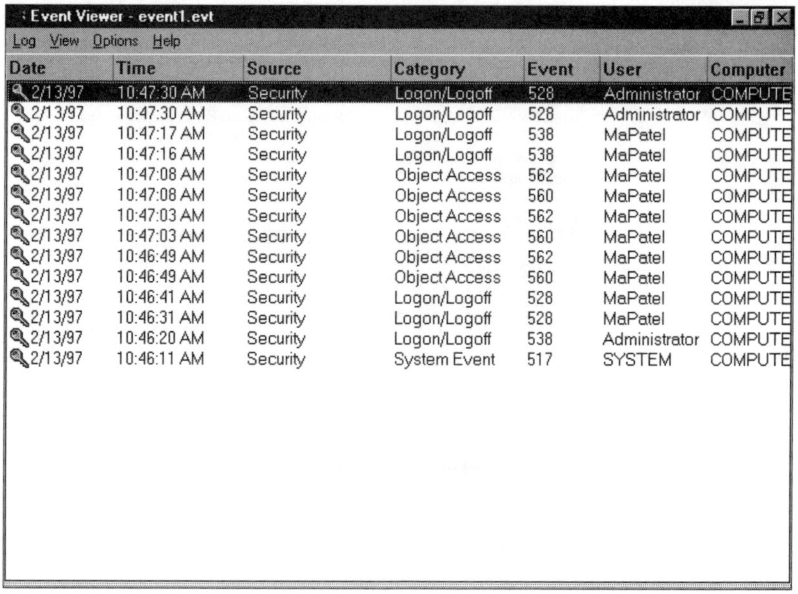

Event Viewer - event1.evt

Log View Options Help

Date	Time	Source	Category	Event	User	Computer
2/13/97	10:47:30 AM	Security	Logon/Logoff	528	Administrator	COMPUTE
2/13/97	10:47:30 AM	Security	Logon/Logoff	528	Administrator	COMPUTE
2/13/97	10:47:17 AM	Security	Logon/Logoff	538	MaPatel	COMPUTE
2/13/97	10:47:16 AM	Security	Logon/Logoff	538	MaPatel	COMPUTE
2/13/97	10:47:08 AM	Security	Object Access	562	MaPatel	COMPUTE
2/13/97	10:47:08 AM	Security	Object Access	560	MaPatel	COMPUTE
2/13/97	10:47:03 AM	Security	Object Access	562	MaPatel	COMPUTE
2/13/97	10:47:03 AM	Security	Object Access	560	MaPatel	COMPUTE
2/13/97	10:46:49 AM	Security	Object Access	562	MaPatel	COMPUTE
2/13/97	10:46:49 AM	Security	Object Access	560	MaPatel	COMPUTE
2/13/97	10:46:41 AM	Security	Logon/Logoff	528	MaPatel	COMPUTE
2/13/97	10:46:31 AM	Security	Logon/Logoff	528	MaPatel	COMPUTE
2/13/97	10:46:20 AM	Security	Logon/Logoff	538	Administrator	COMPUTE
2/13/97	10:46:11 AM	Security	System Event	517	SYSTEM	COMPUTE

Figure 12.21a

Details of 10:46:49AM object access

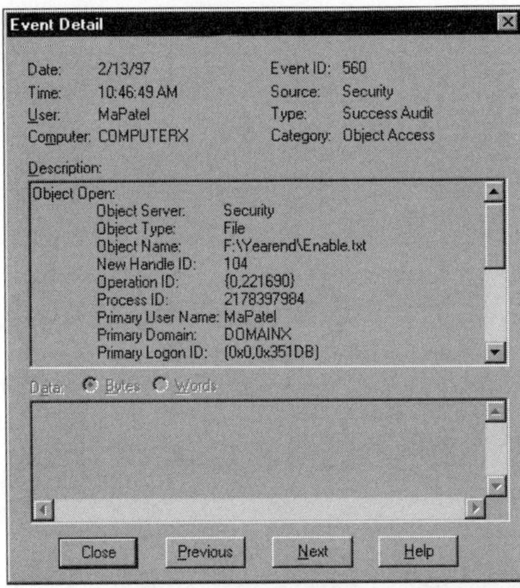

Figure 12.21b

Additional information describing 10:46:49AM object access

Event Detail
Date: 2/13/97
Time: 10:46:49 AM
User: MaPatel
Computer: COMPUTERX
Event ID: 560
Source: Security
Type: Success Audit
Category: Object Access
Description:
Primary Logon ID: (0x0,0x351DB)
Client User Name: -
Client Domain: -
Client Logon ID: -
Accesses READ_CONTROL
SYNCHRONIZE
ReadData (or ListDirectory)
ReadEA
ReadAttributes
Data: Bytes Words
Close
Previous
Next
Help

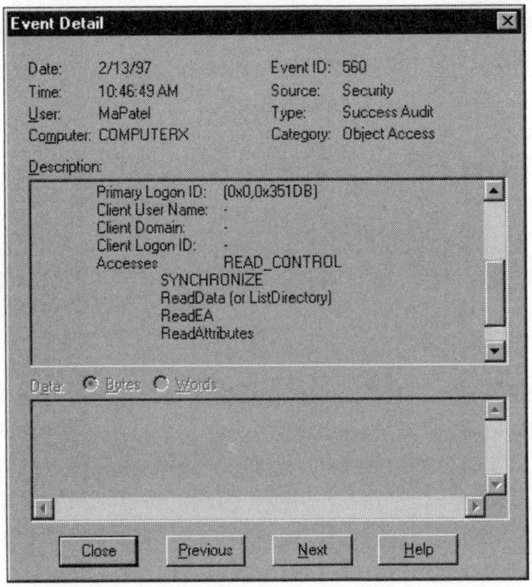

Figure 12.22

Object handle closed

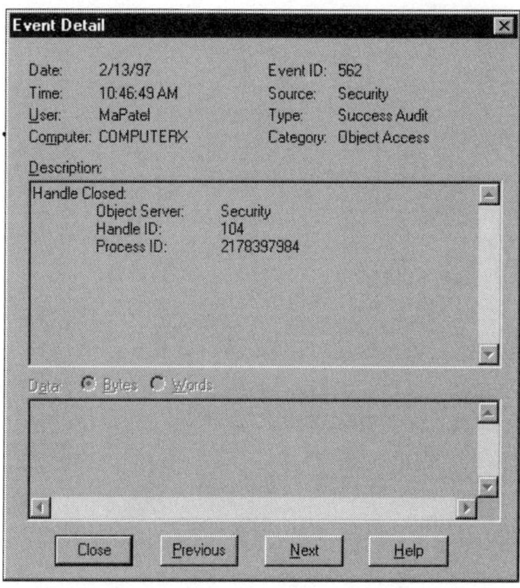

File and Object Access Event Details

Looking back at Figures 12.21a and b and Figure 12.22, let's discuss the entries in the Event Detail dialog.

Object Server This is the name of the NT subsystem process calling the audit function.

Object Type This is the type of object being accessed in this file.

Object Name This is the name of the object—in this case, the filename.

New Handle ID This ID enables the event to be associated with future events. For example, to determine how long a file has been opened, you can look at the handle ID assigned to the file. Then find out when the handle is closed, which is another event in the Log with the same handle ID. Comparing the times on each event will tell you how long the file was open. (This is only true for applications that maintain the handle on the file during work operations.)

Operation ID This unique identifier associates multiple events within a single operation. In the architecture of NT, responsibilities for access validation and handle creation are split. The Object Manager does handle creation. Object type-specific code (the file system) is responsible for access validation to objects of that type (files). Specifically, the NT File System (NTFS) calls audit events based on access validation to file objects, and the Object

Manager later calls another, *related* audit event specifying that a handle to the file object has been created. The objects are related via the Operation ID.

Process ID This is the client-side process that is accessing the object. Determining who is actually behind an access operation (writing to a file) is one of the most important aspects of security. In NT, however, a thread that requests access to a resource is identified by the user ID, and that thread may be impersonating someone else. Thus, it would be ambiguous to log events only by user ID. To handle this, the Windows NT audit function uses two levels of subject identification: the primary logon ID (user ID) and the *impersonation* or process ID (client ID).

This also enables the tracking of processes, what they do, and what programs they call or run.

Primary User Name This is the server-side process. It's usually the same as the client user unless impersonation is taking place.

Primary Domain This is the name of the computer or domain that validated the user—unless the Primary User Name entry is SYSTEM, in which case SYSTEM would be listed here also.

Primary Logon This is the unique logon ID assigned during the user logon process. See "Logon and Logoff Events" section earlier in the chapter.

Client User Name This is the client-side username—the user on whose behalf the Primary User Name is performing the operation.

Client Domain This is the name of the computer or domain where the user is logged on.

Client Logon ID This is the unique identifier by which the client-side user is logged in.

Access This is the type of access attempted or requested.

The Object Access Auditing Process

Applications handle audit events in various ways. Consider this scenario: Suppose we are auditing for success and failure events for both read and write operations on the enable.txt file. MaPatel logs on and opens enable.txt, makes a change, and closes the file. What events are logged? The events are analyzed in the following table.

This explanation gives you a start on the process of file auditing—but remember that you should always test what you are auditing. If you were to execute this auditing process a Word or Excel document you would get

Event ID	Events	Analysis
Event 560 Event 562	Object is opened. Handle is closed.	In this series of events, the process opens the enable.txt file for reading. Next, a handle to the file is allocated and then closed. It is clear in the Security Log that Notepad does not keep an open handle to the file; it loads and keeps a copy of the file in memory.
Event 560 Event 562	Object Open Handle Closed	When MaPatel makes a change to the file and then saves it, a new process is spawned that opens the object for reading and writing. Since the event is successful, the new data is written to the file. The handle is then closed.

similar results, but possibly numerous more entries. (Word and Excel make temporary files and grab more rights up front, not to mention Directory Read access rights and network connections that may also increase the number of audit entries.)

Directory Audits

When you right-click on a folder or directory and choose Properties, finding your way to the Directory Auditing dialog, you will see a remarkable resemblance to the Directory Security Permissions dialog. See Figure 12.23.

Figure 12.23

The Directory Auditing dialog

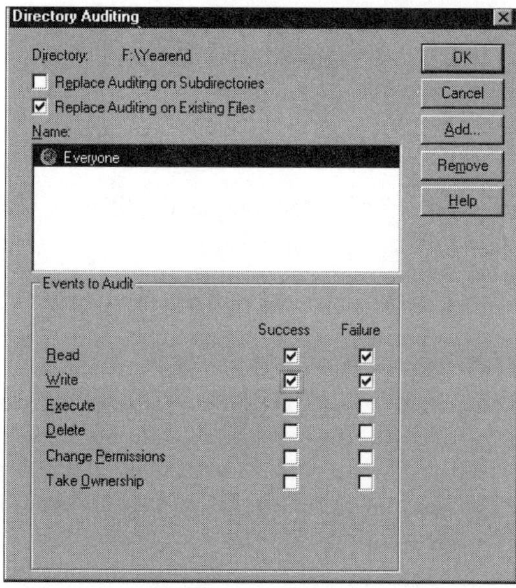

In this dialog, notice that you can change existing auditing settings by checking one or both of the options at the top: Replace Auditing on Subdirectories, or Replace Auditing on Existing Files. These options work exactly like their counterparts in the dialogs for setting security permissions.

When you designate auditing on directories, the auditing settings are propagated automatically to all new objects created in the directory. You can see that, if the directory growth is left unchecked, enormous amounts of auditing events will start showing up. On the other hand, certain directory structures will be very well protected and well secured.

In deciding whether you need to audit these areas, consider whether you need the advantage of being able to audit the activities of authorized users in these directories. In that case, you should audit them. Also, you may need an audit trail to follow should a password become known to and used by unauthorized personnel; this trail can show you what the invader accessed.

There are nearly endless possible scenarios of object auditing—and not near enough time to think them up or space enough in this book to write them up. As you consider your object-auditing needs, you may find some assistance in the decision-making grid in Figure 12.24.

Use of User Rights/Privilege Use Events

The category of Privilege Use in the Security Log is known as Use of User Rights in the Audit Policy dialog (see Table 12.1). This category of events records the users' "hits" on their user rights as assigned from the User Manager's User Rights policy. These rights are assigned to users upon logon, and most uses of these rights can be captured through the other auditing components. One use that cannot be captured is the shutting down of the system, which is audited through this mechanism.

Generally, by auditing for changes to the User Rights policy and audit policy, you can gain the data you need. When you audit Use of User Rights in the Security Log, you audit the times when users exercise specifically granted rights or their attempts to change such rights. An example of this event is a user's changing the system time, or loading and unloading device drivers.

User and Group Management Events

When you audit User and Group Management, you audit events when changes are made to User or Group accounts. Some examples include when a User account or Group is created, changed, or deleted; when a User account is renamed, disabled, or enabled; or when a password is set or changed.

In the Security Log, the Account Management category of events corresponds to the User and Group Management category in the audit policy. The Log records changes made to Window NT users and groups. Event ID 642 records both the changed account (target) and the user making the change

Figure 12.24

Determining your object auditing needs

■ Creates audit event
□ Does not create audit event

To record this ↓ Audit for these →

Actions on Files

	Read	Write	Execute	Delete	Change Permission	Take Ownership
Displaying Data	X	O	O	O	O	O
Displaying Attributes	X	O	X	O	X	O
Display Owner and Permissions	X	X	X	O	O	O
Change Data	O	X	O	O	O	O
Change Attributes	O	X	O	O	O	O
Execute or Run	O	O	X	O	O	O
Delete	O	O	O	X	O	O
Change Permissions	O	O	O	O	X	O
Change Owner	O	O	O	O	O	X

Actions on Directories

	Read	Write	Execute	Delete	Change Permission	Take Ownership
Displaying File Names	X	O	O	O	O	O
Display Attributes	X	O	X	O	O	O
Change Attributes	O	X	O	O	O	O
Create Sundirectories and Files	O	X	O	O	O	O
Changing to a Subdirectory	O	O	X	O	O	O
Display Owner and Permissions	X	X	X	O	O	O
Deleting Directory	O	O	O	X	O	O
Change Directory Permissions	O	O	O	O	X	O
Change Directory Owner	O	O	O	O	O	X

(caller). The target ID is the SID of the user, and the caller ID is the logon ID of the user attempting to make the change.

Audit event 636 is generated when you add a user to a local group (see the Event Detail dialog in Figure 12.25); event 637 is generated when you remove a user. Event 632 occurs when you add a member to a global group, and 633 when you remove a member. The Global Group Changed event 641 will also appear, and event 642 will accompany a change to a local group. Further, event 624 (see Figure 12.26) is the creation of a new account, and 633 is the deletion of a user. You get the point.

Don't forget to test your audits, so you know what you will be logging.

Figure 12.25

Audit Event 636, Add User to Local Group

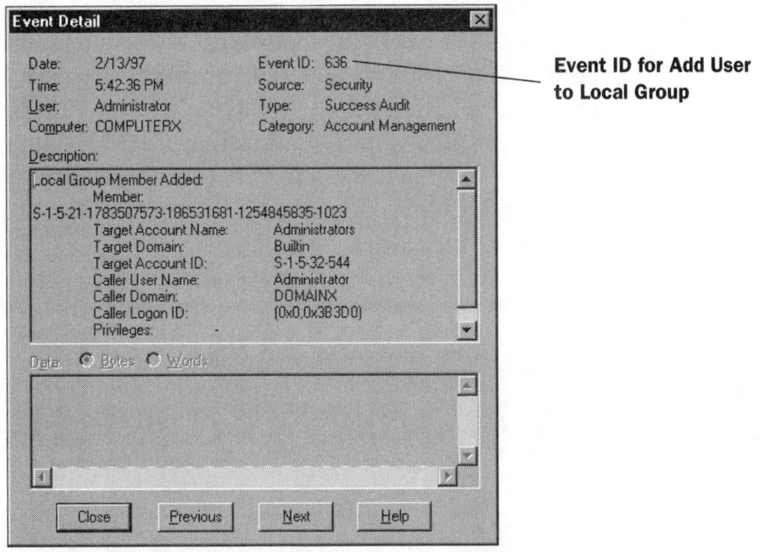

Figure 12.26

Audit Event 624, Create New User

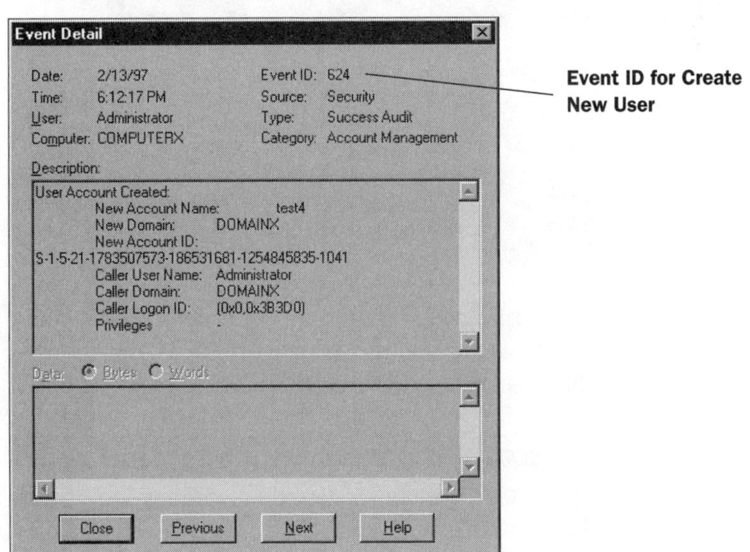

NOTE. *In trust relationships, NT internally creates and deletes user accounts for the trust's use. The account names will end in $ and will not appear in User Manager. The events will be normal 624 and 630 (add and delete).*

Security Policy Change Events

You definitely want to audit policy changes! Also known as Security Policy Changes in the audit policy, this category watches over the use of the User Rights policy and the audit policy itself. The Security Log will contain changes made to the User Rights, Audit, and Trust Relationships policies.

Figures 12.27 and 12.28 illustrate the detail on a Log entry for event 612, an audit policy change. Notice that the entire policy is listed (under the heading New Policy). And if you scroll down (see Figure 12.28), you can see who made the change, including logon ID.

Figure 12.27

Detail of event 612, an audit policy change

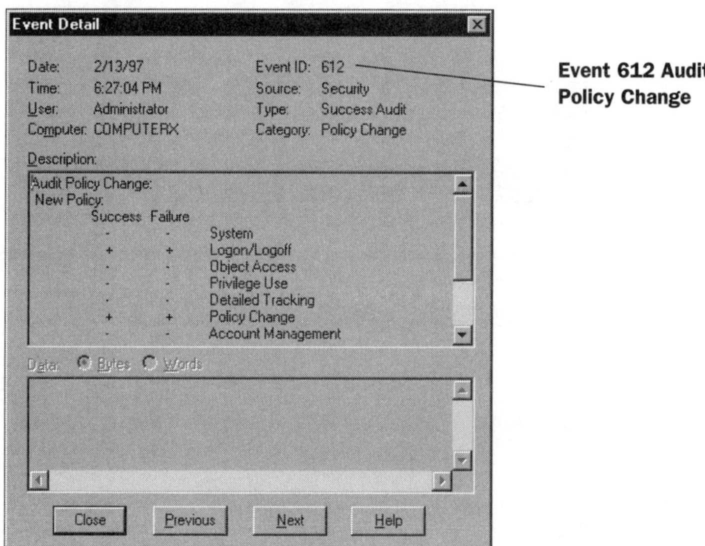

Turning this category of auditing off in the audit policy does not log an event, but turning the category on does; therefore, you can tell when any changes to the audit policy occur.

Restart, Shutdown, and System Events

This category includes general system events such as a user restarting or shutting down the computer, or events that affect system security or the Security Log. Anything that affects the security of the system or the audit functions is recorded as a system event.

Note that if this is the only category audited, audit records for Logon\ Logoff and Detailed Tracking are not generated for the Security Log.

Figure 12.28

Detail of event 612, scrolled down

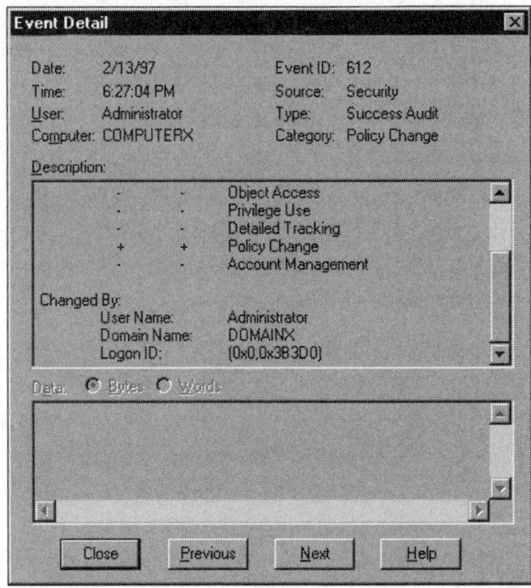

This category (called System Events in the Security Log) shows the all-important system startup and shutdown events (512 and 513). You always want to audit these events—not only to discover who is restarting the system, but (depending on your recovery mode of operation) because the system may shut down due to a stop error and then restart during off-hours. This may be an indication of serious system problems that all administrators need to be aware of.

Process (Detailed) Tracking Events

Process Tracking events (called Detailed Tracking in the Security Log) provide detailed information about programs and internal NT processes. These events include program activation, some forms of handle duplication, indirect object accesses, and process exit. Detailed Tracking is a more precise view of what each process is doing.

Auditing this category is not for the faint of heart. Although it's useful for tracking down program anomalies and even virus attacks, you must remember that when Detailed Tracking is enabled, *audit event records are generated every time a new process is created.*

The following events can be generated from Detail Tacking:

- Event 592, the New Process Has Been Created record.
- Event 593, the Process Has Exited record.
- Event 594, Handle Duplicated, refers to kernel objects. It occurs when a handle is duplicated with the same or lesser access rights.
- Event 595, Indirect Access To Object, is used to indicate a specific event involving the LPC (Local Procedure Call). Connecting to an LPC port causes an access check on one object when creating another object. Event 595 records this action.

The Detailed Tracking information, though esoteric, can provide in-depth views of the internal workings of NT and thus help identify anomalies. For example, if several users in the last 36 hours tried and failed to create a new user account, you would be wise to monitor process creation for every attempt. If the failed attempt to create a user account occurs when users are running some program other than User Manager, you may suspect foul play.

Detailed Tracking Event Components

Specific components recorded Detailed Tracking are as follows:

Creator Process ID This is the process ID of the original process that is spawning another process.

Domain This is the name of the "home" computer or domain for the user account generating this event belongs.

Image File Name This is the name of the file that contains the executable code of the process.

Logon ID This is the user logon ID (primary logon), as explained earlier.

New Process ID This is the process's unique ID.

Process ID This is the ID of the exited process (original).

User Name This is the name of the user trying to start the process or the NT system.

Summary

In this chapter, you explored the seven Windows NT auditing categories and the events they generate. An auditing plan that blends these categories together effectively will define an important element of your Windows NT security.

You should be auditing events in the following categories:

- Logon and logoff
- File and object access (only on sensitive data)
- Use of user rights (in high-security environments)
- User and group management events
- Security policy change
- Startup, shutdown, and other system events
- Process tracking (for experienced auditors who need to uncover complex issues or sequences of events)

NOTE. *Remember that auditing of files and objects requires not only a setting in the audit policy, but also the appropriate selections in the Security tab of the Properties dialogs for files, folders, and directories.*

Auditing is perhaps more art than science. The science is in the planning. The art is in the interpretation of what the system is telling you.

- *Windows NT Internet Services*
- *Securing Internet Services*
- *World Wide Web Security*

CHAPTER

13

Internet Security Basics

THE WORLD HAS BOTH EMBRACED AND OVERWHELMED THE Internet. Business has found the Net to be a valuable sales and marketing tool, tapping new markets that many businesses could never reach until now. For individuals, there is a rich store of information. It's rare that we don't find exactly what we were looking for within the Net's vast data deposits.

The melding of these titanic forces is not as simple as many think. We will not discuss physical security in this chapter; however, we are going to consider the security concerns associated with relationship between the Internet and its customers. Whenever two or more people face each other, there will always be the possibility of one or more of them misrepresenting themselves. And in online communication it becomes even more of a possibility. This misrepresentation may or may not be intentional, but generally can be harmful in some way. As an administrator, charged with the task of placing your Windows NT Server on the Internet as a host, there are several things to look at.

This chapter examines some security issues that arise when you install the Microsoft Internet Information Server that comes bundled with Windows NT Server. Addressing every single possible security hole is beyond the scope of the book, of course, and probably impossible anyway. What's the worst that could happen if your Internet security is breached? Someone could place unsolicited information on your Web site (pornography, graffiti, or obscenity). Or confidential or proprietary data could be stolen. Also, your system could be used for the storing and distributing of pirated software, or your valuable customers could be denied access.

As an administrator, your job is to cover up as many of these holes as you can, and make it as tough as possible for new ones to occur.

Windows NT Internet Services

Microsoft has been striving hard to make Windows NT a strong and viable solution in the Internet marketplace. Internet Explorer, Microsoft's Web browser offering, is one of the first products the company developed to further its Internet strategy. Microsoft Explorer is a graphical tool used to view the various available Internet services. However, it is only the client piece to the big puzzle.

The other major piece is Microsoft's Internet Information Server (IIS). Designed to provide several Internet services, IIS is the back-end piece to the solution.

And Microsoft has shown its commitment to the Internet world by providing support for both its Explorer and IIS products in the Windows NT Enterprise solution. No additional software is required to get the Internet services working on Windows NT.

Internet Information Server and the Peer Web Server

Microsoft has created two separate Web server products: IIS, which we've already mentioned, is included with Windows NT Server. The other is the Peer Web Server (PWS), which is included with Windows NT Workstation.

There are some differences between the two Web servers. IIS offers everything that PWS does, and a few more things:

- Ability to block specific IP addresses or subnets
- Advanced database logging via SQL/ODBC
- 128-bit encryption support in Secure Sockets Layer (40-bit in PWS)
- Control of bandwidth usage
- Support of virtual servers for different domain names
- Support for caching of repeatedly used file handles
- CPU scaling for threads
- Remote IIS Server discovery

In the rest of this section we will discuss only the IIS, since it is geared toward large enterprise intranets. All of the security practices for IIS can also be applied to the PWS.

Location of IIS

The first thing you must decide is whether the server you are going to use will be accessible from your corporate environment and the Internet at the same time. If your users need access to the Web server, then you may want to use a firewall such as Microsoft's Proxy server. If your users do not require access to the Web server from within the company, then you may consider placing the server on a separate network. By doing these simple things, you can contain any possible damage from intruder attacks to your Web server, and keep it away from your corporate intranet.

IIS-Supported Services

Internet Information Server supports three main Internet services: WWW (the HTTP protocol), FTP, and Gopher. These three items constitute a large portion of what the Internet is used for.

The World Wide Web (WWW) is a service that allows a graphical and easy way to view information in hypertext format.

File Transfer Protocol (FTP) is designed to allow users to upload and download files. Not covered in this book.

Gopher provides the ability to locate files on the Internet. (Not covered in this book.)

These three services are not the only ones available on a Windows NT Server, of course. Through add-on products, you can implement all types of Internet-related services. NNTP (Network News Transfer Protocol), IRC (Internet Relay Chat), Telnet, and e-mail are just some of those available.

Microsoft offers many of these services through BackOffice components such as Microsoft Exchange.

Securing Internet Services

Microsoft's IIS leverages Windows NT's powerful security model to provide the highest level of security. Each of the supported services requires mandatory logon, checks a user's access token against the object's ACL, and can provide a meticulous audit trail. IIS also comes with some of its own security administration functions

World Wide Web Security

There are several basic security options that can be put to work when using the WWW services. Because its interface is so easy to use, WWW is the most popular way to surf the Internet. Most of your users will most likely be employing this method for connectivity. Fortunately, Web browsers have many new security features that make WWW publishing more secure than on some of the other services.

To set WWW security options, follow these steps:

1. Start Internet Service Manager.
2. Double-click on the WWW service. Figure 13.1 shows the WWW Service Properties dialog that appears.
3. From the Properties dialog, click on the tab you need to set the important WWW security options. These options are described in the following sections.

Service Properties

The Service properties allow you to identify the off-ramp from the Internet superhighway to your World Wide Web server. You can control port access, anonymous logon, directory access, and encryption methods. Together these components help confine incoming users to specific access rights.

TCP Port

When applications use the TCP transport, they use a port number to identify the connection. TCP 80 is a common port for the HyperText Transfer Protocol (HTTP). This is where Web browsers will look by default for the Web server.

Setting the correct TCP port allows applications to communicate via the HTTP. You may want to change this to another port number for security reasons. If you do change the number, be warned that users will need to type in

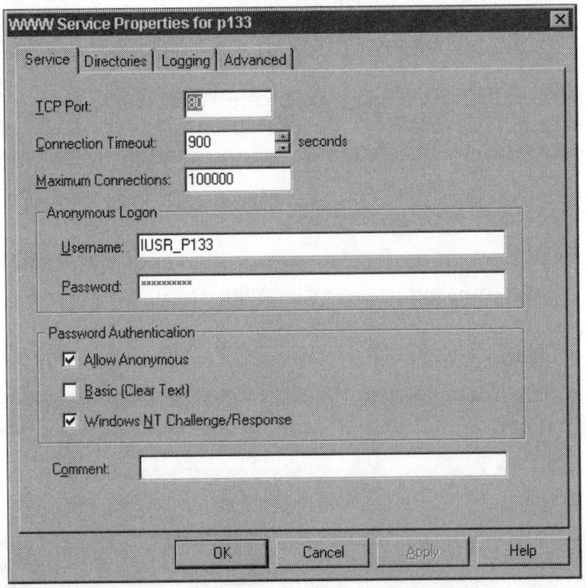

Figure 13.1

WWW Service Properties dialog

the port number when connecting to the site. This is because the WWW service monitors only this port for traffic.

For example, say you choose the number 1050 for the TCP port. When users make a connection to your Web site, they will have to not only enter the site's IP address, but also the TCP Port value you specify here in this dialog. Thus a typical address entry of 131.107.2.201 becomes 131.107.2.201 **1050**—an extra four digits to type.

Anonymous Logon

Users typically make a Web-based connection using *anonymous* connections. This type of connection does not require users to enter any valid information about themselves. Instead, the Web server will default to a specific account and use that account for determining their access rights. Using this approach allows a large number of users common access to resources. On the other hand, it prevents any type of explicit permission or audit trail from being applied.

The default user account created by IIS during installation is called IUSR_*computername.* It is granted the right to Log On Locally. This account is a member of the Local Guest group on stand-alone Windows NT Servers, and of the Global Domain Users and Local Guest groups on Windows NT domain controllers. IIS also generates a random password for this account. This IUSR_*computername* account is used every time a user tries to gain anonymous access to the Web server via WWW service.

As a suggestion, you may want to create different anonymous logons for each IIS service. By default, all the services use the same default account. This does not, however, allow Web administrators to grant exclusive access to a resources based on which service is being used. For example, you might create a user called AnonFTP for anonymous FTP connections, and give this account access just to the FTP directories. Another account called Anon-WWW might allow only access to the Web pages and not the FTP directories.

Password Authentication

It is important to decide an appropriate level of security for the transmission of usernames and passwords over the Internet. The packets are going to be traveling a public superhighway in cyberspace, and we have no idea who is monitoring this area.

As you can see in Figure 13.1, IIS offers three choices of password authentication that will be accepted. These types are described in Table 13.1.

Table 13.1

IIS Authentication Choices

PASSWORD AUTHENTICATION OPTION	DESCRIPTION
Allow Anonymous	Allows anonymous connections to the Web site. The Anonymous Logon account designated in WWW service properties will be used to validate the user.
Basic (Clear Text)	IIS will accept a username and password that is not encrypted. However, it will first try to negotiate a Secure Sockets Layer connection if the Web browser supports this. SSL provides excellent encryption for username and password. Web browsers such as Microsoft Internet Explorer and Netscape Navigator support SSL.
Windows NT Challenge/ Response	The strongest security option for IIS. Uses the username of the person who is logged on to the client running the Web browser, and passes that information encrypted just like a regular NT network. Only Microsoft Internet Explorer supports this feature currently.

You must choose at least one of these three password authentication methods. You may also choose more than one of them. When multiple options are selected, IIS tries Windows NT Challenge/Response first, then Basic (Clear Text), and finally anonymous connections if neither of the first two succeeds.

IIS handling of multiple authentication schemes depends largely on what kind of information it retrieves from an authentication header. The Windows NT Challenge/Response is first in the header, and that is what clients will attempt first. If the Web server receives a client request that contains no username and password, IIS will try to validate with the anonymous account.

If this fails, it sends back a notice of this failure to the client Web browser. It also notifies the browser that the Web server supports additional, more secure methods of authentication such as the Secure Sockets Layer.

Directories Properties

Once you have decided to allow users to access your WWW service, you will definitely need to address the security of the files on your server.

When IIS sets up the WWW service, it places all the WWW files in a directory called \InetPub\WWWroot. When a user connects to the WWW service of the Web server, IIS defaults to this location and looks for a file called default.htm. If this file is not found, then the IIS server looks at your setting of the Directory Browsing Allowed option in the Directories tab (see Figure 13.2). If this option is enabled, then the WWW service will simply drop the user into the root directory. If directory browsing is not allowed, the user will get an "Access Forbidden" response.

Figure 13.2

You may want to leave Directory Browsing turned off.

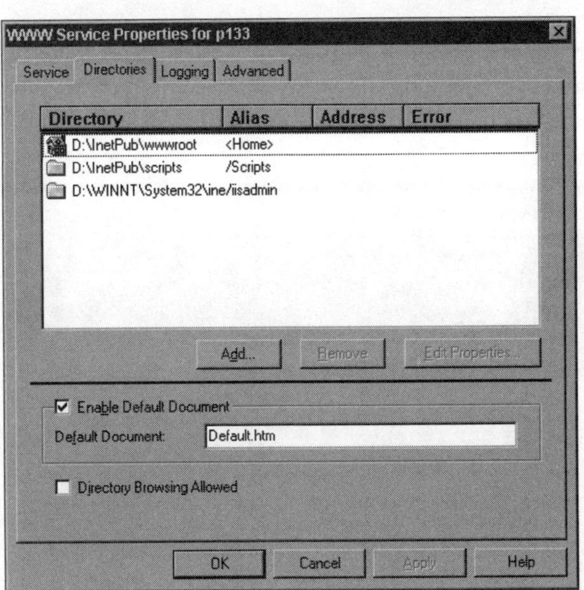

The use of virtual directories is an alternative to allowing directory browsing. A *virtual directory* appears as part of the Web server's directory tree structure but is physically located elsewhere. For example, say you have a directory D:\Newsletters that contains your company newsletters. By using a virtual directory, you can make the Newsletters directory seem to be in \InetPub\wwwroot. This shields the true physical location from users.

Virtual servers, another alternative to directory browsing, allow Webmasters to create more than one Web site on the same machine. You can have two separate domain names—www.tips.pacts.com and www.sales.pacts.com, for instance—pointing to the same physical server.

Helpful Tip

> *Make sure that you use NTFS partitions on your Web server. By doing so, you will allow Windows NT's robust security model to protect your resources at the file-system level. See Chapter 4.*

Logging Properties

It is through the use of WWW logging mechanisms that Webmasters using Windows NT Server can determine who accessed data, what kind of data was accessed, and when it was accessed.

When setting up WWW logs, you have two choices. Figure 13.3 shows the Logging tab of WWW Service Properties. On the left are the options for logging to industry-standard ASCII text files. On the right are the options for logging to an ODBC database such as Microsoft SQL Server. The latter logging arrangement allows greater flexibility; you can set up easy-to-use, powerful reports.

Figure 13.3

Choose text files or a database as your Logging mechanism.

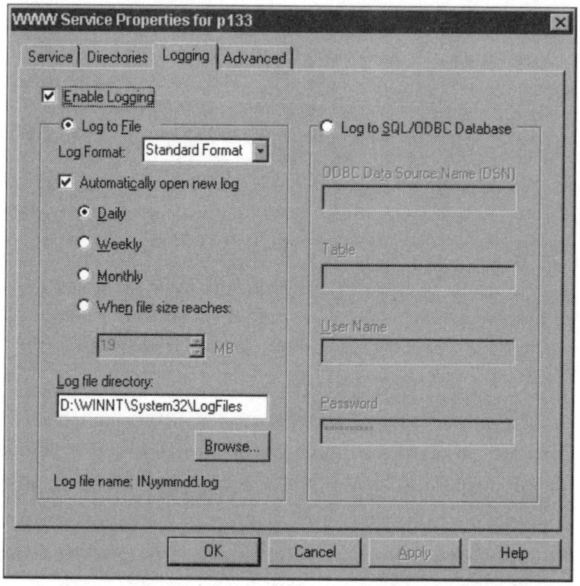

Advanced Properties

The Advanced properties (see Figure 13.4) for WWW Service allow administrators to grant or deny specific hosts access to the Web server. This type of security is one of the most fundamental barriers to malicious use that an Internet server has to offer.

Figure 13.4

Advanced settings for the WWW Service

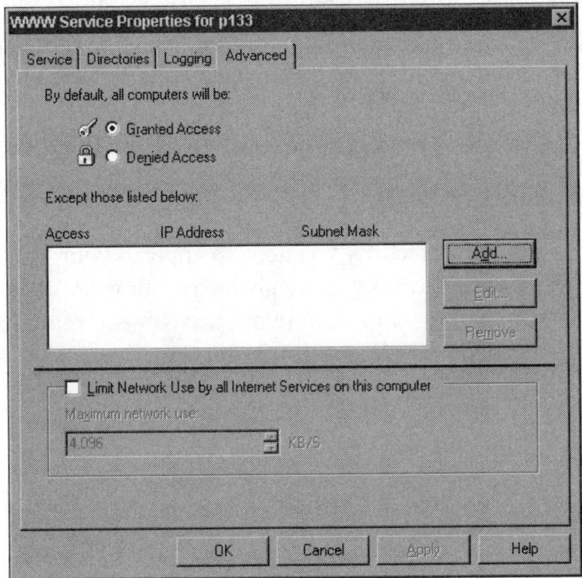

To configure the Advanced security options:

1. In the WWW Service Properties dialog, click the Advanced tab.
2. Choose Granted Access.
3. In the large text field labeled "Except those listed below," you can specify the exceptions to your Granted Access setting. Start by clicking the Add button.
4. Next you will see the Deny Access On window. Choose a single computer or a group of computers on which to deny explicit access. Click the Add button and enter the requested information.
5. Click OK to make the changes final.

Network Monitor Security Issues

The Windows NT Network Monitor allows system administrators to watch packets as they come and go from their servers. This is commonly referred to as *packet sniffing.* When a Windows NT server performs this function using the Network Monitor, it can track all packets that it sends and receives.

There is also a version of Network Monitor that supports the ability to watch packets going between any workstation on the network. This version only comes with Microsoft Systems Management Server.

NOTE. *Since packet sniffing can pose potential risks, it is suggested that you place a password on the Network Monitoring Agent located in the Control Panel applet.*

Summary

The amount of security you need to apply to your Internet server depends upon the amount of access you are giving to your network, and the type of access.

Web pages—and all network access—are more dangerous to your system than a stand-alone Internet server.

- *Security for Services*
- *Systems Management Server*
- *SQL Server*
- *MS Exchange Server*

CHAPTER

14

BackOffice Security Integration

MICROSOFT HAS A COMPLETE SERVER APPLICATION SUITE OF products called Microsoft BackOffice. The products that make up BackOffice 2.5 are

- NT Server 4.0
- SNA Server 3.0

- Internet Information Server (IIS) 3.0
- Proxy Server 1.0
- Systems Management Server (SMS) 1.2
- SQL Server 6.5
- Exchange Server 4.0

BackOffice 2.5 is shipping, yet is always undergoing changes. Exchange Server 5.0 has recently been released and will be included in the next issue of BackOffice. For that matter, it is expected that by fourth quarter 1997 Microsoft will have updated SQL Server, IIS, and SMS. NT Server 5.0 is in beta testing now.

In this chapter you'll see how to manage security for several of Microsoft's BackOffice products. Specifically, we will discuss SMS 1.2, SQL Server 6.5, and Exchange 5.0 in terms of their security features and integration with NT Server.

Building on the NT Powerhouse

NT Server is the foundation for Microsoft's other Server products. Microsoft develops its server applications for one platform, Windows NT. This strategic positioning allows the company to integrate the BackOffice server application suite seamlessly with the operating system. By drawing on NT's wealth of capabilities, Microsoft's engineers can work on core product enhancements for the BackOffice suite without having to reinvent features that NT has covered.

Let me expand on this point. As we have discussed throughout this book, NT has exceptional security features. Consider the following situation: Suppose you must create a relational database management system (RDBMS) for the NT platform. Knowing that the RDBMS must have tight security, would you create a discrete security system within the database? Or would you leverage the security mechanisms already inherent in your operating system? The answer is obvious.

On the other hand, if you had to create this RDBMS for other OS platforms as well, you might not have the luxury of integration with each OS you must support. In fact, to allow your RDBMS to integrate with other versions on different supported platforms, you might not be able to integrate it into the OS at all.

What gives Microsoft its advantage in the corporate arena is that its products are, hands down, the best on the NT platform because of their integration with the OS.

Security for Services

In a domain environment, you may be running several processes on more than one machine. The primary domain controller needs to replicate its Export directory to other domain controllers. You may have one server receiving events from several other servers (Event Forwarding). Perhaps a task-scheduling Server controls when and where certain tasks occur for a collection of NT machines. You may have backup software connected to several servers in order to back up their systems.

In each of these examples, more than one machine is engaged. And to do this in NT, you must have a valid logon in order to connect with and do work on NT Servers. Rather than maintaining an account for each machine or several accounts for each task, using the NT security and domain models we can create one account to accomplish all these tasks, or services. Often you create one account for each major service—for example, a replication account, a backup account, a task management account, and so forth.

Microsoft defines a service as a process that performs a specific system function, and often provides an application programming interface (API) that can be called for other processes. Windows NT services are RPC enabled, meaning that their API routines can be called from remote computers. I like to think of services as components that integrate tightly with the NT OS, runs as a background task, and performs functions automatically.

Services can be viewed in Control Panel, Performance Monitor, and in the Registry. Control Panel depicts services by their name, as shown in Figure 14.1. Performance Monitor depicts them by the executable(s) that make up the service. And the Registry displays services in the cryptic directory format that you have seen throughout this book and in particular Chapter 10.

Figure 14.1

Services in Control Panel

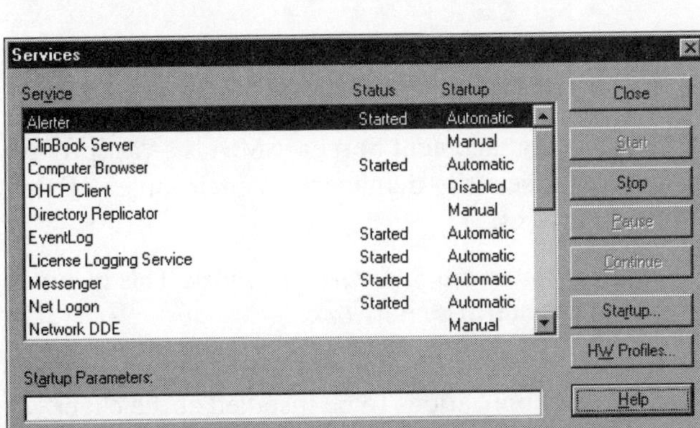

All accounts that are assigned to services need to have the right to log on as a service. This right is established and maintained in User Manager for Domains with Policies/User Rights.

In Control Panel we can configure services to operate under specific security accounts (user accounts). This allows us to track the account through auditing and to control which accounts can have access to multiple machines. Figure 14.2 is the dialog for starting up a service (Control Panel/Services, select a service, and choose Startup).

Figure 14.2

Starting up a service includes establishing its logon security.

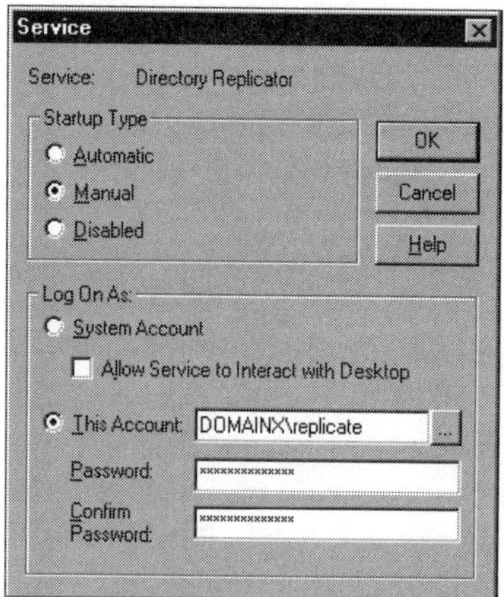

In the Service dialog, you specify whether you want to run the service under a system account or another existing account. In Figure 14.2, the user named Replicate from DOMAINX is being used for the Directory Replicator service.

Systems Management Server

Systems Management Server (SMS) is a vast product that affects your entire enterprise security-management environment. Briefly, SMS provides four main services:

- *Hardware and Software Inventory.* This includes clients and servers for your enterprise network.
- *Software Distribution to Clients.* This manages the shipping out of software applications to be installed at the client. These services can be scripted to run unattended.

- *Shared Application Distribution.* This is similar to the software distribution service, but in this case we leave the bulk of the program on the server, and clients attach to the server to run the application. This service is also known as Network Shared Applications.
- *Support.* This service includes Help Desk support tools such as memory configurations, and remote control of all Windows, Windows 95, and NT machines. Also included are tools such as Network Monitor.

NOTE. *For this section, we have assumed you know what SMS is and how to deploy it.*

SMS Security

You cannot even install SMS without getting the NT security subsystem involved. You need to have Administrator rights to install the product. During its installation, you must give SMS an account to use that has Administrator rights on the machine where SMS is being installed. This account must also have Administrator rights throughout the enterprise.

SMS uses this assigned account to log on and perform work on all the servers in your enterprise. SMS views all servers in the enterprise as one or more of the following: Site Servers, Logon Servers, Distribution Servers, or Helper Servers.

A Site Server is an NT Server domain controller with SMS installed. The Site Server can be a primary or secondary site. A primary site is used in SMS for site administration. The secondary site is more of a tool to control large enterprise installations that are geographically dispersed. In terms of security, primary and secondary sites do not differ much.

The Site Server is a major center of activity and is often the source of such activity. The service account that is assigned to SMS during installation is sent out to do work based on instructions from the Site Server. The Site Server carries out this work on different levels, and uses background processing services to accomplish these tasks.

When installing SMS, you are asked to supply a service account for SMS to use during operation. What SMS does, in fact, is install a bunch of services and assign the security account to each of them. Figure 14.3 lists the services installed by SMS, and Figure 14.4 shows you the Startup properties of the SMS Executive service. Notice that the account named smsadmin is assigned to this service; this same account is assigned to all of the SMS services, according to what was entered during SMS installation.

To understand exactly what each service is and what it does, you have to delve pretty deep into SMS. We won't do that here; what matters to us is the big picture—that SMS uses its group of services to do its work throughout the enterprise. SMS inventories other servers by connecting to them and running some software that queries the machines as to hardware and software

Figure 14.3

The group of SMS services

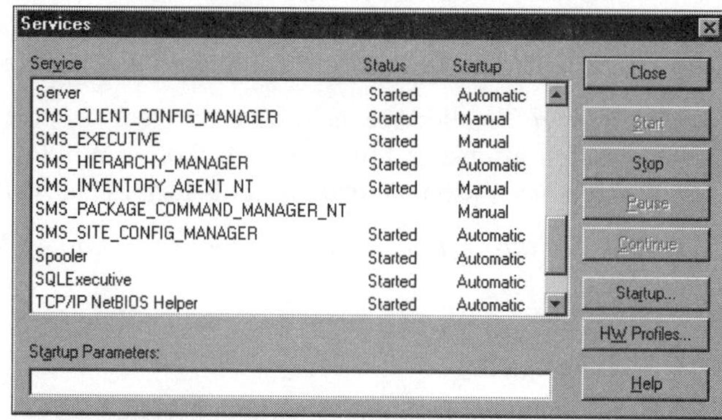

Figure 14.4

The startup information for SMS Executive

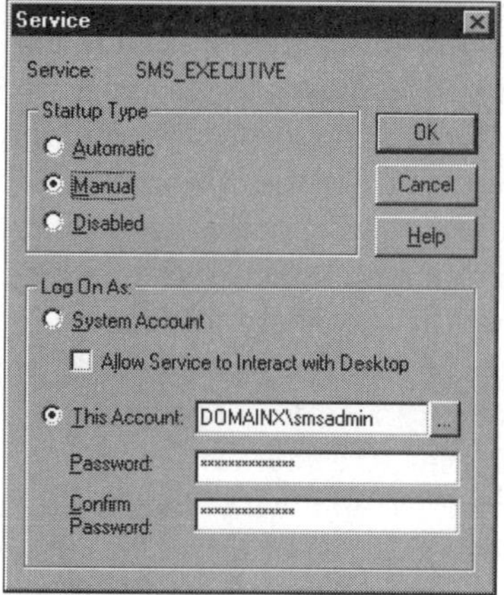

configurations. To do this, SMS must supply an account that has the rights to log on to the queried machine and access it.

Obtaining such access requires Administrator privileges on NT machines and Supervisor privileges on NetWare machines. Since SMS is integrated with NT and uses the domain model, we can create one account for accessing all of our NT machines. The same account with the same password can be created on the NetWare machines, thus allowing NT and SMS to access the NetWare servers. The trick here is to coordinate password changes between the NetWare and NT servers whenever you change the SMS service account password.

In SMS, most frequently you will find that the reason for jobs' failing to process is either a network connectivity problem or a security problem—that is, the SMS service account did not have sufficient rights to carry out the actions attempted.

Troubleshooting SMS

As you learn more about SMS, you will find it easier to troubleshoot and discover simple solutions for seemingly difficult problems. For example, say you have a particular SMS installation that is supposed to inventory five NetWare servers. But one of these servers is not showing up in the inventory. What is wrong?

Well, in SMS, the Maintenance Manager (a miniservice that operates beneath the Executive Services) is responsible for collecting inventory information from NetWare servers. The Maintenance Manager makes network connections to the NetWare server and queries the machine for hardware and software information. To scope out this missing-server problem, first you'd want to ensure you have included the NetWare server in the Servers list box in the Site Properties Domains dialog. (If you didn't tell SMS to go get the server, then of course it won't.) You must also check connectivity (communication) capabilities between the servers. Third, verify that the SMS service account has sufficient rights on the NetWare Server and that the passwords are the same.

SQL Server

Microsoft SQL Server is an RDBMS now in version 6.5. SQL Server started off as a cooperative effort between Sybase and Microsoft, in which Microsoft resold the Sybase Server product under the Microsoft brand. This relationship fostered the sharing of code and technology between the two companies—however, as happens with most relationships in the IS industry, this one came to an end. Subsequently Microsoft has taken the core product they acquired and rewritten it pretty much from the ground up. SQL Server 6.5 is the current incarnation.

SQL Server is very well integrated with NT. Memory architecture components interact, as well as file system components and, of course, security components.

SQL Server has three login security modes: Standard, Windows NT Integrated, and Mixed. All three modes operate on the concept of monitoring where logon validation occurs, and who performs the validation. Let's take a closer look at each of these modes.

Standard Security in SQL Server

Standard security is installed by default. The Standard Security mode is compatible with prior versions of SQL Server and common to RDBMS. Logon validation is done solely by SQL Server. NT in this case plays no role in security validation. This allows the SQL administrator to create, within SQL

Server, accounts that can access the SQL databases. These accounts may not have any other rights on the NT machine or, for that matter, even exist in User Manager for Domains.

This is not a security breach. Files outside the database system cannot be affected. Nevertheless, this arrangement does not provide the tightest of security nor the cleanest. What it *is* really good for is placing an NT Server into a heterogeneous environment where the majority of clients will obtain access to the databases through untrusted connections. These are connections across which NT cannot or does not validate, or clients that you don't want logging on to an NT Server or domain in order to access the database. An example is a UNIX client.

Windows NT Integrated Security in SQL Server

The Windows NT Integrated Security mode allows for the total integration of NT users with SQL Server. When Integrated Security is enabled, you have the capability of allowing users from an NT Server or domain to access the SQL server and its databases through the users' single logon. Once they log on to the NT network, they will have rights to use the database, as allowed by the DBA (database administrator).

Once integrated security is established, you use the SQL Security Manager (found in the SQL Folder) to set up your users. Figure 14.5 is the SQL Security Manager before any users have been established. Here you can select groups of users and give them rights to databases, as well as set defaults for databases.

Figure 14.5

Use SQL Security Manager to manage user accounts under Integrated Security Mode.

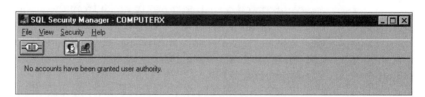

There are two main views in Security Manager: User Privilege view and SA Privilege view (SA is System Administrator in SQL Server). You use these views to add users from the NT system into SQL Server.

Be careful when you are setting up user accounts from SQL Server. First you'll want to create groups in User Manager for Domains that will be specifically for user access to SQL Server. Use no fewer than two groups, one for database administrators and one for database users. If you have more than one database and have a specific set of users for each, you may want separate groups for each database. Also, you can have separate groups for users of the same database if they are to have very different roles in the use of that database. You *must not*, however, place any of the users in more than one group that will have rights to the SQL Server and its databases.

Caution

> *SQL Server assigns rights to users upon creation of user accounts. When you create users from Security Manager, the last group that was used to add users could—and probably will—override any previous user information. You can seriously affect user rights in the databases by adding the same user to more than one SQL group. Avoid this.*

Assigning Rights to SQL Server Groups

So let's assume we have created two groups, SQL Admins and SQL Users. We have several users in each, but no duplicates across the two groups. First we will assign Administrator or SA rights. In Security Manager, choose the SA Privilege view (see Figure 14.6).

Figure 14.6

SA Privilege view in Security Manager

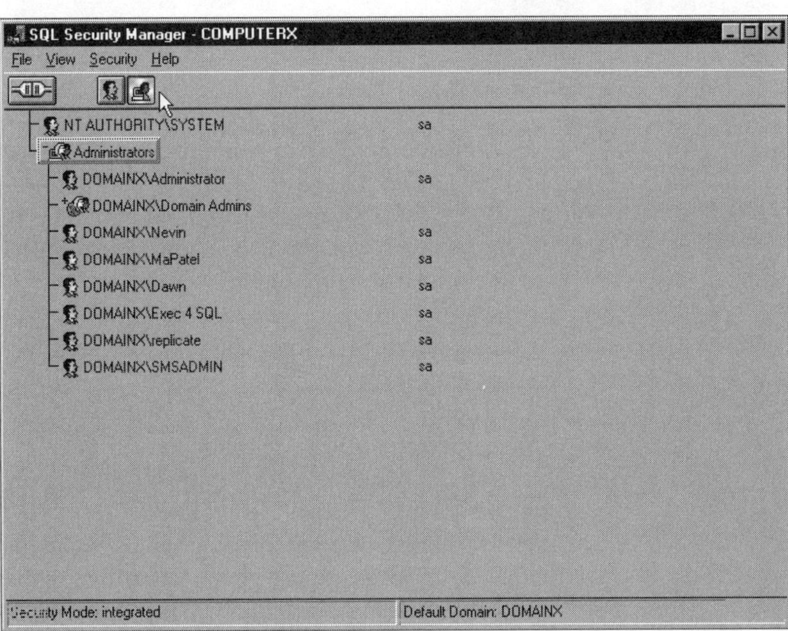

You can see that the Administrators group is listed under SA privilege. Also, notice how each member of that group has specifically been granted SA rights. This is done so that you do not accidentally lock everyone out of SQL Server. When moving into the integrated security mode, all users must be validated by NT before they can use SQL. Yet they also must be granted SQL Access through Security Manager. See the catch 22? If SQL Server did not default some group to SA rights, then no one would have any rights to SQL.

It may happen that soon after installation of SQL Server and after switching to integrated security mode, you may decide you no longer want all Administrators to have SA rights to the SQL Server and the data it holds. In fact, in many environments the DBAs do not allow NT Administrators SA rights; nor do NT Administrators allow DBAs to have Administrator rights to the domain.

To change the rights, in User Manager for Domains you first create a group for SQL Server administration; name it something like SQL Admins. Next, populate it with NT users that you want to be SAs in SQL Server. Then, in Security Manager, you pull down the Security menu and choose Grant New, as shown in Figure 14.7.

Figure 14.7

Choose Grant New to set up SA rights

From the Grant System Administrator Privilege dialog, select the NT group that you want to have SA rights. In this case, we'll select a global group, SQL ADMINS, from the default domain (DOMAINX). Click on the Grant button, and note the Permission Granted dialog. Select OK and then Done to close both these dialogs.

Now notice in Figure 14.8 that we have two groups with SA rights. Before you go any further, write the following sentence down somewhere so you won't ever forget it: *Do not remove the Administrator Group until after you have added another group and granted it SA rights.* Think about it!

When you're sure you're ready to continue, you can revoke the SA rights from the Administrators group by clicking on the Administrators group and selecting Security/Revoke. Figure 14.9 is the confirmation dialog that lets you think twice before you revoke login permissions from the Administrators group, and Figure 14.10 shows the results of choosing Yes.

Granting rights to users follows basically the same process as for groups. First choose the User Privilege view, Figure 14.11, and select Security/Grant New.

Just as you did for granting SA privilege, select a group (SQL Users) from the default domain (DOMAINX), as shown in Figure 14.12. Select Grant to assign the privilege.

Figure 14.8

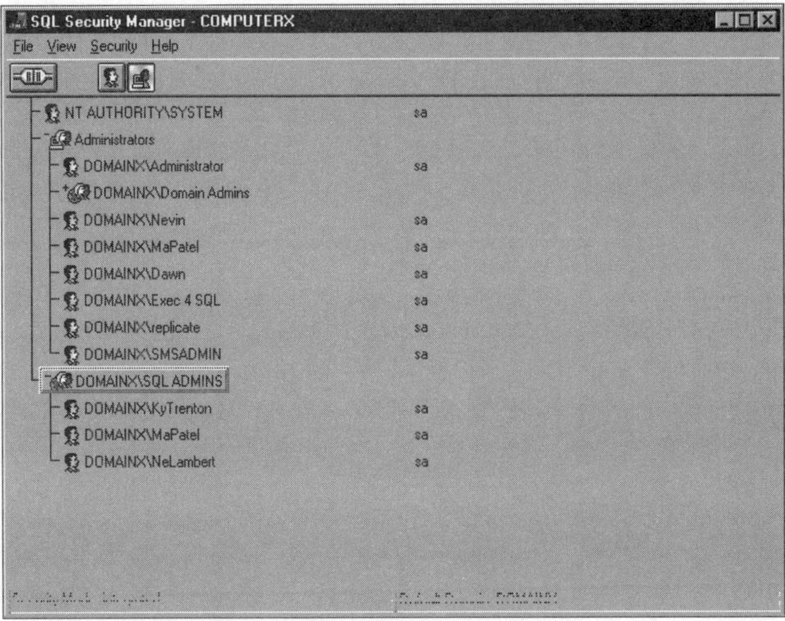

Two groups are granted SA rights.

Figure 14.9

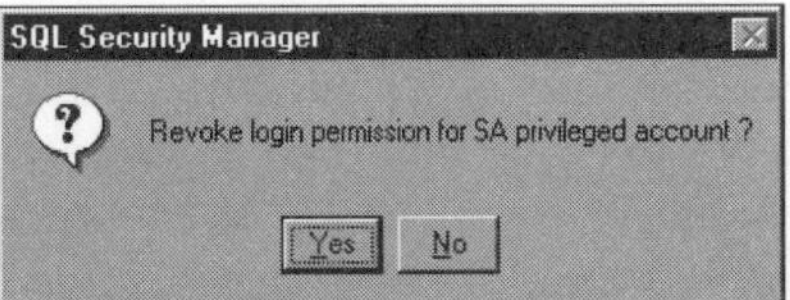

Before clicking Yes, *be sure* you are ready to revoke the Administrators group SA privilege.

Figure 14.10

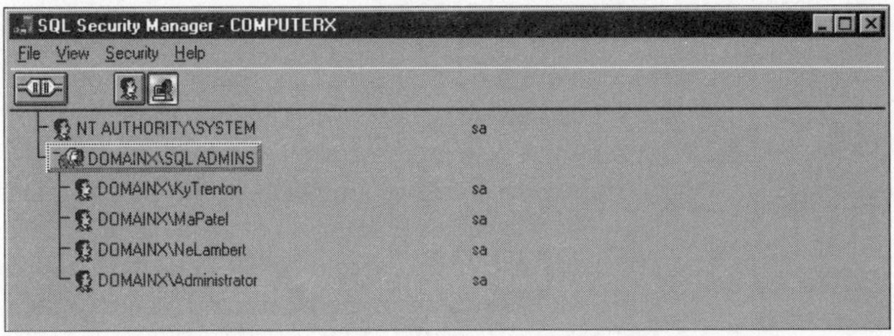

The Administrators group no longer has SA privileges.

Figure 14.11

User Privilege view

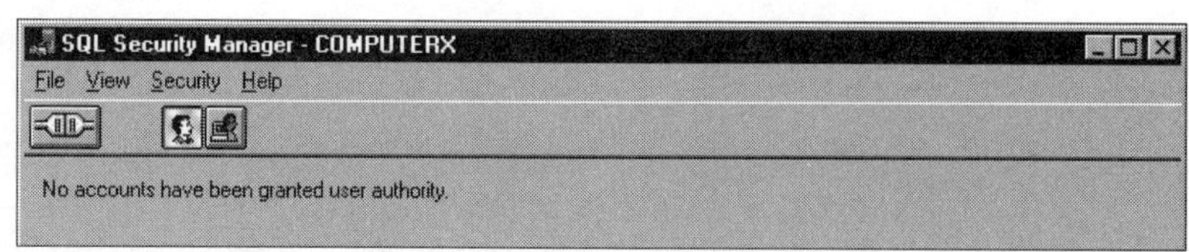

Figure 14.12

Granting user privilege to a group

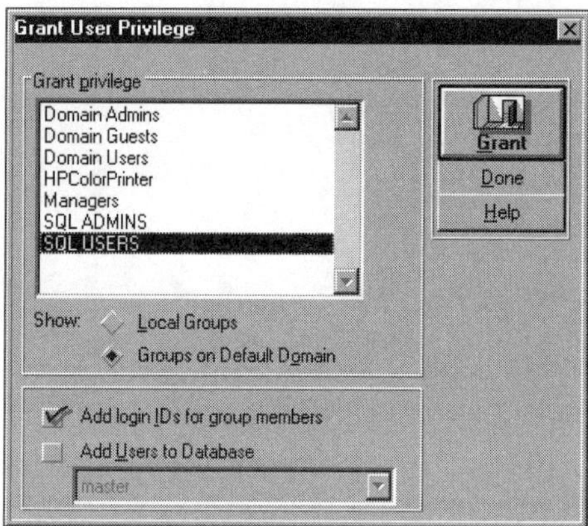

NOTE. *In Integrated Security mode, only trusted accounts are allowed access. SQL Server trusts NT to log on and validate the users who are granted access through Security Manager. No rights will be checked upon SQL Server Login through DB-Library or ODBC. The only check that is done is to ensure that the user has been granted permissions via Security Manager and has a valid access token.*

Mixed Security Mode in SQL Server

In Mixed Secure mode we have the best of both worlds. This mode allows us to set up trusted accounts as we did in Integrated mode, but also allows us to set up some untrusted accounts as well.

Let's say you have a network environment that is mostly made up of trusted users (users that log on to an NT Domain Controller); yet you have a few users who connect from UNIX machines. In Mixed mode you can carry out all of the actions in the Integrated security mode section and just add the UNIX users directly in SQL Server.

What SQL Server does is check to see if the user logging on is using a trusted logon name (that is, a user who is in a group that exists on the domain and has been granted rights from Security Manger). If the user logging on is a trusted user, then SQL Server insists that the connection be trusted, previously validated by NT, and that it provide to SQL a valid access token. No trusted user accounts can log on from an untrusted source. For example, MaPatel is a trusted user account but Tim is not. Any user can supply the correct name and password for Tim and gain access to SQL. But only a user logged on as MaPatel can gain access to the database as MaPatel.

Changing the Security Mode in SQL Server

There are several ways to change the security mode for SQL Server. I find that using the Enterprise Manager is the quickest way. In Enterprise Manager, select Server/SQL Server/Configure. Figure 14.13 illustrates the Server Configuration/Options dialog that appears, and Figure 14.14 shows the Security Options tab you will use.

Figure 14.13

Server Configuration/Options dialog

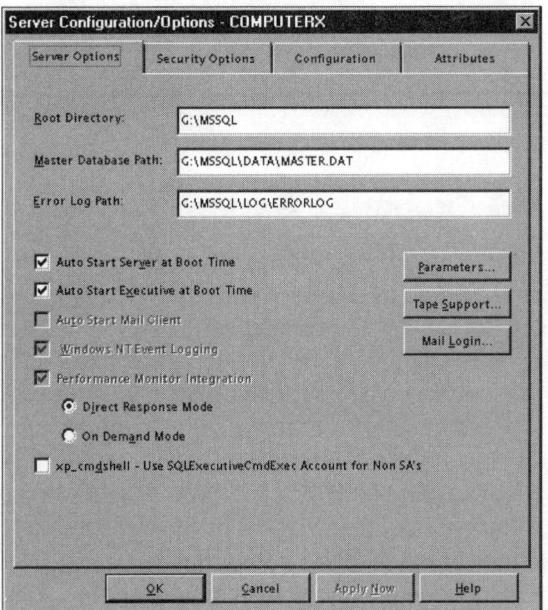

Changing the security mode is as simple as clicking the radio button for the mode you want and then clicking Apply Now. Although this takes effect immediately most of the time, it is always recommended that you shut down and restart SQL Server after making changes to server configuration.

Figure 14.14

Security Options tab contains the Login Security Mode choices.

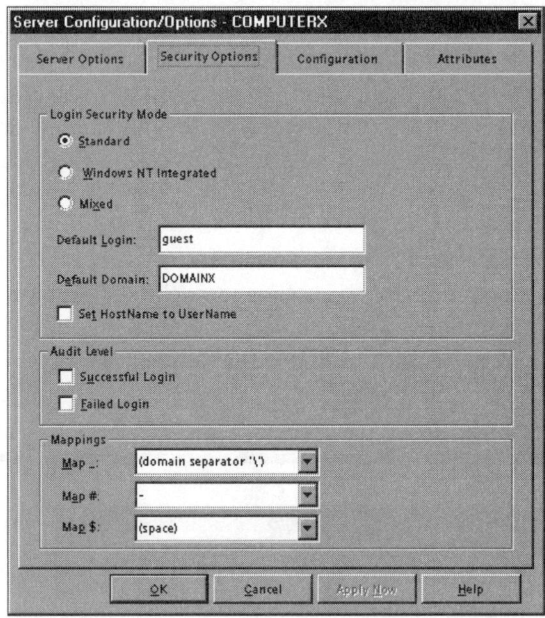

■ MS Exchange Server

E-mail systems have rapidly become a primary method of delivering data from one person to another. As users type away, sending messages and attaching documents, the security of the information must be considered.

Historically, telephone systems have provided a secure method of delivering information. When I pick up my phone and call my business partner, I do not expect someone to be listening in on my conversation and even altering it by the time it gets to my partner's ear. There are some exceptions, but these typically are outside the bounds of everyday practice—such as a court-sanctioned wiretap. The same type of security should be expected by and provided to every user sending electronic mail.

When I install a phone system in my house, I also expect that no one will be able to use the phone system without my permission. E-mail systems must provide similar security to the networks on which they function. Once a messaging system has been placed on-line, I do not want any intruder to access internal data or cause any other type of harm via the e-mail system.

The interception of data typically can occur when a user places a network "sniffer" on your network; data packets are captured and then put together to decipher your data.

Let's take the Ethernet protocol as an example. This protocol works by sending packet information to all machines on the same segment. The packet header contains the appropriate MAC address of the destination machine. Only the machine with the right MAC (Media Access Control) address is supposed to accept the packet. A machine that is accepting all packets, no matter what the packet header MAC address, is said to be in promiscuous mode. If someone were to place a machine with, say, Microsoft Network Monitor on the network, that person could capture all the packets. Some of these will have account and password information; others will contain data. Ethernet and TCP/IP do not have the ability to protect data while it's on the network.

Microsoft Exchange Server offers several solutions for these risks to your data. Security for messaging systems comes in four flavors:

- Data encryption
- Digital signatures
- Firewalls
- Account security

This section examines each one of these security areas, and how Microsoft Exchange Server provides a robust security architecture and leverages Windows NT's existing model as well.

Data Encryption

Encryption of e-mail messages is a mechanism by which data and messages can be stored and transmitted securely. Exchange Server uses a 64- or 56-bit encryption system to establish this security in North America. Outside North America, a 40-bit encryption is used.

Encryption is achieved through the use of public/private keys. These are symbolic of real keys that would lock or unlock a safety deposit box, for instance. Encryption requires both items to be distributed by a single authority considered 100% secure. MS Exchange Server 5.0 allows clients to exchange these keys without going through a central authority, thus bypassing administrative controls.

Here is how the encryption process works:

1. The user chooses to encrypt a message through an enabled client.
2. The client uses a Bulk Encryption Key to scramble the data that are being sent.
3. The client takes the Bulk Encryption Key itself and scrambles it, using the Public Encryption Key. (This is a 512-bit encryption. Since we are not encrypting data, it does not violate any federal restrictions.)

4. The two scrambled items are sent to the recipient.

   While the scrambled data are in transit, anyone using a “sniffer” to capture data would need to have the proper algorithms to unseal the Bulk Encryption Key first, and then use it to unseal the data. The chances of breaking both a 512-bit scheme and 56/64-bit scheme are pretty slim.

5. When the client receives the data, the user must type in a password. The client verifies that user/password combination and compares it to the EPF file (security profile) that was set up. See Figure 14.15.

6. The client then uses its Private Encryption Key to unseal the Bulk Encryption Key and in turn uses that to unseal the data.

Figure 14.15

Key exchange

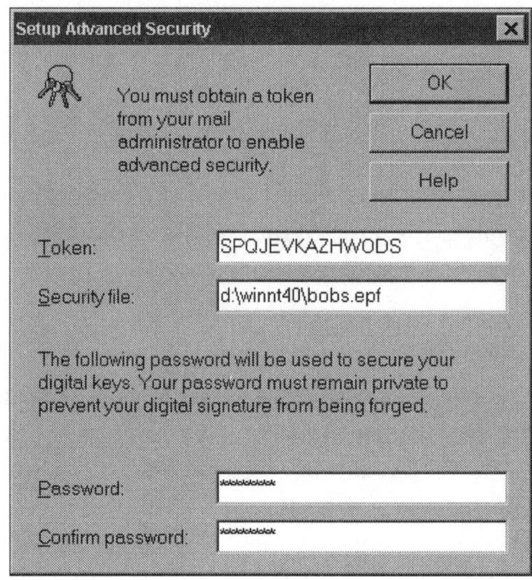

The Key Management Server (KMS)

Clearly, the success of encryption as a security mechanism relies on one thing: The two clients must have been given these keys from some central authority. Exchange Server uses a Key Management Server (KMS) to issue encryption keys.

Caution

The KMS must be installed separately on only one Exchange Server per organization. This may seem limiting, but absolute control must be kept on a single server. All the keys are internally generated and stored in an encrypted database on the server. By use of the KMS, Exchange Server guarantees that no other server can issue the same information to other clients by chance.

To Install the Key Management Server, go to Setup\<platform>\Exchkm on the Exchange Server CD, and run the Setup program. See your MS Exchange Server documentation for more detailed information. And always remember—there should only be *one* of these servers. Period.

On the client end, you will need to perform a few steps to get KMS up and running.

1. Click on the Tools/Options.
2. Open the Security tab (see Figure 14.16).

NOTE. *If the Security tab is not present in the Options dialog, either you have not set up KMS server or you have not enabled the mailbox to have security options. Check the Exchange Server documentation for more information.*

Click the button labeled Set Up Advanced Security. You'll see the dialog shown in Figure 14.17.

3. Provide a 14-character password (assigned by the Exchange Administrator), click OK, and a security profile (*.EPF) will be generated.

Figure 14.16

Security tab of Tools/Options

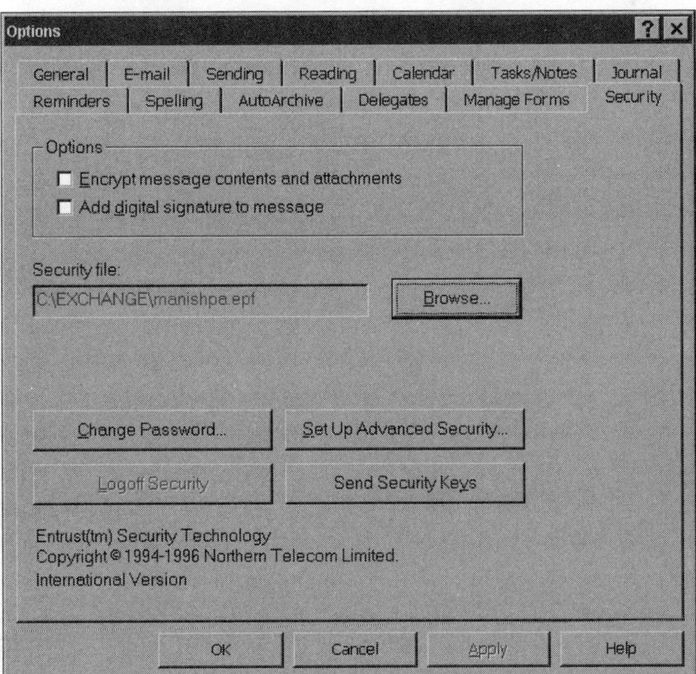

Figure 14.17

Enter the password to generate a security profile.

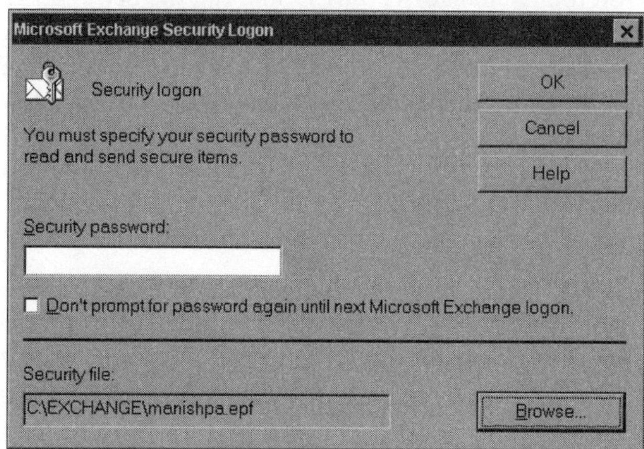

One of the major benefits of Exchange Server is that it is a client/server-based messaging system. The entire system uses RPCs to communicate between the servers themselves. All of these communications are encrypted by default.

Exchange Server uses an RC4 Algorithm from RSA Data Security, Inc., with a 40-bit key. User authentications, mailbox access, directory replication, and remote administration are completely encrypted and safe even across the Internet. You can also encrypt client-initiated RPC communication.

Bear in mind that, although security is heightened with KMS, there is overhead to both the client and the network because packets are going to be a bit larger.

Here are the steps to configure your MS Exchange client to encrypt all RPC traffic:

1. Select Tools/Services.
2. Choose Microsoft Exchange Server service.
3. Open the Advanced tab (see Figure 14.18) and choose one of the Encrypt options to enable RPC encryption for that session.

Digital Signatures

Digital signatures are used to verify that no tampering of data has occurred in transit and that the person who claims to have sent it is indeed the person who sent it.

Digital signatures do not protect the data in the packet; rather, they protect the system from intruders who are trying to deceive users or have altered data in some way. For example, after JoPorter sends a message to KyTrenton, KyTrenton verifies that it really was JoPorter who sent the message.

Figure 14.18

RPC encryption options

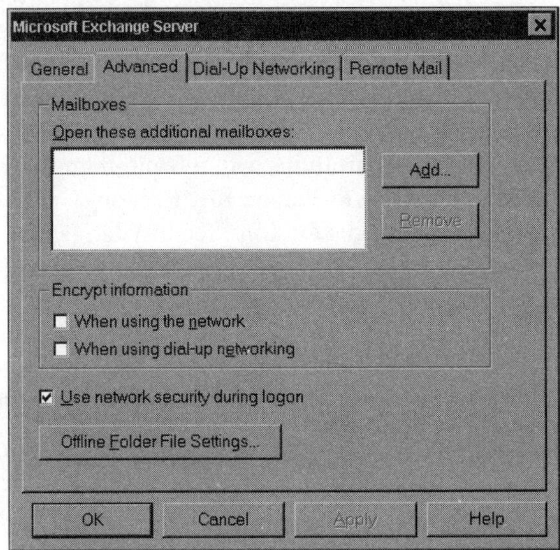

Digital signatures work as follows:

1. The user must first choose to "sign" the message.
2. The client performs a hashing routine (discussed in Chapter 15 on Cryptography). This produces a checksum value on the data.
3. The hashing value, known also as the Message Digest, is then encrypted using a Private Digital Signing Key.
4. The two items, hashing and checksum values, are sent in transit.
5. If the data have been altered in any way, the checksum value of the data will be altered.
6. The recipient then uses a Public Digital Signature Key to unseal the Message Digest and compare it to the one the Key generates on the data. If they match, the message is considered verified.

Person-to-Person Key Exchange

Microsoft Exchange Server 5.0 has added an additional security mechanism. If users in corporations want to send digitally signed or encrypted messages, but the corporations are not in the same MS Exchange organization, Person-to-Person Key Exchange is the answer. With this solution, a user can send his or her public security key to another user. This relieves the other client from having to go to a central authority (KMS). The Person-to-Person Key Exchange is only available under the MS Exchange 5.0 client and MS Outlook client.

There are some security implications with this Person-to-Person arrangement. Since KMS is bypassed, administrators will have less control of the keys. First of all, they will not be able to cancel or revoke the certificate because the client is outside the current organization. A user could very well be accepting messages from another user whose digital signature has been compromised, and the administrator may never be aware of this. Thus this is useful for small organizations or organizations with full autonomy at the user level.

To enable Person-to-Person Key Exchange, click on the Send Security Keys button in the Tools/Options/Security tab (shown earlier in Figure 14.16). In the Security Key Exchange Message dialog (see Figure 14.19), fill in the information about the person you want to receive public security keys. Click the Send button to send the keys to the other person via e-mail.

Figure 14.19

Arranging Person-to-Person Key Exchange

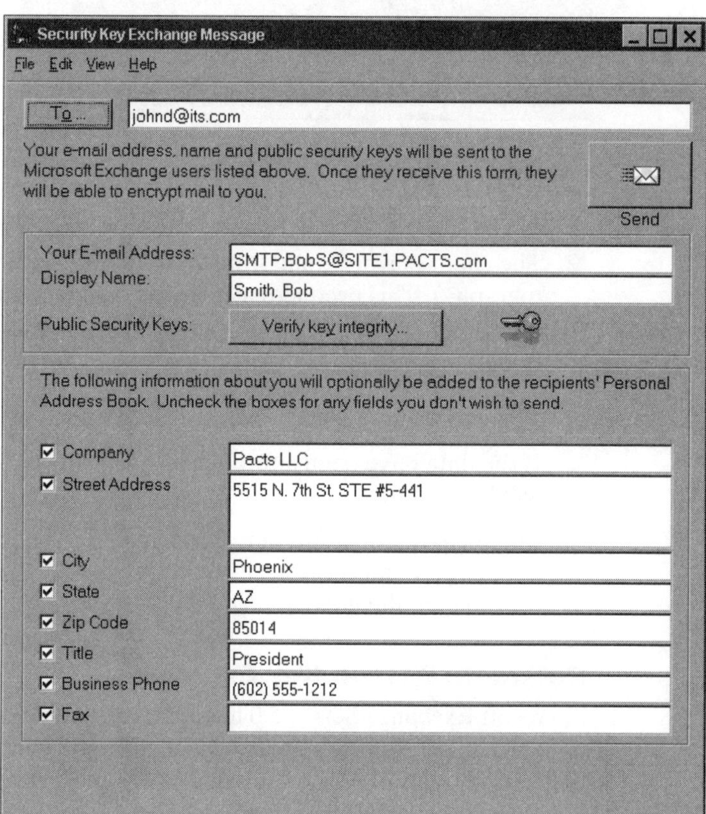

Firewalls

It's likely that you already know this security term. Firewalls allow administrators to filter out data or specific packets that are unwanted within an organization. Essentially, the firewall shields your intranet from the public networks. This mechanism can prevent outsiders from crashing systems and bringing your internal messaging infrastructure to a halt. Firewalls can also be used to block incoming/outgoing messages to certain destinations.

Microsoft Exchange offers some of these firewall-type services within the product. For example, you can prevent messages to certain Internet domains from being transmitted, or you can channel all your e-mail traffic to a single server.

Account Security

Microsoft Exchange fully leverages Windows NT's robust security model. Any user who wishes to send or receive e-mail must have a valid Windows NT user account. NT provides all the authentication for the user accounts, and uses Windows Challenge/Response security to help with secure authentication.

The user's password is never sent across the network. Instead, a challenge is sent to the client, and the client encrypts it using its password as a key. The server then uses the password on its side to decrypt the response. If successful, then a proper password was used initially to perform the encryption.

Administrators must have rights on both the Exchange and Windows NT environments to have complete control over enterprise security. However, in a distributed environment, these roles could be split up to match job functionality.

Exchange uses a service account to communicate between servers. It is important to have the same account context within an organization (use the same account). Trust relationships may have to be created to allow this in a multiple domain model.

■ Summary

Microsoft BackOffice is the best suite of server applications we have ever seen or worked with. The extent of integration of the BackOffice components with NT is outstanding and, in fact, astonishing.

Each of these BackOffice products is a complete and powerful applications in its own right. It is not possible to address all of the security aspects for each application without providing in-depth explanation of the product itself. What we have attempted in this chapter is to establish a baseline of knowledge so that you are prepared to incorporate these products into your security scheme more readily.

Keep this chapter in mind when you read Chapter 17, "Windows NT Distributed Security Services," in which we talk about new feature sets for Windows NT 5.0. Project the new security features of NT 5.0 into the BackOffice product set and see what you come up with. It may just be the best Internet/intranet, secure-transaction, application/file/print server product yet created.

- *Encryption and Decryption*
- *Algorithms and Their Keys*
- *Ciphers*
- *Authentication and Data Integrity*
- *Is Cryptography for You?*
- *The Microsoft Cryptographic Application Interface (CryptoAPI)*

CHAPTER

15

Cryptography

NOW THAT YOU HAVE SECURED YOUR SYSTEM, YOUR USERS, AND your network, it's time to decide if and how you want to secure your transmitted data—whether that data is transmitted across your own network, your company intranet, or the Internet. When transmitting data across phone lines and the Internet, your data is vulnerable to break-ins. The only way to maintain the integrity and security of your transmitted data is by using cryptography. This is the process of encoding data to protect it from prying eyes while it is stored or being transmitted.

The use of codes to keep messages secure is not new, but technology today offers very sophisticated means of data encryption. You can accomplish a high level of security with a fairly simple implementation.

In this chapter you'll find very general information about encryption, decryption, digital signatures and hashes, and cipher types, as well as Windows NT's CryptoAPI.

The field of cryptography is vast and clearly far beyond the scope of this book. This chapter serves as a reminder to consider this aspect of securing your system, and give you a little information on cryptography itself. In addition, Chapter 14's section on Exchange Server, Microsoft's client/server-based messaging system, discusses cryptography as it applies to a messaging service.

Encryption and Decryption

Encryption is the process of taking readable text—*plaintext*—and, using an encryption key, rendering it as gibberish—*ciphertext*. *Decryption* is returning the ciphertext back to its original form using a decryption key.

The encryption/decryption process, with the help of computers, is simple. The hard part is not letting any unauthorized persons learn the keys. The encryption key and decryption key can be the same key, as in symmetric ciphers, or different, as in the public/private key pairs.

Encryption can be set up to protect your data across the network, across the nodes of an intranet, and across the Internet. Encryption can also be configured to ensure authentication; that is, making you confident that the message is from who it claims to be from, and that the message has not been altered.

Algorithms and Their Keys

Encryption (or cipher) *keys* are used to create and access encrypted data. When you encrypt data, an encryption key is used to scramble or cipher your message. When the data is ready for decryption, you use the decryption key like the combination to a safe, to unscramble or decipher the message. Often, the same key is used for both encryption and decryption. It is vital that these keys only be given to the authorized parties. As mentioned previously, keeping the keys secret is undoubtedly the hardest part of this process.

Cryptographic service providers (CSPs) store all keys. They also create, destroy, and use keys for various operations. (More on CSPs shortly.)

An algorithm is a long and complicated mathematical equation or process that encodes your plaintext into ciphertext. Here's a simple analogy: List the alphabet from A to Z:

```
A B C D E F G H I J K L M N O P Q R S T U V W X Y Z
```

Now make a different alphabet. List it backward from Z through O, and then start with A again and finish with N, like this:

```
Z Y X W V U T S R Q P O A B C D E F G H I J K L M N
```

Now spell out your name using the "new" alphabet. Here is "Windows NT Security" spelled with your new alphabet:

```
Krbwcg BH Gvxifrhm
Windows NT Security
```

The foregoing alphabet example is a *very basic* example of an algorithm. In this case, the key to breaking the code is knowing that the normal alphabetical order was substituted with one of reverse order. Computer-generated algorithms use symbols and numbers and are significantly complex—much too complicated for a person to decipher.

Two primary encryption algorithms are used in computer cryptography: symmetric keys and private/public key pairs.

Symmetric Keys

Symmetric algorithms are often considered the conventional algorithms. With symmetric algorithms, the same key is used for both encryption and decryption. Symmetric keys are changed often and are called *session keys.*

Because of their speed, symmetric algorithms are preferred for encrypting large amounts of data. RC4, Data Encryption Standard (DES), and International Data Encryption Algorithm (IDEA) are popular symmetric algorithms.

Your CSP creates the session keys but does not preserve them after each session. If you plan to reuse a key, you will need to export it out of the CSP.

Private/Public Key Pairs

With private/public key (P/PK) algorithms, there are two keys: the *public key* and the *private key.* The two are known as a *key pair.* The owner of the key pair is the only one to possess the private key. The public key is just that, public; it's the one you can safely give out to anyone by any method. Either key can be used to encrypt data, but its opposite is required for decryption.

- *Key exchange pairs* (aka *exchange keys*) are used for encrypting session keys, allowing for secure key exchanges.
- *Digital signature key pairs* (aka *signature keys*) are used for signing hashes. (See "The Hash Function" later in this chapter.)

CSPs provide and save two sets of public/private key pairs for each user, one algorithm for key exchanges and another for digital signatures. Using the same key for encrypting and signing a message could pose some security risk.

The P/PK algorithms are much slower than symmetric algorithms and are therefore used for smaller jobs, such as encrypting and sending symmetric keys. For example, suppose MaPatel needs to send NeLambert a large amount of data and wants to be sure that no one else sees it. MaPatel decides on a symmetric algorithm and sends a message to NeLambert, using NeLambert's public key, telling him to expect the large data package and giving him the symmetric key code. NeLambert will be the only one able to read the public-key transmission, so it is ensured that he will be the only one to receive the key for the package MaPatel is sending him.

Key Lengths

The length of encryption keys will vary depending on the encryption algorithm used. The longer, more complex the key, the harder the code is to break. Windows NT 4.0 uses RC4 40-bit encryption, which when broken down supplies approximately one trillion possible keys. There are encryption programs that are more substantial, but they are subject to a number of laws governing their import/export. For instance, the 128-bit programs cannot be exported. Remember this if your intranet is international.

Exporting (Exchanging) Keys

The two primary reasons for exporting keys are to save session keys (CSPs do not save them), and to send a key to another person. Exported keys are kept, encrypted, in *key blobs.*

When planning to send encrypted data to and receive encrypted data from another person, you will need to exchange your public keys. Now, public keys are not secret, so theoretically you could just as well call the person on the phone, send e-mail, or even use the Postal Service to exchange the keys. But when you don't know the party with whom you are exchanging keys, and you want to be sure you are receiving the correct information, you can exchange keys using a *certification authority.* Certificates can also be used to validate public keys you may already have or receive through less secure means. (There's more on certificates coming up in a later section.)

Key Blobs

Unlike session keys, private/public keys are saved by and stored in the CSP. But what if you want to move a key to another CSP? *Key blobs* are keys that are taken out of the CSP to be saved for later use.

Key blobs are typically used for moving keys between providers. Using an existing key to export the key you are moving out of the CSP creates a key blob. Once exported and saved, you can import the key blob into another CSP, and thus have an identical key in the new CSP.

A *simple* key blob is a session key encrypted using the receiver's public exchange key. This blob is for transmitting session keys. There are also *public* key blobs, which are public keys and are not encrypted; and *private* key blobs, which are actual P/PK pairs used by advanced Crypto APIs for storing and transmitting the pairs. Since the private key, obviously, is highly confidential, private key blobs are encrypted.

Ciphers

There are several different types of ciphers. The two we are going to discuss here are Block Ciphers and Stream Ciphers.

Block Ciphers, as their name implies, encrypt the plaintext in block units, usually of 64 bits. Stream Ciphers encrypt the plaintext one bit at a time, keeping the plaintext and ciphertext the same size. Block Ciphers are considered more secure than Stream Ciphers, but Stream Ciphers are quicker. Also, if an error occurs and the encrypted data is compromised, the Block Cipher will lose an entire block, as compared to the bits lost by the Stream Cipher.

Windows NT supports the RC2 Block Cipher and the RC4 Stream Cipher; both were created by RSA Data Security, Inc.

Cipher Modes for Block Cipher

All CSPs use the same basic concepts for their encryption/decryption methods. This section describes the *cipher modes* that can be specified when using a Block Cipher.

All of the modes but one use *initialization vectors.* An initialization vector is a random number with the same number of bits as the block size. It is the starting point of plaintext encryption. This is what allows identical plaintext segments to be encrypted with the same cipher but look entirely different. It is recommended that a different initialization vector be used for each transmission.

- The *Electronic Codebook* mode encrypts each block individually. Any blocks containing the same plaintext will contain the same ciphertext. This mode does not use initialization vectors.
- The *Cipher Block Chaining* mode encrypts each block with a different ciphertext, so blocks containing the same plaintext will not look the same. This is called *feedback.* This mode is the default when using Microsoft RSA Base Provider, included with Windows NT.
- The *Cipher Feedback* (CFB) mode allows small pieces of plaintext to be encrypted, instead of blocks. CFB uses a *shift register.* A shift register is the size of one block but is divided into sections depending on the amount of bits being processed at a time.
- The *Outback Feedback* mode is much like the Cipher Feedback mode, except that the shift register is filled differently.

Secure Sockets Layer

The Secure Sockets Layer (SSL) protocol is being used on most World Wide Web (WWW) browsers and servers for the various credit-card transactions taking place more and more on the Internet. It epitomizes today's network encryption technology.

SSL is a protocol, not cipher. It uses ciphers to secure communications between the users and servers on the Internet. SSL essentially enhances the security programs you are currently using to transmit data across the Internet by means of a browser such as Internet Explorer.

Authentication and Data Integrity

Now that you have encrypted your data, how can you verify the sender and the receiver? What means do you have of making sure that no one has had unauthorized access to and/or altered the data?

The Hash Function

A one-way hash function is an algorithm that takes a text of arbitrary length and changes it to a fixed-sized *hash.* The hash is a "stamp" of the original text. The purpose of a hash is for signing your transmissions.

Once a hash is created, it gathers the message that is to be signed and adds it to the hash. When the hash has gathered all the data, it can be signed. A message summary may be added at this time. Once you have the digital signature, you should destroy the hash.

You can sign hashes with a private key or a private exchange key. The owner of the message should use his/her private key signature, but if you are sending data that is not yours, you should use the exchange private key.

Digital Signatures

Digital signatures allow you to place a "seal," like the old wax seals, on a transmitted message. A digital signature is used when data is sent in plaintext form, but you want the receiver(s) to be able to verify where the data came from and whether it's been altered after sending. Signing the data won't change it; it only guarantees the integrity of the data.

Digital signatures are bundles of binary data, about 256 bytes, generated with public-key signature algorithms. The private key generates the signature, and the public key validates the signature.

Creating a Digital Signature

To create a digital signature, you must create a hash value of the message and sign it with your private key. For verification of a signature, you must create a hash value of the message. Then the value is checked against the signature, using the signer's public key. If both the value and signature match, it is likely that the message is secure.

Certification Authority and Certificates

Certificates are used to verify the validity of public keys. They contain the key owner's name, public key, validity dates, name and signature of the issuer of the key, serial number, and any restrictions on the key itself. All certificates are signed by an application known as a Certification Authority.

Many public keys are widely distributed, in newspapers and such, so that they are easily verified. But not all public keys have that kind of exposure. The Certification Authority is like the Better Business Bureau. You can use it to check the validity of the public key. Why is this necessary? Suppose someone e-mailed their public code to you. How could you be sure that the e-mail had not been intercepted, and a false public key inserted? Your e-mail responses would wind up in dishonest hands, and your messages could be decrypted, changed, re-encrypted and sent on to your unsuspecting correspondents.

This may seem to be overkill, but not all hackers have a "purpose." Their sneaking around and making "harmless" changes to your data could wreak havoc on your organization. Just as you would not load unchecked software on your system, you should not accept a key at face value.

Is Cryptography for You?

To answer this question, let's take a closer look at the possible threats to your transmitted data. That will help you decide if your data needs protection.

Communication lines such as phone cables have always been insecure because they can be tapped. Any good hacker can access your lines and copy, change, destroy, or steal your data. This is also true of the Internet. When the data has been encrypted, however, the hacker may be able to see your data but won't be able to read it.

If you have decided to use cryptography as part of your security plan, there are many providers for you to choose from. The Cryptography Service Provider architecture gives you a safe way to have your applications access cryptographic and signature services. CSPs are autonomous programs that authenticate the user and check for consent to actions. Each provider has its own guidelines for key exchange algorithms, digital signature algorithms and formats, and key length specifications. There are many types of CSPs to choose from, all of which have their own "specialties." Some are faster, some have more powerful bit-encryption schemes, and so forth. We recommend that you research this area more thoroughly before making a decision on the type of provider you need.

The Microsoft Cryptographic Application Program Interface (CryptoAPI)

The Microsoft Cryptographic Application Program Interface (CryptoAPI) comprises functions that provide access to common cryptographic functions such as hashing, encryption/decryption capabilities, and key generation and exchange.

What the CryptoAPI does is keep the coding applications separate from the CSP, so that you can use various providers as needed. This service allows access to CryptoAPI functions, without your having to know about the underlying implementations. Because of this, if you decide to take advantage of some new cryptographic technology or to change your CSP, and each CSP provides a different implementation of the CryptoAPI, you can change your provider without having to change the application.

Another safety feature provided by Microsoft is the requirement of Microsoft's digital signature on all CSPs in order for the operating systems to recognize them. This requirement protects the integrity of your system. Windows NT verifies the signature periodically to make sure that the CSP has not been changed.

Summary

As you can see, there are many ways for your data to be compromised—but there are many solutions, as well. Through the use of cryptography and related technology, your stored and transmitted data can be fairly secure. There is a lot to cryptography and its applications, but with the service of a trusted Cryptography Service Provider (CSP), cryptography can be an easily implemented part of your security plan. And remember, the CSP does all the work—you won't have to worry about the actual mechanics of cryptography.

- *Passwords*
- *Secure Path*
- *Untrusted Programs*
- *Special Groups*
- *Creating and Managing Groups*
- *Multidomain Groups*
- *Administrator Account Strategies*

- *Domain and Network Full Administrators*
- *Per-User Account*
- *General Account Setup*
- *Security Auditing*
- *Disk Formats*
- *Printer Access Policy*
- *Remote Access Service*
- *ACLs*

CHAPTER

16

Enterprise Security Policy

A JOURNEY OF A THOUSAND STEPS STARTS WITH THE FIRST ONE. IN making NT Security Policy, you have a lengthy journey and actually a somewhat daunting task. If you spend too much time looking at the enormity of the project, you'll never get started. So get started.

To start a plan for your enterprise's security policy, you must determine your criteria for the policy. What follows is a condensed "must use" list of concepts, standards, and mechanisms. These items are critical to the security policy for any enterprise. The plan you make to achieve these goals will be a minimum requirement to setting up security in your environment.

If you're unsure about where to go from this point, then just start implementing the items in this chapter. Learn as you go. But realize that this is just the beginning. We suggest you write a Site Security Policy and Procedures document. This chapter's list of items will give you a good head start.

Passwords

- Know the means to set passwords, to allow users to change their own passwords, and to prevent users from changing their passwords. Know how to construct sufficiently strong passwords and when to change them.
- Decide which users will be responsible for changing their passwords and which ones will be restricted from this task.
- Do allow the responsible users to change their passwords. Consistently and periodically change the passwords of restricted users.
- Never lend a password, but ensure that users will tell administrators when they are forced by circumstances to do so.
- Administrators should immediately and always change their password whenever there is even a chance that it may have been compromised.
- Set password uniqueness to the maximum allowed, and minimum age to a few days.
- Set the expiration date based on your site security. We recommend 90 days for Low security; 30 days for Medium security; and 15 days for High security.
- Set all account passwords to expire, but exempt full Administrators.
- Set password lockout and minimum length to values as high as will be functional at your site. You should always set password lockout, even at low-security sites where you can set the values very liberally.
- Users with more power need to have stronger passwords.
- Define and distribute site policy for the strength of passwords.

Secure Path

- Windows NT never presents the Security window (Secure Path) unless the user keys in the Trusted Path. Hint, hint: That means that any other time a password request pops up, you should be suspicious.
- Use the Security window exclusively for changing a password, locking the workstation, and logging off.
- Never enter a password, except through the Secure Path. The exception is when you connect to a network resource where your account is matched to a remote account with a different password.
- Use the Windows NT Security window for locking a workstation or server. (Use it as a screensaver.)

Untrusted Programs

- Each program you use operates on the same system as you do. It obtains your full capabilities and can sometimes use them without your knowledge. Know the applications you are installing. Do not implement odd or esoteric applications without fully knowing how they function.
- Keep in mind that even common programs may have side doors. For instance, Office 97 is integrated with Outlook, which is integrated with Exchange, and all of which is integrated with Web services. Could a Word macro access a Web page and violate your security?

Special Groups

- Understand the use of special groups, the difference between the Users and Everyone groups, and the implications of access control with the NETWORK, INTERACTIVE, and SYSTEM Special Groups.
- Do not enable the Guest account unless you cannot operate without it. If you must use it, use a password and do not allow the password to be changed.

Creating and Managing Groups

- Understand why you create user groups: to provide file, directory, and network access; to assign rights; and to allocate and monitor resource use.
- Know how to exploit profiles to ensure basic consistency of rights when creating new users.

- Make sure the Policy has clearly defined the criteria for group membership.
- Use group names and descriptions that intuitively describe the intended membership. Try to avoid using a group name already used, particularly if it's used across the entire network.
- If possible, include the name of the group creator or group manager in the group's description.

Multidomain Groups

- Use UGLY (see Chapter 3).
- Understand your naming conventions.
- Consider whether some local groups need to include one or more domain global groups for the same purpose. For example, a Domain Print Managers group in each domain and a Print Managers local group on each workstation that includes the Domain Print Managers groups from some or all visible domains. See Chapter 3.

Administrator Account Strategies

- Make the Administrator account the account-of-last-resort. Do not simply rename the account and use the same password on every workstation on the network, including domain controllers. Make this password long and random and complex. This is extremely important if you are depending on account lockout.
- As a variation on the password standard, vary the password; for example, give the Administrator account a different password in each domain.
- Another alternative is to assign the Administrator account to individual users, renaming them accordingly. This works well for small networks.
- Remember to write down Administrator passwords and secure them, especially for the first and second scenarios in this list.
- If the local Administrator account is exempt from account lockout, you can deny RAS access to this account or even remove its right to access the computer from the network. Currently this does not preclude IIS access.

Domain and Network Full Administrators

- Decide which accounts are going to fully administer particular domains. Decide if any workstations within the domain need exceptions to this scheme, and adjust their Administrators group accordingly.
- Create at least two accounts for each administrator: one to use only during Administrator activities and another for other activities.
- Name Administrator accounts and groups so that it is apparent they are administrative—except in maximum-level security environments. In this case, camouflage Administrator accounts by naming them similarly to other users and groups.

Per-User Account

- Decide if and when you need to set the account's logon-to-workstations list. This is limited to eight entries.
- If restrictions are required for logon hours, determine if you want each domain controller to suspend services forcibly to a remotely connected account when the account logon hours expire. Users are notified that they have five minutes before being disconnected.

General Account Setup

- Decide which groups you want to have the right to log on locally (primary logon), and which ones to have the right to access this computer from the network (secondary logon). Make this decision early, since you assign rights on each workstation; use global groups when appropriate.
- Decide which workstations can be shut down by users, and which accounts or groups shall have the right to shut down the system.
- Choose a consistent scheme for account names and descriptions that will explicitly identify the person who uses the account.
- Avoid establishing accounts that are used regularly by more than one person, even in situations such as job sharing.
- In general, you should set up a home directory for each new user with proper access-control rights.
- If you have a large installation, create a few account templates. Disable each template account, give it a complex and useless password, and allow yourself to forget it. Set Temporary accounts to expire after an appropriate time.

- Give the Replicator account a strong password. There is no need to remember it.
- Decide whether you wish to post the logon banner, either for legal reasons or as a security reminder.

Security Auditing

- Formulate an auditing policy, and practice it over a period of time (months). Start small and grow into broader auditing schemes.

Disk Formats

- Use the NTFS disk format wherever possible.
- Floppy disks and many other removable and recordable media often are not formatted with NTFS. Control the access and use of these devices.

Printer Access Policy

- Determine if there are any printers with access that must be strictly limited for security reasons. For example, printers that do pre-signed checks.
- If a certain group's data is extremely sensitive, you may need to limit the group's access to physically secure printers only.

Remote Access Service

- Install the Remote Access Service only on required machines.
- Don't allow cleartext logons, and always choose to encrypt RAS traffic.
- Install PPTP if you run RAS across the Internet (Virtual Private Networks). Try to avoid allowing access to the entire network for dial-in clients.
- Set the RAS policy parameters to be as secure as is reasonable. Consider that a RAS environment will almost certainly have a more critical need for account lockout.
- Limit the number of accounts that can have remote dial-in access. Use two accounts for users who can dial in; one for in-office work and one for out-of-office dial-in access.
- Ensure that dial-in users have the right to log on remotely, and use callback to predefined numbers where possible.

ACLs

- Understand the mechanics of ACLs. At a minimum, know how to set up a typical home directory.
- When you first inhabit your home directory, set up its ACL securely. When in doubt, disallow.
- Put ACLs on directories that by default properly protect their entire, subsequently created directory tree.

Summary

Remember: It's important to get started. The fact that there is much work to do is no excuse for not doing anything. Tackle the elephant, one foot or toe at a time. Take that first step. Take the Nestea Plunge. I don't care what slogan you use, Just Do It!

This chapter is a great place to start. Find a section that appeals to you and start working on it. Document what you do. Keep adding more items from this chapter—soon you'll be branching out into other areas. Remember to come back and check these lists. Next thing you know, you'll have a security policy. And a good grasp on your enterprise security implementation and issues to go along with it.

- *What Is NT Distributed Security Services?*
- *Multiple Security Protocols*
- *Domain Trust Relationships*
- *Authentication Transition from NT 4.0 to 5.0*
- *A Smooth Migration to the Next Version of Domains*

CHAPTER

17

Windows NT Distributed Security Services

WINDOWS NT 4.0 IS A HIGHLY SECURE AND RELIABLE OPERATING system. Yet in today's high-paced industry, Microsoft cannot afford to sit back and revel in its glory.

Today's enterprise is opening up to the Internet. Businesses need to interact with partners, suppliers, and customers using Internet-based technologies. Security is essential for controlling access to resources in the enterprise's network, its intranet, and its Internet-based servers. Companies today allow outside parties to have access to nonpublic business information, in order to more effectively share information for many different business relationships. Correct configuration of user accounts for the business's "extended family" members is critical to controlling proper access to company data. Such expanded business relationships are redefining the trust that once applied only to employees who used corporate assets, but now includes many more people. The old model of security becomes more difficult to apply to these new relationships.

Remote access over public networks as well as Internet access for interbusiness communications are driving the evolution of security technology. And those security technologies are changing rapidly. For instance, public-key certificates and dynamic passwords have quickly and effectively evolved to meet higher-level security needs in today's environment. Windows NT's modular design and security architecture is uniquely positioned to take advantage of these and other technology advances. Windows NT combines ease-of-use for the user, excellent administration tools, and a solid security infrastructure that supports both the enterprise and the Internet.

Although NT scales well, today's large organizations need substantial flexibility to delegate account administration and manage complex domains. The Internet has exploded, and Internet security concerns are driving the development of public-key security mechanisms that must be integrated with Windows NT security. To meet these ever-changing needs, Microsoft is working on technology called the *Distributed Security Services.*

Before we discuss these "future technologies," let us sneak in a disclaimer. The shipment date for Windows NT 5.0 has not yet been scheduled as this book goes to print. Speculation has it as early as October 1997 and as late as October 1998. We believe it's best to consider NT 5.0 as an OS for 1998, and if we get an early winter gift we'll be thankful.

Like a sign indicating a curve in the road ahead, a little knowledge of what lies ahead for Windows NT will help you plan how to implement what you have today. Although there will undoubtedly be improvements in the next release of NT, everything you learn about 4.0 security is likely to be directly applicable in any future NT releases.

And a final point: Microsoft reserves the right to call the next release of NT anything they desire. For simplicity, we will call it Windows NT 5.0.

What Is NT Distributed Security Services?

The Windows NT Distributed Security Services (DSS) technology has many new features to simplify domain administration, improve performance, and integrate Internet security mechanisms based on public-key cryptography. Although it had not been released at the time this book went to press, through working with Microsoft I have gathered information on this new security model. Microsoft anticipates it will be included in NT 5.0.

What follows are an overview and highlights of an emerging new technology that Microsoft is introducing. I cannot vouch for any of it. Microsoft has the right to change plans and directions regardless of what is written here or of what other information has been released. I expect all of the following features will be in the new DSS, yet I do not doubt that some changes will occur.

Many changes are coming to NT—in Directory Services, the Security subsystem, and even Administrative Tools. In the following sections we discuss the changes to the next generation of security in Windows NT.

Understanding Windows NT Server Directory Services

In future implementations, the Windows NT domain model changes, using the Windows NT Directory Services to support a multilevel hierarchy tree of domains. Management of trust relationships among domains is simplified through treewide, transitive trust throughout the domain tree—another short sentence that has major repercussions! In a tree- or hierarchy-based security system, you can have layers of rights and responsibilities that mimic your corporate infrastructure. This will provide scalable, flexible account management for large domains, with fine-grain access control and delegation of administration. Yes, Microsoft has finally brought a real directory service to NT and to the enterprise.

Today Windows NT account information is maintained inside a secure portion of the Registry on domain controllers. Using domain trust and pass-through authentication, a simple two-level hierarchy of domains provides some flexibility for organizing account management and resource servers. Within a domain, however, accounts are maintained in a flat namespace with no internal organization and one set of administration rights.

To improve on today's model, the next version of Windows NT security will use the Windows NT Directory Services as the repository for account information. Directory Services provide significant improvements over the Registry-based implementation in areas of performance, scalability, and feature-rich administrative environment.

Figure 17.1 shows a hierarchical structure for a tree of Windows NT domains, and the hierarchical (tree) name context within each domain using Organizational Units (OUs) as directory object containers.

Figure 17.1

The new hierarchical structure of Windows NT 4.0

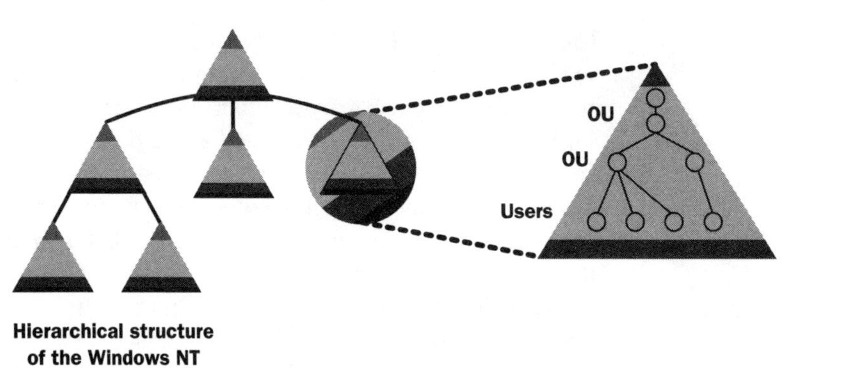

Advantages of Directory Services Account Management

Windows NT Directory Services provide the store (or database) for all domain security-policy and account information (policies and user accounts). Directory Services also furnish replication and availability of account information to multiple domain controllers, and are exposed for remote administration. The advantages of integrating security account management with the Windows NT Directory Services are many; they are described in the following sections.

Accounts

Windows NT Directory Services support a hierarchical namespace for user, group, and machine account information. Accounts can be grouped by Organization Units rather than by the flat, domain account namespace provided by earlier versions of Windows NT. And this means significant impact for large organizations.

Accounts for users, groups, and machines can be organized into directory containers; these are the OUs. Within a domain you can have any number of OUs organized in a tree-structured namespace. Businesses can organize the namespace for account information to represent the departments and organizations in the company. User accounts, as well as OUs, are directory objects that can easily be renamed within the domain tree as people move to different departments in the organization.

Administrator rights to create and manage user or group accounts can be delegated to the level of OUs. This allows the integration of autonomous departments or groups into the enterprise.

Performance and the Registry

The Directory Services support a much larger number of user objects (well over a million objects), with better performance than the Registry. Individual domain size in the past was limited by performance of the security account database that had to reside, in full, on each domain controller. This is no longer a limit. A tree of connected Windows NT domains can support much larger, complex organization structures.

Administration

Advanced graphical tools for Directory Services management will be used for account administration and information. In addition, OLE Directory Services' support for scripting languages will allow common tasks to be implemented using batch scripts to automate administration.

Directory Replication

Windows NT Directory Services replication allows account updates to be made at any domain controller and not just at the PDC. In SQL Server this is called Multi-Master Replication. Directory Services replicas at other domain controllers—what used to be known as backup domain controllers—are updated and synchronized automatically.

The LDAP protocol and directory synchronization support provide the mechanism to link the Windows NT directory services with other directories in the enterprise and allow for replication across heterogeneous platforms. Directory replication supports multiple copies of the account information store; thus, updates can be made at any copy (domain controller), not just at the designated PDC.

Access Rights

Security account, user, and group information is now represented as objects in the Directory. Read and write access to objects in the Directory can be granted to the object as a whole, or to individual properties of the object. Administrators have fine-grain control over who can update user or group information. For example, a Printer Operator group can be granted write access to only user account properties related to Printers, without requiring full Account Operator or Administrator privileges.

This refines the Administrative controls that you can give to others, possibly allowing certain managers specific rights to their staff user accounts. For example, you might allow a specific individual or group to have just the right to reset passwords, but not to modify other account information.

While maintaining complete backward-compatibility, the new Security Services concept of groups has become simplified, because local and global groups are both represented by *group objects* in the Directory. Groups defined in the Directory can be used for domainwide access control to resources or only for "local" administration purposes on the domain controller.

Relationship Between Directory Services and Security Services

A fundamental relationship exists between the Directory and Security Services integrated into the Windows NT operating system. The Directory Services store domain security policy information, such as domainwide password restrictions and system access privileges that have direct bearing on the use of the system. The security-related objects in the Directory must be securely managed to avoid unauthorized changes that affect overall system security. The Windows NT operating system implements the object-based security model and access control for all objects in the Directory. Every object in Directory Services has a unique security descriptor that defines access permissions required to read or update the object properties.

Windows NT authentication service stores encrypted password information in the secure portion of the Directory user objects (user accounts). The operating system trusts that security policy information is stored securely and that account restrictions or group membership is not changed by anyone without authorized access. In addition, security policy information for overall domain management is kept in the Directory.

This fundamental relationship between Security and Directory Services is only achieved by complete integration of Directory Services with the Windows NT operating system.

Integrating the security account repository with the Windows NT Directory Services provides real benefits to manage the enterprise. Performance, ease of administration, and scalability for large organizations are the direct results.

■ Multiple Security Protocols

The next version of the Windows NT Security infrastructure will support three primary security protocols:

- Windows NT LAN Manager (NTLM) authentication protocol is used by Windows NT 4.0 and previous versions. NTLM will continue to be supported and used for pass-through network authentication, remote file access, and authenticated RPC connections to earlier versions of Windows NT.
- The Kerberos Version 5 authentication protocol replaces NTLM as the primary security protocol for access to resources within or across Windows NT domains. Kerberos is a mature industry standard that has advantages for Windows NT network authentication. Some of the benefits of Kerberos protocol are mutual authentication of both client and server, reduced server load during establishment of connection, and support for delegation of authorization from clients to servers through the use of proxy mechanisms.

- Distributed Password Authentication (DPA) is the shared, secret authentication protocol used by some of the largest Internet membership organizations, including Microsoft Network and CompuServe. This authentication protocol is part of Microsoft's Membership System. It is specifically designed for users to use the same Internet membership password to connect to any number of Internet sites that are part of the same membership organization. The Internet content servers use the Microsoft Membership System authentication service as a back-end Internet service, and users can connect to multiple sites without reentering their password.

Public-key-based protocols offer privacy and reliability over the Internet. Secure Sockets Layer is the de facto standard today for connections between Internet browsers and Internet information servers. (An IETF standard protocol definition based on SSL3 is forthcoming, currently known as the Transport Layer Security Protocol, TLS.) These protocols use public-key certificates to authenticate clients and servers and depend on a public-key infrastructure for widespread use.

Windows NT 4.0 provides secure channel security services that implement the SSL/PCT protocols. The next version of Windows NT security will have more enhanced feature support for public-key protocols, as described later in this chapter.

Domain Trust Relationships

As explained earlier in this chapter, the next version of Windows NT domains will be organized into a hierarchical tree. The purpose for trust relationships between domains is to allow users with accounts defined in one domain to be authenticated by resource servers in another domain. In Windows NT 4.0 (and earlier versions, as well), interdomain trust relationships are defined by one-way trusted domain accounts among domain controllers. Management of large networks with many such trust relationships among account domains and resource domains is a complex task.

The next generation of Windows NT Directory Services supports two forms of trust relationships:

- Explicit one-way trust relationships to Windows NT 4.0 domains
- Two-way transitive trust between domains that are part of the Windows NT domain tree

Transitive trust between domains simplifies the management of interdomain trust accounts. Domains that are members of the domain tree by default define a two-way trust relationship with the parent domain in the tree. All domains implicitly trust other domains in the tree. If there are specific domains that do not want two-way trust, *explicit one-way trust* accounts can be defined.

For organizations with multiple domains, the management of trusts is simplified, and the overall number of explicit one-way trust relationships is significantly reduced.

Authentication Transition from NT 4.0 to 5.0

The transition from NTLM authentication, used in Windows NT through version 4.0, to the next version of the Kerberos domain authentication will be very smooth. Windows NT services can support client or server connections using either security protocol.

The transition from enterprise-based services using Kerberos authentication to Internet-based services using public-key authentication is completely transparent to the user. Windows NT support for multiple user credentials makes it possible to use secret-key authentication technology for enterprise application services with very high performance, as well as public-key security technology when connecting to Internet-based servers. Most application protocols that support authentication, such as LDAP, HTTP/HTTPS, or RPC, are designed to support multiple authentication services. They select those services during connection establishment.

Rather than relying on one single authentication technology and one single authentication protocol, Windows NT will use multiple protocols as needed, to fit the application requirements and the user community's requirements for secure network computing.

A Smooth Migration to the Next Version of Domains

Migrating from the current Windows NT 4.0 domain model to the new hierarchical model will be easy, because of backward compatibility for existing Windows NT security and account replication protocols. A smooth migration is available because Windows NT has the following interoperability features:

- The new domain controllers will play the role of Windows NT 4.0 BDCs and receive domain account replication from an existing Windows NT 4.0 PDC.
- The new domain controllers will establish trust relationships with Windows NT 4.0 domains and support pass-through authentication among domains. This means not all domains in an enterprise are required to upgrade to the next revision of the Windows NT domain security at the same time.

In addition, the new domain controllers will eventually replace Windows NT 4.0 domain controllers in a gradual upgrade of Windows NT 4.0 BDCs. Windows NT 4.0 account management tools are used on the primary domain controller as long as the PDC is running NT 4.0. Eventually, all domain controllers can be switched to use the Windows NT Server DSS for account management and multimaster account replication.

Summary

The Windows NT DSS that we will see in NT 5.0 provides flexible solutions for building secure, scalable distributed applications. Security administration and management will have richer feature sets for delegation and fine account control. Windows NT 5.0 Directory Services will support domains with many more accounts in a structured naming environment of Organizational Units. Interdomain trust management will be simpler, providing greater flexibility.

The new Windows NT security architecture is specifically designed to incorporate new security technology. NT 5.0 will make the migration from 4.0 a viable, smooth transition, yet it will not make the Sun rise in the West. What I want to remind you of is *security basics*—they don't change. Everything you use and learn in NT 4.0 will relate to the next version of NT. New products and features are interesting and useful for perspective, but right now it is time to start implementing security. So get started!

Appendix A

Helpful Internet Sites

Here are some locations on the Internet where you can find more information about security, in terms of Windows NT and in general. Also, bear in mind that the Internet sites are often very timely with the data they release. It's usually the best place to go when you want to stay informed about the changing environment.

Helpful Tip

We strongly recommend that you visit the site http://ntbugtraq.rc.on.ca/index.html and subscribe to the NTBugTraq mail service, as described in the Mailing Lists section of this appendix.

Internet Resources

- Microsoft's Web page entitled "What is C2 Evaluation? Microsoft Sets the Record Straight."
  http://www.microsoft.com/NTServer/c2bltn.htm
- Microsoft sales data sheet on NTFS that describes it from a security perspective.
  http://www.microsoft.com/ntserver/ntfs_mb.htm
- Online version of the "rainbow" documents: Red Book, Orange Book, and many more.
  http://www.pinsight.com:80/~royg/security/dod/rainbow.html
- Microsoft's document titled "C2 and Beyond."
  http://www.microsoft.com/ntserver/c2char.htm
- A proposed ISO Standard on a new information technology security standard, called *common criteria.*
  http://csrc.ncsl.nist.gov/nistpubs/cc

Cryptography

- RSA RAQ on cryptography issues.
  http://www.rsa.com/rsalabs/newfaq
- Consensus has a FAQ on the Secure Socket Layer, SSL.
  http://www.consensus.com/security/ssl-talk-faq.html
- International Cryptographics Software Pages for Encryption, Decryption, Cryptoanalysis, Stenography, and related methods.
  http://www.cs.hut.fi/ssh/crypto
- Introduction to cryptography.
  http://www.cs.hut.fi/ssh/crypto/intro.html
- A collection of pointers to cryptography software.
  http://www.cs.hut.fi/crypto/software.html
- The U.S. Army cryptography manual is on line.
  ftp://hubert.wustl.edu/pub/armycryp.zip
- The Computer Emergency Response Team, CERT.
  http://www.cert.org
- U.S. DOE Computer Incident Advisory Capability, CIAC.
  http://ciac.llnl.gov
- First: Forum of Incident Response Teams.
  http://www.first.org/first
- Telstra security pages.
  http://www.telstra.com.au/info/security.html
- COAST home page.
  http://www.cs.purdue.edu/coast/coast.html

Mailing Lists

- CERT advisories.
  <cert-advisory-request@cert.org>
- Best-of-Security BoS.
  <best-of-security-request@suburbia.au>
- NTBugTraq.
  <Listserv@rc.on.ca>

  To subscribe, send a message with "subscribe ntbugtraq firstname lastname" in the message body. You can leave the subject line blank. Turn off any automatic signature that might be added by your mail program.

- Internet Security Systems, ISS, sponsor an NT security mailing list.
  <ntsecurity-request@iss.net>

Articles on NT Security Components

- Microsoft's article on SIDs.
  http://www.microsoft.com/msdn/sdk/platforms/doc/sdk/win32/sys/src/security_14.htm
- Microsoft's article on privileges.
  http://www.microsoft.com/msdn/sdk/platforms/doc/sdk/win32/sys/src/security_15.htm
- Microsoft's article on Access Control Lists, ACLs.
  http://www.microsoft.com/msdn/sdk/platforms/doc/sdk/win32/sys/src/security_9.htm
- Microsoft's article on Access Control Entries, ACEs.
  http://www.microsoft.com/msdn/sdk/platforms/doc/sdk/win32/sys/src/security_10.htm

Virus Software Web Pages

- Symantec has a Web page called "Understanding Virus Behavior in the Windows NT Environment."
  http://www.symantec.com/avcenter/reference/vbnt.html
- Sophos SWEEP for Windows NT.
  http://sophos.com/Marketing/ntgui.html
- WinGuard from Dr Solomon.
  http://www.drsolomon.com
- Symantec's Norton Antivirus for NT.
  http://www.symantec.com/nav/fs_nav20nt.html
- Datafellows F-PROT.
  http://www.datafellows.com

■ Appendix B

■ NT Security Resources

We hope this book has been helpful to your understanding and deployment of security on Windows NT. We also believe that you will need ongoing references and other tools to help you maintain your network. In this appendix is a set of such tools offered by Intrusion Detection, Inc., that will help you in implementing and testing your NT security policies.

Other tools are available, as well. Intrusion Detection, Inc., was the only company to respond with material in time for this book to go to print.

■ The Kane Security Analyst (KSA) for MS Windows NT

The KSA will thoroughly assess the overall security status of a Windows NT network and report security in six areas: password strength, access control, user account restrictions, system monitoring, data integrity, and data confidentiality. The KSA provides the expertise of seasoned security specialists and streamlines the analysis process.

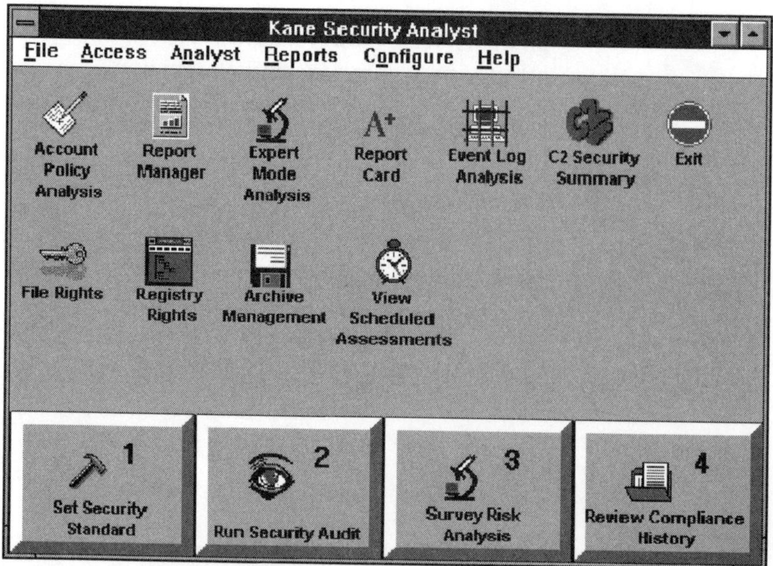

The expert knowledge base embedded in KSA will thoroughly analyze the following:

- Password cracking test
- User/group permissions across domains
- C2 security
- Password strength
- Trust relationships
- Event logs
- Scripted passwords
- Nonsecure partitions
- Audit policy compliance
- UPS status
- Excessive rights
- Security report cards
- Registry security settings
- Guest ID configuration
- Logon violations
- NT services
- Domain security
- Domains that can't be administered
- Security logs
- Down-level authentication

Some other features include an interactive registry assessment, ACL Maps, and the Kane File Rights for NTFS volumes. The Kane File Rights is an interactive tool included with the KSA that allows users to investigate rights and privileges associated with various users, groups, and directories. This is an important feature, because it would take a great deal of time to investigate every user ID manually.

1. **The KSA provides a complete security assessment in MINUTES!** The KSA is the only enterprise-wide security assessment tool that allows users to check the total security soundness of Windows NT and Novell NetWare networks, in minutes.

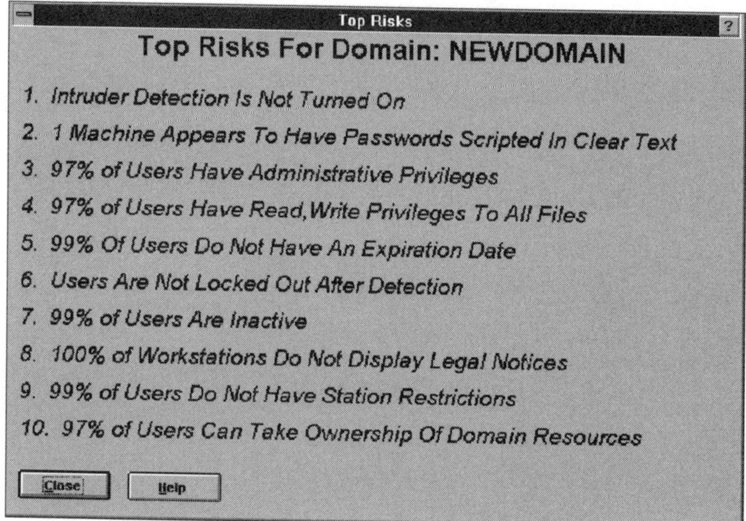

2. **The KSA compares your network security against a set of industry best practices.** The KSA brings the expertise of seasoned security specialist to your network, encapsulating years of security consulting, research, and direct work with customers. A primary component of the KSA security methodology is a set of best practices built into the product.

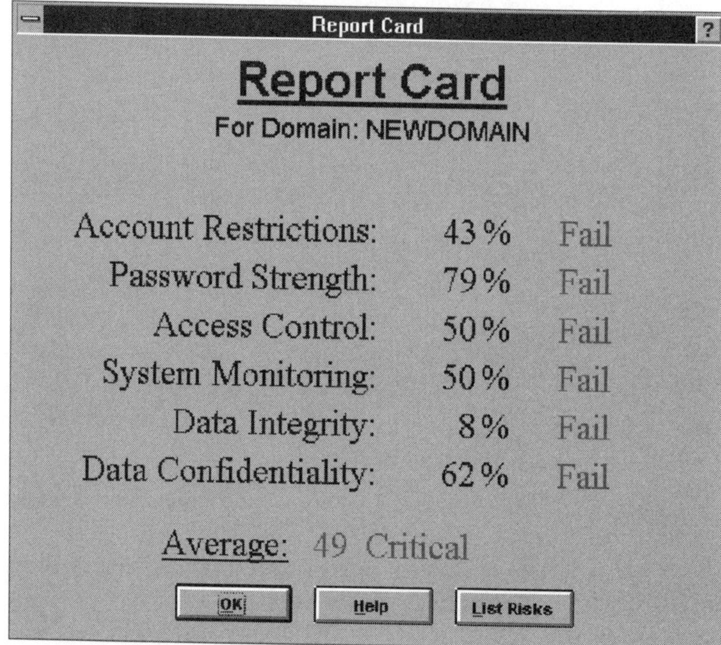

3. **The KSA security investigation can be customized.** You can even configure the KSA to perform according to your needs, from producing a high-level overview to digging as deeply as necessary to investigate specific areas and/or users. You can even customize the security best practices with your own corporate policy.
4. **The KSA produces professional security reports, all in plain English.** The KSA includes a set of detailed security reports that are easy to understand. All you have to do is press "print" and everything is produced, from a cover page and management overview to very detailed security reports.

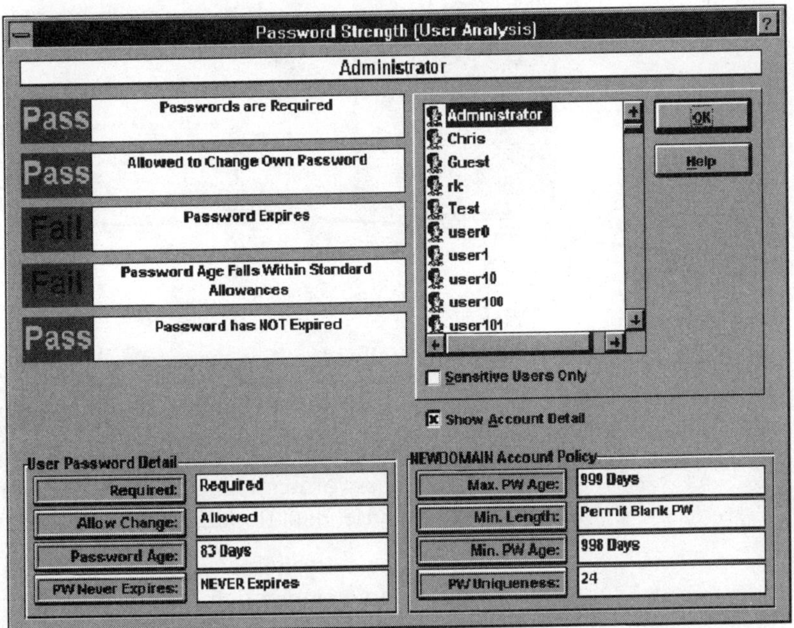

■ SHADOWARE

SHADOWARE is an intrusion detection system that provides sophisticated network security monitoring for Novell and Windows NT networks. Using artificial intelligence, SHADOWARE identifies both subtle and obvious security violations caused by outside hackers or even inside authorized users. Once a violation has been identified, the System Administrator or Security Officer is alerted with the details.

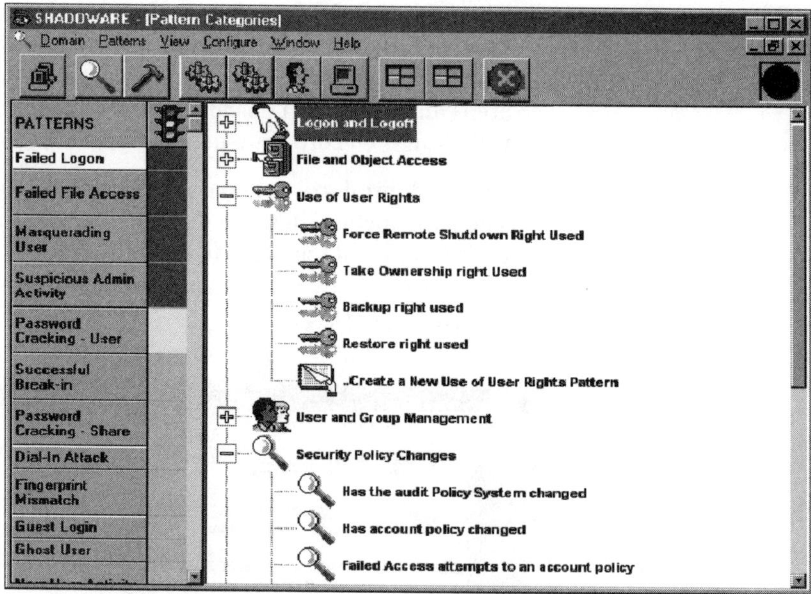

Features

- Automatically identifies security violations.
- Uncovers security break-ins before they occur.
- Uncovers password guessers, curious users, file browsers, compromised user IDs, password-cracking attempts, network doorknob attacks, privileged ID abuse, data flooding, and packet browsing.
- By providing a psychological deterrent against system abuse by insiders, allows you to maintain tighter control over privileged users IDs such as the Administrator or Supervisor.
- Focuses special attention on the most sensitive Users, Workstations, and Files.
- Minimal setup time, with the built-in time-saving, self-populating database of expert security information.
- Security officers, auditors, and LAN administrators can be automatically alerted about unauthorized access.
- Centralized security monitoring of all NT machines (file servers and workstations) from one workstation.
- Seamless integration with the Kane Security Analyst, Intrusion Detection's network security assessment product.

How Can SHADOWARE Help You?

SHADOWARE uses artificial intelligence to filter through security data and audit data to create digital signature fingerprints of all network users. As network audit data is monitored, both subtle and obvious unauthorized activities can be identified and tracked to outside hackers or even inside users.

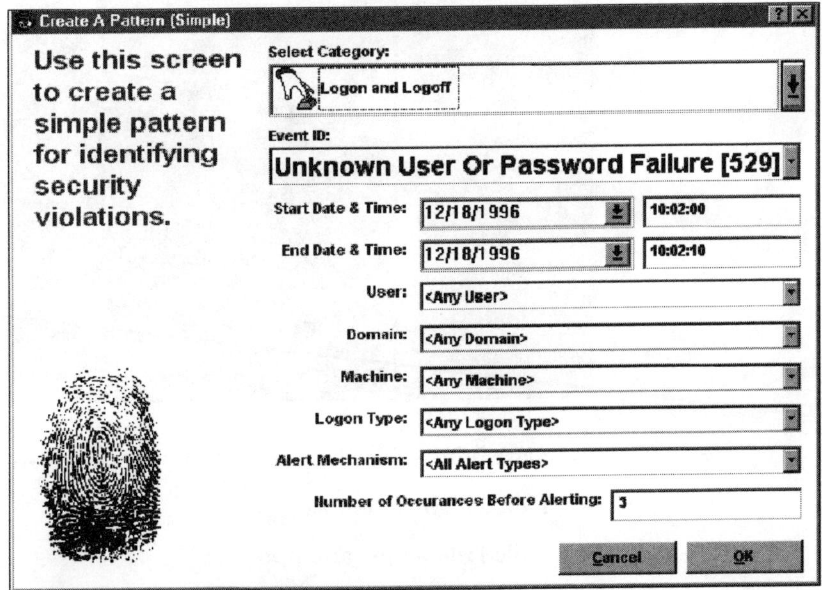

Create Your Own Attack Pattern

An administrator or security officer can designate what events should receive a system warning. For example, the administrator might want to be notified when a new administrative account is created or deleted; or when the administrative account turned off the audit trail, reset a password, or accessed the CEO's desktop and copied several directories worth of data. SHADOWARE can easily be configured to send out alerts for this and many other actions, as decided by the user.

Identify Anomalies

SHADOWARE can identify any unusual activity on the network. By analyzing network activity, SHADOWARE establishes a baseline or average network usage. When a particular activity exceeds that average, SHADOWARE knows. For example, if a particular user ID has an unusual number of logon violations, SHADOWARE will alert the security officer or system administrator via page, fax, e-mail, or printout to investigate further.

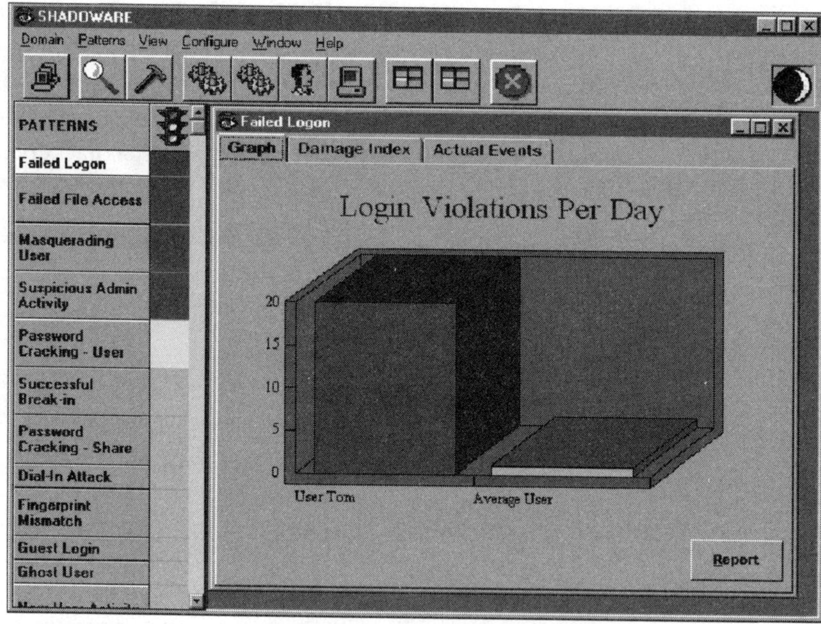

SHADOWARE identifies security break-in patterns, including

- Failed logon attempts
- Failed file-access attempts
- Browsing and curious users
- Denial of service
- Excessive privilege granting
- Ghost IDs
- Masquerading users
- Password cracking
- Administrative ID privilege abuse
- Supervisor privilege abuse

Q & A

Q: Does the KSA affect the production environment?
A: No, the fundamental design of the KSA is its passive operational nature. The KSA does not make any changes to the operating environment.

Q: What platforms does the KSA run on?
A: Windows NT 3.51 and later.

Q: Is the KSA a Windows NT service?
A: No. Instead, the KSA operates from any PC workstation attached to the network. Server resources are not required.

Q: What kind of logon is required?
A: An administrator- or supervisor-equivalent logon is required.

Q: What other platforms is IDI working on for the future?
A: IDI currently has a Novell NetWare 3.x and 4.x NDS product. Future platforms include UNIX, Internet, Lotus Notes, Firewalls, Oracle, ASP, OS/2.

About Intrusion Detection, Inc.

Intrusion Detection, Inc., the leaders in NT and Novell security, specialize in network security software development. This company is privately held and located in New York City.

For more information please contact:

Intrusion Detection, Inc.
217 East 86th Street, Suite 213, New York, NY 10028
Ph: 212-348-8900, 800-408-6104
Fax: 212-427-9185
WWW.intrusion.com

Glossary

ACE *Access Control Entry.* An entry in an ACL containing access rights and a SID.

ACL *Access Control List.* Controls security permissions attached to objects.

Administrator The Administrator account is a special user account with the ability to maintain a workstation.

API *Application Programming Interface.* A high-level language binding that enables a programmer to easily use functions in another program.

Application Log File containing information on errors and warnings; generated by software when security auditing is enabled.

Attack An electronic assault that attempts to breach the target system's security mechanisms.

Auditing Windows NT feature that records the security-relevant audit events into a security log.

Audit Policy Determines the type of security events that are logged.

Authentication A systematic method for establishing proof of identity between two or more entities, usually users and hosts.

Authorization The predetermined right to access an object or service based on authentication information.

Binding Process that establishes the initial communication channel between the protocol driver and the network adapter card driver.

Boot Partition For NTFS or FAT file systems, a formatted volume containing the NT operating system and its support files.

Built-In Groups Default groups provided with Windows NT, which have been granted various rights.

Certificate Authority A trusted entity that digitally signs certificates in order to validate ownership of public keys.

Ciphertext Plaintext converted into a secretive format through the use of an encryption algorithm and encryption key. Ideally, only those who know the algorithm and decryption key can unlock the original plaintext from ciphertext.

Client Computer that accesses shared network resources provided by a server.

Computer Name A unique name that identifies a computer to the network.

Cryptography The science of enabling secure communication through encryption and decryption.

Datagram A package of data and its delivery information.

Decryption The inverse of encryption; the process of converting ciphertext into plaintext.

Default A variable that is assigned automatically by an operating system and that remains in effect unless canceled or overridden.

Desktop The screen background on which the icons, windows, and dialog boxes of an interface appear.

Device Driver Program that allows a specific piece of hardware to communicate with Windows NT.

Digital Signature An unforgettable electronic signature that authenticates a message sender and simultaneously guarantees the integrity of the message.

Directory Structure for organizing files on a disk. Directories contain subdirectories and files/folders.

Discretionary Access Control *DAC.* A term for the kind of access control that ACLs provide.

Disk Mirroring Maintaining a complete copy of a partition on another disk.

Disk Striping Using more than one disk to write data across a volume created from free space.

Domain A network of computers that share a database and security policy.

Domain Name The name by which a domain is known by the network.

DNS *Domain Name System.* A database used to map IP addresses to host names.

Domain Controller An NT Server that controls and stores certain data for a domain, including domain accounts and global groups.

Encryption The process of converting data from an easily understandable format into what appears to be random gibberish until it is later decrypted.

Event An occurrence in the system that requires users to be notified, or an entry to be made to a log.

Event Viewer Standard NT program that lets an administrator view and manage the security log.

Explorer Standard NT program that allows management of logical disks and their files/folders and directories.

FAT *File Allocation Table.* The traditional and standard file system; has no security.

Fault Tolerance The ability of a computer and an operating system to overcome events such as power outages or hardware failure.

File Sharing The ability of a workstation or server to share files with remote clients.

File System The overall structure in which files are named, stored, and organized.

Firewall One or more packet filters and gateways that shield "internal" trusted networks from "external" untrusted networks such as the Internet.

FTP *File Transfer Protocol.* An application-layer protocol used primarily to copy files between systems. Also refers to the client program that implements the FTP protocol.

Gopher An information retrieval service often provided on intranets, as on the global Internet. Gopher makes geographically diverse libraries of information appear to be organized into a single directory tree, so that the libraries appear much like a logical drive.

Group NT supports *global groups* and *local groups.* Global groups exist only on domain controllers and include only the accounts on the controller. Global groups are visible and usable throughout the domain and all trusted domains. Local groups are visible and usable only on their own workstations.

HTTP *HyperText Transfer Protocol.* An application-layer protocol used to deliver text, graphics, sound, movies, and other data over the World Wide Web via the friendly hypertext interface of a Web browser.

Integrity Characterizes data in an unimpaired state; as in "the e-mail message retained its integrity," or "the integrity of the data was not compromised."

Intranet A wide area network consisting of many local area networks. Modeled after the global Internet, an intranet implements a common base of communication protocols.

Interactive Logon The act of a user typing at the keyboard in response to a dialog box displayed on the screen by the operating system.

Internet An extensive and worldwide series of connected networks that reaches universities, government research labs, commercial enterprises, and military installations in many countries.

IP *Internet Protocol.* Responsible for addressing and delivering datagrams across the Internet.

IP Address A 32-bit address that uniquely identifies a node on an IP network.

Kernel Driver A driver that accesses hardware.

Key The only correct value of all possible values that can be applied to convert to and from plaintext via an encryption algorithm.

LAN *Local Area Network.* A communications network that spans small geographical areas.

Layered Protocols Stacked protocols, where the "lower" protocols provide services to the "higher" protocols.

Local Security Authority *LSA.* Creates a security access token for each user accessing the system.

Logon and Logoff The process that NT uses to identify a user account and its access.

Network Layer On the Internet, the layer that implements IP and provides services to the transport layer.

NTFS *NT File System.* A highly secure file-system structure designed specifically for the NT operating system.

Object Any piece of information created by using a windows-based application with object linking and embedding (OLE) capabilities; this object can be linked or embedded into another document.

One-Way Hash A function that takes plaintext of arbitrary length as input, and outputs a small fixed-length value that is a unique stamp of the message.

Owner Part of the account identity attached to each object that has an ACL. The object's creator is the "owner" of the object, until the owner designates another to take ownership.

Partition A portion of a physical disk that functions as though it were a physically separate unit.

Password The word or phrase, kept secret, that allows the user to gain access to resources.

Permissions Capabilities that an account has toward an object protected by an ACL; for example, permission to read a file object.

Printer Driver Program that controls interaction between the computer and the printer.

Protocol A set of rules and conventions used to govern the transmission and receipt of data across a network.

Redirector Software that accepts I/O requests for remote files and then sends them to a network service on another computer.

Registry The critical and substantial collection of parameters on each workstation, which governs the workstation's operations.

Rights A capability assigned on each workstation to accounts and/or groups visible from the workstation.

SAM *Security Accounts Manager.* Element of Windows NT that collects user account and group account definitions and accesses; used to create access tokens.

SID *Security Identifier.* A unique name that identifies a user or group to the security system.

Server Term for a computer that provides services to other computers.

Share To make resources such as printers and directories available to network users.

TCP *Transmission Control Protocol.* A connection-oriented transport protocol that provides reliable, full-duplex data transmission between two entities, often a client and a server.

Transport Layer On the Internet, the layer that implements TCP (Transmission Control Protocol) and UDP (User Datagram Protocol) over the network layer.

Transport Protocol Defines how data should be presented to the next receiving layer in the networking model and packages the data accordingly.

User Account Consists of all the information that defines a user to Windows NT.

User Manager Standard NT workstation program for managing accounts and groups, and the Account, Audit, and Rights Policies.

User Manager for Domains Standard NT Server tool used to manage security for a domain.

Virtual Memory Space on a hard disk that Windows NT uses as if it were actually memory.

Volume A partition or collection of partitions formatted for use by a file system.

WAN *Wide Area Network.* A physical communications network that spans large geographical distances. WANs usually operate at slower speeds than LANs because communication occurs over telephone lines.

Workstation A stand-alone computer, whether connected to a network or not. Uses server services.

WWW *World Wide Web.* A cohesive and user-friendly view of the Internet through many protocols, especially HTTP.

Index

D

H

I

K

L

R

S

T

U